Winner of the 2014 Charles Tilly Award for Best Book,
Collective Behavior and Social Movement Section, American Sociological Association

"Martin, a sociologist at the University of California, San Diego, says today's tea party is just the latest manifestation of another American tradition: the mobilization of wealthy and middle-class citizens in an effort to cut their taxes and contributions to the state.... But these movements sell their efforts as not just benefiting the rich alone – that would be too transparent, too tacky. Instead, they claim to protect freedom, promote growth, safeguard the Constitution or fend off an ever-more-intrusive government." —*The Washington Post*

"For anyone interested in understanding the history of American anti-tax activism, this book is essential reading." —*Democracy*

"A worthy counterpart to Frances Fox Piven and Richard Cloward's classic *Poor People's Movements*." —*Publisher's Weekly*

"An important contribution to understanding the contentious politics of today." —*Kirkus Reviews*

"It is the unlikeliest of political banners: the rich are taxed too much. In this timely, innovative, and fascinating book, Isaac Martin unravels the mystery of why mass movements have repeatedly appeared with the demand that the costs of financing government be redistributed in favor of the nation's most privileged citizens" —Paul Pierson, co-author of *Winner-Take-All Politics*

"Isaac Martin's powerful work of historical discovery reveals how the tradition-building of generations of grass-roots, anti-tax entrepreneurs helped bring about the Tea Party victories in 2010. His archival research and theorizing brilliantly resolve the paradox of how movements 'to untax the one percent' have achieved success in a democratic political system." —W. Elliot Brownlee, University of California, Santa Barbara

"Rich people also march on Washington; sometimes they even convince less-than-rich people to march on their behalf, and sometimes it works. Martin chronicles the efforts of the affluent to protect their interests—or at least their money—over the past century. This indispensable book convincingly demonstrates that social movements aren't only for people who can't get what they want in any other way. By showing the connections between big money, political organizations, social protest, and public policy, Martin raises troubling questions about the nature of democratic politics in America. We ignore them at our peril." —David S. Meyer, University of California, Irvine

"*Rich People's Movements* testifies to the power of understanding a crisis before it repeats. In a revelatory project begun well before "the One Percent" became a centerpiece of political contention, Martin documents the power of outsider protest when practiced by often-unlikely coalitions among the wealthy and powerful: rural mortgage bankers, business leaders, married professional women, public officials concerned over tax-exempt investments, and many others. Through a rich and original historical analysis of the work of political entrepreneurs, Martin locates the roots of our present conflicts are in a long and surprising history of political maneuver and policy crafting." —Elisabeth Clemens, University of Chicago

STUDIES IN POSTWAR AMERICAN POLITICAL DEVELOPMENT

Steven Teles

Series Editor

Series Board Members
Paul Frymer
Jennifer Hochschild
Desmond King
Sanford Levinson
Taeku Lee
Shep Melnick
Paul Pierson
John Skrentny
Adam Sheingate
Reva Siegel
Thomas Sugrue

The Delegated Welfare State: Medicare, Markets, and the Governance of Social Policy
Kimberly J. Morgan and Andrea Louise Campbell

Rule and Ruin: The Downfall of Moderation and the Destruction of the Republican Party, From Eisenhower to the Tea Party
Geoffrey Kabaservice

Engines of Change: Party Factions in American Politics, 1868-2010
Daniel DiSalvo

Follow the Money: How Foundation Dollars Change Public School Politics
Sarah Reckhow

The Allure of Order: High Hopes, Dashed Expectations, and the Troubled Quest to Remake American Schooling
Jal Mehta

Rich People's Movements: Grassroots Campaigns to Untax the One Percent
Isaac William Martin

Rich People's Movements

Grassroots Campaigns to Untax the One Percent

ISAAC WILLIAM MARTIN

OXFORD
UNIVERSITY PRESS

OXFORD
UNIVERSITY PRESS

Oxford University Press is a department of the University of Oxford.
It furthers the University's objective of excellence in research, scholarship,
and education by publishing worldwide.

Oxford   New York
Auckland   Cape Town   Dar es Salaam   Hong Kong   Karachi
Kuala Lumpur   Madrid   Melbourne   Mexico City   Nairobi
New Delhi   Shanghai   Taipei   Toronto

With offices in
Argentina   Austria   Brazil   Chile   Czech Republic   France   Greece
Guatemala   Hungary   Italy   Japan   Poland   Portugal   Singapore
South Korea   Switzerland   Thailand   Turkey   Ukraine   Vietnam

Oxford is a registered trade mark of Oxford University Press
in the UK and certain other countries.

Published in the United States of America by
Oxford University Press
198 Madison Avenue, New York, NY 10016

Library of Congress Cataloging-in-Publication Data
Martin, Isaac William.
Rich people's movements : grassroots campaigns to untax the one percent / Isaac William Martin.
pages cm
ISBN 978-0-19-992899-6 (hardback : alk. paper); 978-0-19-938999-5 (paperback : alk. paper)
1. Income tax–United States.   2. Repeal of legislation–United States.   3. Social movements–
United States.   4. Tax credits–United States.   5. Rich people–United States.   I. Title.
HJ4652.M386 2013
336.24086'21–dc23
2012049410

9 8 7 6 5 4 3 2 1

Printed in the United States of America
on acid-free paper

I dedicate this book to my parents, Ann Wadsworth Martin and
Peter William Martin.

Behind every great movement, especially in the field of taxation,
there is a story of human interest, because taxes and death are certain.

—J. A. Arnold

CONTENTS

PREFACE

On tax day, April 15, 2010, hundreds of thousands of Americans turned out to rallies and demonstrations around the United States to protest against taxes and big government. The protesters included disaffected conservatives representing a variety of groups and causes, but they united in expressing hostility toward the taxation of income and wealth. Spokespeople for the demonstrators demanded, among many other things, an end to progressive income tax rates, a permanent repeal of the estate tax, an extension of temporary income tax cuts for the richest Americans, and a constitutional amendment that would require a supermajority vote in Congress to increase any tax on anyone, for any purpose, ever. Protesters held up picket signs denouncing taxes and the redistribution of wealth. Many asserted that the government was redistributing resources from the rich to the poor, and objected that this was unfair to the rich.[1]

To outsiders, the so-called Tax Day Tea Party demonstrations seemed to present a paradox. Here was an outpouring of collective protest, yet it was protest on behalf of competitive individualism. These were public-spirited civic gatherings, yet their purpose was to celebrate the spirit of private acquisitiveness. The protesters were using traditional tactics invented by the poor and dispossessed—the march on Washington, the rally, the mass meeting—but they were using those tactics to assert the moral and economic worthiness of the rich. Commentators could not agree on what to make of the protests. But whatever else they saw in the events of that day, they agreed that here was something that needed to be explained.

One common explanation, embraced by many of the protesters themselves, pointed to a series of large federal government interventions in the economy, culminating in the Patient Protection and Affordable Care Act that Congress had passed just three weeks earlier. The health care law included subsidies to help low-income people buy health insurance, and paid for those subsidies with new payroll and excise taxes on high-income people and people with expensive insurance plans. Many protesters denounced "Obamacare" as an unprecedented expansion of government powers, and cited it as the reason for their opposition.[2]

Another explanation pointed to an opposite conclusion: It was not the expansion of government, but rather its retreat, that paved the way for protest, by creating a "winner-take-all" economy in which even most rich people felt like losers. People who sympathized with the Tea Party protests were more affluent than the typical American, but few if any of the protesters were among the super-rich. The dismantling of progressive tax rates, labor unions, and financial regulations since the 1980s has allowed the rich to pull away from the middle class, and allowed a few super-rich superstars of finance to pull away from everyone else. Whereas a typical upper-middle-income person in 1980 might look up at the rich and think that the pinnacle of material success was achievable, a typical upper-middle-income person looking up in 2010, in the words of the economist Brad DeLong, "sees as wide a gap yawning above him as the gap between Dives and Lazarus."[3] Even the merely rich now feel that they have been left behind. Perhaps the protesters were simply affluent people who did not know how good they had it.

A third common explanation for the protests pointed to a racial backlash against the president. Many white middle-income and high-income people are conservatives who might dislike a liberal presidential administration under any circumstances. But some of them may have been particularly resentful in 2009 and 2010 because the president was black. Surveys and interview studies show that sympathy for the Tea Party and for its defense of the rich often go together with expressions of resentment and hostility toward African Americans, and at least some influential Tea Party supporters seem to believe that the president's policy agenda is somehow distinctively African.[4] Perhaps racial resentment also explains why so many Tea Party sympathizers turned out to protest on April 15, 2010.

Still a fourth explanation for the protests pointed to the role of new media. The proliferation of cable channels and websites in the twenty-first century allows people to pick and choose their information sources to an unprecedented degree, and the result has been a partisan self-segregation of the media audience that encourages conflict. The protests were certainly promoted by new media: By most accounts, the Tea Party movement began in February 2009 when a cable news commentator named Rick Santelli recorded a video at the Chicago Mercantile Exchange calling for "capitalists" to demonstrate against government redistribution, and it became a national movement when that video went viral on the Internet. Commentators have described the Tea Party as a leaderless network loosely coordinated by websites, e-mail lists, and the Fox cable network.[5] "[U]nlike demagogues past, who appealed over the heads of individuals to the collective interests of a class," the historian Mark Lilla explained in 2010,

"Fox and its wildly popular allies on talk radio and conservative websites have at their disposal technology that is perfectly adapted to a nation of cocksure individualists who want to be addressed and heard directly, without mediation, and without having to leave the comforts of home." The result, he wrote, is the "new form of populism" that was on display at the Tea Party protests of April 2010.[6]

Underlying all of these explanations is a shared premise: Regardless of whether the commentators sought the causes of the movement in the provision of national health insurance, the deregulation of finance, the fear of a black president, or the rise of new electronic media, they agreed fundamentally that populist protests against progressive taxation are something new, and that their causes must therefore also lie in some recent transformation of American society. This book will show that this common premise is mistaken. The Tea Party protests of 2010 were new only in the sense that they were the newest expression of an old tradition.[7]

Social movements that explicitly defend the interests of the rich and the almost-rich have been a recurring feature of American politics. Such movements shook the American polity before the Obama era, before the Reagan era, and before Barry Goldwater ran for president—before, even, the New Deal. The protest movements described in this book had all the characteristics that commentators have found so puzzling about the Tea Party protests of the twenty-first century. They displayed the same paradoxical embrace of collective action and competitive individualism. They offered a similarly forthright defense of capitalists and the rich using the grassroots tactics of the poor and dispossessed. And they were similarly puzzling to their contemporaries.

In 1925, for example, progressive congressmen did not fear tea parties but "tax clubs." These were grassroots associations convened to plead for policies to benefit the wealthiest Americans. Business owners formed clubs, convened hundreds of protest meetings in big cities and small towns throughout the South and Midwest, and petitioned their representatives for lower taxes on the nation's richest citizens. They deliberately copied the tactics and rhetoric of the Populist movement. Yet their specific demands for steep cuts in the top rates of the progressive income tax and for the permanent abolition of the estate tax were directly at odds with the agrarian radical tradition of the original Populists. The tax clubs left an enduring imprint on the American tax system, and their peculiar mix of populist tactics and militant anti-egalitarian demands would reappear again and again in the twentieth century. Like Rick Santelli, they were particularly incensed by federal subsidies for mortgage-backed securities. Their complaints would not sound out of place at a twenty-first-century Tea Party rally.

This book tells the stories of the tax clubs and other forgotten rich people's movements of the twentieth century. The title of the book is intended to pay homage to the classic study of *Poor People's Movements* by the sociologists Frances Fox Piven and Richard Cloward. That book presented a general theory of movements for government aid to the poor. The theory addressed why such movements sometimes emerge, why they sometimes win, and how they typically fail. Piven and Cloward illustrated their theory, and tested it, with case studies of four movements of poor people and their allies from twentieth-century U.S. history. Their book remains a classic work of social science, and many of its arguments have withstood decades of criticism by other sociologists and political scientists.[8]

My purpose in writing this book was analogous to theirs: I set out to understand the emergence and policy impact of movements that demand policies to benefit the rich. Like Piven and Cloward, I set out to test my theory with several case studies from twentieth-century U.S. history. Also like them, I limited the scope of my theory to a small class of movements, defined on the basis of their intended beneficiaries' relative position in the economic order. Piven and Cloward focused on poor people's movements, rather than social movements in general, because they assumed—correctly, as it turns out—that poor people's movements might be different from other movements in theoretically important ways. Movements of the poor have distinctive and characteristic forms, because poverty affects the political opportunities for, and constraints on, collective action. I began this study with the parallel assumption that affluence may affect the political opportunities for, and constraints on, collective action, much as poverty does, but in ways that are not just the mirror image of the effects of poverty. The most surprising thing about poor people's movements is that they sometimes win against all odds; the most surprising thing about rich people's movements is that they even feel they must bother. Rich people, like poor people, are an unpopular minority in the United States.[9] But rich people, by virtue of their money and the political resources that their money can buy, such as education, organizational assistance, and legal advice, have more and different kinds of political leverage than poor people have. My conclusions about rich people's movements therefore differ from the conclusions Piven and Cloward drew about movements of the poor. Theories developed to explain poor people's movements, or all social movements in general, will miss some important characteristics of rich people's movements.

My reason for telling the stories of these movements goes beyond an antiquarian fondness for the American past. I am trained as a sociologist, and I started this project because I wanted to understand an influential social movement of my own time by developing a more general theory of movements like it. I went into the archives in order to test and refine that theory against the accumulated evidence of the past. Because my purpose was comparison, and because social scientists and historians have published so little about rich people's movements,

I first approached my historical project in the spirit of a specimen collector on the trail of an exotic animal: This movement is an interesting beast. Maybe we can learn more about where it comes from by studying the species. How was this movement born, how long might it live, and what environments nourish it? I had an inkling that I would find evidence of several other such movements in the archives, and I assumed that by comparing them I could discover recurring conditions that helped to explain why such movements sometimes emerged and thrived, and why they sometimes did not.

What I found was both less and more than I expected. Less, because I sought to collect many case studies, but by the end of my research, I had found evidence of substantial continuity from one campaign to the next, so that, in some respects, I had only a single case study of one more-or-less unbroken movement tradition. More, because I sought only to describe a species, and instead I found evidence of evolution. Each of the movements described in this book survived and thrived in part because of characteristics it acquired from its predecessors. I have come to the conclusion that the environment that nurtured the twenty-first-century Tea Party is an environment richly littered with the remains of movements past, including such cultural detritus as model policies, surviving organizations, personal relationships, and specific movement-building skills. The great political sociologists Seymour Martin Lipset and Earl Raab, in their own study of right-wing movements, called this kind of detritus "cultural baggage"; I prefer to think of it as tradition. I think that the role of tradition may be even more important for explaining the emergence of rich people's movements than for explaining the emergence of other movements. If the idea of a social movement did not exist, poor people would have to invent it, or something like it; and in fact they seem to have done so independently on many occasions.[10] In contrast, rich people have many other ways to protect their interests, and if the tradition of protest politics did not lie ready at hand, there is little reason to think that they or their allies would have picked it up. Still, I have come to suspect as a result of this study that history and tradition ought to be a good deal more central to the study of all social movements than social scientists usually acknowledge, and certainly more than the metaphor of "baggage" would suggest. Tradition is not just the suitcase we drag along behind us. It is the toolkit we reach for when we want to change the world.[11]

Many of the protesters described in this book were conscious of themselves as part of a tradition. They were clever people who learned from their predecessors, and who passed down concrete policy proposals and lessons in grassroots politics to the protesters who came after them. I will frankly admit here that I do not sympathize much with their policy proposals, or agree much with the use they made of those lessons. Nevertheless, I will also admit that I came to respect these protesters, and to admire some of them a great deal. I hope that this book conveys their stories—their shared *history*—with the respect that they are due as the carriers of an important and poorly understood tradition, that of the grassroots libertarian right. It is a tradition that exercises a major influence on American politics in our time.

ACKNOWLEDGMENTS

I would like to begin by acknowledging a special debt to Andrea L. Campbell, a colleague without whom this book would be very different, and probably much worse. People who know her scholarship will recognize the obvious influence of her ideas on this book; she also helped by inviting me to visit the Massachusetts Institute of Technology, introducing me to colleagues, and giving me just the right mix of incisive criticism and supportive comments on the manuscript when the first draft was nearly complete. Thank you, Andrea.

The funding for this book consisted mainly of the salary paid to me by the University of California–San Diego. In-kind support was also provided by the department of political science at the Massachusetts Institute of Technology, for whose hospitality I owe particular thanks to Rick Locke and Helen F. Ray, and by Christina Hanhardt, Seth Karpinski, Ann Zeidman-Karpinski, Cathy Rion, Mike Rion, and Nancy Rion, who housed me, fed me, and kept me entertained on my trips to archives in their towns. Thank you all.

Andrew Anderson and Andrew Cheyne provided outstanding research assistance in the earliest stages of this project. I also thank Clark Radatz, Tiffany Paige, Meghan Cochrane, and Greg Facincani, reference librarians who all were kind enough to track down obscure legislative histories for an out-of-state library patron.

For preserving and cataloguing the records I used for this project, I thank the archivists and special collections librarians of the Lyndon Baines Johnson Library, the National Archives and Records Administration, the University of Oregon Special Collections, the University of Connecticut Special Collections, the University of Houston Special Collections, the John Fitzgerald Kennedy Presidential Library, the University of Iowa Special Collections, the University of Kansas, the Brown University Special Collections, the Hoover Institution, and the Everett M. Dirksen Congressional Center. I would like to single out Bruce Tabb and the rest of the University of Oregon Library Special

Collections department for special thanks. I am also grateful to the library staff of the Boston Public Library, the Massachusetts Institute of Technology, and the University of California–San Diego. I thank Adam Berinsky for providing me with weighted Gallup poll data from the Berinsky-Schickler Data Reclamation Project.

The following people all read and commented on early drafts of various chapters. I was not able to answer all their questions or take all their advice, but they still deserve thanks for making this book better than it would have been without their input: Marisa Abrajano, Amy Binder, Amy Bridges, W. Elliot Brownlee, Bruce Carruthers, Cheris Chan, Maria Charles, Tony Chen, Meghan Duffy, Julia Elyachar, John H. Evans, Peter Gourevitch, Zoltan Hajnal, Jeff Haydu, Robert Horwitz, Tomás Jimenez, Greta Krippner, Mirella Landriscina, Jack Jin Gary Lee, Clarence Lo, Thomas Maloney, Michael Mann, Bill Maurer, David McBride, Ajay Mehrotra, Kwai Ng, Paul Pierson, Monica Prasad, Dylan Riley, Ákos Rona-Tás, Bill Roy, Ronnee Schreiber, Tad Skotnicki, John Skrentny, Jim Sparrow, Steven Teles, and Dilara Yarbrough.

Portions of the introduction, chapter 3, and chapter 4 appeared in the *American Journal of Sociology*. Portions of chapter 2 appeared in the *Journal of Policy History*, and an early version of chapter 8 appeared in the *Berkeley Journal of Sociology*. I am grateful to all of these journals for permission to reprint.

This manuscript was much improved by anonymous peer review, and by the face-to-face criticism of students and faculty who heard me present drafts of various chapters at the University of Arizona, Northwestern University, the University of California–Berkeley, the University of California–Irvine, the University of California–Los Angeles, the University of California–San Diego, the University of Wisconsin–Milwaukee, and Oberlin College, as well as at the conference on "Two Political Economies in Crisis" organized by Eisaku Ide and W. Elliot Brownlee at Keio University. I also benefited from attentive and critical audiences at the annual meetings of the American Sociological Association and the Social Science History Association. The people who offered constructive criticism on these occasions are too many to list individually, and I do not know all their names, but I owe them thanks.

Steven Teles and Dave McBride kept after me to finish the book and welcomed it into their series on American political development. I am delighted to be in such good company.

Amaha Kassa promoted this project from the beginning. He also taught me a lot of what I think I know about organizing. The ideas in the book are not his fault, but the book surely would not exist without him.

My parents supported the writing of this book in countless ways, just as they have supported every other endeavor of mine. I would like to thank them for—well, for everything—but on this occasion most especially for inspiring me with a lifetime of examples of personal and civic courage. I am tempted to go on for pages here explaining why they are awesome and what that has to do with why I wrote this book. Instead, I just ask you to believe me, and I dedicate this book to them.

ABBREVIATIONS

The following abbreviations for archives and manuscript collections are used in the endnotes.

CCGE   Committee for Constitutional Government (Ephemera), University of Iowa Right Wing Collection, microfilm, reel 36.

CEM   Clarence E. Manion Papers, 1922–1979, Chicago History Museum Research Center.

CLM   Research Collection on Conservative and Libertarian Movements, series III, University of Oregon Library Special Collections.

DAR   Daniel A. Reed Papers, Collection No. 1907, Department of Manuscripts and University Archives, Cornell University Libraries, Ithaca, New York.

EAR   Edward Aloysius Rumely Papers, University of Oregon Library Special Collections.

EC   Papers of Emanuel Celler, Library of Congress, Manuscript Division.

ED   Everett M. Dirksen Papers, Working Papers, 1957–1969, The Dirksen Congressional Center, Pekin, Illinois.

FEG   Frank E. Gannett Papers, Collection No. 1900, Department of Manuscripts and University Archives, Cornell University Libraries, Ithaca, New York.

HH   Hall Hoag Collection, Brown University Library Special Collections, Ms. 76.60, Box 60-1, Tax Rebellion Movement.

JBS   John Birch Society Records, Brown University Library Special Collections.

JFK   Papers of John F. Kennedy, Presidential Papers, Presidential Office
          Files, John F. Kennedy Presidential Library and Museum.

JHK   John Henry Kirby Papers, 1885–1939, ID 03/2006-008, University
          of Houston Library Special Collections

MF   Milton Friedman Papers, Hoover Institution Archives, Stanford
          University.

PKR   Polly King Ruhtenberg Papers, University of Oregon Library Special
          Collections, Coll. 081.

RBD   Robert B. Dresser Papers, Hoover Institution Archives, Stanford
          University.

RG 56   National Archives and Records Administration, Record Group 56,
          Office of the Treasury, Entry 191, Correspondence of the Office
          of the Secretary of the Treasury, Central Files of the Office of the
          Secretary of the Treasury, 1917–1932.

RHH   Richard H. Headlee Papers, 1976–1992, General
          Correspondence–1977 Folder, Bentley Historical Library,
          University of Michigan.

SBP   Samuel B. Pettengill Papers, University of Oregon Library Special
          Collections, Coll. 15.

TCA   Thomas Coleman Andrews Papers, University of Oregon Libraries
          Special Collections, Coll. 119.

TI   American Taxpayers' Association Tax Information series, Univerity
          of Iowa Right Wing Collection, microfilm, reel 8.

VK   Vivien Kellems Papers, Archives and Special Collections at the
          Thomas J. Dodd Research Center, University of Connecticut
          Libraries.

WC   Wilcox Collection, University of Kansas Libraries.

WES   Willis E. Stone Papers, 1955–1982, University of Oregon Library
          Special Collections, Coll. 118.

WIK   Willford Isbell King Papers, University of Oregon Library Special
          Collections, Coll. 89/88/6.

WP   Personal Papers of Wright Patman, Lyndon Baines Johnson Library.

Rich People's Movements

INTRODUCTION: THE RIDDLE OF RICH PEOPLE'S MOVEMENTS

On September 4, 1962, hundreds of conservative activists crowded into the Wilshire Ebell Theatre in Los Angeles for a protest meeting that they called the California T Party. These protesters were unusually well-heeled and unusually radical. They were there to support a constitutional amendment that would outlaw all federal taxation of income and inherited wealth, and would further require the federal government to sell off virtually all its assets in order to pay for a massive, one-time transfer of wealth to the richest Americans. There were two more California T Parties that week, followed by a national gathering in Chicago two weeks later, at which activists from around the country met, sang protest songs, and attended workshops on grassroots organizing for income tax repeal.[1]

When we think of a social movement, we usually picture poor people marching in the streets, not rich people sitting in a theater.[2] But the California T Parties were part of a vigorous movement tradition. Since the early twentieth century, a small but vocal minority of Americans has fomented nonviolent rebellions—founding protest associations, holding press conferences and mass meetings, petitioning, demonstrating, and sometimes even engaging in civil disobedience—to demand that government redistribute resources to the rich. These movements sometimes won partial concessions and sometimes failed to make any impact at all, but they always came back, with peak episodes of mobilization around 1925, 1943, 1951, 1957, 1979, and 1995. Figure 1.1 illustrates the episodic rise and fall of rich people's movements in two ways: first, in black, the number of state legislatures passing resolutions in support of the demands of rich people's movements; second, in gray, the number of *New York Times* articles mentioning any of the principal social movement organizations affiliated with the rich people's movements described in this book.[3] In every one of these cases, the protesters had more income and wealth than the average American, and the policies they demanded explicitly singled out people with the most income and wealth to receive the greatest benefit.

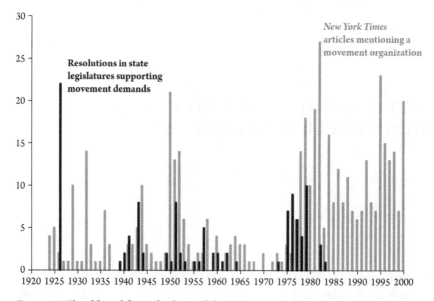

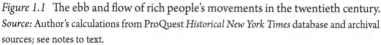

Figure 1.1 The ebb and flow of rich people's movements in the twentieth century.
Source: Author's calculations from ProQuest *Historical New York Times* database and archival sources; see notes to text.

These were rich people's movements. Their distinguishing characteristic was not only that they mobilized relatively affluent people; many conservative causes in American history, from the anti-abolitionist mobs of the early nineteenth century to the anti-suffragists of the early twentieth century, have mobilized relatively affluent activists.[4] Nor were rich people's movements distinctive for being bankrolled by wealthy donors. Even poor people's movements have had their philanthropic patrons.[5] What made the rich people's movements different—what made them rich people's movements, instead of environmental movements, or women's movements, or labor movements—is that they defined the rich as the constituency they sought to benefit. They were disproportionately movements of the rich and by the rich, but the reason that I call them rich people's movements is that they were distinctively, especially, and categorically movements *for* the rich.[6]

The twentieth-century United States was a fertile field for rich people's movements, because the industrial revolution produced more riches there than ever before, or in any other society. Those who had great wealth, as well as those who merely aspired to it, saw the successes of a few rich families as a sign that the American experiment was working. Even many socialists saw the accumulation of a few great fortunes as a happy sign that a golden future awaited everyone. On the eve of the twentieth century, for example, the American socialist Edward Bellamy wrote a best-selling novel, *Looking Backward,* about a future in which anyone who wanted to could live like a Rockefeller. The hero of the story went to sleep in 1887 as a wealthy man from the upper crust of Boston society, only to awaken in the year 2000 in a society where everyone was guaranteed a minimum income sufficient to live in luxury. "I suppose ... that no reflection would have cut the men of your wealth-worshipping century more keenly than the suggestion that they did not know how to make money," a citizen of the fictional twenty-first century remarked to this modern Rip Van Winkle; "Nevertheless, that is just the verdict that history has passed on them." Bellamy was right that the American economy of the twenty-first century would be unimaginably productive. The rapid economic growth of the twentieth century would yield incomes even greater than he predicted in his wildest utopian fantasies—and also more unequally distributed.[7]

Although the rise of great fortunes created optimism, the great inequalities that arose in their shadow fueled a more pessimistic and mistrustful strand of American political culture. The wider the gap that separated the wealthy few from the impoverished many, the more that some wealthy people feared that an envious democratic majority might rise up against them. "In the United States, where the poor rule," Alexis de Tocqueville wrote in his 1832 classic *Democracy in America*, "the rich have always some reason to dread the abuses of their power." It was a commonplace among rich people in the nineteenth century that unrestrained majority rule could threaten their property or their personal safety. Tocqueville called such abuse "the tyranny of the majority," and wealthy observers of American politics who came after Tocqueville debated whether the tyranny of which he had warned was already coming to pass.[8]

Many in the poor majority, for their part, feared that great fortunes might be used to undermine democracy. The promise of democracy in America was that politicians could ascend to office without inheriting wealth or title, but precisely because American politicians were not independently wealthy, their loyalties could sometimes be purchased by other people who were. (Tocqueville had warned of this problem too: "In democracies statesmen are poor, and they have their fortunes to make," he wrote. "The consequence is, that in aristocratic states the rulers are rarely accessible to corruption, and have very little craving for money; while the reverse is the case in democratic nations.") By the early 1900s, Populist and progressive critics of inequality thought that the corruption of democracy by the rich had reached a critical level, and they began to sound the alarm in books with titles such as *Plutocracy*, *The American Plutocracy*, and *The New Plutocracy*. Both rich and poor thought inequality could erode democratic virtue, but whereas the rich and their allies feared envy, the poor and their allies warned of greed.[9]

The clash between these competing forces would shape the course of American political economy in the twentieth century. One of the first fateful encounters was the battle over progressive income taxation. The idea of a progressive tax—one that took a progressively greater percentage of income from the rich than the poor—was born in the democratic fervor of the French revolution. The first person to use the term "progressive taxation" in English appears to have been Thomas Paine, whose 1792 tract *The Rights of Man* argued for a progressive tax on estates in order to protect democracy against the corrupting influence of large fortunes.[10] American Populists and progressives a century later revived the idea of progressive taxation because, like Paine, they saw it as a bulwark of democracy. By limiting the excessive concentration of wealth in private hands, they thought, a progressive tax could prevent the re-emergence of monarchical privilege and power. The fearful rich, in contrast, saw proposals for progressive taxation as evidence that their own worst fears were coming true: The democratic majority was turning tyrannical. The congressional enactment of a progressive income tax in 1913 did not end the conflict. Instead, it set the stage for a century-long tug-of-war over the limits of private property and public power.

By the end of the Second World War, many observers and intellectuals thought that the struggle was over. The federal government had fought the Great Depression and won the Second World War by means of massive interventions in the market economy. Progressive taxation had proven its usefulness as a means for controlling inflation, and it funded federal spending on everything from widows' pensions to warplanes. In December 1954, the president of the American Economic Association, Simon Kuznets, delivered a presidential address in which he even went so far as to describe progressive taxation as the inevitable result of modernization. We should expect the people of any society to become less tolerant of income inequality as their society grows richer, he said, because an affluent society need no longer depend so much on "income inequalities as a source of savings for economic growth." Kuznets thought it was a law of history that there was "an increasing pressure of legal and political decisions on upper-income shares"—that is, greater taxation of the rich—"increasing as a country moves to higher economic levels."[11]

He was wrong. Progressive taxation was not an inevitable law of history. It was a temporary settlement in a struggle between competing forces. The progressives had won some temporary victories in the United States, but the advocates for the rich were not defeated. They had not even gone away. During and after the Second World War, some conservative businessmen and businesswomen led a broad-based grassroots campaign to reduce progressive income taxes. Even as Kuznets delivered his address, a growing number of activists affiliated with that movement were beginning to make the new and radical demand that progressive taxes on income and wealth be not only reduced, but abolished, and not only abolished by statute, but constitutionally prohibited for all time. These activists called on the revolutionary rhetoric of Tom Paine and used tactics pioneered by Populists and progressives. Their demands for greater economic inequality, however, stood Paine and the Populists on their heads. In the coming decades, these activists on behalf of the rich would emerge from obscurity to play a major role in the politics of economic inequality in the United States.

Who is rich, of course, is a matter of dispute. Official statistics will not settle the issue for us: The federal government maintains a definition of poverty for the purpose of counting poor people, but there is no official income threshold or wealth threshold for the purpose of counting rich people. Most social scientists who study the rich have taken one of two approaches. The first common approach is to define an absolute dollar threshold, usually some multiple of $1 million, and to define anyone whose net wealth exceeds that threshold as "rich." The second common approach is to set a relative threshold by defining the rich as a fixed portion of the income distribution or the wealth distribution—such as the wealthiest 400 people or the highest-income 1 percent of the population or some other such criterion. I follow the latter approach. These movements were rich people's movements because they favored those who had *either* great wealth *or* great income *relative to others* in their society.[12]

There were several such rich people's movements in the twentieth-century United States. The episodes selected for this study were twentieth-century campaigns for tax cuts that were explicitly targeted to high-income or high-wealth households, led by special-purpose associations, unaffiliated with a particular political party or administration, that attempted to get their way by mobilizing demonstrations of civic support for their demands far outside the halls of power in Washington, D.C., and that had active campaign operations in multiple states. Table 1.1 lists the campaigns.[13] The list includes every such campaign I could discover mentioned in several standard histories of taxation and of the American right, and some that I discovered only after immersing myself in the primary sources. All of these movements had sufficient visibility or cultural influence to be noticed by historians and social scientists, but in other respects the sample is as unbiased as the archival record permits.[14]

The participants in every one of these movements defined their constituency explicitly on the basis of riches. They did not demand special benefits for any group defined on the basis of geography, industry, gender, religion, or race. Instead, they drew a line across the income distribution or the wealth distribution, and argued for policies that favored everyone above it. Different movements drew the line in different places, but they all drew a line. They ranged from the movement for the Mellon plan, which would have benefited only 3 percent of "income tax units"—that is, single adults or married couples—to the movement to repeal federal income taxes, which promised at least some financial benefit to everyone who owed personal income tax, amounting to 68 percent of tax units

Table 1.1. **Rich people's movements in the twentieth-century United States**

Campaign	Dates	Principal social movement organizations	Initial demands	Potential beneficiaries	
				Top... % of the income distribution	Top...% of the wealth distribution
The campaign for the Mellon plan	1924–1929	American Bankers' League, aka American Taxpayers' League	Abolish estate tax, cut top personal income surtax rate to 25%	3%	1%
The campaign for constitutional tax limitation	1936–1957	American Taxpayers' Association, Western Tax Council, Committee for Constitutional Government	Limit top marginal rates of personal income tax and estate tax to 25%	4%	1%
The campaign to repeal federal income taxes	1951–1964	Liberty Belles, Organization to Repeal Federal Income Taxes, National Committee for Economic Freedom, aka Liberty Amendment Committee	Abolish estate tax and personal income tax	68%	2%
The campaign for a tax limitation/ balanced budget amendment	1978–1989	National Taxpayers' Union, National Tax Limitation Committee, American Tax Reduction Movement	Limit top personal income tax rate to 25%, limit growth of income tax	24%	N/A
The campaign to repeal the estate tax	1993–2001	Family Business Estate Tax Coalition, Americans for Tax Reform, 60 Plus Association	Abolish estate tax	N/A	1%

at the time that the movement began. The latter movement was the only one that promised benefits to a majority constituency. It obviously included people we would not ordinarily call rich among its intended beneficiaries. Even in this case, however, most of the financial benefit would have accrued to a small minority of the population, consisting of its very highest-income people—who were also among its very wealthiest people. These protesters argued for policies that would collectively benefit the rich, *all* the rich, and the richer, the better.[15]

The spokespeople for these movements spoke up frankly and unabashedly in favor of more economic inequality. They typically claimed that a policy of unequal rewards was in the universal interest, much as spokespeople for movements of the poor and downtrodden have often claimed that the redistributive policies they seek are in the shared interest of all humanity. In other words, the spokespeople for rich people's movements almost always denied that they were looking out *only* for the interests of the rich; but they usually made no bones about the fact that they *were* looking out for the interests of the rich, and they even took the trouble to explain why. The most prominent spokespeople for rich people's movements gave speeches and wrote manifestos defending the special moral worthiness of the wealthy. The rich were "necessary to any economy"; they were "persons of admittedly superior ability" who had a special role as "trustees for the public"; they were the only ones who could "build the fires and start the wheels of industry." The rich were the hardest-working citizens. They were the vanguard of the movement for individual freedom and the front-line defenders of human rights. Or so the activists said.[16]

In every case, the activists themselves probably included a disproportionate number of people in the top 1 percent of households by wealth; but in every case, the protesters certainly included many more people who were not that rich, and the pool of sympathizers was broader still. In practice, the historical record rarely permits a very precise picture of the finances of the activists in these movements or their sympathizers. I rely of necessity on indirect indicators of socioeconomic status—whether a Gallup pollster coded survey respondents as "wealthy," for example, or whether a list of contributors to a social movement organization could be matched to a list of corporate executives and directors. The activists themselves, as we will see, were usually business owners. We can say with certainty that at least some of them were very rich indeed in both wealth and income, but it is likely that most of them were merely somewhat richer than the average American. In other words, most of the activists were pleading on behalf of people even richer than themselves—another respect in which rich people's movements present something of a sociological curiosity.[17] Almost all of the activists were white. In other respects they were a varied bunch. Some were frankly elitist and believed in the principle of political aristocracy. Others were passionate democrats. Some, including men and women, objected to woman suffrage, and others were feminist supporters of the Equal Rights Amendment. Some acknowledged that they were rich by the standards of their society, and others thought of themselves or described themselves as middle class. Several had been poor at one time in their lives. The nature of their wealth and the sources of their income were varied as well. The tax club activists of the 1920s were mainly country bankers in the South and Midwest; the crusaders for constitutional tax limitation in the early 1940s were preponderantly industrial and financial capitalists and managers from the Northeast; the activists for income tax repeal in the 1950s and 1960s included an unlikely coalition of California heiresses, Southern entrepreneurs, and ranchers from mountain states; and the late-twentieth-century campaigns for tax limitation and estate tax repeal mobilized homeowners and small businesspeople from old and new industries all over the country. Political sociologists have sometimes tried to explain variation in rich people's political behavior by constructing typologies based on industry sector or geography—new money versus old money, new industries versus old industries, locals versus multinationals, small business versus big business, "cowboys" versus "Yankees"—but members of all of these groups sometimes participated in rich people's movements, if not always in the same ones.[18]

This book traces the history of rich people's movements in the twentieth-century United States in order to discover why movements like these sometimes occur, and what impact, if any, such movements have on American society. The answers to these questions should interest anyone who cares about the history of the United States. But they will be of particular interest to students of social science. Sociologists have made considerable progress in understanding protest movements by the poor and the powerless, but our best theories of social movements still leave us ill-equipped to understand protest movements that align themselves explicitly with the rich and powerful. Why would anyone protest on behalf of the rich? When rich people and their allies take collective action to defend wealth and privilege, why do they sometimes use the tactics of political outsiders, instead of the tried-and-true technique of trading money for influence behind the scenes? And why would those outsider tactics—including tactics such as demonstrations, petitions, and mass meetings, whose sole raison d'être is drawing attention to a worthy cause—ever work for a cause as unpopular as giving away public resources to people who are already rich?

Policy Threats

Let us begin with the first puzzle: Why would anyone protest on behalf of the rich? It is easy to find examples in American history of altruistic rich people who have supported protest movements for one or another worthy cause, but you might think that rich people would seldom have much reason to protest *their own* material circumstances. After all, as the political scientist Frank Baumgartner once said of the wealthy, "[I]f they really wanted something, they probably already have it."[19] It is not only material goods that the rich enjoy. High incomes can also insulate people from environmental hazards, everyday discrimination, and various other unpleasant shocks that sometimes lead people to protest.[20] Being rich also has intrinsic satisfactions. Research shows that people whose incomes are high relative to others in their society consistently report that they are happy. The key to their happiness seems to be the satisfaction that comes from being richer than other people, rather than the satisfaction that comes from high levels of material consumption.[21] In light of this research, it is hard to understand why people who are already at the top of the heap would sometimes protest in order to demand even more income and wealth for themselves. It is even harder to understand why other people who are not quite at the top of the heap would side with those above them.

Some of the obvious solutions to this puzzle involve popular stereotypes about the motives of the rich—such as ambition, insatiable greed, or hunger for status—that turn out on closer examination to provide no solution at all, even if they otherwise contain a grain of truth. It is probably true, for example, that greed (or financial self-interest, to use a non-pejorative term) is an especially prevalent motive among the rich.[22] It can take a lot of determination to make a lot of money, after all, and the people who achieve great wealth probably include a disproportionate share of people who simply care more than the average person does about the acquisition of money. You might think that this motive is sufficient to explain why already-rich people would sometimes protest to demand even more money. Maybe they are the kind of people who just cannot get enough. But greed cannot really explain the occurrence of protest movements like this, because social protest for *collective* financial benefits is never the path to individual financial success. A person who was merely greedy would let others protest on her behalf while she got on with the business of making money.[23]

It is also probably true that many rich people are unsatisfied with their wealth because they are motivated by status competition with other rich people. In other words, they may be trying to keep up with the Joneses. This status competition hypothesis may help to explain why so many people with lots of income and wealth appear to think they are deprived. It may also help explain some kinds of acquisitive behavior among people who appear to have more than enough wealth already. But it does not help to explain the emergence of social movements that are defined by collusion, rather than competition, among the rich. The puzzle is not just why rich people would want more wealth; it is why anyone would want to protest on behalf of more wealth for all rich people, *including* the Joneses.[24]

The solution to this puzzle requires us to recognize that it is not the individual experience of absolute hardship, but instead the collective threat of increasing hardship, that motivates affluent people to protest. Rich people and their allies protest collectively when they perceive a common threat to their economic standing. This pattern results from a general psychological propensity that is not unique to the rich. Threats, defined as anticipated losses of economic or personal security, can create new incentives for people to take collective action, regardless of whether those people are rich or so poor that they are on the brink of starvation.[25] Threats make it rational to engage in protest by reducing the opportunity cost of mobilization: If people weigh the expected costs and benefits of protest before deciding on a course of action, then the threat of adversity can alter their calculations by increasing the perceived cost of doing nothing.[26] But even apparently small threats sometimes motivate people to protest more than this sort of rational decision calculus would lead us to expect. One reason why even small threats provide a big stimulus to protest is that a threat can produce uncertainty about one's future well-being. People may experience small changes in their economic standing as signals that larger losses are yet to come. Another reason why small threats produce big behavioral reactions is a psychological tendency called the endowment effect. Most people see an asset as more valuable when they see it as their own. An important consequence of the endowment effect is to change people's evaluations of risk and reward. People who would not risk much to acquire a new benefit will often undergo much greater risk to keep it once it is in their hands.[27] The applicability of this finding to social protest—usually a high-risk form of political activity with a low probability of any reward—should be clear. You do not have to be one of the have-nots to protest. Nor do you have to believe that the odds are on your side. You just have to believe that you might lose what you have if you sit idle.

This general psychological propensity to respond disproportionately to threats, however, is an insufficient explanation for the existence of rich people's movements, because it is normal for the economic fortunes of the rich to fluctuate wildly without producing much protest. Many well-to-do people lose substantial income every time there is a recession, and even a small stock-market downturn may destroy millions of dollars of financial wealth, including the wealth of many rich investors. In a competitive market economy, moreover, a substantial fraction of high-income people may experience downward income mobility relative to others even when the stock market is booming and the economy is growing. Longitudinal studies from the late-twentieth-century United States, for example, show that roughly a quarter of families from the top fifth of the income distribution fell into a lower quintile in a typical year. Published estimates from the 1980s suggest that rates of downward wealth mobility are comparable to these observed rates of downward income mobility, and there is evidence that both income and wealth mobility may have been increasing since then, particularly for the very richest people.[28] In short, the threat of losing income and wealth is part of the experience of many rich people. Maybe that threat motivates them to take risks, but most of the time that risk-taking appears to mean starting a new job or starting a new business. Rich people do not ordinarily respond to economic threats by starting protest movements.

This book will show that it usually takes a special kind of threat called a *policy threat* to trigger collective protest on behalf of the rich. Scholars refer to a policy threat when the loss of economic or personal security is attributable to a real or anticipated change in public policy.[29] Policy threats have two crucial characteristics that make them different from other threats—and more likely to motivate protest.

First, policy threats are especially likely to provoke collective action because they affect many people at once. Other common events that trigger income shocks—such as business failure, job loss, and divorce—are less potent causes of social movements, because they threaten different people at different times. (By the time that the threat of bankruptcy motivates me to act, you may be out of danger.) A movement requires that a sufficient critical mass of potential protesters share the same grievance at the same time. Particularly if you belong to a small and economically privileged elite, it can be hard to find a critical mass of others in your elite group who feel aggrieved at the same time. Changes in public policy can catalyze a critical mass by providing a common and simultaneous threat.[30]

Second, policy threats are also particularly conducive to protest because policymakers provide a convenient and legitimate focal target for protesters. In order for people to persuade themselves and each other that an adverse condition is remediable by protest, they must attribute the adverse condition to the actions of a blameworthy agent.[31] That task is hard when the sources of economic insecurity are diffuse. A downturn in the stock market, for example, can threaten the economic security of many rich people at once, but the source of the threat is difficult to target, because the institution of the market aggregates the decisions of individuals in a way that diffuses responsibility for any particular change in prices. Which of the tens of thousands of buyers or sellers should we blame when prices fall? The institution of the state, in contrast, aggregates decisions in a way that concentrates authority and thereby concentrates perceived responsibility. Laws, no less than prices, depend on many people for their realization. But when policymakers threaten your economic security, you know who to blame: the officials who made the law and who have the authority to change it.

This explanation for protest differs from our leading theories of social movements, because those theories were developed to fit social movements on behalf of the poor and powerless. Political process theory, for example, tells us that people protest when they think they can achieve something by protesting, which generally means that they protest when they think elites will be responsive; and so they are most likely to protest when the appearance of new allies in positions of authority opens a window of political opportunity. This theory might help to explain protests by people who were previously excluded from politics, but the rich never wanted for political access. Resource mobilization theory, another influential theory of social movements, reminds us that protest takes resources, including intangible resources like free time, knowledge of the political system, and civic skills, but also such tangible resources as a place to meet or money for gas to get to a demonstration. The most put-upon people in any society, precisely those who might ordinarily have the most reason to protest, usually do not protest because they are also the people who are most deprived of resources like these; and social movements are therefore most likely to emerge when deprived people experience an infusion of new resources. This theory has proved helpful in explaining the emergence of protest among the poor. But no influx of mobilizing resources can help to explain protest by people who did not lack such resources in the first place.[32]

Comparisons of the rich people's movements described in this book will show that policy threats were necessary to trigger mobilization on behalf of the rich. If it were simply the prospect of losing wealth that motivated rich people's movements, then we would find rich people's movements waxing and waning in time with the movements of the business cycle. If it were the threat of losing political power, then we should expect mobilization to ebb and flow with the shifting electoral fortunes of political parties. Neither of these alternative hypotheses fits the historical record. Instead, we find that mobilization followed on the heels of policy threats. These threats were various, but in all of the cases examined here, they included acts of Congress that increased taxes on at least some high-income or wealthy people. Such policies were often perceived as threats even by many people who did not themselves have sufficient income or wealth to be affected directly, when such people had, or thought they had, reasons to fear that they would be next. Policy threats thereby created a critical mass of people who felt they had a common interest in mobilizing to cut the taxes of the economic elite.

The Political Behavior of the Rich

Policy threats may provide even rich people with shared grievances. But why would aggrieved rich people start a protest movement? Social movements are collective challenges to authority. They press their demands on the powerful, not by promising dollars or votes, but instead by repeatedly and publicly demonstrating their worthiness, unity, numbers, and commitment through such tactics as civil disobedience, "creation of special purpose associations and coalitions, public meetings, solemn processions, vigils, rallies, demonstrations, petition drives, statements to and in public media, and pamphleteering."[33] Many scholars have assumed that people resort to these tactics because they lack better options.[34]

Rich people usually have easier ways to make their voices heard. High-income people participate in politics more than others, at least in part because their money confers access to other resources, such as education and leisure time, which make political participation easier. Money also confers routine access to political authority in the United States through the medium of campaign contributions. Such contributions do not always allow the rich to buy the policies they want, because there are often ample donations on both sides of an issue that cancel each other out. But the bidding war for political access does tend to shut out the perspectives of people who do not have any money to give.[35] Recent public opinion scholarship suggests that American elected officials are most responsive to the preferences of their high-income constituents, and almost totally unresponsive to the preferences of people at the bottom of the income distribution.[36] Elected officials often go beyond mere responsiveness to the rich and eagerly solicit the opinions of their wealthy and high-income constituents. Rich people, in short, rarely need to take collective action to get their way.

When the rich do feel it necessary to act collectively, there are many other ways that they can get their way without resorting to protest. They may found corporations, civic associations, or political action committees. They may jointly hire a public relations firm or pool their political contributions to influence public policy.[37] There are sound reasons to think that rich people will ordinarily prefer strategies like these that require large amounts of money rather than large numbers of people. One such reason is the principle of comparative advantage. Rich people often have the education, time, and confidence that would allow them to make very effective activists, but in a competitive political environment, they get the greatest payoff from using those political resources that the fewest others possess. That means relying on their money.[38] A closely related reason is the efficiency gain from specialization. Wealthy businesspeople may moonlight as amateur lobbyists on their own behalf if they want to. But unless they are expert lobbyists, their economic interests are probably better served by spending their time making more money, and hiring experts to do the lobbying. This kind of delegated, professional, inside lobbying is, in fact, the usual pattern: When wealthy people want to use the political process to protect their assets, they typically hire someone else to lobby behind closed doors for a special tax break.[39]

Why, then, would advocates for the rich ever turn to grassroots tactics that rely on the direct participation of large numbers of people? The answer has two parts: The first part of the answer is that they turn to movement politics when their usual tactics break down. Most rich people usually find elected officials responsive to their preferences, but "most rich people" is not the same as "all rich people," and "usually" is not the same as "always." Policymakers in the twentieth century sometimes acted in ways that threatened the resources of some rich people. This often happened as the result of a crisis (such as a war or a depression) that interrupted legislative business as usual and imposed new priorities on policymakers. Rich people turned to grassroots movement tactics in part because they interpreted these policy threats as signals that the familiar channels of political representation had failed to protect their economic interests.[40]

The second part of the answer is that the advocates of tax cuts for the rich turned to grassroots tactics in times of crisis only when they knew how, and they knew how only when they had been taught. Such tactics as civil disobedience, demonstrations, and petitions all require skill. Access to the relevant skills is a non-trivial necessary condition for the emergence of a social movement. Historical sociologists remind us that the particular repertoire of tactics we think of as 'a social movement' is a recent invention peculiar to a few democratic societies. Aggrieved and dispossessed people in other times and other societies have had their own peculiar modes of collective action that little resemble what we think of as a social movement; they might tar and feather unpopular officials rather than petitioning them for redress of grievances, surround the baker and seize his bread rather than demonstrating for lower prices, or head up to the hills to take up uncivil banditry rather than heading down to the courthouse to practice civil disobedience.[41] Such modes of protest are learned. Few people today know how to tar and feather someone effectively, just as few people in the eighteenth century knew how to write and circulate a petition. Even today, in the era of mass literacy and the Internet, the skill to organize an effective petition is scarce. Still scarcer is the ability to organize a press conference, or a protest meeting, or a tax strike.

Most activists in rich people's movements did not have these skills until they learned them from experienced movement entrepreneurs. By a movement entrepreneur, I mean a leader who initiates a new campaign, organization, or tactic.[42] The movement entrepreneurs who initiated rich people's movements in twentieth-century America were people with exceptional social skills. They also had several specific skills associated with the social movement repertoire.[43] They were the ones who taught other affluent people how to set up a telephone tree, how to solicit a resolution of support from a local club, and how to write a press release. Some of them brought more rarified skills to the movement: how to draft a legislative petition, how to start a new federation of dues-financed clubs from the ground up, even how to attract attention to the cause by charming reporters and courting arrest.

The existence of such movement entrepreneurs is not peculiar to rich people's movements. Indeed, the entrepreneurs who initiated rich people's movements all acquired these skills in other contexts and especially in other social movements. It is a commonplace of social movement scholarship that one movement may have a "spillover" effect on the tactics of the next, in part through the specific skills and experiences that movement entrepreneurs carry with them.[44] Even when activists improvise new tactics and organizational forms, these inventions are usually based on transposing and recombining other tactics and forms with which they have had some practice in another context.[45] The entrepreneurs who first taught rich people how to emulate grassroots protest fit this common pattern: As we will see, they were activists who had acquired their know-how in movements of the left. By the latter half of the twentieth century, however, rich people's movements had begun to incubate their own movement entrepreneurs, and thereby grow a movement tradition of their own.

The existence of skilled movement entrepreneurs willing to organize rich people's movements is a necessary condition for such movements to emerge. Without the efforts of these entrepreneurial activists, many of the policy threats of the twentieth century might still have provoked rich people to political action, but that action would have not have taken the form of a social movement, which is, after all, neither the easiest nor, for most rich people, the most familiar form of political participation.[46]

The evidence for this argument takes two forms. The first is narrative. This book follows the life histories of many influential movement entrepreneurs, sometimes in considerable biographical detail. I hope these stories are engaging—many of these movement entrepreneurs were fascinating people—but my main purpose in telling these stories is not to entertain you; it is to show how the activists who organized and led rich people's movements all acquired their know-how in previous social movements. Such narratives show that skilled entrepreneurs were central figures in every rich people's movement of the twentieth century. They do not show that skilled entrepreneurs were *necessary* to get these movements started. For that we need a second kind of evidence: comparison. The chapters to come will show many instances in which policy threats produced a pool of aggrieved rich people, but no movement was forthcoming, because no skilled entrepreneur was organizing such a movement. In many cases it is even possible to identify entrepreneurs who tried, and failed, to mobilize a movement because they lacked the skills that could be acquired through previous movement experience. By comparing episodes, we can see that skilled movement entrepreneurs were critical.

It is also instructive to compare the people who participated in rich people's movements with their socioeconomic peers who did not join in. In every campaign, those who participated were a small subset of the people who shared a potential interest in, and sympathy for, the cause of cutting taxes on the rich. The identity of that activist subset varied from one rich people's movement to the next—one time, Southern country bankers; another time, Northeastern urban industrialists—but there was one overriding commonality. In every case the joiners were disproportionately those who had been contacted and recruited by skilled movement entrepreneurs.[47]

Finally, the importance of movement entrepreneurs can also be seen in the comparison across episodes of mobilization. The forms of protest—styles of activism, models of organization, tactical choices, and even rhetorical tropes—varied from one movement to the next, sometimes dramatically, in accordance with the styles of activism promoted and taught by the particular entrepreneurs active in each movement. The tax clubs of the 1920s looked like Populist organizations, because the organizers followed the template they had learned from radical agrarian protesters; the business-backed tax limitation effort of the 1930s and 1940s modeled its demands and tactics on the movement to repeal Prohibition, because that is the model that the leaders knew and the model that they copied; the movement for income tax repeal in the 1950s had many organizational and tactical similarities to the women's club movement and the movement for woman suffrage, in part because it was led by former suffragists and clubwomen. Without *any* such activists to teach them the ropes of social protest, it is likely that the aggrieved rich would have stuck with the inside lobbying tactics that they knew.

Crafting Policy to Reward the Rich

Rich people resorted to grassroots politics when inside lobbying failed, and when skilled movement entrepreneurs showed them an alternative. But they stuck with it because they found that protest sometimes worked. This is the third and last puzzle of rich people's movements. It is not surprising to find rich people getting their way in American politics. Generations of political scientists have shown an unmistakable bias toward business and the rich in American policymaking.[48] What *is* surprising is to find rich people winning *new* policies that explicitly provided collective benefits for *all* the rich—and what is especially surprising is that they did so by means of a social movement.

Social movements work by drawing attention to themselves. Most of the time this is exactly what does *not* work for rich people in democratic polities. The rich are a small minority of the polity. Tax cuts or other benefits targeted to all rich people (and big enough to be appreciated by those who, after all, have expensive tastes) do not come cheap. Such upward redistributive policies often offend widely held norms of fairness, and they always conflict with other, more popular budget priorities. Under these circumstances the best move for rich people who want to protect their resources is usually to contain the scope of the potential conflict. Advocates for particular rich people usually avoid broad, class-wide appeals in favor of identifying themselves with narrowly defined interest groups such as "prestigious professions or businesses" to which they may belong. They often lobby for tax breaks so narrowly crafted that they apply only to a particular industry, firm, family, or individual. They pursue these tax breaks by lobbying quietly behind the scenes, "within the smallest and most exclusive governmental forums, as far out of public view as possible," as the political scientist Jack Walker put it. Above all, they avoid attention.[49]

Elected officials in the United States are so responsive to the rich precisely because they are usually smart enough to confine themselves to these hidden forms of influence. Political scientists have shown that the exchange of campaign contributions for narrowly targeted tax breaks is in fact the most common pattern in business lobbying. American political institutions provide many opportunities to tinker with the tax code: Tax bills must originate in the House of Representatives, and they pass through two houses and many committees before they become law. American political institutions also favor industry- and geography-specific coalitions, because representatives who want to be reelected must attend to the influential interest groups in their districts. That is why elected officials are so eager to vote for tax breaks narrowly targeted to a particular industry, a particular firm, or even a particular individual. Such particularistic tax breaks are also politically appealing because they are easily concealed from the publics that might oppose them.[50] In contrast, a proposal to cut taxes for all wealthy or high-income people across the board would be hard to keep out of the headlines. Even a sympathetic elected official—one who might reward a wealthy campaign donor with an earmark or two—will be tempted to look the other way when a grassroots group comes knocking at the front door with a petition that openly demands tax cuts for all rich people.

But sometimes elected officials did not look the other way. Activists repeatedly got their demands on the policy agenda. And on a few occasions, Congress responded to rich people's movements by providing tax cuts targeted to the rich. Whether the movements were successful depends on what you mean by success; activists sometimes disagreed with each other about whether they could or should claim any credit for these tax cuts, and measured against the benchmark of the protesters' most radical demands, the tax cuts typically fell short. But measured against the benchmark of what would have happened in the absence of any rich people's movements, the benefits were sometimes substantial indeed. In at least a few cases—including some of the largest income tax cuts in American history—there can be little doubt that rich people's movements affected the scale of the tax cuts passed by elected officials. Protesters had an impact, even when they did not succeed on their own terms.[51]

Under what conditions did they have an impact? Mainly they did so when the reins of federal government were already in the hands of a programmatic political party that was openly allied with the interests of the wealthy. In practice, this meant that it happened when the presidency and both houses of Congress were unified under the conservative wing of the Republican Party.[52] This favorable circumstance arose only a few times in the last century, notably under Presidents Calvin Coolidge and George W. Bush. The Republican Party also briefly controlled both houses of Congress during the first term of President Dwight D. Eisenhower, but Eisenhower's pragmatic accommodation to the welfare state and his express opposition to the demands of the rich people's movements of his day provided a less favorable environment. It was not the Republican Party label that mattered; it was the ideological content and consistency of the party in control of government. This pattern is the mirror image of the conditions that favor poor people's movements: Such movements have had the most influence on public policy when the governing party has been programmatically committed to redistributive reform.[53]

Ordinarily, however, rich people's movements could not count on partisan allies controlling all the levers of power. Even when their allies were in charge, those allies often needed political cover if they were to enact a policy that so obviously favored the rich. For these reasons, activists in rich people's movements found that getting their demands on the policy agenda required careful legislative drafting; they wrote their own policy proposals and crafted them to appeal to a bigger constituency than the rich. This practice of strategic policy crafting is a special kind of persuasive communication. Sociologists have pointed out that activists in any movement have to come up with a culturally resonant "frame," which is a definition of the situation that diagnoses a social ill and implies a particular solution. Much of the work of activism consists of framing the problem in a way that will attract allies and demobilize potential enemies.[54] Typically this means finding ways to characterize the problem that make its solution seem beneficial to a big coalition. Policy crafting allows activists to create their own coalitions by manipulating these benefits directly.

Activists in rich people's movements had tremendous latitude to craft their policies because there were many ways to write a policy that would achieve the same collective benefits for their constituency. The same distribution of benefits, for example, can be achieved by any of several different policy instruments, from regulation, to taxation, to spending, and each of these tools in turn involves several parameters that can be manipulated independently of each other. Several different policies can be packaged together to lure in other interest groups that might otherwise have no interest in redistribution to the rich.[55] Such policy crafting is more than just spin. Scholars who study framing and public policy most often address the strategic use of rhetoric (or "crafted talk") to sell a policy proposal after it has been written.[56] But activists know that some policies are more easily spun than others, and they need not limit themselves to crafting talk about their policy proposals after the fact. They can and do write their policies to manipulate policy tradeoffs directly, and to make some of the costs harder to perceive and evaluate. The rich people's movements described in this book crafted their policies deliberately to reduce and obscure the budgetary and political tradeoffs involved in expensive transfers to the rich.[57]

By crafting their own policy proposals, activists allied with the wealthy can make it substantially easier for policymakers to meet their demands. Lawmakers often struggle with information overload. Without some strategy for coping with the sea of information, a conscientious person of ordinary intelligence could take forever to narrow the infinite universe of possible policies down to a definite set of alternatives. Policymakers cope with this potentially overwhelming task by relying on simple decision-making heuristics, and one of the most reliable is to choose from the options that come most readily to their attention. They rely on lobbyists and other advocacy groups to suggest policies; they copy parts of policies that they have previously applied to different target groups or problems; they imitate other, highly publicized policies, or policies that exist in nearby jurisdictions with which they are familiar. The participants in the rich people's movements of the twentieth century played to these coping strategies. They improved their chances of getting on the agenda by presenting lawmakers with ready-made proposals that were partly copied from other policies that they knew legislators would find familiar.

The protesters also manipulated or obfuscated the costs of their proposals by packaging tax cuts for the rich with other policies. One tactic was to package them together with tax cuts or giveaways for other groups, as when Iowa tax clubs in 1925 demanded abolition of the estate tax on large fortunes together with tax cuts for small corporations. Another tactic was to package several options in a single proposal that included the desired outcome as one alternative among many, with the political incentives rigged so that it was bound to be the most appealing option when it came time for implementation. Proponents of income tax limitation, for example, proposed a constitutional amendment that allowed high tax rates on the rich as long as Congress was willing to impose similarly high taxes on the vast majority of voters. This amendment would have achieved their policy ends, not by legally prohibiting high taxes on the rich, but by making such taxes politically prohibitive. This way of crafting their demands allowed activists to downplay the revenue costs of their proposals. Such policy obfuscation can be an effective way for an advocacy group to win legislative support even if legislators are undeceived: It may be sufficient to craft a policy proposal in a way that persuades legislators that *voters* will not perceive substantial budgetary tradeoffs.[58]

The activists in these movements sometimes made shocking or radical proposals that would require the dismantling of virtually the entire federal government. They were not always naïve or utopian enough to think that their most extreme proposals would become law, but often it was enough merely to get such proposals on the agenda. The mere presence of radical proposals provided negotiating leverage to lawmakers who backed less extreme benefits for the rich. Sympathetic economic conservatives in Congress often found it useful to treat movement proposals as a starting point for negotiation with their more liberal colleagues. They sold regressive tax cuts to moderates as a way to co-opt or forestall the more extreme demands of the movement. Sociologists have found that poor people's movements sometimes provided a "radical flank" for establishment liberals and thereby helped to legitimate greater redistribution from the rich to the poor.[59] This book will show that radical flank effects were not only for the left. Sometimes rich people's movements provided a radical flank for establishment conservatives that helped to legitimate less extreme conservative measures—and thereby helped to pull American tax policy toward the right.

Finally, when partisan ideological allies were not in charge, and when policy crafting was not enough to sway more votes to their side, some activists embarked on a long-term project to take over the Republican Party. The conservative takeover of the Republican Party is one of the best-known stories of late-twentieth-century American political history. It is worth underscoring here, however, because the role of the party is too often neglected in studies of social movements. Social movement scholars describe dramatic conflicts between protesters and policymakers in which political parties usually figure as part of the terrain—sometimes presenting protesters with obstacles, sometimes presenting them with opportunities. In the late twentieth century, however, the Republican Party was not just an obstacle or an opportunity, but also an instrument. Rich people's movements ultimately swayed the state by seizing the party.

Making a Movement Tradition

The movements described in this book sometimes persuaded democratically elected policymakers to reward the rich. This result would seem surprising to those theorists of democracy from Aristotle to Karl Marx who argued that rational politicians in a majoritarian system will redistribute property from the rich, who are few, to the poor, who are many. The victories of rich people's movements would seem to pose a challenge for *any* democratic theory that assumes politicians tailor their decisions to please a rational, well-informed, and self-interested voting majority.[60]

The argument I have presented here is that rich people's movements have shaped American politics precisely because of the *limitations* of human rationality, information, and self-interest—including endowment effects that led many affluent people to react disproportionately to threats; cognitive limitations that forced rich people and their allies to choose tactics and arguments from a limited repertoire taught to them by movement entrepreneurs; and limitations on policymakers' information-processing abilities that allowed the activists to obfuscate the costs of their policy proposals. This argument should not be confused with the view that people who support tax cuts for the rich are all dupes. The people who supported the demands of rich people's movements were not hyper-rational calculating machines, but neither were most of them fools, and they usually knew where they stood in the American economic order every bit as well as their political opponents did. Nor should the argument presented here be confused with the popular view that the rich are puppet masters who pull the strings of American politics. The activists who led the rich people's movements were not far-seeing master manipulators who knew just how to get their way. They, too, were only human, and they improvised within their limitations using the materials at hand.

The materials that these activists found at hand were the detritus of other movements past. They picked up policy models, templates of organization, and protest tactics from previous challenges to authority. At first they had few previous rich people's movements to learn from, so they drew on their experiences and observations of other early-twentieth-century movements, including movements of veterans, workers, farmers, and women. But they passed on the lessons they learned, so that later activists could and did draw on the accumulated lore of previous rich people's movements. That is why certain policy proposals reappeared again and again in the twentieth century, evolving over time as they were tailored to new circumstances. The statutory tax limit proposed by the tax clubs in 1924, for example, was revived by business-backed tax associations in 1936 as a tax limit amendment to the Constitution, and again in 1975 by their successors as a combined tax limitation and balanced budget amendment. The activists stocked their rhetorical arsenals, too, with arguments and tactics forged in earlier struggles, even as they recombined them in new ways to suit the times.

Through this process of borrowing and patchwork, the rich people's movements of the twentieth century gradually stitched together a grassroots libertarian tradition. It was a practical tradition that encompassed a distinctive style of action. The grassroots libertarian style included reliance on paid organizers to recruit and knit together local chapters of volunteers who engaged in outsider tactics including petitions, public demonstrations, and occasional celebrations of civil disobedience to tax authorities. It also encompassed styles of argument and rhetorical tropes. True to its agrarian populist roots, the rhetoric of the grassroots libertarian tradition celebrated producers and disparaged idlers. It depicted the income tax as the linchpin of the post-New-Deal order—the "root of all evil," in a phrase that many mid-century activists liked to repeat—and it embraced remedies up to and including amendment of the Constitution. This tradition had little to do with the intellectual libertarianism that we today associate with

the names of Friedrich Hayek, Ludwig von Mises, and other academic thinkers. The ideological content of the tradition was a grab bag of arguments rather
than a coherent body of ideas or political philosophy, because this tradition was
practical rather than scholastic; with few exceptions its carriers were not intellectual system-builders, but instead activists and organizers who treated ideas
as tools to win arguments. Thus the tradition came to include both utilitarian
arguments that justified tax cuts for the rich as a way to stimulate investment,
and rights-based arguments that implied a moral duty to cut taxes regardless of
utilitarian considerations. It came to include the classical liberal idea that taxation of capital is bad because it distorts investment decisions, alongside the classical republican idea that the taxation of capital is bad because it leads to tyranny.
It came to include arguments that taxing the rich is bad because it generates too
little revenue, and arguments that taxing the rich is bad because it generates too
much revenue. Like other practical traditions in American politics, the grassroots libertarian tradition is not always logically coherent, but it is *sociologically*
coherent: It is a real set of tactics and arguments suited to a particular position
in social relations. The grassroots libertarian tradition lives on today. Its features
will look and sound familiar to any observer of American politics in the early
twenty-first century.

The history of rich people's movements, in other words, is an important chapter in the development of the American right. The rise of the right, we now know,
was one of the major stories of twentieth-century American history. Twenty-
first-century historians and social scientists have taught us a great deal about how
conservative economic policy ideas came to exercise such influence in American
political life, and about the conservative social movements that reshaped the
Republican Party in the last decades of the century. But the story of rich people's
movements is still little known—perhaps because, with few exceptions, our histories of economic conservatives have focused on thinkers and ignored social
movements, while our studies of conservative social movements have focused
on social, rather than economic, conservatives.

Recent studies of the pro-business strand of American conservative thought,
for example, have enriched our understanding of economic conservatism by
tracing its roots to early-twentieth-century boardrooms and late-twentieth-
century classrooms. But such studies have told us very little about grassroots
political behavior. They have focused instead on the history of libertarian or
neo-liberal ideas. Most histories of economic conservatism in its American vari-
ant are therefore peopled with intellectuals, writers, and publishers—the Ayn
Rands and Friedrich Hayeks—and the businessmen who gave them grants.
Such intellectual histories are valuable. By training our attention on book learning to the neglect of the practical lore that generations of activists passed down,

however, they neglect everything that made the libertarian strand of American conservatism more than just a debating society.[61]

Other studies have filled in our picture of conservative social movements, but they have focused with few exceptions on a subset of such movements that aim to resist cultural change. The classic sociological studies of conservative social movements explicitly restricted their attention to cultural preservationist movements—such as the Temperance movement, the Ku Klux Klan, and the Religious Right—and set aside the politics of economic redistribution. Even within this narrow focus, most sociological scholarship on conservative movements has focused on the most explicitly racist or nativist movements, and disproportionately on the most violent or extreme even among these. These studies, too, are valuable, but they tell us little about those conservative movements that have accepted the American pluralist order and worked within its constraints to shape public policy for the benefit of the rich.[62]

This book joins a recent turn in historical scholarship on conservatism that corrects this partial view of American conservative traditions. The last decade has seen a proliferation of suburban community studies by historians who aim to explain the conservative resurgence in the late twentieth century.[63] It has also seen new studies of conservative business elites and the institutions they funded to propagate their beliefs.[64] And it has seen a dramatic resurgence of political history focused on conservative Republicans in office and the party activists who put them there.[65] All of these new histories of conservatism tell us a great deal about the philanthropists who funded rich people's movements, the rank and file suburbanites who supported them, and the conservative Republican politicians who took up their banner in the late twentieth century. But these histories still have told us too little about the movement organizations that solicited the donations, recruited the members, and made the banners in the first place. That is the story told in this book. It is a story of movement entrepreneurs and the personal and organizational networks they knit together, thereby transforming ideas, money, and scattered local constituencies into actual campaigns.[66]

The story begins in 1913, with the ratification of the Sixteenth Amendment, which authorized the federal government to levy a direct, personal income tax. If the spokespeople for the rich people's movements were to be believed, this was the greatest catastrophe in the history of American government, perhaps in the history of the world. Generations of activists likened the ratification of the Sixteenth Amendment to the biblical fall from grace. We begin, then, in their Garden of Eden.

CHAPTER 1

The Revolution of 1913

The activists who campaigned to untax the rich in the twentieth-century United States told a common story about the origins of their crusades. It all started, they said, when a singular catastrophe befell the American polity in 1913. The story was handed down from generation to generation. Writing in 1938, J. A. "Pappy" Arnold remembered it as "the greatest calamity in the evolution of government." In 1952, Frank Chodorov recalled it as "the revolution of 1913." In 1974, Robert Charlton published an article describing it as a "disaster" that undermined the American republic. In 1989, Lewis Uhler characterized it as the beginning of big government in America, as the end of an era of freedom, and as the first step on the road to serfdom. In 1997, Larry Arnn and Grover Norquist portrayed it as a betrayal of the founding fathers and as the beginning of a new federal policy of "terror and torment."[1]

The calamity these activists were describing was the ratification of the Sixteenth Amendment. Passed by Congress in 1909, the Sixteenth Amendment to the Constitution consists of a single sentence: "The Congress shall have the power to lay and collect taxes on incomes, from whatever source derived, without apportionment among the several states, and without regard to any census or enumeration." It became part of the Constitution in March 1913, after forty-two state legislatures voted to ratify it. To understand why so many Americans thought it necessary to write this sentence into their Constitution, and what it has to do with the origins of rich people's movements, it helps to understand something about inequality in the early-twentieth-century United States.

At the top were a few rich men. In 1913, Andrew Mellon was one of the richest of them all. Caricatures of that era depict the stereotypical capitalist as a smug, fat man who towered over the poor, but Mellon did not fit the stereotype. He was medium in height and slight of frame; in photographs of the period, he looks like he might bend under the weight of his impressive mustache. Contemporaries described him as modest and unassuming, an impression that arose partly because he was a man of few words who rarely socialized. Instead, he worked. Mellon rose early every day and spent the morning in his office at the downtown Mellon National Bank. In the afternoon he returned to his house in the highlands for a dinner of mush. That house, a three-story red-brick home on a medium-sized garden lot within the Pittsburgh city limits, was hardly opulent by the standards of the day. But it was filled with gilt-framed paintings, expensive furnishings, the most modern indoor plumbing, and more than enough rooms for Mellon, his two children, and a small household staff.[2]

And who was at the bottom? Down in the riverfront wards of Pittsburgh, the immigrant laborers who filled the lowest-paid jobs in the city's steel mills were crowding by the dozens into dilapidated houses a fraction of the size of Mellon's home. A typical workman might rent a single room for himself, his wife, and his children—and then sublet half of the room to another worker to help with the rent. People commonly slept four to a room, and ten to a room was not unheard of. When beds were too few they slept in shifts. Many slum tenements in Pittsburgh still had no running water or sewer access in 1913. If the residents were lucky, they might share a single indoor tap with one or two other families. Often they made do with an outdoor hydrant. And often many families, sometimes amounting to well over a hundred people, shared the same latrine. Working-class Pittsburgh was ill-served by sewers, and middle-class reformers wrote horrified reports about the slum privies that were little better than covered pits, frequently "full to the brim and overflowing." Those who could afford to lived uphill.[3]

But it was the downhill residents who paid a greater share of their income in taxes. The federal government levied tariffs and excise taxes on alcohol and tobacco that pressed most heavily on the poor. The state and local governments taxed property in ways that perversely favored the rich. Mellon, for example, like other homeowners in the highlands, enjoyed special tax treatment on his estate—until 1912, the spacious garden homes in the old Nineteenth Ward of Pittsburgh were taxed as if they were no more valuable than rural farms—and lived in a district where real property tax rates were low. In contrast, the unskilled laborers in the Eighth Ward, who paid their landlords' taxes indirectly whenever they paid rent, had no such luck. They lived on urban land that was assessed at a greater share of its true value and then taxed at a higher rate than land in Mellon's neighborhood.[4]

From top to bottom, American society before the income tax was a picture of inequality, and taxes made it worse.

The Price of Inequality

This picture of Andrew Mellon's Pittsburgh is only a partial image of American inequality in the Progressive Era. The country had hundreds of men richer than

Mellon, and millions as poor as the poorest Pittsburgh slum dwellers. Andrew Mellon's wealth on the eve of the Great War probably made him one of the richest 0.01 percent of the population, an elite circle that would have numbered about 6,000 people. Together they owned almost 10 percent of all the wealth in the country. Draw a slightly wider circle to include the wealthiest 2.5 percent of Americans, and you would have encompassed the owners of more than half of the property in the United States. Visitors from abroad in this era marveled at the material wealth of the American republic, from the stock markets and skyscrapers of Manhattan to the mountains and gold mines of California to the endless miles of fertile farmland in between. But the owners of most of that wealth would have fit into a city smaller than Chicago.[5]

Indeed, although statistical evidence on inequality before the twentieth century is fragmentary, the limited available data suggest that the ownership of wealth on the eve of World War I was as unequal as it ever had been, and more unequal than it ever has been since. The Civil War had briefly seemed to promise economic equality: The war had wiped out much of the wealth held by the Southern elite—by destroying much of their capital and by abolishing a great share of their wealth that consisted of property rights in enslaved people—and emancipation had also conferred on many of the poorest Americans for the first time the right to own property. But the war had also laid the groundwork for new inequalities of wealth that replaced the old. In the North, war production incubated the new industries that would produce great fortunes in the Gilded Age, including the railroads that would make the fortunes of Pittsburgh's steel industry (and with them the fortunes of Andrew Mellon). In the South, freedmen, no matter how thrifty, began accumulating wealth from a baseline of zero. Most Southern farm tenants stayed poor. Many, black and white, grew even poorer, as the small sums of money they borrowed to carry them through the planting season compounded from year to year until they found themselves trapped in a permanent condition of debt peonage. By 1913, wealth inequalities in the United States yawned wider than ever.[6]

Income was less unequally distributed than wealth, but it was still comparatively unequal by any historical standard. The richest 1 percent of people claimed 18 percent of the personal income before taxes. Their share after taxes and transfers may have been even greater. Andrew Mellon's annual income would have been around $1 million in 1913, putting him in the top 0.01 percent of the income distribution too.[7] On the other side of town, an unskilled laborer for U.S. Steel, by toiling ten hours a day for six days, might expect to earn $12 in a week—when he could find work. Pittsburgh was known as one of the best labor markets in the country for the unskilled. By comparison, a black sharecropper in the Mississippi Delta could expect to earn $333 annually from his share of the crop. Andrew Mellon sometimes spent a hundred times as much on a single painting to hang in his house.[8]

Poverty was everywhere. Social investigators had only begun the work of surveying incomes and quantifying the budgets necessary to sustain life, but the fragmentary picture that emerges from their findings is sobering. One famous study by Robert Hunter aimed to draw what he called a "poverty line" at the income level just above starvation for a family of average size in 1904. He pegged it at $460 in the North industrial states (higher in cities, where the cost of living was greater) and $300 in the rural South. Hunter guessed that perhaps one American in five was poor by this standard. Most historians who have looked at this question have concluded that this was a conservative guess at the percentage below his poverty line, and moreover that his poverty line was unrealistically austere. Other contemporary investigators judged something like a third to a half of Americans to have been poor on the eve of World War I. Social historians who have tried to derive a more exact poverty rate by applying the official poverty measure of the late-twentieth-century United States to early-twentieth-century incomes have generally given up on the exercise, not only because the data are too poor to permit precise measurement, but also because the overall picture is clear. Regardless of the precise estimate, it is plain that what is now defined as absolute poverty in our official statistics was so widespread that it would have been seen as the normal condition of a majority of the population.[9]

State and federal governments did little to moderate the extremes of inequality, and much to exacerbate them. A handful of Southern states had income taxes on the books that were not effectively enforced. Wisconsin was the only jurisdiction that had the administrative capacity to effectively assess and collect a tax on the incomes of the rich, with the result that high-income people could easily avoid the tax by avoiding the state.[10] Most state and local governments supposedly taxed wealth, but in practice the general property tax was a tax on real estate only, because real estate was the only form of wealth that could not be hidden or carried over county lines when the assessor came calling. Almost no one reported their household effects to the tax assessor, and intangible wealth represented by stock and bond certificates generally escaped scot-free. "The country grows apace, and wealth and numbers accumulate at a rate unexampled in the world's history," the economist Franklin Taussig wrote in 1899. "But the tax returns, if any one believed them, would indicate that personal property is barely holding its own—nay, is commonly decreasing—and that a veritable blight has fallen on this form of wealth." In 1913, fully $10 billion worth of property escaped taxation in New York State alone.[11]

Public spending, too, did little to alleviate poverty. The poorhouses of the nineteenth century had mostly closed down. Local budgets for so-called outdoor relief were meager and shrinking.[12] States spent little on relief. Some Southern states had paltry pensions for disabled or indigent veterans of the Confederate Army, but eligibility was limited by a test of moral character that county officials administered arbitrarily, and the amounts were inadequate to support life: In Georgia, the most generous state, an indigent Confederate veteran could expect $60 a year.[13] A group of determined reformers in Northern states were campaigning for the creation of public pensions to support poor widows with children. The Illinois mother's pension law, passed in 1911, was the first, and until 1913 the only, such pension law, and it illustrates their shortcomings. The Illinois law did not mandate public pensions, much less fund them, but merely authorized counties to provide such pensions out of their own funds at their own discretion. Thus, for example, Cook County opted to provide pensions, upon application, to those widowed mothers who were judged by county officials to be of suitable moral character and otherwise unable to support their families by work. The few women who risked the scorn of their neighbors by applying, and who met the stringent criteria of morality and disability, were then required to submit to a detailed examination of their household budgets, so that they could be provided with a pension that was carefully calibrated to be *insufficient* for their needs; the purpose was to supplement, but emphatically *not* to replace, a wage from domestic service. Eighteen more states would pass mothers' pensions in 1913. Such laws obviously would not make a big dent in poverty.[14]

At the national level, the only substantial transfer program was the Civil War veterans' pension. Congress had created this pension to provide income for disabled veterans of the Union Army, and generations of election-minded politicians had liberalized the eligibility rules to include anyone who could plausibly claim to be a Union veteran, or the survivor of a deceased Union veteran. It was a comparatively generous social insurance scheme by the standards of the day, many times more generous than state-level veterans' or mothers' pensions. In 1913, the pension expert Isaac Max Rubinow noted that this pension enrolled hundreds of thousands more people and redistributed more than three times as much money as the British old-age pension scheme. But Rubinow also noted that the federal Civil War pensions were not much of an income-equalizing measure. The Northern native-born veterans had enjoyed an advantaged position in the labor market before their retirement. They also had received many other government benefits, from preferment for government jobs, to extra allotments of free land under the Homestead Act. Compared to most elderly Americans, the typical recipient of a veterans' pension was probably already comparatively well off.[15]

The Union Army pensions may even have exacerbated income inequality because they were financed by the tariff. This method of financing was doubly regressive. First, the tariff was a tax on consumption that took a greater share of income from the poor than the rich. Legally, it was the importer who paid the tariff. In practice, importers passed the costs along in their prices. These price increases allowed their domestic competitors to raise prices as well. Although imported and import-competing goods made up a small share of the average family's household budget, this hidden tax could still amount to an economic burden on the poor.[16]

Second, and more important, the tariff also discriminated among industries, providing protection to investors (and higher wages to workers) in some import-competing industries of the urban North, but leaving out most agricultural products and therefore most agricultural workers. The result was that the net burden of paying for Civil War pensions fell most heavily on farmers and farm workers, and disproportionately on the defeated South, where almost no one had fought on the side of the war that would have qualified them for benefits. The tariff-and-pension system transferred money from the poorest part of the country to the richest, and from the working poor to the middle-income elderly.[17]

These economic institutions did little to equalize incomes for American society as a whole. The result was economic inequality on a scale that may be difficult for twenty-first- century readers to grasp. Contemporaries thought that the great inequalities of the Progressive Era were something altogether new in the history of the human species. "So much wealth, so much luxury, such a bewildering display, such a concentration of the power for which money is only a symbol has not been known in the records of the race," wrote the socialist newspaperman Charles Edward Russell in 1908. Some saw the new concentrations of wealth as evidence of the unprecedented opportunities now open to Americans, and a great vindication of the promise of democracy. Others, like Russell, saw the potential for new dynastic families to corrupt American democracy and transform it into "plutocracy."[18]

Inequality this extreme had many undesirable consequences, not just for the poor, but also for the rich.[19] One such consequence was economic volatility. Financial crises were a frequent fact of life, because the availability of large fortunes fueled speculative bubbles that eventually burst. In the absence of any taxes on income or financial wealth, the economy lacked an important automatic stabilizer that could help to moderate the extremes of the business cycle, although no one knew it at the time. Andrew Mellon regarded it as natural and inevitable that a catastrophic recession should follow years of growth; his father's maxim was "five up and five down." This rollercoaster ride was worst for the poor. As the sociologist W. E. B. DuBois noted in 1899, a single business depression could push most residents of Philadelphia's black ghetto below the level of subsistence. But the big swings of the business cycle were also unsettling and often ruinous for the rich, who experienced extreme fluctuations in their fortunes. Mellon, who was generally a conservative investor, lived in dread that a financial panic might wreck his business without warning, as the Panic of 1873 had nearly done.

When he wanted to describe a particularly unpleasant experience, he compared it to "a panic day at the bank."[20]

Another consequence of economic inequality was economic segregation. The development of streetcar lines allowed cities to spread outward, and the economic elite used the opportunity to pull away from the poor in the first decade of the twentieth century. Class segregation exacerbated the social distance between rich and poor. A resident of a new garden suburb on the outskirts of Pittsburgh, for example, described it as a "magic circle ... where life is worth living and nature smiles sweetly, undefiled by smoke and grime," and contrasted his charmed neighbors with the "devilish" working-class majority he had left behind. Mellon's six-year-old son Paul, leaving for a family vacation in Europe in the summer of 1913, was stunned by the sight of working-class people who were not his fathers' servants. "I had never seen people as poor and as dirty as that before," he wrote in his memoir. "They were huddled together, looking strangely at us." He stood looking strangely back at them. The rich and the poor regarded each other with incomprehension.[21]

Class segregation also bred disease. The crowded riverfront slums of Pittsburgh, ill-supplied with sewer lines and clean water, were unhealthy places to live. The root of the problem was not just poverty and poor hygiene, but also economic inequality: Most of the rich withdrew to the suburbs and resisted incorporation rather than pay for sewers, a water filtration system, and rubbish removal in the Pittsburgh slums.[22] Mellon was atypical because he still lived within the city limits. Most of those who could have afforded to tax themselves for a municipal hospital chose instead to live outside the city and endow private institutions far from the slums. When the sick poor managed to get to these private hospitals, they often found that they were refused treatment. By one estimate, in the winter of 1908, the city had some 3,000 tuberculosis sufferers "in a sufficiently advanced stage to be a peril to all with whom they came in contact," of whom 1,800 received no hospital or home care whatsoever. The illnesses that plagued the Pittsburgh slums did not always stay contained. Pneumonia, for example, was endemic in the city, and though it mostly killed poor people, it did not discriminate too carefully. In the winter of 1911, it almost felled Andrew Mellon.[23]

Less easily quantified, but perhaps also as corrosive, was the effect of inequality and economic segregation on social trust. Sociologists of the era marveled at the growth of large cities where even the simplest tasks—going to work, getting the news, finding your next meal—required daily negotiations with countless strangers. Such negotiations worked when there was a baseline of trust. Between people who were desperate to get ahead and people who were anxious to protect their wealth, however, there was ample room for misunderstanding. Men and women of Mellon's station in life had to be constantly on guard against thieves, kidnappers, and hustlers of all kinds. Mellon's wife Nora, for example, who was understandably bored with the dour banker she had married, met a dashing stranger on a trip to England in 1902 and thought she had found true love; but it turned out that the handsome stranger with the upper-class accent was a con man from a very poor background who was after her husband's money. Protecting oneself against such scams could be costly and time consuming. Mellon once said that he had to do a more thorough background investigation to hire household staff than to hire a new chief executive for one of his companies. It was a revealing admission, because the stakes were immeasurably higher in the latter case: A wrong move by a captain of the Mellon banking empire could have been enough to wreck the economy of Pittsburgh, and Mellon's household with it. Apparently Mellon simply found it harder to identify a trustworthy job candidate across the chasm of mutual suspicion that separated rich and poor.[24]

The mistrust was mutual, and it often erupted into open class hostility. Mellon well remembered that in 1892, his best friend, Henry Clay Frick, one of the richest men in the country, had been shot and stabbed nearly to death in his own home by a penniless anarchist named Alexander Berkman, who saw himself as an avenger for the poor. On another occasion, a passing stranger had recognized Mellon as a famous millionaire and shoved him in front of an oncoming trolley car. He narrowly escaped with his life. On September 6, 1901, an unemployed steelworker named Leon Czolgosz had shot President William McKinley, because, he said, "McKinley was going around the country shouting about prosperity when there was no prosperity for the poor man."[25] It may seem a stretch, or even a perverse denial of personal responsibility, to attribute such acts of terrorism to something as diffuse as economic inequality. But that is how people, including McKinley's patrician vice president and successor, Theodore Roosevelt, interpreted these attacks at the time. In October 1912, when Roosevelt was running for the presidency again, and on his way to give a campaign speech, he was shot by a would-be assassin of his own. After checking his wound to be sure that it was non-fatal, Roosevelt strode on stage, threw aside his prepared text, unbuttoned his jacket to show his bloody shirt, and delivered a speech describing the assault as evidence that inequality was tearing society apart:

> Friends, every good citizen ought to do everything in his or her power to prevent the coming of the day when we shall see in this country two organized greeds fighting one another, when we shall see the greed of the "Have nots" arraigned against the greed of the "Haves." If ever that day comes, such incidents as this tonight will be commonplace in our history.

In this case, Roosevelt guessed wrong. His would-be assassin was no have-not, but rather a saloon owner who claimed to be acting on instructions from the ghost of William McKinley.[26] But the fact that Roosevelt assumed his assailant was poor illustrates just how pervasive was the atmosphere of mistrust at the time. The rich and powerful were ready to believe the worst of the poor. The haves saw the have-nots as an ever-present terrorist threat.[27]

Inequality, in short, was not an unmitigated good even for the rich. It brought new dangers. It made their lives uneasy. Sometimes it may have even made their lives shorter. But men like Mellon welcomed it anyway. They saw inequality as inevitable in a competitive economy that rewarded excellence, and they had no doubt that their own riches were a sign that excellence and virtue were rewarded.

The Best Citizens

Who were these men like Mellon? All of the top wealth holders in his rarified circle were white, and the first tax returns filed under the new federal estate tax in 1917 indicate that most of them were men in late middle age.[28] Like Mellon, these wealthy people held the vast majority of their assets in the intangible form of stocks and bonds, which were mostly safe from state tax authorities. Mellon's peers were also children of wealth. Most of the truly great fortunes, like Mellon's, were accumulated over generations, and the super-rich were generally beneficiaries of their parents' luck and prudence as much as their own business acumen.[29]

Even the wealthiest Americans on the eve of the Great War did not usually describe themselves as rich. Mellon's son Paul grew up thinking that "millionaire" was an impolite word. When pressed to describe their station in life, men of Mellon's elite status used the same words as business owners in the middle and upper middle of the income distribution. They described themselves as gentlemen of good character, businessmen, and substantial citizens. The common vocabulary did not always translate into harmonious relations. The new corporate elite usually had little regard for the merchants and proprietary manufacturers who fancied themselves small-town big shots. The latter, for their part, sometimes loathed the big corporate firms, and frequently indulged in parochial snobberies of their own. The old elite of Boston, for example, were particularly keen to stress their Puritan roots; the wealthy of Philadelphia, true to the Quaker traditions of their city, were especially suspicious of ostentation; the elite of San Francisco harped on those virtues that they thought they shared with all white men (as opposed to the vices that they attributed to the Chinese). Despite these differences, wealthy men everywhere in the United States, from the small business owners to the men whom the press called "captains of industry," shared a sense of distinction from the working classes. The substantial citizens were the guardians of property and propriety. They were respectable businessmen foremost, and they thought of themselves as trustees of the social order.[30]

For the most part, their political behavior was correspondingly staid. The party loyalties of the rich were sectional. Most fortunes were Northern, and most of the fortune-owning Northerners were Republican. Since the Civil War, the Grand Old Party had developed an identity as the party of business. That identity was beginning to change, as the discovery of oil in the Gulf of Mexico had begun to make new fortunes in the South, and rich Southerners meant rich Democrats. North or South, however, the party loyalty of the wealthy only went so far. The rich in both regions gave their money to *particular* political party bosses, and they expected deference from politicians in return. When party organizations grew too demanding, the rich often threw their influence behind plans for nonpartisan reforms.[31]

The typical political behavior of the rich in the earliest years of the twentieth century could be fairly described as buying influence. Politics in Mellon's Pennsylvania presented a notorious, if extreme, example. It was an open secret that Mellon acquired his streetcar lines through bribery of local officials. He occasionally paid cash for favorable state legislation too. When Nora Mellon asked for a divorce, for example, and Andrew wanted to avoid a scandal, he simply paid state legislators to rewrite Pennsylvania's divorce law so that he could end his marriage with a minimum of publicity.[32] The exchange of cash for favorable government action did not always work quite so smoothly, particularly at the national level, where the price of favorable action was higher, and where many issues were sufficiently complex that party bosses could find willing purchasers of influence on both sides. But even here the exchange of cash for favors must have worked with some regularity, because Mellon and his peers were surprised and outraged on the occasions when it failed. When President Theodore Roosevelt began to enforce the antitrust laws in 1902, Mellon's friend and fellow Republican contributor Mr. Frick was heard to complain that "we bought the son of a bitch and he did not stay bought."[33]

By the middle of the first decade of the twentieth century, many rich people were finding that politicians all too rarely stayed bought. Perhaps there were too many buyers bidding up the price. Rich businessmen responded by organizing new civic associations and municipal reform leagues that sought to restrain the anarchy of the political marketplace and reduce the power of political party bosses. They sponsored lectures, published reports, and raised funds for candidates who favored standardized nonpartisan ballots, civil service reforms, and streamlined administrative agencies designed to reorganize government and make it more "businesslike." Such local campaigns for good government were generally backed by businessmen, although they typically pitted reform-minded businessmen against others of their class, including some very rich men like Mellon who had the old party machines in their pockets.[34]

Wealthy businessmen also acted collectively outside of the political arena when they perceived collective threats to their economic position. With the integration of national markets, for example, businesspeople in industries that were threatened by increased competition responded with new forms of organized cooperation. These ranged from informal price-fixing agreements sealed with a handshake after dinner to formal mergers sealed with incorporation papers. Historians speak of a merger movement that swept the American economy after 1897. Contemporaries described it as the rise of "the trusts." Andrew Mellon himself was a consummate organizer of trusts who used his influence as a lender to cajole and browbeat investors into ever-larger coalitions. By 1913, he sat on dozens of corporate boards representing interests in dozens of industries, and his Union Trust financed almost half of the investments in the Pittsburgh region.[35]

Business owners and managers also organized in response to threats from their employees. Local trade associations representing particular industries often arose in response to trade union mobilization; even the most jealous of competitors could discover common interests when their workers all threatened to go on strike at the same time. Such business associations were hard to sustain, but while they existed, they could provide collective goods ranging from strategic advice to strike insurance.[36]

Local business elites, who were mostly men well below Mellon's exalted station, occasionally even formed militias or irregular vigilante groups. Much of the time, such militias and vigilante committees did little more than parade their arms in public, and by the twentieth century, their rituals had begun to seem somewhat passé. People of Mellon's stratum, who also prided themselves on their modernism, would not have participated.[37] When local elites believed their control over the local economy was seriously threatened, however, many otherwise respectable businessmen in the South and West were not above organizing the occasional vigilante mob to go after the troublemaker. Hangings of African Americans and Mexican Americans were most common; Chinese Americans and white ethnics—particularly when they were socialists or union organizers— were sometimes also selected for brutal treatment.[38] Contemporary accounts emphasize that the "best citizens" often took a leading role in such mobs. On May 16, 1912, for example, a committee of San Diego's leading businessmen hustled an anarchist agitator named Ben Reitman into a car at gunpoint, drove him into the desert, and proceeded to strip him, kick him, gouge his eyes, twist his testicles, brand him with a lit cigar, tar him, and attempt to rape him anally with his cane.[39] Such collective, politically motivated assaults by businessmen were rare—and rarely described so explicitly in the euphemistic reportage of the period—but they were by no means unheard of. Maybe the men who did crimes like these thought their actions were a legitimate response to the threat of class warfare from below.

Such vigilante action was as close as the business elite came to a social movement in defense of wealth, and it was not very close. Action like this obviously took place well outside of the usual civic channels. It was politics by other means, but it had little in common with the phenomenon of the social movement. Vigilante assaults were focused on asserting control directly by threatening or exercising violence, rather than on protesting or demonstrating moral worthiness in the eyes of properly constituted authorities. Often the local notables who took part *were* the local authorities.[40]

Peaceful collective protest, in short, was not part of the repertoire of the rich. They did not even really have a word for it. "The social movement," in the American language of the day, was still often used as a proper name for what we now call the labor movement. Contemporaries had begun to speak of other movements, such as the "woman movement" and the "progressive movement," but these terms designated trends in fashionable opinion or the world of ideas as much as anything else. The picture of the social movement that we have after the twentieth century—as a style of mass political behavior based on nonviolent, demonstrative protest tactics such as public assembly, petition, and civil disobedience—was just beginning to come into focus. It was not a picture in which the best citizens of the Progressive Era could recognize themselves. Even when they thought they had a collective interest in defending their riches against a threat from below, even when they dared to assert that interest in ways that broke all the rules of decorum and everyday morality, they did not think of starting a rich people's movement. They did not know how.[41]

The Social Movements and the Income Tax

They were about to learn. The Progressive Era was a time of frenzied invention in American politics. The flood of rural migrants into American cities, the increasing integration of national markets, and the tremendous growth of business corporations all outstripped the capacity of local party organizations to meet the political challenges of the day. People responded by inventing new forms of political organization. Historians have shown that the lobbying firm, the interest group, and the candidate-centered presidential campaign organization all came into their own in the early years of the twentieth century. So did the social movement organization. Members of one social group after another began to form new special-purpose associations, independent of party, for the purpose of pressing their claims on authority by means of petitions and nonviolent public demonstrations.[42]

The inventors of these social movements drew on what they knew. Farmers, for example, invented new movement organizations by recombining elements from an older tradition of nonpartisan agrarian protest. Many older activists remembered their bitter disappointment in the presidential election of 1896, when the charismatic William Jennings Bryan had led the Populist party in a frontal assault on the farmers' traditional enemies—usurious mortgage lenders, price-gouging railroads, and tax-dodging urban sophisticates—and the party had gone down to defeat. Chastened by this failure, activist farmers gave up on the dream of third-party politics and refocused their efforts on nonpartisan organization of the style they began to call "grass roots."[43] Farmers in the first decade of the twentieth century flocked to the Patrons of Husbandry, reviving the "Grange" of their grandparents' generation. Other veterans of the Populist party founded new organizations to agitate on behalf of farm interests, including the Society of Equity and the militant Farmers' Educational and Cooperative Union.[44] As the latter name suggests, the new generation of agrarian activists eschewed party politics and candidate endorsements in favor of forming cooperatives, educating farmers, and mobilizing farm voters for issue-oriented campaigns at the state and national levels. In meeting halls from Stockton, California, to Springfield, Missouri, assembled farmers met the new industrial century by "whereasing and resolving" for cooperative organization, railroad regulation, cheap credit, and political reform.[45]

Industrial workers too met the new century by reinventing their protest traditions. Their fathers and grandfathers had fought a long and losing battle to preserve the craftsman's traditional authority over the pace and organization of his work. By 1913, many industrialists had finally wrested control over the work process away from their employees. They broke traditional crafts into small tasks that could be timed with a stopwatch and taught to workers who had less skill—and who were therefore more easily replaceable if they worked too slowly or asked for too much money. Industrial workers who were subjected to this new regime of scientific management eventually gave up the fight to control their work. They began to focus instead on exacting a higher wage as a price of their consent. To that end, they organized trade unions and metropolitan labor councils that cut across traditional lines of craft, gender, and industry. Unions, many representing unskilled industrial workers, almost doubled their share of the workforce in the decade from 1900 to 1910. A "living wage movement" uniting unions and Christian socialists petitioned and demonstrated for minimum wages in the early years of the twentieth century. The Socialist Party grew rapidly in this period, and unskilled workers launched a wave of strikes in the years from 1910 through 1913 that socialists called "the revolt of the laborers."[46]

Women began organizing collectively for causes as various as civic reform, mother's pensions, and woman suffrage. Foremost among the new women's movements was surely the movement for Prohibition. The Women's Christian Temperance Union (WCTU), founded in 1876, revived in the early twentieth century.[47] In contrast to earlier temperance crusades, which had encouraged voluntary abstention from liquor as a sign of Christian morality (and therefore as a badge of status), the WCTU campaigned for the outright prohibition of alcohol as a way to protect the safety and well-being of women. It was an understandable position: At a time when divorce was difficult and a husband's income was the sole source of income for most women, the risk that a husband could become alcoholic was a serious threat indeed.[48] Men also joined the movement for Prohibition out of some mix of piety and self-interest; many native-born businessmen saw the saloon as a threatening space where working-class immigrant men could gather and talk party politics away from the civilizing and Americanizing influence of their native-born betters, and some industrialists came to see the prohibition of drunkenness as a way to improve the efficiency of their workers.[49] Still, women activists were the foot soldiers of the temperance movement, and because women did not have the vote, the movement exhibited the full panoply of peaceful protest tactics, including petitions, prayerful public demonstrations, and sometimes nonviolent direct action. The latter was typically limited to a noisy and disruptive prayer gathering in the middle of a saloon, but sometimes God moved his flock to pick up rocks or hatchets and destroy the booze. This was usually a last resort. For example, Carry Nation, the president of a Kansas WCTU chapter, became notorious for destroying the inventory of an illegal dive bar in the town of Kiowa in July 1900; but she only heard God's voice telling her to "go to Kiowa and smash" after a peaceful mass meeting of the WCTU in that town had failed to move the state or local authorities to action. "You refused me the vote and I had to use a rock," she later explained to the Kansas legislature.[50]

Women were also organizing to demand the right to vote. Many of the woman suffrage activists were inspired by their experiences in the other movements of the era. The temperance movement in particular was so closely linked to the woman suffrage movement that it could fairly be called a school for suffrage activists: Many of the leading activists for women's voting rights were religious crusaders who had concluded that granting women the vote was the most direct path to Prohibition. Still other activists came to the suffrage movement through the women's club movement. The General Federation of Women's Clubs, founded in 1890, claimed a million members by 1910, more than 2 percent of all adult women in the United States. Middle-class urban women founded social clubs as places for literary discussion or friendly debate on civic questions, but after discussing and sometimes voting on the political issues of the day in a club meeting, it was a short step to demanding the right to vote on those issues in local, state, and federal elections.[51]

By the beginning of the twentieth century, at least some activists in all of these movements had begun to converge on a common agenda that they called "progressive." The term was appealing to so many activists in part, no doubt, because it was so nebulous. "Progress" was the watchword of the labor law reformers and the scientific management men; of the Western activists who sought to extend voting rights to women and of the Southern "reformers" who sought to take voting rights away from African Americans and poor whites; of settlement house workers who embraced new European immigrants and of the nativist agitators who sought to exclude immigrants from the country. Historians have sometimes despaired of finding any common cause or constituency underneath the chaotic welter of people and groups who styled themselves as progressives in this period. Many of the self-styled progressives, however, were part of a common intellectual world that included social reformers in Europe and the United States, and even when they did not all agree on precisely which policies progress demanded, they seemed to have chosen many of their proposals from the same short list. Among the policies that commanded the most widespread support in the progressive social movements was a graduated federal tax on personal income.[52]

Activists in each social movement had their own reasons for supporting what came to be called the "progressive income tax." For farm activists, the income tax was a way to shift the tax burden off of agricultural land. As long as state and local governments relied on general property taxes, farmers paid far more than their legal share of the burden. Such tax injustice had long been a sore point. The farmers' complaint was not only that the owners of intangible property could more easily escape the assessor; it was also that the worst tax cheats were precisely the creditors and middlemen who were already exploiting agriculturalists. The farmers paid tax on their heavily mortgaged land; the bankers who held the mortgage notes paid none. Farmers paid sometimes exorbitant railroad fees to get their produce and livestock to market; then the railroad shareholders stuck farmers with the tax bill too. Of all industrial capitalists, the railroad barons might have been expected to pay a fair share of the property tax, because railroad companies, unlike some other businesses, could not easily conceal their property from the tax assessor without tearing up the tracks. But the railroad companies found other ways to dodge taxes. Railroad agents bribed assessors, traded free tickets for favorable treatment, and sometimes just refused to pay. The railroads' tax avoidance and outright evasion of the law left small landowners, and disproportionately farmers, to pay the cost of state and local government. Organized farmers lobbied for state and federal income taxes in order to remedy what amounted, in some cases, to naked exploitation.[53]

For activists in the industrial workers' movement, the income tax was a way to remedy great inequalities of wealth. It was also a way to relieve the burden of import tariffs and alcohol excise taxes on working-class consumer budgets. But perhaps most important, it was a way to unite labor across industrial lines. Many socialists in the labor movement saw the tariff as a tool that the Republican and Democratic parties used to divide and conquer the working class. Local craft unions representing high-wage workers in protected industries such as steel and glass could sometimes be, and often were, bought off by high tariffs on their products. Industrial unionists who sought to organize workers across industry lines therefore rejected tariffs as divisive and iniquitous—or, in the words of one labor journalist, as "a source of interminable strife, an inexhaustible fountain of injustice, and one of the chief means by which colossal fortunes have been built up at the expense of labor." Many union activists had come to see the graduated income tax as the fairest alternative. The progressive income tax was a center-piece of the Socialist Party's program. Even the anti-statist American Federation of Labor embraced a progressive federal income tax in the first decade of the twentieth century.[54]

The leaders of the temperance movement also saw the progressive income tax as a solution for their grievances. The income tax, wrote the leaders of the WCTU, was "the most just and equable arrangement ever made for the equaliza-tion of governmental burdens." In particular, they argued, it was a superior substi-tute for the alcohol excise tax, as the latter gave government officials a pecuniary interest in the continued sale of alcohol. A federal income tax could cure the fed-eral government of its dependence on revenues from liquor. Temperance activ-ists hoped that it might thereby make Congress more amenable to Prohibition.[55]

Many suffragists also came to see the progressive income tax as "a women's issue." It was a commonplace among free traders and protectionists alike that women acted as purchasers for the household, and could therefore be expected to feel the burden of import duties and other consumption taxes more acutely than men. Suffragists made much of this burden. "Indeed, so large a tax is paid through various avenues of 'home consumption,'" wrote the suffragist Carrie Chapman Catt in 1898, "that if it were possible to suddenly remove the home without the pale of government it would find its chief source of support gone."[56] A graduated income tax, to this way of thinking, would benefit most women by shifting the tax burden off of household consumption. Many wealthy anti-suf-fragists agreed, and urged opposition to woman suffrage because they assumed that most women, if enfranchised, would vote to increase taxes on the rich.[57]

Some suffragists also hoped that the progressive income tax might provide a weapon in the struggle for the vote. Catt and other woman suffrage advocates frequently argued that women deserved the right to vote because they paid taxes, and taxation without representation was tyranny. This argument was most effec-tive at the state and local levels, where property-owning women could, and did, sometimes protest their lack of voting rights by refusing to pay taxes.[58] Although only thirteen states granted full suffrage to women by 1913, activists using some version of this argument had persuaded another five states to grant at least some voting rights to *taxpaying* women. But the tactic of trading taxation for representation did not work at the federal level: Short of withdrawing from the market economy, there was no way a suffragist could protest her disfranchisement by refusing to pay the tariff.[59] In the United Kingdom, where there was an income tax, well-to-do women suffragists founded the Women's Tax Resistance League in 1909 in order to agitate for the right to vote. Hundreds of Englishwomen risked seizure of their property and even jail rather than pay an income tax to a government that deprived them of the vote. Some leading American suffragists were watching their British sisters-in-arms with interest. They hoped for an income tax of their own so that they too might refuse to pay it.[60]

The Coming of the Income Tax

The activists in all of these movements would get their wish for a federal income tax. But first Americans would have to amend the Constitution. The last time Congress had enacted a personal income tax, the legislators had failed to persuade the Supreme Court to go along with them. The law in question was a 2-percent tax on incomes above $4,000 that had been enacted as a largely symbolic response to the Populist agitation that swept the South and West in 1894. The following year, a Massachusetts investor named Charles Pollock—with the backing of what one newspaper called "a large body of public-spirited New York merchants and businessmen," including some of the country's wealthiest families—had brought suit to stop the Farmers' Loan and Trust Company from complying with that law. Pollock was a shareholder in the company. His lawyers had argued that the company had no business providing the federal government with information about his income because the tax law was unconstitutional. The Supreme Court had ruled in his favor. Overturning a century of precedent—indeed, reversing its own decision in the first hearing on the very same case just one month before—the Court had decreed in *Pollock v. Farmers' Loan and Trust Company*, 158 U.S. 601 (1895), that the personal income tax was a "direct tax" within the meaning of the Constitution. Because the Constitution required that any direct tax be apportioned among the states according to population, the personal income tax law was therefore unconstitutional. A federal personal income tax would require a constitutional amendment.[61]

The story of how the American people got that amendment is a story of miscalculation. The core constituencies of the Democratic Party, including most of the white South and working- class Northerners, favored an income tax. Pro-income tax Democrats and progressive Republicans in Congress had introduced versions of the amendment dozens of times since 1896. After a decade of frustration, however, many of them concluded that it was futile. Radicals began to argue that Congress should simply pass an income tax bill and dare the court to overturn *Pollock*. In 1909, with the backing of a new crop of so-called insurgent Republicans elected with the votes of militant Midwestern farmers, it appeared that they finally had the votes to pass a personal income tax.[62]

It was the conservative opponents of the income tax who introduced what would become the Sixteenth Amendment. The idea came from President William Howard Taft, who hoped thereby to head off a direct confrontation between Congress and the Supreme Court. Conservative Republican senators embraced Taft's proposal because they hoped a bill to amend the Constitution would peel away some insurgent Republican votes and buy time. By making a personal income tax conditional on ratification by three-fourths of the states, they could delay the introduction of the tax and create forty-eight new opportunities to vote it down. Many Republicans in Congress voted for the amendment in hopes that the drive for ratification would fail and thereby kill the tax for good.[63]

They failed to anticipate how quickly the progressive movements would change the electoral landscape. The drive for ratification began slowly and predictably: Seven of the first nine legislatures to vote for ratification were impoverished states of the former Confederacy, whose residents had little income to tax. Then, in November 1910, voters turned against incumbent Republicans, whose policy of high tariffs got the blame for a weak economy. Pro-income tax Democrats swept into office in state legislatures throughout the country. After the election, another twenty-four states ratified the amendment in quick succession. Even high-income New York got on the income tax bandwagon. And that was only a prelude to the election of 1912. Many voters aligned with the progressive social movements bolted the Republican Party to join the ranks of the Socialist Party and especially the new Progressive (or "Bull Moose") Party. The latter was an alliance of social reformers, woman suffragists, living wage advocates, and farm activists who backed a new presidential bid by former president Theodore Roosevelt.[64] The Democratic presidential candidate Woodrow Wilson took advantage of the split in Republican ranks and did his best to woo progressives. Voters elected dozens of Socialist and Progressive Party candidates and, once again, hundreds more Democrats to state and local offices throughout the country. Now state legislators who supported the income tax were the majority almost everywhere.[65]

The final ratification of the amendment in 1913 did not appear to contemporaries as a revolution or as a catastrophe, but rather as an anticlimax. Thirty-four states had already ratified the income tax amendment by the beginning of the year. The only interesting question left was which state would be the one to put the amendment over the top. The legislatures of Delaware, Wyoming, and New

Mexico tied for the honor on February 3, thereby ensuring that the income tax amendment would become law; legislators in four more states went on to ratify before the end of March, just to make a point. President Wilson signed the first income tax into law on October 3, 1913. It was a symbolic measure that targeted only the top 3 percent of incomes.[66]

The importance of the income tax amendment became clear only in retrospect when the United States joined the First World War. Congress financed its participation with new taxes on inherited wealth, profits, and incomes. The most controversial of these was the "excess profits" tax, which was intended to counter public outrage over war profiteering. But the most lucrative of these war taxes was the personal income tax. The rates in the Revenue Act of 1918 were, in the words of the economist Edwin Seligman, the highest income tax rates "in the annals of civilization."[67]

Many of the wealthy hoped that they could roll back the taxes after the armistice. They would have their chance. On November 2, 1920, the voters elected Warren Gamaliel Harding to the presidency, on the strength of his promise to restore "normalcy." And on February 1, 1921, Harding appointed the unassuming millionaire Andrew Mellon as his secretary of the Treasury.

If Andrew Mellon had been a rich man before the war, by 1921, his savvy investments in the munitions industry had made him something even more. His wealth overawed President Harding, who described him hyperbolically as "the second-richest man in the world" and "the ubiquitous financier of the universe." As secretary of the Treasury, this astronomically rich man would now be in charge of the Bureau of Internal Revenue (BIR), which administered federal taxes on income and wealth.[68] Many progressives, such as Wisconsin Governor John J. Blaine, doubted that the new secretary could be trusted to "scourge the profiteer and the millionaire with the same vigor that he does the lesser criminals."[69] Mellon seemed determined to prove the skeptics right. One of his first acts in office was to authorize the administrative staff of the BIR to interpret the law with more deference to taxpayers. Another was to put the staff lawyers to work devising plans for income tax reductions in the top brackets. Some wealthy conservatives even dared to hope that Mellon would use the prestige of his office to lobby for the repeal of the estate tax and the income tax.[70]

The appointment of Mellon to the Treasury was the beginning of the long counterrevolution. Mellon would remain secretary of the Treasury through twelve years and three presidencies. He would use his influence to push for the elimination of the estate tax, but not the personal income tax; although he might have liked to see the latter abolished, he did not think it could be done. Nevertheless, he would prove to be an influential ally and inspiration for rich men and women who protested against income taxes on the rich. As secretary, he would encourage, advise, and support their protests. After his retirement from office and even after his death, his writings and his memory would continue to inspire them.

These activists protested against the progressive taxes on income and wealth. But in their organizational style, in their tactical choices, and even in their rhetoric, they copied the progressive social movements that had put those taxes on the books. It was the collision of these two legacies of the Progressive Era—a new tax policy and a new social movement repertoire—that set the stage for the era of rich people's movements.

CHAPTER 2

Populism against the Income Tax

In September 1924, a rubber company executive named Jacob Pfeiffer went to visit the secretary of the Treasury with a proposal to solicit private funding for a grassroots movement. Pfeiffer was alarmed at the growing tax burden on "business and rich men." He blamed social movements of farmers, industrial workers, and veterans who had begun to demand benefits from the federal government. "The unorganized taxpayer is the victim of the bloc movement throughout the nation, organized to promote the special benefit of one class at the expense of all others," he said. High tax rates on incomes and inherited wealth were only the beginning. In Russia, a revolutionary movement of farmers, workers, and veterans had recently toppled an entire regime and abolished private property altogether. If something was not done, Pfeiffer told the secretary, it could happen in America too. The solution he proposed was to imitate the movements. The workers and farmers organized unions to promote their special interests. Very well: He would organize a union that represented the *general* interest—a national union of taxpayers.

Secretary Mellon was sympathetic but skeptical. He made no promises of assistance. He pointed out to Pfeiffer that organizing a movement was a matter of building state and local chapters, and that this would take deep knowledge of state and local conditions. He argued that it was a job for skilled and dedicated organizers. Mellon also seems to have recognized that Pfeiffer was the wrong person for the job, because his parting advice was to hire someone else to manage the effort. "Find a man who loves work and will work all the time," he said.

Mellon proved to be surprisingly knowledgeable about grassroots politics for someone who spent his life behind a desk. He heard nothing more from Pfeiffer for months, and when he did, it turned out that the United Taxpayers Union was nothing but a pipedream. Instead of hiring an organizer who loved work, or even organizing the taxpayers union himself, Pfeiffer had retreated to his office and spent months writing a memo about it. The document he produced was like a prospectus for investors. It outlined the union's mission, its dues schedule, its organizational chart, even the procedures for handling its bank account—everything, in fact, except for the niggling detail of what the union would actually *do*. Pfeiffer said nothing about how the United Taxpayers Union would recruit any members. Even less did he say about how it would mobilize them into action. In truth he had no clue. Pfeiffer knew how to run a rubber company, but he did not know how to start a movement.[1]

The boardrooms of America in 1924 were filled with Pfeiffers: rich men who were scared of progressive taxation but did not know how to fight it. These rich men had expected Congress to trim the high wartime tax rates once peace came. Instead, they had watched as Congress kept tax rates high and found new ways to spend the money. In April of that year, Congress caved in to pressure from organized veterans who were petitioning, marching, and holding mass meetings to demand a "soldier's bonus"—preferably one that would be paid for by extending the high wartime tax rates on the rich.[2]

Secretary Mellon wished for a countermovement. On the eve of the bonus vote, he tried to stir up public sentiment by publishing a mass-market book called *Taxation: The People's Business* that made the case for cutting taxes on the rich, and against paying the servicemen's bonus, in popular language with folksy anecdotes that anyone could understand. The subtitle of the book was an obvious play on the rhetoric of the old Populist movement, and the afterword was a call to action by President Coolidge for "the people" to rise up and demonstrate their support for tax cuts, in order to counteract the veterans' movement. Major business organizations took up the call with a massive public relations buy. They flooded magazines, movie theaters, vaudeville houses, and railroad cars with advertisements that sought to win the public over to the cause of tax cuts for the rich. It was in vain. After voting to support a veterans' bonus over Coolidge's veto, a coalition of Democrats and insurgent Republicans in Congress blocked the administration's tax proposal, and passed a substitute bill that cut income tax rates much less than the administration requested—while further *increasing* estate taxes on the rich.[3]

To produce a movement against the taxation of rich people, it would take more than advertisements and wishful thinking. It would take a new policy threat—in this case, a change in farm credit policy that threatened rural mortgage bankers with intensified competition and motivated them to join in protesting against income taxes on men much richer than themselves. And it would also take an experienced movement entrepreneur—in this case, a person who could knit those protesters together using organizing strategies he had learned from the Populist movement.

The Populist Education of J. A. Arnold

James Asbury Arnold—or J. A. Arnold, as he preferred to be known—lived his whole life in the shadow of Populism. He was born to William Arnold and

Eva Jones Arnold on January 15, 1869, in the township of Foster, Illinois, just a few miles away from the brick farmhouse where an eight-year-old boy named William Jennings Bryan was taking his first lessons in elocution.[4] Foster was at the edge of the prairie, where scattered woods gave way to rolling grasslands. It was also a hotbed of radical agrarian protest.

Radicalism followed the railroads. In the middle of the nineteenth century, public and private investment propelled railroads outward from urban centers into the country. The arrival of the new roads created the conditions for collective action by bringing farmers together wherever the trains stopped. The rails attracted farmers because rail transit provided them with new access to urban markets. Railroads also brought new people, new investments, and new ideas. The result was often a minor real estate boom, as when the railroad put in a new stop at Kinmundy on the east side of Foster Township in 1857; by the time of J. A. Arnold's birth, a lonely railroad platform had grown into a bustling little town of 1,200 people. Much of this growth resulted from frontier farmers' abandoning remote settlements to move in closer to the train station.[5] The arrival of the rails drew together the scattered homesteads of the district. The result was a critical mass of farmers in one place, which allowed them to forge new social bonds that they could use for political mobilization.[6]

The railroads also gave farmers new reasons to demand radical reforms. Farm income had always been subject to unpredictable fluctuations. Railroads made it worse. Production for the urban market was potentially very profitable, but only if farmers specialized; and specialization increased the risk that a bad year for one crop could wipe out the farm. Now too there were identifiable human institutions to blame when calamity struck. It was no longer just the hazards of nature or the hand of God that farmers had to fear. Their incomes also depended on prices set by traders in far-away urban markets. They depended on mortgage rates set by urban banks. And they depended most immediately on freight prices set by the railroads. The railroad companies saw this dependence clearly enough, and often exploited their monopoly position to extract additional rents from remote communities. Farmers, in turn, realized that they were vulnerable to exploitation and fought back.[7]

Throughout the years of J. A.'s childhood, agrarian radicals seemed to spring from the soil of his township and county whenever times got hard.[8] Arnold was never one of them. He grew up on the farm of his uncle, Eli Jones, one of the many farms in Foster Township that had been cleared out of the wilderness a generation before. Eli Jones was a Union army veteran with a generous disability pension. As such he was too loyal to the Republican Party, and probably also too prosperous, to be a Populist.

By the time that Arnold came of age, however, that prosperity had begun to dissipate. The frontier had moved on, and young Midwesterners in the 1880s watched it go with a melancholy sense of vanishing opportunity. "Free land was receding at railroad speed," wrote Arnold's contemporary, the memoirist and Populist frontier lecturer Hamlin Garland, who, like Arnold, was raised by a Union army veteran on a Midwestern frontier farm.[9] There was no more wild prairie on the outskirts of Foster Township, and it was not possible for the young J. A. Arnold to stake a claim of his own near the family homestead.

So he did what many of the Illinois farm boys of his generation were doing: He joined the wage-earning class. He married his neighbor Emma Holt when they were eighteen, and she bore their son Lloyd a year later.[10] To support his new family, J. A. Arnold first moved to the town of Marion, where he found work at a newspaper called the *Marion Democrat*. Before long he left to take a secretarial job. At that time and place, clerical work was a moderately high-status occupation, requiring more literacy than most people had, and many young men saw it as a pathway into management. Still, most jobs lasted a short time, and workers moved often.[11] Arnold moved more often than most, because he went to work for the railroad.

His new job took him right back to Populist country. Later in life, Arnold would recall his itinerary only vaguely, but it is clear that his first stop was Kansas, and that he must have arrived there during the peak years of the Populist rebellion.[12] Throughout his youth, Kansas had been marketed to farmers and land speculators as a lush prairie paradise. By the time that Arnold got there, the rain had stopped, the speculative bubble had burst, and the state was in the throes of a farm mortgage foreclosure crisis. Impoverished farmers rose up with all of the familiar complaints against creditors, railroads, and rich city folk.[13] Organized farmers founded the People's Party in 1890, and lecturers like Mary Lease traveled from town to town organizing protest meetings at which they urged farmers to raise less corn and more Hell. The farmers' rebellion reached a fever pitch in Kansas that had not been seen elsewhere; after disputed elections narrowly deprived Populists of a majority in the state House of Representatives in 1892, it almost came to armed conflict between dueling legislative bodies that denied each others' legitimacy.[14] By 1896, when the Populist program had penetrated the national Democratic Party under the leadership of William Jennings Bryan, the Kansas journalist William Allen White complained that a parade of Populist radicals in power had made Kansas a "plague spot" as far as businessmen were concerned. "Every month in every community sees someone who has a little money pack up and leave the state," he wrote.[15] J. A. Arnold was one of them. Sometime around the end of the decade, he left Kansas and moved with his family to Missouri, where they lived briefly before moving on again.

Arnold's last stop was Beaumont, Texas, where he arrived in 1903—once again, just as the farmers were stirring. Led by a handful of old veterans of the Farmers' Alliance and the Populist party, the farmers of East Texas held the founding convention of the Texas Farmers' Union in 1904. Their radicalism was somewhat chastened by the defeat of the People's Party in 1896, but their grievances were the same. They were particularly incensed about tax injustice. Farmers paid property tax on their land, even when it was heavily mortgaged, but the bankers who held the mortgage notes paid none. The Farmers' Union demanded progressive taxes that could reach the incomes and intangible assets of the urban rich.[16]

Arnold was not a farmer, but he had grown up on a farm, and he might have been expected to sympathize with the downtrodden. To this point he had spent his whole life in hotbeds of Populist agitation on behalf of the poor. The arc of his own career did not point toward great material success. While his cousins stayed in Marion County and took their places in the local establishment, he was living the life of an itinerant clerical worker. And he was bad at it. His coworkers from his later career described him as perpetually nervous, easily distractible, and sometimes short-tempered. His surviving correspondence shows him to be a mediocre typist and a poor speller. He was also a slovenly record-keeper, according to people who had occasion to look at his files.[17] He evidently had no talent for organizing paper.

But he would discover in Texas that he had a talent—a genius, said some—for organizing *people*.[18] This discovery would launch him on a new career that would prove to be quite lucrative. And if it did not quite make him famous, it certainly earned him some notoriety. Before his retirement he would be hauled before a Texas grand jury and four hostile congressional committees. The progressive Republican Congressman Fiorello LaGuardia would denounce him as "the evil Arnold."[19] The great political scientist E. E. Schattschneider would immortalize him as a scam artist. Long after Arnold's death, twenty-first-century historians would describe him as "sleazy" and "criminal."[20]

The puzzling thing about this chorus of condemnation is that it concerns his political methods, when it was really his political *ends* that were distinctive. In an age of reform, J. A. Arnold set himself against almost every cause that Progressives held dear, from woman suffrage, to Prohibition, to the reform that he regarded as the root of all other political evils, the reform that even today bears the name of the Progressive Era, the graduated tax on personal incomes. His overriding goal, if he had one, seems to have been to wind back the clock and return to the era of the frontier yeoman farmer.

But there was nothing very original or distinctive about the means he used to pursue this goal. Sleazy or criminal though they may have been, they were techniques he learned from the Populist movement.

From Populism to Income Tax Protest

Arnold's new career began in Beaumont. He was thirty-four years old, and he had hit rock bottom. He was in between jobs. His wife Emma was ill. He hoped that the move to Texas would improve her health, and no doubt he also hoped that he would find a job.[21]

What he found was even better than a job: a talent for flattering rich and powerful men. For perhaps the first time in his life, his unpopular political views were in tune with his milieu. In the Texas hinterlands, farmers were agitating in favor of income and wealth taxes, but J. A. Arnold thought that income and wealth taxes unjustly punished success, and in the oil boom town of Beaumont, he found many newly rich men who were pleased to agree. One of them was the oil man William McFadden, who was impressed with Arnold's business-friendly political views. On that basis alone, McFadden arranged for the Beaumont Chamber of Commerce to hire him on as secretary. The experience seems to have impressed Arnold, because he would repeat the trick again and again over the course of his subsequent career—seek out a rich patron, turn the conversation to politics, profit.[22]

Suddenly Arnold was thrust into politics. In his new job he was still a secretary, but he was secretary to a business association, and the dominating fact in the business environment of Beaumont was class conflict. The Texas legislature had just enacted a series of progressive reforms, including new taxes on intangible wealth that were meant to shift the tax burden from farmers onto railroad shareholders and other urban businessmen. In 1906, the businessmen of Beaumont began to politically organize in reaction; they set up the Beaumont Businessmen's League and hired Arnold as the secretary.[23] The next year, Arnold persuaded Ben B. Cain, a railroad builder, to fund a statewide Texas Business Men's Association that would unite all of the local business associations of the state. The plan was to maintain a permanent lobbyist in the state capital, following the organizational model established by organized labor and the Texas Farmers' Union.[24] Arnold got the job, and for the first time, he was in a position to dispense patronage himself. He hired a young woman named Ida Muse Darden when she walked in off the street. Four months later he hired her brother Vance Muse.[25]

The position brought him into closer contact with the remnants of the Populist movement. In June 1912, the president of the Texas Farmers' Union, Peter Radford, approached the Texas Business Men's Association to ask for their help. Radford wanted to do something to stabilize farm incomes in the volatile cotton market, and his plan was to persuade banks to make short-term loans secured by warehoused cotton in order to help farmers through hard times. He needed the help of the businessmen to negotiate with the state's banks.[26] Arnold saw an opportunity, and on October 6, the two organizations established a formal alliance for the purpose of putting the plan into action.[27] Now Arnold's apprenticeship in Populism began in earnest. Radford was a popular leader— a "philosopher of the farm," he was called—and he also seems to have been a skilled organizer. He left the Texas Farmers' Union to become the head of the National Farmers' Union on August 5, 1913. The following year Arnold followed Radford into publicity work, and brought Darden and Muse with him.[28]

The collaboration was an intense period of learning for Arnold. In private Arnold liked to boast to potential financial backers that he could "control" Radford, and through him the Farmers' Union. In public, particularly when he was under investigation for financial improprieties, Arnold likened himself to Radford's humble apprentice. Neither picture seems to have been the whole truth. The two men were both strong-willed and pulled in different directions. Radford was interested in solving the problems of tenant farmers, and Arnold was interested in raising money from wealthy corporate interests. The philosopher of the farm sometimes went off-message and sounded a bit too radical, creating problems for Arnold's relationships to his conservative business backers. But Radford evidently learned to accommodate business interests, and Arnold seems to have learned a lot from Radford about how to run a grassroots organization.[29]

In particular, Arnold seems to have taken to heart Radford's pragmatic lessons about politics. Radford always thought about politics from the point of view of the independent farmer; later in life, Arnold recalled how Radford would actually do sums on a chalkboard to figure out how a particular piece of legislation would affect his constituency. The other lessons Arnold learned from Radford were pragmatic rules for radicals: He listened to his constituents and changed his issues accordingly. He organized on a nonpartisan basis and avoided endorsing candidates. He exploited political jealousies—if one group was offering money or support, then he approached their rivals for support too. He set up local, state, and regional chapters. He paid organizers on commission; funds were too uncertain to maintain a salary, and distances too great to monitor people's work closely, so he needed to give his organizers an incentive to recruit even when they were not being closely supervised. He allowed organizers to subcontract in turn. All this made accurate bookkeeping impossible.

And he took money where he could get it. The mid-twentieth-century historian Richard Hofstadter once wrote that the poverty of independent farmers meant that the radical farmers' movement was always "for sale cheap."[30] So it was. Like the Farmers' Alliance before it, the Texas Farmers' Union was a hybrid of political organization and network marketing, and its publications were a corresponding mix of heartfelt agitprop and thinly disguised advertising for its patrons: the Bolshevik newspaper *Iskra* meets the advertising circular. Arnold and Radford collaborated on newspaper inserts that mixed Farmers' Union propaganda with anti-Prohibition advocacy paid for in secret by brewers and railroads. They distributed their screeds on ready-made boilerplates to hundreds of small-town newspapers throughout the state. Their issue advocacy may have helped to sway the 1914 gubernatorial election. In the process, they made powerful enemies. The state attorney general launched an investigation that led to the dissolution of the Texas Business Men's Association in 1915, and a subsequent congressional investigation into the loyalty of German brewing interests during World War I gave the pro-Prohibition "drys" another chance to put Arnold and his associates on the witness stand in 1918.[31]

Arnold was unfazed. He set out to create a new organization of businessmen, this one spanning the entire South. In 1920, he sought out the patronage of the timber baron John Henry Kirby to do it. Together they started the Southern Tariff Association. The tariff had long been unpopular in the South. It was identified with the Republican Party and the protection of Northern manufactured goods. The embrace of protectionism by Democratic President Woodrow Wilson created an opportune wedge issue, because Democratic voters in the South generally regarded the protectionist tariff policy as an unjust form of regional and anti-agrarian discrimination: In Kirby's words, the tariff put "everything the Farmer produces upon the Free List while compelling him to make his purchases in a taxed market." The traditional remedy proposed by Southern Democrats was free trade, or at least reducing the tariff on Northern manufactured goods.[32] But Arnold saw that there was another alternative: If the farmer must make his purchases in a taxed market, let him sell in a taxed market too. Increase the tariff on Southern farm products.

It was a tough sell, and it required Arnold to use all the tricks of the old Farm Alliance lecturers. With initial backing from Kirby, he hired other organizers on a commission basis to canvass the South for contributions and to organize local tariff clubs.[33] The organizers, including at least one other veteran of the Farmers' Union lecture circuit, traveled around the Gulf Coast seeking out unorganized producers. When an organizer arrived in a town, he or she would make contact with local businessmen, beginning with existing contacts in "chamber of commerce societies, in local boards of trade, and among associations of live stock breeders, pine and lumber producers, and peanut and cottonseed crushers." These local notables would organize a meeting of a local tariff club where the processors of a given commodity could hammer out a common policy.[34] Then, in Arnold's words, the organizer would "get the different localities together to agree upon the rate they want to ask for on that particular commodity," and finally he would take their demands to Washington. The association held a series of state conferences in the early 1920s and lobbied successfully for the inclusion of certain Southern products in the Emergency Tariff Act of 1921 and the Fordney-McCumber Tariff Act of 1922.[35]

It was exhausting work. By January 1923, Arnold was tired of hustling for small donations and ready to quit.[36] It was difficult to build a coalition of tariff supporters on a regional rather than an industrial basis, particularly when the coalition included producers at different stages in the same commodity chain—vegetable oil producers wanted the tariff on their product raised, for example, but soap manufacturers, who bought a lot of vegetable oil, wanted it lowered, and Arnold was in the embarrassing position of trying to work out a policy that would keep both groups in the association.[37] Partisan politics also complicated his job. Democrats in the South remained suspicious of the tariff. Republicans in the South were completely marginalized. There was some prospect for raising funds from wealthy Republican donors in the North, but many of them were industrialists who purchased Southern raw materials, and few of them saw much advantage in funding the Southern Tariff Association. Arnold hoped to raise money through local chapters, but he had begun to discover that the local business elites in many towns of the South and the Midwest were led by bankers who were simply not very exercised about the tariff. They were much more concerned with income tax policy.[38]

So he turned from organizing for the tariff to organizing for Secretary Mellon's tax plan. As outlined in Mellon's recommendations to Congress, this was a plan for income tax cuts targeted to the top brackets, including a maximum marginal surtax rate of 25 percent on personal incomes. Arnold had approached Mellon in early 1923 with a plea to fund the Southern Tariff Association, and had found him unhelpful. Now he showed up with an offer to help Mellon achieve tax cuts for the rich, and he found the secretary willing to listen. The South was strategic ground for the Mellon plan, Arnold pointed out, because it was the region that held the swing vote. Income tax rates were high because Southerners in Congress had voted to raise them. They would return to reasonable levels when Southerners voted to lower them again. Arnold proposed a new organizing drive "to accurately gauge public opinion in the South" on the Mellon plan, "and to locate Southern congressional and senatorial districts that can and will make strenuous efforts to convince their congressmen and senators that the present high surtax rates and inheritance tax rates are burdensome, inefficient and incapable of encouraging capital to invest in productive enterprises."[39] Mellon did not contribute personally, but he did broker a connection to other major Republican donors. On Tuesday, December 18, Arnold met in the Treasury Department with Undersecretary Garrard Winston and a small group of wealthy industrialists, including a representative of the du Pont family, and executives of General Electric, General Carbon and Carbide, Eastman Kodak, and the Swift meat packing company, to discuss the plans for a grassroots lobbying campaign on behalf of the tax cuts. Arnold came away with pledges of $1,000 apiece from five of the men in attendance toward a new venture called the American Bankers' League.[40]

The plan to seed the South with tax clubs succeeded beyond anything Arnold could have imagined. At first, Arnold had privately described the American Bankers' League as a "subterfuge" to raise funds for the tariff work.[41] But it was not long before his grassroots activity on behalf of the tax plan eclipsed the tariff organizing altogether. Historians have attempted to explain the sudden outpouring of organized grassroots enthusiasm for the Mellon plan by depicting the Southern and Western tax clubs as puppets of the Eastern industrial and financial establishment. Most accounts of the tax clubs focus on "corporate elites" or "financiers and industrialists" who used their financial power to create a "vast propaganda machine" on behalf of the tax plan.[42] The truth was stranger. A handful of the country's richest capitalists did indeed give seed money, but the grant of $5,000 was a small sum in relation to the league's budget, most of which seems to have been raised from the tax clubs themselves. The greatest contribution of the Eastern financial establishment was simply the endorsement of Andrew Mellon, the secretary of the Treasury and one of the country's richest men. Arnold found that Mellon's prestige among bankers was such that his name worked magic in local organizing drives.[43] The people who responded to that name, and who founded and joined the tax clubs, belonged to the local elites in their own communities, but they were not the corporate or financial elite of the country. They were far outside of Mellon's circle. Neither were they dupes or paid stooges of the du Pont family or the Mellon Treasury.

They were country mortgage bankers who had their own reasons to favor the Mellon plan. They saw income tax cuts as a way to deprive their competitors of capital. In particular, they reasoned that cutting the top rates of income tax would deprive the newest entrants into the farm mortgage market—the so-called land banks—of a valuable tax exemption.

The Politics of Mortgage-Backed Securities

The menace that threatened the country bankers of Texas was the land bank, a new category of lending institution that was only beginning to penetrate the rural mortgage market in 1924. The land banks were nominally created by the Federal Farm Loan Act of 1916 in order to make credit available to farmers at lower cost. The core innovation of the law was the mortgage-backed security. The law created two new categories of land banks (the federal land banks and the joint stock land banks) that were authorized to issue bonds backed only by mortgage certificates. These banks in effect acted as intermediaries, bundling mortgages together to reduce the risk of nonpayment, and thereby encouraging more lenders to enter the market. Another European-inspired innovation of the Farm Loan Act was cooperative governance: The federal land banks were to be run by associations of farmers, who would use their local knowledge to screen borrowers. (They were also required to collectively co-sign each mortgage note, giving them an incentive to screen carefully.) The banking industry, as represented by the American Bankers' Association (ABA), embraced these innovations.[44]

At the insistence of farmers' organizations, however, and over the protests of the American Bankers' Association, the legislation also included a federal subsidy for the new mortgage-backed securities. In particular, the mortgage-backed securities issued by land banks were exempted from taxation, as were their mortgage assets. The tax exemption for bonds created an incentive for investors to favor the new land banks over existing farm mortgage banks, which could only raise capital by issuing stock or taxable loan instruments such as certificates of deposit. Existing banks could take advantage of the tax breaks only by reorganizing themselves as joint stock land banks, and thereby subjecting themselves to new regulations and lending limits that could substantially curtail their profits. Representatives of the banking industry denounced the tax exemption as "socialistic" and "class legislation." The implementation of the act was delayed by World War I, but when the land banks began to issue loans after the war, the mortgage banks responded with a renewed campaign to repeal the tax exemption. The Farm Mortgage Bankers' Association of America regarded the tax exemption as a "life or death" issue for its members. It distributed a circular warning rural mortgage banks that "the Federal land bank and joint-stock land banks are covering the best fields and loan in such sums of money that no legitimate mortgage company can long meet the competition if the tax exemption feature is allowed to remain." Senator Reed Smoot introduced legislation to repeal the tax exemption, and the Senate Committee on Banking and Currency held hearings on the issue in 1920.[45]

The struggle over the tax exemption almost put an end to the nascent land banking system. In 1919, Charles E. Smith, a shareholder in the Kansas City Title and Trust Company, sued in U.S. District Court to enjoin the company from investing in tax-exempt land bank bonds on the grounds that they were authorized by an unconstitutional law. The suit was intended as a test case on behalf of the entire mortgage banking industry. It effectively froze the land banks' market share by stopping them from issuing their bonds. Although the case took years to wind its way upward to the Supreme Court, in the mean time the mere fact of the lawsuit created the perception of a substantial risk that the land banks might be declared unconstitutional—and therefore that their bonds might not be repaid. It was enough to make the bonds unmarketable until the case was resolved.[46]

But the resolution of the case was not favorable for country bankers. The Supreme Court finally ruled that the land banks were constitutional in February 1921 (*Smith v. Kansas City Title and Trust Company*, 255 U.S. 180), unleashing new federally subsidized competitors in the farm mortgage banking market just as a wave of mortgage defaults hit the industry. High agricultural profits during World War I had led many farmers to expand production, and to finance that expansion with debt that they found they could not pay off when prices fell. The recession of 1920 triggered a wave of mortgage defaults and foreclosures that undermined the solvency of small rural banks. Even after farm prices began to recover, the bank failure rate continued to climb, as small banks that were close to failing sought to recover their losses by betting on ever-riskier investments. It was the first great systemic bank failure of the twentieth century.[47]

Rural mortgage bankers saw the Mellon plan as a solution because it promised to reduce competition in the industry by taking away the advantage of tax-exempt financing enjoyed by the land banks. The promise of abolishing tax-exempt financing was in fact the crux of the plan as Mellon outlined it in *Taxation: The People's Business*. The thesis of the book was what would later come to be called a supply-side argument for tax cuts: Mellon argued that cutting income tax rates would actually bring *more* income tax revenue, not less, because cutting rates would encourage economic growth and thereby give the government more income to tax. But unlike later versions of the supply-side doctrine, Mellon's version asserted that the particular problem with high tax rates was not that they discouraged investment altogether. It was that they encouraged "the flight of capital away from taxable investments" and toward tax-exempt bonds. Mellon's preferred solution was a constitutional amendment to eliminate the tax exemption for government bonds. In the mean time, he argued for lowering tax rates on the rich on the grounds that it would decrease the value of the tax exemption.[48]

As Mellon described it, the point of cutting taxes on the rich was to make taxable investments more attractive, and thereby increase government revenue. If tax rates fell, then more rich people would invest in taxable securities rather than tax-exempt bonds; more income would start to show up on the tax returns of rich investors; and more revenue would start to flow into the Treasury. Many rural bankers agreed that cutting the tax rates on the rich was an important step to lure investors away from tax-exempt bonds. But the way they saw it, the point of luring investors away from tax-exempt bonds was not to increase government revenue, but to take away the unfair advantage enjoyed by the land banks.

The Tax Club Movement

The country bankers' enthusiasm for the Mellon plan took even supporters of the plan by surprise. Arnold had traveled around other states of the South for months trying to stir up sentiment for the Mellon plan without much success. And then he arrived in Texas.

One of his first recruits was G. H. Colvin, vice president of the Farmers and Mechanics National Bank of Fort Worth. On October 30, 1924, Colvin invited a group of fourteen local businessmen to a protest meeting against heavy taxes on the rich. The purpose of the meeting was to demand a reduction in estate taxes and in the highest marginal rates of income tax. The assembled citizens denounced these taxes as "a serious handicap in financing development enterprises necessary to the progress and growth of our section of the country." After discussing the evils of high tax rates and the merits of the tax cuts proposed by Secretary Mellon, they voted to urge Mellon to consider even deeper income tax cuts for the rich—a maximum surtax rate of 15 percent would be ideal, they agreed, instead of the current 40 percent or Mellon's preferred 25 percent. Then they elected a resolutions committee that would draft petitions communicating their demands to the Treasury and to their congressman, Fritz Lanham, who had voted against the Mellon tax cuts the previous spring. They also delegated a group of "leading taxpayers and most active business men" of Fort Worth to meet with Lanham and deliver their message in person. "[W]hile we may not be able to convert him to our way of thinking," Colvin wrote after the meeting had adjourned, "we will at least deliver our souls and discharge our responsibility as citizens to our government." With that, the first Texas tax club was formed.[49]

The meeting in Fort Worth was just the beginning. The tax club idea spread, slowly at first—Dallas on November 6, Houston on November 10, Beaumont on November 25—and then rapidly. From December 30 to the end of January 1925, there were 216 tax conferences in small- and medium-sized towns throughout the state (see figure 2.1).[50] Arnold was stunned at how rapidly the tax clubs took hold, even in the remotest Texas towns. "Remarkable as it may seem," he wrote, "we find small towns show much deeper interest than the large ones, at least they are more expressive."[51]

The growth of the movement followed the organizing model Arnold had learned from his long apprenticeship to Populism. His role was not to represent existing members, as a lobbyist for the Texas Businessmen's Association

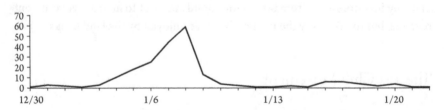

Figure 2.1 Reported Texas tax conferences per day, December 30, 1924, to January 22, 1925. *Source:* Calculated from lists: Nathan Adams to Andrew Mellon, January 10, 1925, and Nathan Adams to Andrew Mellon, January 27, 1925, both in RG 56, entry 191, box 163, Tax (General) Jan.–April 1925 folder.

might, but instead—like a union organizer or a circuit-riding Populist lecturer—to recruit previously unorganized people into new associations. Arnold and the other organizers he hired did not dictate policy to the tax clubs. Instead, they recruited members to an assembly where they could hash out their own programmatic demands. Indeed, the citizens who assembled in tax clubs argued over tax policy and arrived at their own conclusions. Sometimes their demands diverged considerably from the Mellon plan. Sometimes they also diverged from the demands of other tax clubs. The paid organizers provided what little coordination existed. These organizers were paid to recruit on a commission basis, and they sometimes subcontracted their recruiting responsibilities to others. None of these organizational practices resembled the business methods Arnold must have learned in his youth as a secretary for the railroads, or the organizational template he might have acquired from the Texas Businessmen's Association. But these organizational practices were in the pure image of the Texas Farmers' Union and the Farmers' Alliance before it.[52]

The participants in the tax clubs, however, were not farmers: They were overwhelmingly bankers (see table 2.1). These data on the activists are from a petition signed by the taxpayers who chaired the Texas tax conferences. Comparison of their names and towns to the directory listings in the September 1924 edition of *Polk's Bankers' Encyclopedia* yields the conclusion that bank presidents made up the great majority of tax conference chairmen, at 76 percent; other bank officers and directors made up the next largest group, at 17 percent; and all other occupations—comprising 99.9 percent of Texas adults—presumably accounted for the remaining 7 percent of the tax conference chairmen. Some additional information about the gender and ethnicity of the participating bankers could be inferred from their directory listings. Only one of them was a woman (Mrs. Anna Martin, president of the Commercial Bank in Neches). Only one had an identifiably Spanish surname (Mr. F. Vaello Puig, president of the Merchants' Exchange Bank in Victoria). We may infer that none were African American from the fact that none of the tax conference chairmen worked for any of the state's handful of black-owned banks.[53] These statistics represent chairmen who called the tax conferences. The available evidence suggests that the citizens who showed up for the conferences were slightly more occupationally diverse, but not much. A petition from a taxpayers' conference in Fort Worth on October 30, 1924, lists the occupation of every individual on the "resolutions committee"; seven of fourteen were bankers, three were merchants, two were cattlemen, one owned a lumberyard, and one listed his occupation merely as "capitalist."[54] At a Houston meeting on November 15, the thirty-four signatories were all businessmen, and the nine who indicated their occupations more specifically than that were all bankers.[55] Compared to the population of Texas, the tax club activists were a homogeneous group of white male bankers.[56]

Table 2.1. **The social base of the Texas tax clubs: white men in charge of banks**

	Tax conference conveners, October 1924–January 1925	All Texas adults 16 years of age and older, 1920
Occupation		
Bank president	76.3% (167)	0.1% combined
Other bank officer or director	16.9% (37)	
Other occupation	6.8% (15)	99.9%
Gender (banking industry sub-sample only)		
Men	99.5% (203)	52.5%
Women	0.5% (1)	47.5%
Race and ethnicity (banking industry sub-sample only)		
White, non-Spanish surname	99.5% (203)	79.3%
Spanish surname	0.5% (1)	4.8%
Black	0% (0)	15.9%

All of the Texas tax clubs identified high surtax rates on the top income brackets as a threat to business, especially business in Texas. The citizens assembled for the Dallas tax meeting in November asserted that cutting the top rate of income tax was "essential to maintaining our financial equilibrium and to the development of the Southwest."[57] The assembled chairmen of the Texas tax conferences signed a petition to their senators that described high tax rates in the top brackets as "a National emergency" because high tax rates interfered with "the business requirements of the country."[58]

The threat that motivated these activists was not, however, the threat that their own incomes would be taxed away. It was the threat that high tax rates advantaged their competitors in the financial industry. In particular, bankers feared that high tax rates would lead investors to put their savings in tax-exempt bonds—which most rural mortgage banks could not issue, but which their competitors could. Indeed, few of these tax club activists can have been rich enough to expect much of a personal income tax cut from the Mellon plan. Any taxpayer who exceeded Mellon's proposed top marginal rate was making at least $68,000, an income that was far above the pay of the typical Texas bank executive; the Federal Reserve Bulletin reports that the average federal reserve member bank in the Dallas district in 1924 was paying a total of $27,481 in wages, salaries, and dividends to *all* of its employees and investors combined.[59] Fewer than 188 income taxpayers in the entire state of Texas in 1924 would benefit personally from the proposed reduction in the top marginal tax rate.[60] It is safe to assume that most of these rich taxpayers were concentrated in a few big cities. Most of the tax conferences, by contrast, took place in rural counties where at most six people had taxable incomes of $10,000.[61] The tax club activists who spoke up for the rich were mainly speaking up for others.

The activists who spoke for the tax clubs invariably seized on the existence of tax-exempt debt as the first—and sometimes the only—grievance that led them to favor income tax cuts. The tax conference at Fort Worth began its petition for income tax cuts by complaining that the Revenue Act of 1924 had failed to effect "the diversion of capital from tax exempt to productive securities."[62] Businessmen from Houston opened their petition with the same complaint: "At a conference of business men here today, the effect of the present revenue act upon business activity of this section was reviewed and we find that the surtax and inheritance tax rates in the higher brackets are diverting capital into tax exempt securities and discouraging business activities."[63] The chairman of the Dallas tax conference called the assembled citizens to order with a call for "tax reform which will divert the flow of capital from tax exempt securities to private enterprises."[64] The petition of the state's tax conference chairmen to their senators made this demand explicit: Their priority was an income tax reduction; but "[i]f we cannot have tax reduction, then we should have tax reform with the least possible delay with the schedules so revised that the source of revenue will not be destroyed, but rather enlarged, by more nearly equalizing the income from tax-exempt and taxable securities."[65] J. A. Arnold, who had helped to recruit many of the tax club chairmen, wrote to the Treasury to report that this was their top priority: "Our people are as much concerned in reducing the surtax rates to a point where capital will be released for investment in productive enterprises as in tax reduction as such."[66] Ending the tax privilege for bonds was the most important thing; cutting the top income tax rate was a means to an end.

Activists distinguished between investors in "productive" enterprise and investors in tax-exempt land banks, which they implicitly disparaged as unproductive. The letterhead of the American Taxpayers' League drew this line in the sand by describing it as an organization "To Protect and Promote the Interests of Those Engaged in *Productive* Pursuits."[67] This motto was carried over from the Southern Tariff Association, where the adjective "productive" was meant to describe farmers and manufacturers. In the context of banking, the adjective might seem odd, but in the discourse about the Mellon plan, "productive" was used as a term that distinguished equity investment and taxable debt instruments from tax-exempt bonds. Mellon himself called tax-exempt bonds "safe but unproductive forms of investment." In other passages of *Taxation: The People's Business*, he treated "productive" as the semantic opposite of "tax-exempt." So did many tax activists—as in the petition of the Texas tax club chairmen, who spoke of the need to "divert capital from tax exempt to productive securities."[68] To say that the league favored the interests of those engaged in productive pursuits, then, was to say that it did *not* favor the interests of the land banks.

The comparison of the activist bankers to their quiescent banking peers also supports the inference that bankers were more likely to get involved if they were exposed to competition from the land banks. Table 2.2 reports on the profile of the activist banks—those whose officers and directors chaired tax meetings—compared to a representative sample of non-activist Texas banks operating in the fall of 1924. The greatest difference between participating and nonparticipating banks concerned the size of the community. Contrary to Arnold's impressions, bankers in large- and medium-sized towns were no less likely to convene tax conferences than bankers in small towns. The average tax club chairman was in charge of a bank in a town of 7,248 people, compared to 2,938 people for non-activist banks. This pattern probably reflects the size of the local business elite: A tax club required a critical mass of bankers and business owners that simply was not available in the smallest towns. The activist and non-activist banks differed slightly, but measurably, in their ratio of debt to assets, suggesting that large asset-holders were more likely to act in support of the Mellon plan. The groups also differed slightly in the percentage of mortgaged farmers in their counties, suggesting that the participating banks probably held a relatively high proportion of their assets in farm mortgage notes.[69]

The participating banks were also substantially more likely than nonparticipating banks to belong to the American Bankers' Association (ABA), the principal organization that had lobbied against the tax exemption for federal land banks. The national ABA itself did not contribute resources to the formation of tax clubs. Although the national organization endorsed the Mellon plan, the leadership was anxious to distinguish itself from the tax clubs, and even insisted that the latter change the name of their network from the American Bankers' League to the American Taxpayers' League in order to avoid any confusion on the subject.[70] That evidently did not stop the ABA member banks from using their contacts with each other to propagate the tax club model throughout Texas.[71]

In most other respects, participating and nonparticipating banks were similar. Their social contexts were nearly identical. Their counties were comparably white and had comparable proportions of high-bracket income tax payers. Their counties were not politically distinguishable, whether in their propensity to vote for Calvin Coolidge, whose administration produced the Mellon plan, or in their propensity to vote for the Ku-Klux-Klan-identified Democratic Senator Earle Mayfield. It also made no difference whether the bank was located in the congressional district of John Nance Garner, who was a prominent opponent of the Mellon plan on the House Ways and Means Committee. The local availability of rich patrons did not

Table 2.2. **Characteristics of the banks whose officers led the Texas tax club movement**

	Banks whose officers convened tax conferences (N = 187)	All other banks in sample (N = 658)
Characteristics of the bank		
Debt ratio (debt to assets)	1.03*	1.07
Loan ratio (loans to all assets)	0.61	0.61
ABA member	68%*	52%
Contextual characteristics of the town		
Population	7,248	2,938
Contextual characteristics of the county		
Farms mortgaged as % of owner-operated farms in county	39%*	36%
Located in John Nance Garner's congressional district	5%	6%
Coolidge presidential vote share, 1924, as % of county	20%	18%
Mayfield senatorial vote share, 1922, as % of county	67%	67%
Affluent taxpayers (reporting incomes $10,000 and over), as % of county residents	0.07%	0.06%
White native-born people, as % of county residents	81%	80%
County had a Texas Farmers' Union chapter, c. 1904–1906	66%	70%

* Difference is statistically significant at the p < .05 level.

distinguish participating banks; the population of affluent taxpayers in a county (those reporting $10,000 or more in taxable income) made no measurable difference in the likelihood that a banker would chair a tax club meeting.

In short, the tax club movement was a movement of farm mortgage bankers who faced competition from federal land banks. Country bankers thought the Farm Loan Act had tilted the playing field in favor of the federal land banks. They embraced the Mellon plan in hopes of tilting it back.

The Movement Spreads

Arnold spent the winter and spring of 1925 traveling throughout the South. He persuaded bankers to organize themselves into tax clubs in Alabama, Louisiana, Arkansas, Virginia, and Florida. They all endorsed the Mellon plan, though the clubs often set their own priorities and many of them favored even steeper cuts in top tax rates than Mellon had proposed.[72] Arnold then turned his attention to the Midwest, with stops in Minneapolis and Des Moines. The country bankers he met with in Minnesota took a wait-and-see attitude, but the Iowa bankers were enthusiastic. A dozen "leading tax-payers" met with Arnold and founded the Iowa Tax Committee in the summer of 1925. In just a few months, with assistance from Arnold and his field organizing staff, they organized hundreds of tax club meetings throughout the state.[73]

As with the Texans, it was the threat of competition from the federal land banks that motivated Iowa mortgage bankers. This threat was, indeed, just about the only distinguishing characteristic that Texas and Iowa had in common. These were the two states in which the tax clubs took root most rapidly and organized in greatest numbers. They were not high income states. Nor were they set apart by the severity of the farm mortgage crisis; farm mortgage foreclosure rates were among the highest in the country in Iowa, but somewhat below average in Texas. The characteristic that these states shared that set them apart from other states was the market penetration of the federal land banks. The six land banks licensed to lend in Texas had distributed $106 million in mortgage loans by October 31, 1924; the Iowa land banks were next at $51 million; and no other state came close.[74] (See figure 2.2.)

The demands of the tax clubs sometimes deviated from the particulars of the Mellon plan, always in ways that made their program more appealing to farm mortgage banks. The first bulletin of the American Taxpayers' League, issued in January 1925, reported that tax conferences in Texas, Louisiana, and Virginia had demanded even deeper tax cuts than those proposed in the Mellon plan. They may have hoped to extend the top-bracket tax cuts further down the income scale so that more rural bankers would benefit personally, but the bigger issue seems to have been undercutting the competition from the land banks. The bulletin justified its demands by providing careful estimates of how lower income tax rates would affect the high-income investor's choice between stocks and tax-exempt bonds.[75] The organizing committee for the Iowa tax clubs initially endorsed a graduated income tax on corporations—a measure favorable to many smaller country banks—until Arnold persuaded them that it was not just different from but inconsistent with the Mellon plan.[76] Some farm mortgage bankers in Iowa explicitly declined to sign on to the full Mellon plan, which included abolition of the estate tax, precisely because they thought the estate tax

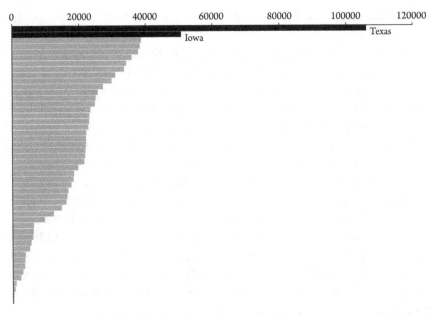
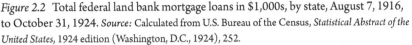

Figure 2.2 Total federal land bank mortgage loans in $1,000s, by state, August 7, 1916, to October 31, 1924. *Source:* Calculated from U.S. Bureau of the Census, *Statistical Abstract of the United States*, 1924 edition (Washington, D.C., 1924), 252.

could be used as an instrument to level the playing field in the mortgage lending industry. "As I interpret their position," Arnold wrote in early August, "they would place a heavy tax upon government bonds, etc., found in the possession of a deceased and tax at a much lower rate or make tax free, all industrial securities or taxable properties belonging to an estate. In this manner they would seek to equalize at death the discrimination in tax levies that may have accrued during the life of the deceased." Farm mortgage bankers seem to have supported the Mellon plan only to the degree that they believed it would help them against their competitors, the tax-exempt land banks.[77]

The Iowa tax clubs circulated literature and organized hundreds of local tax clubs throughout the state in preparation for a mass meeting to coincide with the state fair in Des Moines on September 2. The purpose of the mass meeting was to put pressure on Representative William Green, an insurgent Republican who was chair of the House Ways and Means Committee. The tax clubs, with Arnold's help, recruited some of Green's financial backers to attend as well. Governor John Hammill presided, and Iowa Senator Albert B. Cummins addressed the assembled citizens. Mellon's staff at the Treasury interceded with Commerce Secretary Herbert Hoover to secure special permission for a Des Moines radio station to broadcast the meeting over a larger area than its license ordinarily permitted.

Arnold encouraged tax clubs throughout the country to hold "radio parties" to listen to the address.[78]

The climax of the campaign came on October 22 and 23, when delegations from the Texas and Iowa tax clubs appeared before the House Ways and Means Committee to testify in favor of the Mellon plan. Bankers were overrepresented, but the delegations were also stacked with Democratic and Republican party notables in other lines of business, many of them personally acquainted with Garner and Green. Committee questioning revealed the delegates to be less than unanimous in their opinions on tax matters. They all agreed that they favored the Mellon plan, however, and they argued for it on the grounds that it would encourage investment in taxable business. "[W]e hope that out of your wisdom and your deliberations will come such a revenue bill as will invite men who have converted their capital into bonds and gone to California or Florida and are now pitching horseshoes and playing golf to reconvert those bonds into money and get back into business, build the fires, and start the wheels of industry again," said the Des Moines lawyer Henry L. Adams on behalf of the Iowa tax clubs.[79]

Success and Failure

The campaign worked. Representatives Green and Garner, who had opposed the Mellon plan in 1924, reversed themselves and came out in favor of a tax bill that contained steep income tax cuts for the rich. Ways and Means reported the bill on December 7. James A. Frear, a progressive Republican representative from Wisconsin who had helped Garner oppose the Mellon plan in 1924, remarked wryly that the Texas and Iowa tax clubs appeared to be effective bludgeons. He called their testimony "the blackjack method of intimidating Congress to relieve a handful of wealthy men."[80] The House passed the revenue bill by an overwhelming majority on December 18. The Senate concurred in February.

The Revenue Act of 1926 was a victory for the very rich. It cut the tax rates on the richest Americans more deeply than any other tax law in history. The marginal income tax rate in the top bracket was dropped from 46 percent to 25 percent. The gift tax was eliminated entirely. The estate tax survived only because of the determined resistance of Green and Garner, but in order to preserve the only federal tax on wealth, they bargained away high rates. The maximum rate of estate tax was halved from 40 percent to 20 percent. The law also increased the estate tax exemption from $50,000 to $100,000, and increased the credit for state inheritance taxes paid from 25 percent to 80 percent of the federal estate tax. This package of estate tax cuts fell short of the Mellon plan to eliminate all estate taxes, but it amounted to a substantial tax cut.[81]

Victory only emboldened the leaders of the American Taxpayers' League. With the support of his board of directors, Arnold and his coworkers Darden and Muse set out to organize a new campaign for repeal of estate taxes. This demand did not have the same resonance for his constituency of country bankers. Fewer than 1 percent of all adults were rich enough to owe any estate tax when they died.[82] More than half of all federal estate taxes paid in the years 1917 to 1925 came from the three states of New York, Pennsylvania, and Massachusetts.[83]

The American Taxpayers' League therefore reached out to perhaps the only geographically dispersed constituency that saw the 1926 estate tax legislation as an economic threat: state legislators in the rest of the country. Many state officials resented the federal incursion into a field of taxation that had been their own. The way they saw it, the estate tax credit in the Revenue Act of 1926 was not a give-away to the rich: It was, to the contrary, a new incentive for states to increase their inheritance taxes. States were now free to increase their own estate tax rates up to 80 percent of the federal level without fear of chasing away their rich residents, because residents could now credit those state taxes toward their federal estate tax obligations. Conversely, states such as Florida that had declined to tax estates heavily in hope of attracting rich investors were now deprived of their competitive advantage. The Taxpayers' League propaganda played to their resentment. "The levying of an inheritance tax is a matter that should rest entirely with the state," stated one Taxpayers' League mailer: "Our protest is against Congress coercing a state into levying any tax for any purpose." Another flyer, with the alarming bright-red headline "Socialism in Our Tax System," described all inheritance taxation as a socialistic threat to freedom—and then concluded with the modest proposition that the federal government should leave states free to choose this form of socialism or not.[84]

The campaign combined direct mail petitions with grassroots organizing. The American Taxpayers' League sent postcards to all the state legislators in the country with a resolution for them to sign and return to Congress: "*Resolved,* that we request Congress to repeal the Federal estate (inheritance) tax provision of the revenue law, effective February 26, 1926, and abandon this field of taxation and leave this source of revenue for the State legislatures to deal with as they see fit." Arnold and his employees also took to the road again, organizing committees of businessmen in Southern and Midwestern states in order to pressure state officials to adopt resolutions.[85] The tax clubs succeeded in getting resolutions in favor of federal estate tax repeal on the agenda in twenty-eight state legislatures, and approved by twenty-two of them. In the fall of 1927, Arnold recruited sympathetic officials into a new organization he called the National Council of State Legislatures to lobby on behalf of estate tax repeal. [86]

The climax of the campaign was the Ways and Means Committee hearing on tax revision in October and November 1927. Arnold hoped that the testimony from state officials could sway the leading committee members as the tax clubs had done two years before. The Connecticut tax commissioner William Blodgett acted as spokesman, while Arnold sat in the back of the room, passing notes to him on the order of speakers. Officials from one state after another took the stand to decry the federal estate tax as an unfair infringement on the taxing authority of the states. But this time Representative Garner was ready for them. He attempted to paint the council as a front group for the rich, by querying each of them about who paid their travel expenses. "Did not Mrs. Darden give you a check?" "Do you know anything about Mr. J. A. Arnold?" "Do you know any-thing about the sending out by these various organizations of solicitors who got 40 percent of all the money collected, and some of whom made as much as $5,000 a month?" (This last charge Arnold flatly denied when he finally took the stand to speak for himself. Some of his canvassers were paid on commission, but no one ever made that much money in a month.)[87]

The committee hearings were good theater, and they revealed that many of the state officials had indeed allowed Arnold to pay their expenses. But the hearings did not change any minds. The best efforts of the American Taxpayers' League were in vain. The Ways and Means Committee introduced a bill that retained the estate tax. By an overwhelming majority of 366 to 24, the House voted on December 15, 1927, for a revenue bill that retained the estate tax. The Senate narrowly passed the bill by a party-line vote of 34 to 33 on May 21, 1928, and the president signed the Revenue Act of 1928 eight days later.[88]

Why did the grassroots campaign to abolish the estate tax fail when the campaign for income tax cuts had succeeded? The estate tax seemed an easier target: It was a minor source of revenue, and even its total repeal would have cost the Treasury less revenue than the income tax cuts of 1926 did. The partisan balance of power too was substantially the same in 1928 as it had been two years previously. Elected officials did not have opinion polls to tell them about public opinion, so they relied on representations from their constituents to gauge the mood of the public, and these also might have seemed to favor repeal. Estate tax repeal had the endorsement of thirty-two elected governors, representing the majority of the population of the United States.[89]

Despite the appearance of public support, however, this time there was little mobilized pressure on Congress. In 1925, the tax clubs had been as persuasive "as a highwayman with a blackjack," in the words of Representative Frear, because the bankers they had mobilized included some large campaign contributors in key congressional districts. In 1927, state officials did not wield the same blackjack, and the tax clubs were mostly silent. The tax clubs stayed home because proponents of repeal had gotten much of what they wanted already. Big contributors were not especially worried about the estate tax; the 1926 Revenue

Act had cut estate tax rates substantially. In the absence of a new policy threat, mobilization of influential citizens was hard to sustain.[90]

The tax clubs' failure to sustain constituent pressure also showed a failure of policy crafting. The airiest rhetoric of the movement may have had broad appeal—surely many Americans would have said they favored "freedom" over "socialism" in 1927—but the concrete programmatic demands of the campaign were not well crafted to win allies. The country bankers who formed the base of the tax clubs had favored tax cuts to eliminate the income tax break for investors in land banks. They favored estate tax repeal as long as the Mellon plan was presented as a package deal. Isolated from the rest of the package, estate tax repeal appealed to almost no one except for the wealthiest 1 percent of the public, and the officials of state governments who were competing to attract them. That, it turned out, was not a winning coalition in Congress.

In the aftermath of this episode, progressives painted the tax club movement as a front group for the greedy rich. Representative William R. Green, reflecting on the grassroots campaign for the Mellon plan, called it "the most extraordinary, highly financed propaganda for a selfish purpose... that has ever been known in the history of this country." Progressive historians, following his lead, have painted the tax clubs and the American Taxpayers' League as creations of J. A. Arnold, and they have treated Arnold himself as a mere cats-paw for the Mellon Treasury. This is a mistaken judgment. Arnold was an influential organizer, but he could not have mobilized a constituency if particular policy threats had not already created a latent constituency in favor of tax cuts for the rich. The Taxpayers' League was not a mouthpiece for Mellon.[91]

Indeed, the demands contained in the league's 1927 program went well beyond anything Mellon proposed. They included abolition of state or federal personal income tax ("Income taxes should be levied by either the States or the Federal Government, but not both"), further cuts in corporate income tax rates, and a constitutional limitation on the top rate of personal income tax. "A graduated levy is unequal taxation and should not be permitted without constitutional limitations," the program announced; "it has in it more power than a free people should permit their rulers to employ."[92]

This demand for a constitutional limit on income taxation went unremarked upon in 1927. The tax clubs never made it the object of a large campaign. But J. A. Arnold and his network of taxpayer activists would revive this demand more than a decade later, and it would have a lasting impact on American politics.

CHAPTER 3

The Sixteenth Amendment Repealers

The failure to abolish the estate tax seemed at first like a temporary setback. The mood of the country was still favorable to conservatives, and the calculus of partisan politics still seemed to favor the cause of tax cuts for the rich. The election of 1928 was a Republican sweep. Voters elected the Republican candidate Herbert Hoover to the presidency, and one of his first staffing decisions was to invite Andrew Mellon to continue as Treasury secretary.[1] More than three dozen new Republican congressmen rode into Congress on Hoover's coattails, further reinforcing the conservative majorities in the House and Senate. J. A. Arnold, who regarded the Republican Party as natural allies for the rich, would have perceived this as a window of political opportunity.[2]

Then the stock market crashed. On Thursday, October 24, 1929, an unprecedented wave of panic selling nearly shut down the market. A consortium of big banks stepped in to buy stocks and prop up prices, but the new stability only lasted until Monday, when the bottom fell out. The stocks traded on the New York Stock Exchange lost more than $14 billion of their value in a single day.[3] The economist John Kenneth Galbraith later wrote that wealthy Americans were thereby "subjected to a leveling process comparable in magnitude and suddenness to that presided over a decade before by Lenin"—a substantial exaggeration, but probably a good description of what it felt like to many rich investors.[4]

The crash was bad news for the rich, but for that very reason, it might have been expected to be good news for the movement. Just five years earlier, the financial crisis in the farm mortgage industry had swelled the ranks of the tax clubs in small towns throughout the South and Midwest. Now country bankers were in an even more precarious position than before, and now they were no longer alone. The financial crisis of 1929 spilled over all industrial lines. The stock market crash was only the beginning. Stock prices kept falling, with only temporary reprieves, for the next two years. Production fell in automobiles, steel, and other durable-goods manufacturing industries, as consumers and firms uncertain about the future postponed spending on big-ticket items. Then unemployed and underemployed workers started to spend less on small-ticket items too. Prices fell. Businesses closed. Farmers defaulted on mortgages. Depositors rushed to pull their money out before their banks went belly-up. In October 1930, the spiraling crisis of confidence became a full-fledged banking panic—the first of several. Investors' incomes plummeted. If an economic threat was enough to make a movement, then the tax clubs should have found a flood of eager recruits among the anxious rich.[5]

Instead, the tax clubs began to disappear. Arnold appeared before an investigative subcommittee of the Senate Judiciary Committee a week after the stock market crash to testify about his lobbying for estate tax repeal. Although he claimed that the American Taxpayers' League still had hundreds of chapters, he conceded that most of these local tax clubs were "not so very active." Within the next two years they had all but vanished. The populist organizing model of the league depended on paid field staff to recruit and involve the dues-paying membership, and the expense of keeping such organizers in the field became increasingly hard to justify as the depression wore on. "Everyone's going broke and jumping out of windows," Vance Muse, one of the league's most experienced organizers, wrote home to Texas from Washington, D.C., in 1931: "Thought I might too, so I took a practice leap from a curb. Scared me so bad I knew I'd never make it off a building." His gallows humor suggests the depths of the league's organizational crisis. Muse quit the league shortly thereafter. In 1932, the league incorporated as a not-for-profit to secure a tax exemption, changed its name to the American Taxpayers' Association (ATA), and instituted a new, cheaper dues structure and a direct mail program for membership recruitment. "On Mondays we would open up the morning mail and pour out the dollar bills," recalled John Emmerson, who worked as the ATA's stenographer for a brief spell in 1932. "Finally, the money-raising petered out, and the low-ranking employees—which included me—were summarily fired."[6]

It took a policy threat to spur renewed mobilization on behalf of the rich. Businesspeople rallied in response to changes in tax law that they perceived to threaten them collectively; public policy, unlike the diffuse threat of a financial panic, provided a shared focus of blame for their grievances. The basic dynamic of threat-induced mobilization resembled the tax club movement of 1924. This time, however, the campaign to limit taxes on the rich began among Northern urban industrialists. This time too, the activists could draw on a wider experience of social movements. The movement entrepreneurs who organized these businesspeople drew on skills and policy models that they developed in other campaigns, notably including the campaign to repeal Prohibition. They could also draw on the cultural and organizational legacies of the tax club movement, and they did. And this time the demands of the activists were different from and more radical than the demands of the tax clubs. The businessmen who mobilized on behalf of the rich in the 1930s did not just want to lower the top personal income tax rate. They wanted to repeal the Sixteenth Amendment.

The Rich Soak Back

The "real father of the campaign to repeal the Sixteenth Amendment" (so said a pamphlet that the ATA published in 1944) was Thomas Wharton Phillips Jr. It is strange to picture this man challenging the establishment, because to all appearances he *was* the establishment. His father, T. W. Phillips Sr., was an oil baron, a sometime congressman, and a proud tax fighter. T. W. Sr. had fought successfully for the repeal of a Civil War tax on petroleum and had organized the independent oil producers of Pennsylvania after the war to block a proposed state tax on oil extraction. T. W. Jr. followed in his footsteps. In 1897, he graduated from Yale and went into the family business. In 1912, he inherited his father's company, and in 1922, his father's congressional seat. He also inherited his father's opposition to taxes on wealthy oil men. Phillips became one of the "most active" directors of the ATA, according to one of its pamphlets, and in 1936, he hatched the idea to repeal the Sixteenth Amendment.[7]

It was not a crazy idea; just two years earlier, he had helped to repeal the Eighteenth Amendment. Like many other conservative Protestants, he had been a convinced Prohibitionist at first. But once Prohibition became the law of the land, Phillips was quick to perceive that it was futile, and he came to believe that the federal enforcement budget was a wasteful extravagance. The cost of enforcing Prohibition was a particularly sore point to pious rich people because Prohibition had eliminated federal liquor taxes, and the federal government had made up the lost revenues with income taxes—thereby letting the sinners off scot-free while shifting the costs of their sins onto the rich. Phillips was incensed. Shortly after the First World War, he joined the wealthy brothers Pierre and Irénée du Pont in the Association Against the Prohibition Amendment (AAPA), and in 1926, he became part of the AAPA's inner circle, personally committing to cover a seventh share of its staff budget for five years.[8]

Phillips also helped to steer the anti-Prohibition organization toward a strategy of appealing openly to the pocketbook resentments of the rich. "As I look upon this matter," he wrote to Pierre du Pont in April 1929, "I realize that Prohibition has indirectly cost me already several hundred thousand dollars"—he was referring to his income taxes—"and, of course, if it continues indefinitely, the amount that I will be assessed on account of this religious and reform fanaticism will mount into the seven-figure column. I do not know how this strikes other people, but it is very irritating to me." He proposed a direct mail appeal to people in the top income tax brackets, a strategy that the AAPA embraced the following month in a pamphlet called *The Cost of Prohibition and Your Income-Tax*. This report purported to demonstrate that the repeal of Prohibition would permit complete elimination of the income tax, by increasing liquor tax revenues and decreasing enforcement expenditures. It was the AAPA's most widely distributed pamphlet, and it was distributed by direct mail to a mailing list of high-income people. The office staff addressed each form letter individually, but the original on file at the AAPA's headquarters was made out to "Mr. Multi Millionaire, 100 Park Avenue, New York, New York."[9]

The Cost of Prohibition and Your Income-Tax was not an effective appeal to the common man or woman, who did not pay any income tax. Phillips did not really have a strategy for appealing to them. His best idea was to bully them: Maybe the rich might induce some of the most stalwart Prohibitionists to change their minds by threatening to withhold donations from their churches. Phillips was a sometime trustee and dedicated fundraiser for his church, but if "religious people insist on the Government's carrying out a program to make people holy, religious, and reverent by law," he wrote, then they ought to consider his income tax his tithe and stop asking for donations. "I have about come to the conclusion that I am relieved of much of my moral obligation to continue passing out money to organizations which are politicoecclesiasticisms," he wrote, "or which are run by or closely identified with church people and are responsible for maintaining a situation which has become intolerable with no possibility of accomplishing the desired purposes."[10] This argument was not a winner. In 1930, Phillips ran for governor of Pennsylvania on a single-issue, third-party ticket backed by the AAPA. He lost badly to the dry Republican Gifford Pinchot.[11]

Public officials from both major parties began to find the fiscal argument for repeal more compelling as the depression wore on. Legislators in states that were increasingly stressed to pay for basic public services came to agree that futile efforts to enforce the Prohibition laws were indeed an extravagance they could not afford. The Pennsylvania legislature cut Pinchot's enforcement budget to zero. The AAPA recalibrated its appeals: Instead of describing the legalization and taxation of liquor as a way to relieve the rich of burdensome income taxes, it began pitching legalize-and-tax as a way to provide additional revenue to state and federal governments in crisis. The Democratic landslide election of 1932 gave the "wets" a decisive majority in both houses. In February 1933, Congress voted to repeal the Eighteenth Amendment, and in December, Utah became the thirty-sixth state to ratify repeal, thereby writing Prohibition out of the Constitution for good.[12]

Phillips and his friends were dismayed, however, to find that repeal did not reduce their income taxes. Instead, the Roosevelt administration welcomed liquor taxes as a new source of revenue, and then proposed some more, including an agricultural processing tax, a social security payroll tax, and a new tax on dividends. Congress enacted all of these and adjusted several provisions of the personal income tax code to permit greater taxation of the wealthy.[13] The Supreme Court struck down the processing tax in January 1936, but the rest stood the test of constitutionality. It was time, Phillips concluded, to change the Constitution. Having repealed the Prohibition amendment, he set his sights on the income tax amendment. The best hope for the country, he said in 1936, lay in repeal of the Sixteenth Amendment, "or at least in some drastic modification that will limit the power of the Federal Government to levy destructive and unconscionable taxes."[14] Pierre du Pont agreed. The campaign to repeal Prohibition "should have been directed against the 16th Amendment," he wrote in January 1936, "which I believe could have been repealed with the expenditure of less time and trouble than was required for the abolition of its little brother," the Eighteenth.[15]

Crafting the Amendment

Abolish the Sixteenth Amendment or drastically modify it, but how? These wealthy men left the details to a lawyer named Robert B. Dresser. Tall, blonde, and dapper, he was a Mayflower descendant and heir to a textile fortune who moved easily among the old-money elite of New England. His educational qualifications were impeccable: Phillips Exeter and Yale, followed by Harvard law school, where he served on the law review, and an apprenticeship at the Boston firm of Ropes, Gray. In 1909, he took a position at Edwards & Angell, a boutique law firm tending to the affairs of Rhode Island's wealthiest citizens, including the textile millionaire Frank Sayles, who had amassed the largest fortune in the history of the state. After Sayles died, Dresser was appointed a trustee of the estate, and managing the investments of the Sayles trust became his full-time job. From his downtown Providence law office, he became a corporate director and the acting chief executive of the Sayles Finishing Company.[16]

Dresser did not seem cut out to be a social movement entrepreneur. He was Republican by conviction and conservative by disposition, but he stuck to business. His first forays into lobbying were solely intended to serve the interests of his client. He orchestrated the campaigns for the so-called Sayles Probate Act of 1921, which rewrote state probate law to help the trustees postpone tax payments to Rhode Island until the work of valuing the enormous estate could be completed, and the so-called Sayles Act of 1926, which rewrote Rhode Island's law of evidence to help the estate fend off a lawsuit. As the common names of these acts suggest, Dresser's lobbying was a narrow advocacy on behalf of the Sayles trust. It did not seem to portend any broader advocacy on behalf of the rich.[17]

The experience that broadened his outlook seems to have been the great textile strike of 1934. That spring, Alabama cotton workers struck to enforce the wage and hour provisions of the National Recovery Act; the protest spread throughout the industry during the summer, until the United Textile Workers called an industry-wide strike for September 1. It was the one of the largest and most militant industrial confrontations in American history, and on September 8, it arrived on Dresser's doorstep. Squads of striking workers from other textile mills throughout New England began to picket the Sayles Finishing Company plant outside of Providence. For the next three days, the plant was besieged by thousands of striking workers who threw bricks at windows and engaged in bloody, pitched battles with private security, the police, and eventually the National Guard. From his downtown law office, Dresser found himself thrust into the role of a general—hiring and deploying troops to protect the plant and its workforce, and issuing leaflets to persuade the employees that the strikers' cause was not their own. He struggled for three days to keep the plant open. On September 12, after the National Guard shot and killed three strikers, he caved in to pressure from the governor and closed the plant to prevent further bloodshed. Few if any of his employees joined the strike. It seems likely that Dresser, like the rest of the Providence establishment and the governor, blamed the violence on outside communist agitators.[18]

It seems that Dresser also blamed the Roosevelt administration, for he threw himself into anti-New Deal activity. He joined the National Economy League, a conservative organization founded two years earlier to oppose the expansion of federal veterans' benefits. He got himself elected as a state delegate to the Republican national convention in 1936, where he introduced a plank that called for restraining "the cost of governmental waste and extravagance," and helped to lobby the party for tough platform language that pledged to cut federal expenditures "drastically and immediately." He joined the board of the National Association of Manufacturers and the ATA. And when the ATA set out to repeal the Sixteenth Amendment, Dresser volunteered to draft the new amendment that would do the job.[19]

Dresser had some experience drafting state legislation, but he had never written a constitutional amendment before. The obvious model to work from, the only successful attempt to repeal a previous constitutional amendment, was the Twenty-first Amendment, which had repealed Prohibition. So the first section of Dresser's proposed amendment simply copied its straightforward wording:

"The Sixteenth Amendment to the Constitution"—instead of the Eighteenth Amendment—"is hereby repealed."

But merely repealing the Sixteenth Amendment was not enough to do the job. Repeal might kill the progressive income tax temporarily, but what was to prevent Congress from bringing it back? Before the New Deal, the answer to this question would have been obvious: *Pollock v. Farmers Loan and Trust Company.* For almost two decades, this ruling had stood as an insuperable barrier to the federal personal income tax, and it was precisely to circumvent it that Congress had enacted the Sixteenth Amendment in the first place. The Supreme Court of 1938, however, was not the Supreme Court of 1895. In particular, President Franklin D. Roosevelt's "court-packing" proposal to expand the court by six presumably administration-friendly justices seemed to have cowed the Court into submission to the New Deal. The Court under Chief Justice Charles Evans Hughes appeared increasingly willing to grant Congress power to intervene in the economic life of the country. It even began to overrule its own conservative precedents of just a few months earlier.[20] Dresser thought it was by no means certain that the new, reformed Hughes court would uphold the *Pollock* decision. Maybe it would decide that an income tax was perfectly constitutional even without a Sixteenth Amendment. If the ATA wanted to prevent the reemergence of a steeply graduated income tax, it would be necessary to go beyond repeal of the Sixteenth Amendment and positively limit the future taxing power of Congress.[21]

So Dresser drafted a provision to explicitly limit the income taxing powers of Congress. Having repealed the Sixteenth Amendment in section 1 of his proposed amendment, he restated it word for word in section 2, with the added proviso that "in no case shall the maximum rate of tax exceed 25 per cent." This clause appears to have been a straightforward borrowing from state constitutions. When later pressed to explain himself, Dresser pointed out that many state constitutions had specific, numeric caps on state or local property tax rates.[22] Eighteen states had statutory or constitutional limitations on state or local property tax rates that dated from the Progressive Era, and still more states had acted to limit taxes in response to a wave of local property tax strikes during the depression. By 1939, nine additional states had enacted new limitations on the maximum rate of property tax.[23] Dresser's proposal simply extrapolated the same principle to the federal income tax.

As for the decision to put down 25 percent as the maximum rate, it was easy: The number came from the Mellon plan. Dresser read *Taxation: The People's Business* and consulted speeches by Calvin Coolidge. He also consulted federal revenue statistics and found Mellon's argument to be borne out by experience. Federal income tax revenues increased after the Revenue Act of 1926 lowered the top marginal tax rate to 25 percent, just as Mellon had predicted. Dresser added another section to his amendment imposing the same limit on estate and gift tax revenues. [24]

The resulting proposal was a patchwork assembled from the proposals of prior movement organizations and political campaigns. The board of the ATA approved it in 1937. On December 13, J. A. Arnold wrote a letter to the multimillionaire Irénée du Pont soliciting funds for the ATA's new campaign to repeal the Sixteenth Amendment. "You and your associates did well with the 18th amendment," he wrote. "Why not try a real job and one that will bring happiness and prosperity to all the people as well as perpetuate the Republic?"[25]

The Wealth Tax and the Sixteenth Amendment Repealers

At the time Arnold wrote this letter, his organization was foundering. He had managed to keep the Taxpayers' League on life support only by transforming it into an all-purpose anti-tax lobby for a long list of special interests, including brewers, tobacco growers, utilities, and gas stations.[26] His efforts to mobilize grassroots pressure outside of the capital were feeble and ineffective. In March 1935, he sent a field organizer to open up an office in the Bronx, in hopes of starting a neighborhood-based organizing drive to oppose the new federal agricultural processing tax. After collecting some 5,000 signatures on a petition, he canceled the plans for a mass meeting and closed up shop, because there was simply not much enthusiasm for the campaign among the Taxpayer's League donors.[27] Later that year, Arnold tried to get another community organizing campaign started in Chicago by circulating a petition to stop the growth of federal spending, but, in his words, it "didn't amount to anything."[28]

The campaign for an income tax limitation amendment was a Hail Mary pass. It might revive the organization if it succeeded, but it did not seem likely to succeed. Unlike repeal of the Prohibition amendment, repeal of the income tax amendment was not a popular cause. Most people drank. Most people did not pay income tax. At the time Dresser penned his amendment, only 4 percent of tax units had any income taxed at or above the 25 percent marginal rate. This was an amendment that would provide immediate tax relief only to the very rich.

But it was not just the rich who saw income taxes as a policy threat. The rising federal tax burden led even many businessmen of modest means to fear that they might be next. The New Deal made many business owners fearful of federal controls over private property, but fear of taxes had a special place in their imaginations, and the straw that broke the camel's back seems to have been the so-called wealth tax. Under pressure from Senator Huey Long, a likely presidential challenger who led a movement of "Share Our Wealth" clubs that supported the confiscation of great fortunes, the president introduced a tax bill in 1935 that he said was designed to "prevent an unjust concentration of wealth and economic power."[29] FDR's proposal included an additional new tax on inheritances, a progressive tax on corporate income, and a steep increase in tax rates applicable to personal incomes greater than a million dollars. Businessmen reacted with alarm. Executives decried it as a vengeful proposal to "soak the rich." A spokesman for the U.S. Chamber of Commerce warned before passage that the new tax proposals bordered on confiscation. His counterpart at the Ohio Chamber of Commerce speculated that "some of the oily propagandists whispering around Washington think Russia is a better country to live in than the United States." The Revenue Act of 1935, in its final form, omitted the inheritance tax and moderated the administration's proposed income tax increases, but it still imposed new costs on the rich. It increased marginal tax rates on all personal incomes over $50,000 and added two new tax brackets to permit increased graduation at the top of the scale. It also increased and graduated the rates of corporate income tax.[30]

To business owners of all income levels, the announcement of the wealth tax signaled that property rights were now uncertain. Daniel E. Casey, who was Arnold's successor as the executive director of the ATA, expressed the grievance in terms that would be familiar to his constituency: Uncle Sam was acting like a business partner who demanded a portion of the income, except that "his ideas of how much his portion of the income amounts to changed frequently." Many investors had designed their businesses to take advantage of specific tax privileges that, it now seemed, might be abolished overnight. Conservative oil men, for example, were alarmed in 1935 by talk that Secretary Morgenthau wished to abolish the depletion allowance, a tax rule that allowed them to deduct a share of their oil revenues from taxable income. Other investors simply feared more generally for the rights of property. "The integrity of their businesses, their jobs, was threatened," Casey later recalled of the ATA's constituency: "They feared outright confiscation of their incomes."[31]

The richest of all (who had the most to lose from income taxation) were not, perhaps surprisingly, the quickest to join. T. W. Phillips Jr. launched the campaign by reaching out to other multimillionaire veterans of the campaign against Prohibition. But many of the plutocrats on his mailing list hesitated to campaign against the Sixteenth Amendment, lest they appear too transparently self-interested. Captain William Stayton, the chief executive of the AAPA, argued that "men connected with the world of finance" could not pursue repeal of the Sixteenth Amendment on their own, lest their motives be "misunderstood."[32] It would prove more popular to pose as defenders of the Constitution against the excesses of the Roosevelt administration, he said, rather than to assail the Constitution by campaigning for a new amendment.

Phillips scoffed at this concern: "While those who are now working for repeal of the Sixteenth Amendment will also be subjected to criticism and have their motives impugned," he wrote, "the condemnation will certainly be mild in comparison to that which the repealers of the Eighteenth Amendment endured."[33] Still, the du Ponts and many of the other wealthy wets initially sided with Stayton over Phillips. They made annual token contributions of $10 to the ATA, but they bet much more heavily on Stayton's strategy, and in 1936, announced with great fanfare the formation of the Liberty League, a nonpartisan organization pledged "to defend and uphold the Constitution" rather than to amend it.[34] These men intended the Liberty League to defend those parts of the Constitution that protected wealth—the names that were initially considered for the league included the Association Asserting the Rights of Property, the National Property League, and the American Federation of Business—and they even hired the former ATA organizer Vance Muse to run their field operation. But they deliberately and conspicuously left the Sixteenth Amendment alone.[35] Instead, the league attacked the Roosevelt administration's fiscal policy—followed by its farm policy, its labor policy, its monetary and banking policies, and, with increasingly blunt language, its chief executive. In the spring of 1936, the Liberty League backed Georgia Governor Eugene Talmadge in an unsuccessful primary challenge to Roosevelt. After the June primary was over, they backed the Republican candidate Alfred Landon. After the November election, another Roosevelt landslide, the Liberty League all but disbanded.[36]

The ATA, meanwhile, was just getting started. The ATA seems to have been more successful than the Liberty League at appealing to potential supporters outside the charmed circle of the rich. The activists did so by presenting repeal of the Sixteenth Amendment as a cure for the depression. The argument that tax cuts could spur economic development echoed the rhetoric of the tax clubs; in the context of the depression, however, this argument acquired a new urgency. The vice president of the ATA, Isaac Miller Hamilton, asserted in May 1935 that "the federal income tax has made the largest contribution to the unemployment of labor and capital."[37] Phillips made the same point, but fingered the Sixteenth Amendment as the ultimate culprit. "It can truthfully be said that the adoption in 1913 of the Sixteenth Amendment, giving Congress the right not only to discriminate in taxes, but to levy such high taxes that they become virtually confiscatory, opened the door for a saturnalia of government extravagance, which has much to do with the present Depression," he said in 1938. It was a stretch—in order to pin the blame for the Great Depression on the Sixteenth Amendment, Phillips found himself insisting, contrary to all common sense, that the depression had been "smoldering since 1913 when the Sixteenth Amendment was adopted"—but he seems to have believed that it was true.[38] He also believed it was a politically expedient argument. By asserting a connection between the income tax and the Great Depression, Phillips said, the "Sixteenth Amendment Repealers" could hope to find support not only among rich business owners, but also among wage earners, "forward-looking labor leaders," and anyone else who cared about the good of the country.[39]

The ATA embraced this message. Its 1939 pamphlet on "Labor's Stake in the Tax Battle" explained that "[t]here is not an unemployed man, there is not a struggling farmer, whose interest in this subject is not direct and vital." The depression, it implied, was directly attributable to heavy income taxes on the rich: "Repeal of the 16th Amendment; proper limitation of the Federal taxing power; and restoration of business confidence will coax out of hiding the available billions of private capital for industrial expansion, will launch new enterprises, and thus provide employment for the jobless by putting the free enterprise system back on the rails with a clear track ahead." Another pamphlet addressed itself to the working-class housewife who struggled to make ends meet. "Most of this distress has come because the people in 1912 ratified the 16th Amendment," it explained. "There can be no relief from present conditions until the Sixteenth Amendment is repealed and government returns to its original fundamental principles."[40]

These appeals may have drawn some working-class supporters. In May 1939, the Gallup organization polled a sample of American adults with the question: "Do you think that conditions in this country would be improved if taxes on people with high incomes were reduced so that they could put this money into business?" This was the ATA's message in a nutshell, and fully 50 percent of the public agreed with it, including many wage earners.[41]

Support was strongest, however, among businessmen and property owners. The Gallup poll results show that the proposal unambiguously enjoyed majority support among those whom the pollsters coded as "wealthy," based on the appearance of their homes (77 percent, compared to 43 percent of the respondents whose socioeconomic status was coded as merely "average"); among managers and proprietors (60 percent, compared to 48 percent of their white-collar clerical employees); and among Republicans (58 percent of those who voted for Alf Landon, versus 44 percent of FDR voters). It also enjoyed majority support among black respondents (63 percent, compared to 49 percent of whites). In no other groups did a clear majority assent to the proposition (see table 3.1).[42]

Those who went beyond sympathy to actually join the ATA were especially likely to be corporate executives and directors. The ATA's propaganda materials later described the activists who launched the campaign as "businessmen of varied callings" of whom "few were more than moderately successful."[43] No lists of donors survive from the period after 1938—the ATA, depending on whom you asked, was either sloppy about keeping records or assiduous about destroying them—but a congressional investigation in 1936, on the eve of the tax limitation

Table 3.1. **Social characteristics of Americans who supported reducing taxes on high-income people, 1939**

	Observed percent in favor (95 percent confidence interval)
Gender	
Men	49 (45 to 53)
Women	51 (47 to 55)
Race	
White people	49 (46 to 52)
Black people	63 (53 to 73)
Party	
Voted for FDR	44 (40 to 48)
Voted for Landon	58 (52 to 63)
Voted other	35 (9 to 62)
Did not vote	54 (49 to 60)
Gallup SES category	
Wealthy	77 (63 to 92)
Average Plus	56 (47 to 64)
Average	43 (38 to 48)
Poor Plus	50 (42 to 57)
Poor	56 (50 to 62)
On relief (incl. work relief, home relief, or OAA)	49 (42 to 55)
Occupation	
Professional	49 (38 to 60)
Farmers	44 (38 to 50)
Business	60 (50 to 69)
Clerks	48 (41 to 55)
Skilled workmen and foremen	55 (45 to 65)
Semi-skilled workers	52 (38 to 66)
Farm laborers	38 (0 to 76)
Other unskilled laborers	56 (44 to 68)
Servant classes	50 (34 to 65)

campaign, turned up a list of 159 contributors that was weighted toward corporate executives and directors in manufacturing and finance. Just over half of the contributions (eighty-three) were made in the names of corporations or other businesses, and another forty-four contributions were made by individuals listed in *Poor's Register of Corporations, Directors, and Executives* for 1935.[44] Manufacturers comprised the single largest identifiable group of contributors (at least 26 percent of the total, and 40 percent of those whose industry could be identified from the name of the firm). Executives from finance, insurance, real estate, and professional services firms were next, comprising at least 23 percent of contributors, and they were by far the most generous, accounting for 40 percent of all contributions. Extractive industries—mainly oil and timber— were next, and no other industry came close (see table 3.2).[45] There are no data available on the wealth or incomes of most contributors. It is clear that the list included some very rich men: The du Pont brothers Pierre and Irénée regularly donated small sums, and Andrew Mellon personally gave Arnold a check for $1,000. It is probably safe to assume that these men were the exception, and that

Table 3.2. **Contributions to the ATA by industry, 1936**

Industry	Contributors			Contributions		
	N	% of total	% of those classified	$	% of total	% of those classified
Could not be classified	56	35		4,090	25	
Agriculture, forestry, fishing, and hunting	3	2	3	175	1	1
Mining, oil and gas extraction, utilities, construction	12	8	12	2,250	14	18
Manufacturing	41	26	40	2,715	16	22
Trade, transportation, and warehousing	10	6	10	650	4	5
Finance, insurance, real estate, professional services	37	23	36	6,592	40	53
Total	159	100	101	16,472	100	99

most of the other contributors were mostly well above average with respect to both income and wealth, but also well below Mellon's stratum.[46]

The geographic distribution of contributors reveals the importance of movement entrepreneurs in keeping the ATA going. The majority of contributions uncovered by the congressional investigation in 1936 came from just four highly industrialized states: Illinois, Massachusetts, New York, and Pennsylvania (see table 3.3).[47] New Yorkers contributed the most money, but the largest group of people on the list—21 percent of all contributors—were from the Chicago metropolitan area. The best explanation for this pattern is the importance of personal contact: The single most important factor for predicting who would make a contribution in that year appears to have been proximity to J. A. Arnold, who now lived most of the year with his adult son in Chicago, and who, at sixty-six years old, no longer traveled as much as he once did. ("It costs money to get money, when you go all over the United States to get it personally," he said.) Individuals and businesses from Texas also remained overrepresented, at 13 percent of the total contributors listed, though they included only two of the country bankers who had served as chairmen of the first Texas tax clubs (Jay Welder of Victoria and J. M. Radford of Abilene).[48]

The leadership of the ATA had diversified from its rural roots. The officers included a few old hands from the tax club movement—the banker L. O. Broussard from Louisiana was chairman of the board—but the president was a Chicago industrialist (Laurence Staplin of the Carbonite Metal Co.), and the vice president was a Chicago insurance executive (Isaac Miller Hamilton of the Federal Life Insurance Company of Illinois). The man who replaced Arnold as executive secretary, Daniel E. Casey, had been a field organizer for the American Taxpayers' League in the 1920s, before becoming a lecturer in economics and business administration at Georgetown University.[49]

In short, the tax changes of the New Deal, particularly the wealth tax of 1935, were perceived as threats by businesspeople regardless of industry or region. The social base of the sympathizers with the movement to repeal the Sixteenth Amendment consisted primarily of urban and industrial capitalists. Those who contributed money and effort to the campaign, however, were not a representative sample of sympathizers, nor were they those who had the most to lose; instead, the evidence suggests that they were disproportionately those who were contacted and recruited by skilled movement entrepreneurs. These men (and the few women who joined them) were not likely suspects to participate in a grassroots protest movement. They participated in a rich people's movement because they were recruited by J. A. Arnold and his network. In order to campaign for the repeal of the Sixteenth Amendment, Arnold and his comrades would return to the populist tactics of their youth.

Table 3.3. **Contributions to the ATA by state, 1936**

State	Contributions	
	N	Total amount ($)
Illinois	34	2,075
New York	26	6,558
Texas	21	1,115
Massachusetts	13	775
Pennsylvania	10	1,960
Rhode Island	9	925
Missouri	7	325
Ohio	5	250
New Mexico	5	175
Oregon	5	375
Colorado	4	390
Iowa	3	75
Florida	3	533.35
Connecticut	2	100
District of Columbia	2	125
Georgia	2	115
Oklahoma	2	150
Kansas	1	25
Michigan	1	100
Minnesota	1	150
Kentucky	1	25
Louisiana	1	25
Tennessee	1	100
California	1	25
Total	160	16,471.35

Back to the Grassroots

The ATA first attempted an inside lobbying strategy. In 1938, the ATA approached a Democratic congressman from Brooklyn. Emanuel Celler had come into Congress in 1923 as part of the same class as T. W. Phillips Jr. He was a director of several small banks, and he had voted for some of the aspects of the Mellon tax program most favored by small banks, including the proposal to abolish tax-exempt securities.[50] But he was otherwise a surprising choice to champion a cause dear to business conservatives. He would later make his name as a liberal advocate of antitrust legislation and civil rights. The ATA's reliance on Celler was a mark of their desperation to find even one congressional ally willing to entertain their proposal.

Celler was hardly the legislative champion that these activists hoped for. By his own account, he was at first "enamored with the idea" of constitutional tax limitation, and behind closed doors he let Casey understand that he was sympathetic, if skeptical whether Dresser's amendment could succeed.[51] He put the proposal before the Congress on June 15, 1938. His actions, however, betrayed more ambivalence than he let on. Having introduced the proposal, he did not speak on its behalf and he did not look for a cosponsor. He took pains to distance himself from it even as he put it forward: "Not wishing to sponsor the legislation himself," Casey remembered years later, "Mr. Celler had the words 'by request' inserted just after his name in parentheses."[52] Celler's later behavior confirms that he did not regard the introduction of this bill as his proudest moment. He only spoke of the tax limitation amendment once in public, years later, and then only in order to repudiate the idea. He skipped the episode entirely in his autobiography. He left behind no record of this proposed amendment or of his dealings with the ATA in the papers he deposited at the Library of Congress.[53]

Without even the support of its nominal sponsor, the proposed amendment had no hope of passing in Congress. It did not come anywhere near to a vote. Celler's resolution was perfunctorily referred to the House Judiciary Committee, where it died. He introduced it again the following year, with the same result.[54]

Blocked in Congress, the activists of the ATA turned to an outside lobbying strategy. If they could persuade two-thirds of the state legislatures to petition Congress, they could force a convention for the purpose of amending the Constitution. No one had ever successfully amended the Constitution this way, and it promised to be extraordinarily difficult. Even if the activists could find the requisite number of petitions from the states, their proposal would still have to win a contentious vote on the floor of the constitutional convention, and then they would have to persuade three-fourths of states to ratify. Because this path was untested, moreover, it posed thorny questions of constitutional interpretation. Could a convention be called for the limited purpose of debating and voting on a single proposed amendment, or, once the convention was called, would the entire text of the Constitution be on the table? Would the states' petitions have to be identical in wording in order to count toward the two-thirds quorum? Could a governor veto a petition for a constitutional convention? Could a subsequent legislature in the same state repeal a petition? Even supposing that the ATA were successful enough to reach the quorum of thirty-two states, a Supreme Court challenge seemed all but inevitable. But Dresser and his colleagues were gambling that it would not come to that. They did not actually intend to call a constitutional convention. Instead, they hoped that the threat of a convention would force Congress to act on their proposed amendment before the two-thirds threshold was reached.[55]

This ambitious campaign plan required a return to the populist methods of the tax club movement. Since 1928, the ATA had degenerated into a one-man shop, and Arnold had gradually given up on building local committees or soliciting member involvement. Now the ATA would need to field effective lobbies in at least thirty-two states. It did not have the budget to set up an office and hire a professional staff in each state capital; instead, it would have to depend on volunteers. The budget would have to go toward publishing agitational pamphlets and paying field organizers to inspire and organize local grassroots committees.

The ATA launched its public campaign in 1938 with the publication of a people's manifesto written by J. A. Arnold, a 150-page book called *The Desire to Own*. In contrast to previous ATA newsletters and brochures—which merely compiled economic arguments about taxation for the use of congressional allies, or briefed contributors on the progress of particular legislation—this book was a sweeping piece of agitational propaganda written in a popular style, with big type and dramatic illustrations, for people who were not political insiders. It depicted Celler's introduction of the tax limitation amendment in Congress as the climax of a grand quasi-biblical narrative, in which the Sixteenth Amendment appeared as the fall from grace—"the colossal mistake in the annals of this government, and one that reverberated throughout the nations of the earth"—and its repeal as the path to human salvation.[56]

The book also echoed the producerist ideology that had been current in the Populist milieu of Arnold's upbringing. The "desire to own" of the title was, in Arnold's telling, the divine spark that separated man from the beasts, and that inspired humans to transform the earth by their labor. This view of human nature was far removed from Adam Smith's classical economics, with its assumption of a natural propensity to barter, truck, and exchange; Arnold's natural man was a producer, not a trader. The book also had nothing to say about the economics of taxation or the virtues of the free market. In place of a liberal economic theory, it offered a republican political theory to justify tax limitation. The individual ownership of land, Arnold explained, was the basis for political independence, because only a man who worked his own land could feel free to criticize the powerful without fearing for his livelihood. A society of independent proprietors thus provided a check on the arbitrary authority of rulers. Private property rights were the basis for all civil rights. The free society, in this telling, was not necessarily a market economy, but was instead a society of independent citizen-producers engaged in "cultivating, improving, and building the earth." The Sixteenth Amendment was evil, not because it stifled production, but because it put political freedom at risk: It had eroded the rights of property and therefore paved the way for tyranny. Safeguarding the future of democracy required "diminishing the authority of rulers and enlarging the rights of the people." To realize this goal, Arnold wrote, "the people" would have to take up the weapons of free speech and free association. The echo of Populism in all of this was unmistakable.[57]

The return to Populism was not just a matter of rhetoric. It was also a matter of organizational style. In 1938, the executive board of the ATA, led by the du Ponts, who were fed up with Arnold's habit of "pocketing commissions on contributions" and frustrated with his failure to deliver results, forced him to resign and appointed Casey as his successor.[58] Rather than give up, Arnold began the work of setting up grassroots organizing committees independently. The directors promised him an annuity on the condition that he would permanently retire from tax lobbying; instead, he opened a new office in Chicago and convened an organizing committee to campaign for the 25 percent tax limitation amendment. His first recruits were executives and corporate tax lawyers he knew from his previous lobbying work on behalf of the ATA. They declared themselves the Western Tax Council, and with their contributions in hand, Arnold, now almost seventy years old, took to the roads once again. His strategy had all the hallmarks of grassroots Populism. He deliberately targeted rural states of the South and West, far from the urban and industrial centers of power; he relied on traveling organizers to recruit members and set up local chapters; and, in defiance of the du Ponts, he continued to rely on commissions to incentivize recruitment.

The initial results validated this field organizing strategy. The first state legislature to introduce a resolution in support of the amendment was Wyoming's. The support of Wyoming legislators for the tax limitation amendment might seem puzzling: No more than twenty-five voters in the entire state had incomes above the 25 percent marginal rate threshold. Wyoming was also, like other mountain states, a net beneficiary of New Deal spending.[59] If the movement for federal tax limitation were driven by short-term pocketbook considerations, then one would predict support for federal tax limitation anywhere but here.

But Wyoming had an organized constituency that was up in arms about *state* taxation. To be sure, big landowners in Wyoming had never warmed to the income tax; for the most part, they were sheep and cattle ranchers who liked the tariff just fine, as long as wool and hides were on the tariff schedule. In the

1930s, however, what they were particularly incensed about was state and local property taxes. The state's leading ranchers and mine owners helped found the Wyoming Tax League in 1932 to lead the drive for economy in state government and limit taxation. When the Republican Party reclaimed the governorship and the state legislature in 1938, after a campaign that called for "hewing governmental taxes to the bone," the new Republican majority decided to pass a symbolic resolution in favor of repealing the Sixteenth Amendment.[60] The legislator who introduced the resolution was Representative Ernest Shaw, the Republican editor of the *Cody Enterprise* and a bitter opponent of the New Deal. Shaw identified strongly with what he described as the "pioneer spirit" of Wyoming, and he agreed with J. A. Arnold's view that the absolute property rights of landowners were necessary to guarantee political freedom. Like Arnold, Shaw saw FDR as a would-be tyrant using tax dollars to buy loyalty and suppress dissent. "The more we see and read of the various relief agencies in every city, town, and hamlet of this great U.S.A.," he wrote in one editorial, "the more we are inclined to believe that they were created to give jobs to government employees to build up a vast governmental machine, rather than to render any great relief service to humanity."[61] Shaw introduced a resolution in support of constitutional tax limitation ("by request") on January 30, 1939. The House approved it by a vote of thirty to eighteen; all but one of those who voted in favor were Republicans, and all but one of those who voted against were Democrats. The Senate approved it on February 23, and on March 8, the Republican Representative Frank Horton presented the resolution to Congress. "Since Wyoming has no state income tax and no large income that could, by the wildest stretch of the imagination, come within a mile of the higher brackets, certainly no selfish reasons can explain why this action was taken," he said. The citizens of Wyoming, he explained, wanted to stop "wild federal spending" and safeguard the rights of individuals to keep their earnings.[62]

The next state legislature to act was Mississippi's. In economic terms, this state was, like Wyoming, an unlikely place for a movement against the federal income tax to find purchase. Fewer than 300 high-income Mississippians owed enough income tax to expect any direct tax cut from the proposed amendment. In political terms, the state was if anything even less likely than Wyoming to support federal tax limitation. Mississippians had long favored federal income taxation because they had little income to tax; Mississippi been among the first states to ratify the Sixteenth Amendment. In national politics, Mississippi Democrats and Wyoming Republicans were on opposite sides of the major issues of the day. In Mississippi, a small minority of white landowners monopolized political power through their control over the state Democratic Party, and through devices such as the poll tax and the all-white primary that effectively restricted the right to vote to a small fraction of eligible adults. The Mississippi Democrats' lock on political power gave them seniority in Congress, and their seniority gave them positions of special influence in the New Deal coalition. They used their leverage to cut deals. In particular, they consistently pushed for more federal spending with fewer strings attached, and made sure that most New Deal policies contained no guarantees of rights for African Americans. In exchange, they mostly went along with the administration's tax policies. The finance committee chairman who shepherded the soak-the-rich Revenue Act of 1935 through the Senate was Byron "Pat" Harrison from Mississippi.[63]

But Mississippi was also a state where J. A. Arnold had many contacts from his days organizing the Southern Tariff Association, and it was also a state where many businesspeople and landowners feared and resented the New Deal. Despite their congressional representatives' best efforts to moderate the redistributive effects of New Deal spending, many in the Mississippi elite worried that federal spending threatened their political power. The planters of the delta counties saw the Social Security Act in particular as an invasion of states' rights, and feared that generous relief to the poor would endanger the willingness of the black poor to work for low wages.[64] After the administration came out in favor of the wealth tax, a resolution in favor of the tax limitation amendment was an opportune symbolic gesture of opposition to the egalitarian turn that the New Deal had taken. Senator Evon A. Ford of Taylorsville introduced the tax limitation resolution on February 28, 1940. The Senate passed it on April 29 by a vote of thirty-three to two, with fourteen absent or not voting. The House passed it on the same day by a vote of seventy-seven to forty-eight, with fifteen absent or not voting.[65]

Meanwhile, the ATA failed to get such resolutions introduced in Northeastern industrial states that might have seemed like much more favorable terrain. Top-bracket taxpayers were much more plentiful in New England and the mid-Atlantic states than in the South or the mountain West. Their state legislatures also met more often—New York's met annually, compared to once every four years for Mississippi—creating many more opportunities to pass resolutions in favor of tax cuts for the rich. But without Arnold and his network of organizers, the ATA did not have the networks it needed to mobilize successful campaigns for federal tax limitation. Not a single Northeastern state legislature introduced a resolution in favor of Robert Dresser's amendment, with the notable exception of Rhode Island. It appeared that inside lobbying by financial elites was not effective at pushing for tax limitation.

Rhode Island is the exception that tests the rule. The ATA had exceptional influence here only because Robert Dresser's control over the Sayles fortune and his contributions to the Republican Party had made him a power broker in Rhode Island politics. And even here, in Dresser's home state, he was forced to water down his proposed constitutional amendment in order to attract legislative support. In the winter of 1940, with German troops massing to invade France, Scandinavia, and the Netherlands, many legislators thought that the United States would soon be drawn into the war, and even many conservative Republicans were reluctant to endorse a limitation on federal taxes for fear that it would restrain the government's ability to raise the necessary revenues for national defense. Dresser did not share this concern: Tax limitation would *help* national defense, he thought, because lower tax rates would increase government tax revenues, in keeping with Andrew Mellon's supply-side theory.[66] He nevertheless compromised by adding a new escape clause to the proposed amendment:

> [I]n the event of a war in which the United States is engaged creating a grave national emergency requiring such action to avoid national disaster, the congress by a vote of three-fourths of each house may for a period not exceeding one year increase beyond the limits above prescribed the rate of any such tax upon income subsequently accruing or received, or with respect to subsequent devolutions or transfers of property, with like power, while the United States is actively engaged in such war, to repeat such action as often as such emergency may require.[67]

This escape clause was not much of a concession, because it applied only in wartime, only for a year at a time, and only if large supermajorities in each house agreed. Still, it was enough of a symbolic concession to get the state Republican Party on board. With this proviso, the wealthy Senator Charles Algren of East Greenwich introduced a resolution in favor of the constitutional amendment on January 26. It passed the Senate on February 16, with twenty-one in favor, six opposed, and sixteen absent. All but one of those voting in favor were Republican, and all but one of those voting against were Democratic. It passed the House on March 15, with forty-two in favor, twenty-eight opposed, and thirty absent or not voting. Again, the vote was almost totally along party lines, with all but one of the "ayes" from Republicans, and all but two of the "noes" from Democrats.[68]

The comparison of these three states illustrates the importance of skilled movement entrepreneurs. Although it took a policy threat to inspire a campaign against the income tax, it was not the most threatened who mobilized. The apparently haphazard, hopscotch pattern that the movement followed through the states seems to have reflected the peregrinations of campaign personnel, rather than any shared structural preconditions. The resolution was a Republican Party issue in Rhode Island and Wyoming, but not in Mississippi, where it merely divided Democrat from Democrat. It was backed by industrialists in Rhode Island, but not in Wyoming or Mississippi, where it was favored by ranchers and growers. It was Rhode Island (of the three, the state with the greatest number of rich people) that had the least receptive legislature. These three states were the only ones to pass resolutions in favor of repealing the Sixteenth Amendment before World War II for the simple reason that they were the only three states where such resolutions were introduced.[69]

The comparison also highlights the importance of policy crafting. Even in an otherwise hostile political environment, Robert Dresser managed to get a resolution in favor of his amendment passed by tinkering with the wording of the amendment to obfuscate its costs. It was a trick that would come in handy after the coming of total war. The more that poor and working- class Americans were asked to sacrifice for the war, the more difficult it would become for state legislators to justify a vote in favor of limiting taxes on the rich. But the problem of persuading legislators to limit the income tax even in the midst of a total war was not insoluble. As Dresser had discovered in Rhode Island, it would simply require careful policy design.

Appendix 3.1. Text of the Dresser Amendment,[70] 1939

Section 1. The Sixteenth Amendment to the Constitution is hereby repealed.
Section 2. The Congress shall have power to lay and collect taxes on incomes, from whatever source derived, without apportionment among the several States, and without regard to any census or enumeration; provided that in no case shall the maximum rate of tax exceed 25 per cent.
Section 3. The maximum rate of any tax, duty, or excise which Congress may lay and collect with respect to the devolution of property, or any interest therein, upon or in contemplation of death, or by way of gift, shall in no case exceed 25 per cent.
Section 4. Sections 1 and 2 shall take effect at midnight on the 31st day of December, following the ratification of this Article.

CHAPTER 4

The Most Sinister Lobby

The coming of the Second World War brought a revolution in the taxation of income. In order to pay for the massive military investment necessary to win the war, Congress increased tax rates, lowered exemptions, and instituted new procedures to collect income tax from the majority of American workers and businesses for the first time in history. Many businesspeople perceived the new tax regime as a threat to the security of property. The perceived threat of confiscation brought more protesters and business organizations into the movement to repeal the Sixteenth Amendment.

The war also put new obstacles in the protesters' path. Under Secretary Henry Morgenthau, the Treasury Department mounted a major public relations campaign with rallies, songs, and films to persuade voters that paying income tax was a patriotic duty and a direct contribution to the war effort. The administration sanctified taxes as a patriotic sacrifice and compared the taxpayers' economic sacrifice to the blood sacrifice of the young men drafted to fight the war. In this climate, business conservatives who mobilized against the income tax risked appearing selfish, unpatriotic, or even treasonous.[1]

The new protesters who joined the movement fought back with a public relations campaign of their own. These protesters included experienced movement entrepreneurs who brought new skills and sets of relationships. The most successful of them combined the old populist organizing repertoire with scientific publicity techniques they had learned in the social movements of the Progressive Era.

Progressives against the Income Tax

Edward Aloysius Rumely was the movement entrepreneur who would do the most to transform the movement to untax the rich. Rumely's youth was a tour of the radical progressive movements that traversed the Atlantic world at the beginning of the twentieth century. He was born in La Porte, Indiana, in 1882 to German parents who ran a business manufacturing farm implements. He entered the University of Notre Dame at the age of sixteen, but was thrown out after his freshman year for his participation in the "single tax" movement. The single tax was a radical proposal by the economist Henry George to replace regressive consumption taxes with a tax on land speculators. George was a San Francisco printer and autodidact whose best-selling 1879 treatise, *Progress and Poverty*, had combined Ricardian economics and firsthand observation of the manic California real estate market into an argument that real estate speculation was the ultimate cause of industrial depressions. His followers believed that taxing away the speculative or "unearned" increment of land values would prevent real estate bubbles, free up land for productive uses, and incidentally provide enough revenue to relieve workers of the burden of commodity taxes. It was a reform program that had something for almost everyone, but it was especially popular among urban workers in the late nineteenth century. To the administration of Notre Dame, Rumely's single tax activism on campus smacked of socialism.[2]

Rumely went off to study at Oxford, where he promptly fell in with radicals again. A letter of introduction from one of his single tax friends led him to the working-class cooperative movement. While living in cooperative housing, he became infatuated with the pacifism of Leo Tolstoy and embraced an abstemious lifestyle, wearing modest peasant clothes, consuming only vegetarian food, and abjuring alcohol. He left Oxford after a year in disgust at the economics curriculum—they were still teaching "the *laissez faire* theory of Adam Smith," which was in his view an old-fashioned and inhumane doctrine—and transferred to Heidelberg, where he switched his major to medicine. Despite his fluency in German, Rumely did not fit in with his German student peers. He was a teetotaling, pacifist eccentric, whereas they were fond of their beer, proud of their dueling scars, and conservative in their habits and political views. So he befriended other outsiders. He attended meetings of the German Social Democratic Party and became close to some party and trade-union leaders. He also hobnobbed with Russian exchange students, many of whom were revolutionary socialists. On at least one occasion, Rumely colluded with Russian students to hide revolutionary literature from the authorities, and he may have helped them smuggle Leninist tracts back into Russia. (Rumor had it that Rumely was also distributing subversive leaflets to soldiers in the German army, though he denied it.) By his own account, he excelled at his medical studies, but what he valued most about his medical education was the instruction he received in the German system of social insurance, which he regarded as a model for the United States. He ultimately took degrees in medicine and sociology from the University at Freiburg in 1906.[3]

He was, above all, a Progressive, part of the transatlantic traffic in social reform ideas that has been described by the historian Daniel Rodgers. Like other activists of his generation, Rumely thought the social problems of the industrial era could be solved with an appropriately scientific attitude, and he sought out knowledge of interesting social experiments wherever they were conducted. By the end of his student days he had abandoned his experiments with Tolstoyan living, but he continued to experiment with diet, educational reform, and farm cooperatives. He returned to Indiana to found an experimental school called Interlaken that would combine classroom instruction with hands-on learning, in keeping with the progressive educational philosophy of John Dewey. In 1912, he took over the family threshing-machine business, but his heart was not in it. He spent most of his time and energy organizing cooperative farm credit associations, to the detriment of the firm's bottom line.[4]

In 1912, Rumely's enthusiasm for reform led him into the Progressive Party. Although the party was short-lived, it was one of the defining experiences for many social movement activists of the Progressive Era.[5] For Rumely, it was a crash course in the political role of the modern mass media. As a new party, the Progressives had no district- or ward-based organization, so they set out to bypass traditional machine politics with new tactics that relied on the emerging national media market. They commissioned movies, sound recordings, and magazine articles. They courted the newspapers, including the journalists whom their candidate, Theodore Roosevelt, had once derided as "muckrakers." Rumely offered his expertise on farm policy to the candidate, and in return TR taught him about publicity. Rumely committed the lessons to memory: If you want to move public opinion, first get into the daily papers; then parlay that into coverage by the weekly papers and the periodicals; then, when favorable stories or editorials are printed, have copies printed up in the hundreds of thousands, and mail them to every list of influential citizens you can possibly afford to buy.[6]

After the election, Rumely took what he had learned about publicity and put it to work in the antiwar cause. As preparations for war spread across Europe in 1914, Rumely saw a niche for an American newspaper that would report from an antiwar perspective. He hoped to persuade the United States to remain neutral. His reasons for opposing U.S. entry into the war were many: Like many German-Americans, he sympathized with Germany; he may still have harbored a touch of Tolstoyan pacifism; and he also dreamed of digging the family business out of debt by selling farm implements to the Germans. He found an existing New York paper that was for sale, and he persuaded the muckraking progressive editor S. S. McClure to come on board as his chief editor and business partner. Then he went looking for someone to front the money. American investors balked. (One of the first to turn him down was Standard Oil, which declined to back him, he assumed, because of his association with McClure, who had published

Ida Tarbell's iconic exposé of the company's misdeeds.) Some of his German contacts, however, offered to lend substantial sums on very generous terms from an undisclosed source. Rumely later denied knowing that it was German government money. He seems to have been careful not to inquire too closely about where it came from, however, and after the United States declared war, Rumely misrepresented the identities of his creditors to the Office of the Alien Property Custodian. He was indicted for trading with the enemy, convicted, and pardoned by President Coolidge after a month in prison. In 1925, he returned to Indiana, where he pursued his interests in dietary reform and agricultural credit.[7]

When the Great Depression struck, Rumely put his publicity skills back to work in political advocacy, this time for farmers. He convened the Committee for the Nation to Rebuild Prices and Purchasing Power, an association of industry and farm leaders that agitated for an end to the gold standard.[8] The group included many rich businessmen, and some New Dealers regarded the committee with a jaundiced eye as profiteering speculators in silver, or (in Rexford Tugwell's words) a "curious collection of reactionaries." But they also included representatives of leading farm organizations, and their doctrines, borrowed from Cornell agricultural economics professor George Warren, were pure Populism. The committee argued, like generations of agrarian radicals before them, that the crushing debt burden on farmers was harming the nation, that inflation was the path to prosperity, and that the way to bring about inflation was to reduce the gold content of the dollar. Rumely's speeches on the subject echoed the Populist rhetoric of William Jennings Bryan: "The ox that is goring farmers first and hardest has a golden horn," he said.[9]

This was not the rhetoric of a conservative. But in 1937, when President Franklin D. Roosevelt threatened to reorganize the Supreme Court, Rumely turned decisively against the New Deal. He concluded that the Roosevelt administration's hunger for power made it the "antithesis" of the old progressive movement. In this judgment, he was typical of the middle-class Progressives of his generation, most of whom mistrusted FDR and thought his administration was turning into a dictatorship.[10] Rumely joined the conservative Republican newspaper publisher Frank Gannett in forming a "National Committee to Uphold Constitutional Government" to oppose the court-packing plan. He was joined by many other former leaders of the progressive movement, including McClure and the lawyer Amos Pinchot (author of the *History of the Progressive Party, 1912–1916*). Gannett hired Rumely to be the executive secretary and manage the direct mail publicity program. They claimed credit for the defeat of the court-packing plan in July and decided to continue the fight against encroaching executive power in general and the New Deal in particular, shortening their name to the Committee for Constitutional Government (CCG) in 1941.[11]

That is how, in early 1943, the old Progressive Edward Rumely found himself nodding in agreement as Robert Dresser explained that the progressive income tax would lead to tyranny. Dresser, now a trustee of the CCG, was urging the rest of the board of trustees to sign on to his campaign for a constitutional tax limit. He laid out his proposal and told the story of his successes in persuading state legislatures to endorse it. His pitch persuaded several other wealthy trustees "to put up $5,000 on the spot," as Rumely later recalled, for the purpose of continuing the campaign.[12] Another trustee of the CCG who helped kick off the revival of the tax limit campaign was the statistician Willford I. King, whose early studies of economic inequality had helped fuel the movement for progressive taxation, but who now worried that the cure for too much inequality might be worse than the disease. King thought that the Roosevelt administration was "an almost typical fascist government," and without constitutional limits on the taxation of income and wealth, there might be no check on arbitrary executive power.[13] These men turned to the CCG because of Rumely's expertise in publicity and organizing—which he had acquired in a lifetime of progressive social movements.

Management Men Join the Movement

The business public was ready for his message. The Revenue Act of 1942 mandated the largest expansion of income taxes in U.S. history in order to pay for the war. The bulk of the new revenue came from lower-income taxpayers who had never before paid income tax; and with the addition of a new 5 percent "Victory Tax," even those who had previously paid income tax on modest incomes saw their marginal tax rates nearly double, from 10 percent to 19 percent. But the act also imposed heavy new taxes on the rich. Marginal tax rates formerly applicable only to million-dollar incomes now applied to incomes of $80,000 or more. The top marginal rate was raised to 88 percent. The rate of tax on so-called excess profits was increased to 90 percent.[14]

The kicker was the salary cap. This was a sop to organized labor that enraged business executives. Under pressure to step up war production, the leaders of the United Auto Workers in 1942 gave up their members' contractual right to premium pay for weekend work; in exchange, under the slogan of "Equality of Sacrifice," they pressed the Roosevelt administration to limit the growth of inequality by capping executive pay. President Roosevelt responded with a proposal for a 100 percent "super-tax" that would limit after-tax family incomes to $25,000 per adult. "In this time of grave national danger, when all excess income should go to win the war, no American citizen ought to have a net income, after he has paid his taxes, of more than $25,000," he announced. When Congress failed to act on his proposal, FDR used his authority under a new amendment to the Emergency Price Control Act of 1942 to cap salaries by executive order. The salary cap fell short of the original proposal for a maximum income—it did not apply to dividends or capital gains, for example—but FDR returned to Congress to urge extending the cap to all incomes.[15] The proposal for an income limit was particularly popular with farmers and blue-collar wage earners (see table 4.1).[16]

Businessmen, in contrast, reacted with outrage and alarm. The *Wall Street Journal* ran a series of front-page stories about the hardships of corporate executives affected by the salary cap, titled "The New Poor." The business-friendly *Chicago Daily Tribune* reported that the salary cap "represents further adoption of the Communist party program" by the Roosevelt administration. The Los Angeles Chamber of Commerce distributed a pamphlet that decried the executive order in the name of businessmen who did not make that much money. "We who write this are not in the affected income class nor do we know many whose gross incomes exceed $67,000 (the gross income necessary to net $25,000 after federal taxes), nor are we particularly concerned with their individual financial fate," they wrote. But if the "collectivists" could limit income to $25,000, the chamber asked, where would they stop? (The pamphlet was titled "Why Not $1,900?").[17]

Table 4.1. **Support for limiting the amount of income that each person should be allowed to keep, by occupation of respondent, 1942**

Occupation	Percent in favor of any limit	Percent of those answering "yes" who favor a limit of $25,000 or less	Average limit favored by respondents answering "yes"
Farmers, farm laborers	57 (50 to 63)	64 (56 to 72)	$20,537
Business executives and small business	47 (38 to 58)	55 (41 to 70)	$25,547
White collar	60 (54 to 67)	66 (57 to 74)	$23,453
Skilled workmen and foremen	54 (46 to 61)	58 (58 to 68)	$19,047
Semi-skilled and unskilled labor	60 (52 to 67)	66 (56 to 76)	$17,535
Service workers	51 (43 to 60)	59 (48 to 70)	$19,181
Professional and semi-professional	55 (44 to 66)	76 (64 to 88)	$24,241

The CCG joined the chorus of business opposition. It decried the salary limitation as a "transfer of taxing power from Congress to the Executive" and as a threat to the free enterprise system. Even after Republicans in Congress repealed the executive order in March 1943, many business executives saw the administration as a threat. "A battle [has] been won but not a campaign," the CCG explained in a 1944 pamphlet. "Congress is still under pressure from the redistribution-of-wealth radicals to embody their doctrine in federal taxation. And, unless a 'ceiling' is placed on the taxing power, that pressure will be a continuing menace."[18]

It was not only business owners who rallied to the cause. Salaried managers also thought that the administration's taxing power needed to be restrained. In 1944, the magazine *Modern Industry*—a trade journal "for all management men concerned with making and marketing better products at lower cost"—polled its readers on whether they supported constitutional tax limitation, after running arguments both pro and con. It found more than 82 percent of respondents in favor.[19] A Gallup poll in 1946 asked respondents whether they would favor a limit of 50 percent on the average rate of income tax. In households headed by business executives, support for a tax limit was 68 percent, compared to 36 percent of unskilled and 49 percent of skilled blue-collar wage earners. Support was higher among Republicans than Democrats (it was 53 percent of those who said they voted for Dewey in 1944, compared to 44 percent of those who said they voted for FDR). The biggest gap by far, however, was socioeconomic, with 80 percent of the "wealthy" and 45 percent of the "poor" expressing support for a tax limit (see table 4.2).[20]

There are no systematic data on the active participants who contributed time or money to the campaign. The treasurer of the CCG, Sumner Gerard, claimed in congressional testimony that that the CCG had about 5,000 volunteers engaged in organizing work in 1944. This was almost certainly an exaggeration, but at least that many people were contributing money. An auditor's report for 1943 shows 14,066 contributions, of which 10,974 were in amounts less than $10. Nothing more is known about the contributors' identities. When a congressional investigating committee issued a subpoena for a list of the contributors in 1944, Rumely flatly refused. He feared that Congress would use the list to portray the CCG as a cabal of the rich, which suggests that there were probably some well-known rich people on the list; but we will not know, because the list was never produced. Rumely was indicted for contempt of Congress and acquitted by a jury in 1946.[21]

Stirring the Ocean

Rumely believed that the success of a movement depended on a scientific approach to the problem of publicity. "Most of the wreckage in public movements,

Table 4.2. **Social characteristics of Americans who supported income tax limitation, 1946**

	Observed percent in favor (95 percent confidence interval)
Gender	
Men	44 (41 to 47)
Women	50 (47 to 52)
Race	
White people	47 (45 to 49)
Black people	47 (40 to 53)
Party	
Voted for FDR	44 (41 to 47)
Voted for Dewey	53 (50 to 58)
Voted other	26 (3 to 48)
Gallup SES category	
Wealthy	80 (67 to 93)
Average Plus	52 (45 to 58)
Average	48 (44 to 52)
Poor	45 (43 to 48)
On Old Age Assistance (OAA)	47 (37 to 47)
On relief	56 (40 to 72)
Occupation	
Farmers and farm labor	46 (42 to 51)
Business executive	68 (57 to 78)
White collar	50 (45 to 54)
Skilled labor	49 (43 to 55)
Semi-skilled	46 (41 to 51)
Domestic service	36 (26 to 45)
Protective service	52 (38 to 64)
Other service	42 (34 to 50)
Small business	61 (51 to 71)
Unskilled	37 (30 to 45)
Professional	42 (35 to 50)
Semi-professional	42 (14 to 69)

and political movements, come to men who take a sound stand, go 5% of the way to formulate it so that people understand it, reach 5% of the people, and then lack the ability or courage to drive through to the other 95%," he wrote. The first key to reaching the majority was to pick one's battles carefully. The movement should stick to truly national issues that would not "divide the following" along lines of section or industry. And the second key, he thought, was to rely on direct mail. He liked to quote Theodore Roosevelt's admonition that "America is as vast as an ocean—and you can't stir an ocean with a teaspoon." The way to stir public opinion was with mass mailings that made the ideas and slogans of the movement directly available to tens of thousands of opinion leaders at once.[22]

Direct mail brought supporters, but it also brought attention, and thereby broadened the scope of the conflict. In the summer of 1943, for example, the CCG issued a mass mailing of a brief by Robert Dresser in support of the proposed constitutional tax limitation. The "Dresser Brief" reiterated the pragmatic supply-side arguments from Andrew Mellon's *Taxation: The People's Business* with somewhat less nuance ("in normal times the lower tax rate will produce the greater revenue," it said). It also sounded an ominous new warning: "Whether or not we are witnessing a deliberate attempt to establish Communism or some other form of national socialism in this country, the fact is that measures which have been adopted by the Federal Government in the past few years have had the effect of driving us steadily in that direction, and the most potent means to this end has been the use of the taxing power," Dresser wrote. The CCG had the brief printed in pamphlet form and issued a fundraising letter over the signature of the popular Reverend Norman Vincent Peale soliciting funds for a mass mailing to "have the country seeded" with 1,000,000 copies.[23]

The activists from previous campaigns to untax the rich thought the mailing was a bad move. T. W. Phillips Jr. wrote to the CCG to warn that any such mass mailing would be prohibitively expensive unless the organization relied on rich donors, which would open the movement to charges that it was "only an effort on the part of the rich to avoid high taxes." He also thought increased publicity would draw unwelcome attention to Rumely's criminal record. "It occurs to me that it might be more effective if the Committee for Constitutional Government would not become unduly prominent in this movement," he wrote.[24] The ATA issued a bulletin to its own membership denouncing the CCG's mass mailing technique, which "has served notice upon the 'opposition' that the program was under way and from now on it is definitely going to be much more difficult to secure favorable action on these resolutions than it would have been if the program had been carried on as in the past in a quiet and effective way."[25] The Citizens National Committee, a group of prominent economists and other public figures that had been set up in 1924 to lobby for the Mellon plan, agreed that publicity was going to make things harder for the movement to repeal the

Sixteenth Amendment. "Until quite recently the proposal appears to have had fairly clear sailing," wrote a member of the Citizens National Committee in 1944:

> The campaign for it has been quietly conducted, and has been of such a nature that relatively little opposition has been aroused in state legislatures where it has been up for action.
>
> Within the past year, however, it has attracted more attention. The opposition has begun to organize. As already noted the petition has failed of passage in some state legislatures, and from now on the prospects probably are for more concerted opposition.[26]

Publicity contributed to growing opposition, but the thing that finally provoked the opposition to mobilize was a grassroots organizing project. In the summer of 1943, under Rumely's direction, the CCG began organizing local committees to raise funds and influence elections. The committee's grandiose and unrealistic objective was "to mobilize 1,000,000 constitutionalists, one to four thousand in each Congressional district, organized to support our constitutional system."[27] Although the CCG was nominally nonpartisan, Rumely and his colleagues decided to begin organizing local committees in those congressional districts where New Deal Democrats were vulnerable.

They launched their organizing drive in Texas, where a series of recent actions by the federal government—including oil price controls, pro-labor legislation, and a Supreme Court ruling against the Texas all-white primary (*Smith v. Allwright*, 321 U.S. 649)—had led much of the conservative Democratic elite to break with the administration in disgust. Texas oil men were organizing to refuse the state's Democratic nomination to Roosevelt. Many of them were ready to found a new party if necessary to preserve oil profits and white supremacy.[28] Rumely retained the Dallas public relations consultant Ted Ewart, who had close ties to the oil industry, to organize these men into the cause of tax limitation. Ewart and his staff traveled around the state setting up local clubs, much like a union organizer or an old Populist lecturer. These volunteer-run clubs, in turn, organized fundraising dinners and solicited contributions for the work of the CCG. They also spent a good portion of their time organizing essay contests in the schools on the subject of the Constitution.[29] The campaign was nominally nonpartisan, but it was clearly designed to convey a partisan message. The clubs and contests were arranged to take place in the districts of only those congressmen allied with the New Deal, and they were timed to coincide with primary season.[30] The CCG even distributed targeted mailings to the districts of incumbent New Deal Democrats that stopped just short of explicitly calling for their ouster. One flyer that was distributed in Representative Wright Patman's home town of Texarkana warned of mounting federal debt, calculated the share of interest payments on the federal debt that would be owed by Texarkana residents, and then singled out Patman as "one of those who thinks nothing of debt." In April 1944, former congressman Samuel B. Pettengill showed up in Texarkana to give a speech on behalf of the CCG to "a limited number of business and professional leaders" in order to warn them of the fascist menace and urge them to "send strong right-thinking men to Congress."[31]

In Patman, the CCG found a perfect nemesis. He was a former tenant farmer who still had a Populist's fervor for progressive income taxation. He was also a veteran of the First World War and an American Legion member who had participated in the movement for the soldiers' bonus. Patman had never forgiven Andrew Mellon for opposing the bonus in the name of tax cuts for the rich. One of his first priorities when he was elected to Congress in 1928 was to get the bonus paid early. Another was to hound Mellon out of office. Patman spent years collecting evidence that Mellon was using his position as Treasury secretary to enrich his companies and avoid taxation; in 1932, he finally moved to impeach Mellon, and the ensuing brouhaha precipitated Mellon's resignation as Treasury secretary even before President Hoover left office. Patman was not the sort of person to take it lightly when a bunch of businessmen and bankers met to organize a challenge in his district.[32]

Patman went to war. He persuaded Representative Clinton Anderson (D-NM), chair of the House Committee to Investigate Campaign Expenditures, to subpoena virtually the entire leadership of the CCG in the fall of 1944, setting in motion the chain of events that would eventually lead to Rumely's trial for contempt of Congress. Patman also began a publicity offensive of his own. He went on the radio to denounce the CCG. Patman bluntly described Gannett, Pettengill, McClure, and Rumely as fascists. He characterized the CCG as "the most sinister lobby ever organized" and gave speeches on the floor of Congress that described Robert Dresser's proposed constitutional amendment as "the millionaire's amendment to oppress the poor and benefit the rich." Then he mailed copies of his speeches to state legislators, union leaders, and civic leaders around the country.[33]

Even without Patman's counteroffensive, success brought scrutiny that might have slowed the momentum of the campaign. In the early months of 1943, eight states passed resolutions in favor of the amendment. In the summer, E. P. Dutton published a sensationalistic book called *Under Cover* by the pseudonymous "John Roy Carlson" that named Rumely and the CCG, among many other groups, as fascist sympathizers.[34] In October, the campaign in the states received favorable coverage in the *New York Times*. On February 25, 1944, New Jersey became the sixteenth state to pass a resolution in favor of the constitutional amendment—marking the halfway point toward the constitutional threshold for calling a convention. Republicans on the House Ways and Means Committee began discussing the need for statutory income tax cuts as a way to forestall the movement for a constitutional amendment.[35] Treasury Secretary

Henry Morgenthau Jr. directed his Division of Tax Research to study the effects of the proposed amendment. The report, issued in the summer of 1944, argued that the amendment would eliminate the possibility of a budget surplus, shift the tax burden onto low-income taxpayers, and impair the government's ability to respond to emergencies such as the war.[36]

The new opposition brought the campaign to an abrupt halt. In 1943 and 1944, fifteen state legislatures considered resolutions in favor of the constitutional amendment; ten of them passed the resolutions. In 1945, eighteen state legislatures considered resolutions; not one secured enough votes to pass. No state legislature would endorse the Dresser amendment again until 1949.[37]

A Policy Threat Revives the Movement

The CCG survived the next few years by turning its attention to other issues and by returning to the grassroots. It continued to raise funds by direct mail and urged its subscribers to contact Congress to demand statutory income tax cuts and restrictive labor legislation.[38] As Rumely's direct mail appeals gradually stopped yielding the same income, however, the CCG also turned to volunteer associations to increase its base of support. "Seventy percent of all citizens are opposed to socialistic legislation being driven through by minority pressure groups that would milk the United States Treasury and taxpayers for selfish group interest," one committee publication explained. "But the 70 percent majority is unorganized and unable to project its viewpoint effectively." The solution that the CCG envisioned was a network of local organizing committees of influential citizens in key cities. The CCG placed print advertisements in local newspapers. The advertisements described the creeping threat of communism in vivid terms, and invited interested citizens to send in contributions and add their names to the "Fighters for Freedom" mailing list. The CCG also secured the endorsement of local Kiwanis and Lions Clubs, and sent out mailings on behalf of local sponsoring committees to recruit additional supporters. Trial runs in Knoxville and Milwaukee in 1949 brought in enough contributions to more than recoup the cost of advertising and mailing, and generated hundreds of new recruits. Readers who signed up as Fighters for Freedom thereby pledged themselves to "Pitilessly expose Communism"; protect private property; oppose labor unions; defend the Bill of Rights; "Protest against politicians buying votes by promising Federal Aid for education, socialized medicine, and public housing"; campaign for a balanced budget; and, in the only concrete legislative proposal on the list, "Limit by Constitutional Amendment the peacetime taxing power of the Federal Government." By May 1950, internal documents indicate that the CCG had enrolled 35,000 Fighters for Freedom.[39]

The other organizations in the movement for tax limitation were also return-ing to a grassroots organizing model. By 1948, the Western Tax Council had "gone to seed," in the words of board member Frank Packard, a retired tax attor-ney for Standard Oil of Indiana. J. A. Arnold was approaching eighty, and his failure to get results had alienated many of his business supporters. The long-term donor Pierre du Pont finally prevailed on Arnold to turn over executive leadership of the Western Tax Council to Packard, who shared Arnold's enthu-siasm for the methods of the Populists and their radical agrarian successors.[40] Although Packard did not have Arnold's direct organizing experience, he had been a tax commissioner for North Dakota in the 1910s; this gave him a front-row seat from which to observe the formation and grassroots lobbying efforts of the Farmers' Nonpartisan League, one of the most famous and successful of the post-Populist farmers' social movement organizations. The league left him in awe. He told other tax lawyers that he regarded its founder A. C. Townley as a "genius" and the league itself as "the most perfect political organization of which I have any knowledge." Packard made a careful study of the league's grassroots organizing model. In place of farm cooperatives or political parties, he noted, A. C. Townley had undertaken to organize farmers into a grassroots interest group, or "a nonpartisan movement to influence the already existing political parties." Rather than hiring a professional lobbyist to communicate their con-cerns to legislators, the Farmers' Nonpartisan League used their dues to hire professional organizers to build their membership; when it came to communi-cating their interests, the assembled farmers of the league spoke for themselves. These were the same organizational features that J. A. Arnold had copied from the Farmers Union in the early years of the tax club movement. Packard would attempt to copy them when he took over the Western Tax Council.[41]

The ATA, meanwhile, under the leadership of Daniel E. Casey, continued to eschew mass publicity. While the CCG invited anyone who read its advertise-ments to sign up as a Fighter for Freedom, and the Western Tax Council returned to the grassroots, the ATA preferred to court a few influential citizens. The ATA continued to employ a field organizer who lobbied state legislatures through per-sonal contacts with business and political elites. But in the late 1940s, the ATA also began to formalize its organizing model, creating a new "Southern Division" in 1950, for example, that consisted of an advisory board of "outstanding busi-ness leaders" in twelve Southern states.[42]

These efforts finally bore fruit in 1950 when a new policy threat inspired another wave of business opposition to the income tax. The crucial events seem to have been the large tax increases in the Korean War and Revenue Act of 1950 and the Excess Profits Tax Act of 1950. Support for tax limitation swelled (see figure 4.1). A new crop of conservative multimillionaires, led by the former Prohibition repealer and DuPont executive John Raskob, joined the

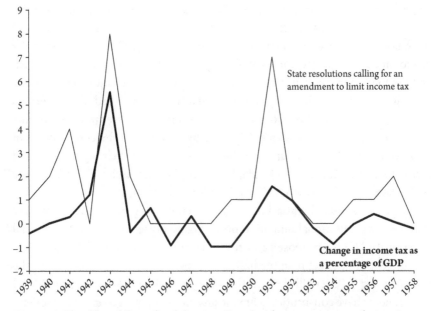

Figure 4.1 The ebb and flow of mobilization: State legislatures passing resolutions in favor of constitutional tax limitation. *Source:* Change in income tax as a percentage of GDP calculated from the National Income and Product Accounts, Tables 1.1.5 and 3.4; total resolutions calculated from sources described in introduction, note 3.

CCG.[43] Eight state legislatures endorsed the call for a constitutional tax limit in 1952. The campaign began to go mainstream. The U.S. Chamber of Commerce endorsed the tax limit. So did the American Legion, the National Association of Manufacturers, the National Small Business Men's Association, and the American Bar Association. The matter was sufficiently pressing that the new Treasury secretary, John W. Snyder, once again detailed the Treasury staff to issue a critical report. The Republican presidential candidate Dwight D. Eisenhower even weighed in on the issue with a letter to the Lafayette, Louisiana, *Daily Advertiser*, dated October 6, 1952, in which he asserted that "a prudent and positive administration should be able to approach the goal which the amendment seeks without the difficulty and dangers involved in the adoption or continuing operation of such an amendment to our Constitution." The movement did not have Eisenhower's support, but it had his attention.[44]

Crafting a Tax Limitation for Wartime

How did the movement take what was once a fringe political issue and get it on the agenda of mainstream politicians? Policy threats made businesspeople responsive to a campaign for tax limitation, and movement entrepreneurs mobilized them; but it was clever policy crafting that allowed these activists to get their tax limitation amendment on the policy agenda. Dresser designed the proposed amendment to copy state-level precedents, and the advocates of federal tax limitation made use of the analogy between state and federal policies in their arguments. When opponents argued that it was a bad idea to write a maximum tax rate into the Constitution, for example, Dresser pointed out that it was already done in the states: "It is worthy of note that the constitutions of [nineteen] states contain curbs on the taxing power of their legislatures, and that in four of these states—Florida, Louisiana, North Carolina and Utah—the curb relates to taxes on income."[45] An ATA leaflet of 1944, apparently directed at state legislators and influential businessmen, echoed his point: "Practically every state has a constitutional limitation on its taxing power. So should the federal government." Of the proposed constitutional amendment, the leaflet said, "It is no different in its effect than the limitation now found in many states upon the power to tax."[46] Pettengill thought the analogy obvious: "Many state and local governments have constitutional limitations on their power to tax or incur debt. The federal government has none."[47] The point was echoed by a national committee of state legislators who supported the resolution. These "State Legislators for the XXII Amendment" urged their colleagues around the country to apply the familiar policy of constitutional tax limitation to federal government: "If it is sound to limit the taxing power of State and local government, it is doubly sound to limit with respect to income, gift, and inheritance taxes, that power in the hands of the Federal Government."[48] All of these proponents argued that the proposed federal tax limitation amendment was analogous to state limitations on state and local taxation.

Robert Dresser rewrote his amendment again and again. Some of these revisions were merely technical changes meant to make it more effective. He introduced successive revisions, for example, in order to clarify that Congress could not circumvent an income tax limitation simply by adding a second income tax, or by redefining an income tax as an "excise tax" on salaries or business activities. He also hardened his position on the estate tax, revising the amendment in 1951 to abolish federal estate taxation altogether, on the grounds that taxation of inheritance was best left to the state level. He thought competition among states could be counted on "to keep the rates within reasonable bounds."[49]

Other revisions were more obviously designed to make the amendment appealing to potential allies. In particular, he sought to reassure otherwise-sympathetic businesspeople who worried that tax limitation would jeopardize national security. Lammot du Pont wrote to Rumely in October 1951 to say that rich businessmen of his acquaintance had doubts about the wisdom of limiting income taxes in wartime. He was not alone. "Within the past year," Packard wrote in 1951, "as during 1942–46, we have received many letters asking whether our proposal would cripple the war effort." Dresser answered such worries by redesigning his policy proposals.[50] In 1940, he had introduced the emergency clause permitting Congress to suspend the tax rate limit by three-fourths vote of both houses in the event of a national emergency; in 1951, he revised it to relax the income tax limitation further, permitting Congress to temporarily raise top marginal tax rates even in peacetime, up to a maximum of 40 percent or even 50 percent, upon a three-fourths vote of both houses.[51] In 1952, he revised it again to permit raising the top rate to any level, provided that the rate "does not exceed the lowest rate... by more than fifteen percentage points," a provision designed to make high rates politically impossible even though they were constitutionally permitted.[52] Other activists, including Rumely and King, fretted that these provisions were unnecessary giveaways, and wished to make the amendment more, rather than less, restrictive. But these revisions were useful concessions that allowed the campaign to win the support of people who did not share Dresser's faith in the power of tax cuts to spur economic growth.[53]

This careful approach to policy crafting was effective. After the Second World War, no state legislature seriously considered the proposal without the wartime emergency clause. But the version with the emergency clause proved popular when the campaign picked up again during the Korean War. Three of the states that had already endorsed the early version of the proposal voted to rescind their earlier resolutions of support, and replace them with resolutions that called for a tax limit with the wartime emergency clause.[54] The activists' willingness to reconsider basic aspects of their policy design also helped them get their demands back on the congressional agenda. Representative Chauncey Reed (R-IL) and Senator Everett Dirksen (R-IL) introduced a version of the amendment in the House and the Senate in 1951 that included the 40 percent maximum rate. The bill died quietly in committee, but Reed and Dirksen persisted at the request of the CCG, introducing a less restrictive version in 1953 and again in 1955.[55]

As the activists approached the threshold for calling a constitutional convention, some of them began to get cold feet. By the end of 1951, legislatures in twenty-six states had endorsed the call for a constitutional convention. Only six more states were needed. Some business conservatives began to express concern that instead of forcing Congress to introduce an amendment, their grassroots campaign might actually call a constitutional convention and thereby open Pandora's box.[56] Dresser shared their concerns. "It has been my opinion from the start that our objective should be to get Congress to propose the amendment itself, and not to call a convention," he wrote to Rumely. This course would be "safer," he opined, because a convention might do anything: "It is probable that the convention would not be limited to a consideration of this one proposal, but could consider any other changes in the Constitution it might see fit. Moreover, there would, I believe, be no obligation on the part of the convention delegates to adopt the amendment proposed by the 32 states." Dresser seems to have been particularly concerned that a constitutional convention would be subject to communist influence. It might undermine the protections for private property in the Constitution rather than strengthening them.[57]

Opposition to the campaign had also picked up. In 1950, the House of Representatives Select Committee on Lobbying Activities issued a subpoena for a list of major donors to the CCG. Rumely thought the request unconstitutional. True to the Tolstoyan ideals of his youth, he resolved on a course of civil disobedience (over the objections of Robert Dresser, who counseled obedience to the law). On June 6, 1950, Rumely appeared before the Select Committee "under protest," supplying account books and photostatic copies of checks from various wealthy contributors, including the du Pont brothers Pierre, Lammot, and Irénée. But he refused to supply the names of individuals who made bulk purchases of books and leaflets for distribution. He was cited, tried, and convicted for contempt of Congress. An appellate court overturned his conviction on the grounds that the CCG's attempts to influence the public were outside the statutory authority of the Select Committee. The Supreme Court finally upheld the appellate court ruling on March 9, 1953. The case did not provide the constitutional test that Rumely had hoped. In particular, the Court did not rule on the issue of whether the CCG's book sales had First Amendment protection. But the ruling did vindicate his contention that the CCG was not a front group for the Republican Party, nor was it engaged in lobbying, which the Court defined as "representations made directly to Congress, its members, or its Committees." The Committee was a grassroots social movement organization—in Rumely's words, "the biggest and most important movement ever projected."[58]

By the time that Rumely was acquitted, it was a movement in decline. After the armistice of July 1953, there were no new tax increases to keep anti-tax mobilization at a high pitch. Packard, on behalf of the Western Tax Council, continued to lobby state legislatures to call for a constitutional convention, insisting that a convention posed no danger; but other activists began to rein in their campaign.[59] Dresser, testifying before the Senate Judiciary Committee on behalf of the Reed-Dirksen bill in 1954, took pains to distinguish that proposal from earlier versions of his amendment. "I do not think anybody expects today or advocates the amendment that there will be any limitation of 25 percent at the present time," he said. The proposed amendments were "very different," he said, and states endorsing different versions of the amendment should not count towards the same two-thirds quorum.[60] The ATA also distributed booklets arguing for the new and less restrictive Reed-Dirksen amendment in place of its earlier proposals, and argued that "the odium of calling a convention to amend the Constitution instead of submitting a Resolution of its own to be ratified by the

State Legislatures in the customary manner, would rest squarely on the shoulders of Congress." By 1957, the campaign in the states had petered out.[61]

Meanwhile, other activists had begun to eclipse Dresser on the right. His policy crafting made the cause of tax limitation increasingly palatable to mainstream conservatives, but it alienated militants on the right who thought that his increasingly elastic tax limitation proposals missed the whole point of repealing the Sixteenth Amendment. Several activists broke away from the campaign for tax limitation in order to push for a new amendment that would do away with federal income taxes altogether. "[Y]ou cannot get rid of a weed by cutting it off at just grass level," one of them explained to a reporter.[62] The next campaign to untax the rich would try to uproot the income tax once and for all.

Appendix 4.1. Text of the proposed Reed-Dirksen Amendment

1951 version (H. J. Res. 323)[63]

Section 1. The Sixteenth Amendment to the Constitution is hereby repealed.

Section 2. The Congress shall have power to lay and collect taxes on incomes, from whatever source derived, without apportionment among the several States, and without regard to any census or enumeration. The maximum top rate (a term which shall mean the aggregate of all top rates) of all taxes, duties, and excises which the Congress may lay or collect on, with respect to, or measured by, income shall not exceed 25 percent; *Provided, however,* That Congress by a vote of three-fourths of all the Members of each House may fix a rate in excess of 25 per centum, but not in excess of 40 per centum, for periods, either successive or otherwise, not exceeding one year each. In the event that the United States shall be engaged in a war which creates a national emergency so grave as to necessitate such action to avoid national disaster, the Congress by a vote of three-fourths of all the Members of each House may, while the United States is so engaged, suspend, for periods either successive or otherwise, not exceeding one year each, such limitation with respect to income subsequently accruing or received.

Section 3. The Congress shall have no power to lay or collect any tax, duty, or excise with respect to the devolution or transfer of property, or any interest therein, upon or in contemplation of or intended to take effect in possession or enjoyment at or after death, or by way of gift.

Section 4. Sections 1 and 2 shall take effect at midnight on the 31st day of December following the ratification of this article. Nothing contained in this article shall affect the power of the United States after said date to

collect any tax on, with respect to, or measured by, income for any period
ending on or prior to said 31st day of December laid in accordance with
the terms of any law then in effect.

Section 5.   Section 3 shall take effect at midnight of the day of ratification of
this article. Nothing contained in this article shall affect the power of the
United States after said date to collect any tax with respect to any devolution or transfer occurring prior to the taking effect of section 3, laid in
accordance with the terms of any law then in effect.

1953 version (H. J. Res. 103, S. J. Res. 23)[64]

Section 1.   The Sixteenth Amendment to the Constitution is hereby repealed.

Section 2.   The Congress shall have power to lay and collect taxes on incomes,
from whatever source derived, without apportionment among the several
States, and without regard to any census or enumeration. The maximum
top rate (a term which shall mean the aggregate of all top rates) of all taxes,
duties, and excises which the Congress may lay or collect on, with respect
to, or measured by, income shall not exceed 25 percent; *Provided, however*, That the Congress by a vote of three-fourths of all the Members of
each House may fix such a maximum top rate in excess of 25 percent, for
periods, either successive or otherwise, not exceeding 1 year each, if such
rate so fixed does not exceed the lowest rate (a term which shall mean the
aggregate of all lowest rates) by more than 15 percentage points. Subject
to the foregoing limitations, the rates of tax applicable to the incomes of
individuals may be different from the rates applicable to the incomes of
corporations, which term shall include also associations, joint-stock companies, and insurance companies. The determination of income subject to
tax shall be by uniform rules of general application which shall not vary
with the size of the income.

Section 3.   The Congress shall have no power to lay or collect any tax, duty, or
excise with respect to the devolution or transfer of property, or any interest
therein, upon or in contemplation of or intended to take effect in possession or enjoyment at or after death, or by way of gift.

Section 4.   Sections 1 and 2 shall take effect at midnight on the 31st day of
December following the ratification of this article. Nothing contained in
this article shall affect the power of the United States after said date to collect any tax on, with respect to, or measured by, income for any period
ending on or prior to said 31st day of December laid in accordance with
the terms of any law then in effect.

Section 5. Section 3 shall take effect at midnight of the day of ratification of this article. Nothing contained in this article shall affect the power of the United States after said date to collect any tax with respect to any devolution or transfer occurring prior to the taking effect of section 3, laid in accordance with the terms of any law then in effect.

CHAPTER 5

The Power of Women

On September 27, 1951, a congressional staffer forwarded to Wright Patman a clipping from the *Washington Times Herald* that heralded "support of the Millionaire Amendment coming from two new quarters." The clipping was from the society pages, for, as the reporter Ruth Montgomery noted with incredulity, a new assault on the income tax was being launched from the drawing rooms of society women. Corinne Griffith was a former movie star also known to Washington high society as the wife of Washington Redskins owner George Marshall. Vivien Kellems was a factory owner and fashion icon—"the bombshell lady industrialist"—who had made herself notorious by resisting taxes during the war. Montgomery reported that Griffith and Kellems were mobilizing women for "an all-out-drive next month against—of all things—Federal income tax." In the short run, she reported, these women wanted a constitutional limit on the top tax rate. In the long run, they wanted to repeal the federal income tax altogether. "If the Griffith-Kellems plan succeeds," Montgomery wrote, "women all over the country will shortly be organizing to warn 1952 candidates for the Presidency, the Senate and House: 'No women's votes unless you pledge to support repeal of the 16th amendment.'"[1]

The announcement heralded a broader transformation in the movement to repeal the Sixteenth Amendment. Postwar changes to the income tax code threatened the economic security of many women and thereby inspired a new wave of protest against the income tax. The activists and leaders of the new campaign included wealthy women like Kellems and Griffith who had acquired new fortunes as a result of the war. But the activists also had the sympathy of many women who were not especially rich themselves.

The influx of women activists changed the movement against the income tax. The new leaders included movement entrepreneurs who brought with them skills, rhetoric, and relationships they had acquired in previous women's movements, including the club movement, the isolationist "mothers' movement," and the movement for woman suffrage.[2] Kellems was a particularly influential movement entrepreneur, but her influence depended on her access to a network of thousands of other women who had experience organizing together. These activist women pushed the movement in an increasingly radical direction. Among their contributions to the movement against the Sixteenth Amendment were a new tactical repertoire that embraced civil disobedience, a new rhetorical framing that portrayed the income tax as a violation of fundamental rights, and a new policy strategy to remedy that violation. Under their influence, the movement to repeal the Sixteenth Amendment abandoned the idea of a tax limitation amendment and embraced the radical demand to ban federal income taxes altogether.

Women, War, and Wealth

Corinne Griffith was an unlikely activist on behalf of the rich. Born in Texarkana in 1894, she was, she once said, "the last of a long line of seedy nobility, gone to pot." She remembered her mother as an heiress who married for love, and her father as a kindly but improvident alcoholic who squandered the last of the family fortune. On more than one occasion she was sent away to live with relatives because her family could not afford to support her. When she was an adolescent, her ailing father took her aside to tell her that there was no money left, and she would have to work to support the family. She quit school after eighth grade and went to work in movies at age fifteen.[3]

Her career was an object lesson in the high cost of sexism in the entertainment industry. At first, she parlayed her beauty and acting talent into a successful film career. At age twenty-five, she was one of the highest-paid silent film stars in Hollywood, appearing in five pictures a year and earning $12,500 per week. But her economic position was fragile. The roles began to dry up when she turned thirty. Then came the talkies, which demanded a different style of acting. Griffith had trouble making the transition. Critics panned her first two voice roles, accusing her of talking "through her nose" and complaining of her "tired voice" and "listless manner." The *Los Angeles Times* ran a feature story about how her legendary beauty had been eclipsed by younger women. Her contract with Warner was not renewed. Griffith was subsequently offered a contract by another producer, but only on the condition that she have sex with him. She refused, and he told her that she would never work in movies again. She believed that he followed through on his threat and had her blacklisted out of spite for her refusal. Her movie career was over.[4]

Griffith had saved for this day. But the stock market crash of October 1929 wiped out most of her savings. Most of what was left was taken by the federal government the following year, when a judge ruled that she owed almost $20,000 in unpaid income taxes. She later described this period as her "own private stock market crash." The long slide bottomed out in 1932, when she returned from her final film shoot in England to find that her assets were reduced to "$3,000 cash and vacant lots on South Beverly Drive in Beverly Hills, California." So she went to work in a touring theater company at less than a tenth of her former salary, and in 1936, she accepted an offer of marriage from George Marshall, a wealthy man whom she barely knew and, by her own account, barely liked.[5]

It was the war that made her fortune back. Beverly Hills turned out to be a good place to own two vacant lots. Los Angeles was a center of war production, and the flood of federal money and defense industry employees produced a real estate boom. Prices continued to rise after the war, as many discharged military personnel and war industry workers decided to settle there for good. After the war's end, Griffith saw properties in surrounding neighborhoods increase their value fivefold within a year. Her vacant lots were valuable. So she borrowed against them to finance the development of a commercial building, and soon she had enough to finance the development of another building, and another.[6]

By 1950, she was financially secure once more. Her marriage to Marshall had provided entrée to Washington society. Although he was active in Democratic Party circles, she also met and mingled with Republican critics of the New Deal and the Fair Deal. She came to realize that many rich people had experiences like her own private stock market crash—experiences of economic insecurity compounded by heavy tax liabilities—that made them resentful of the personal income tax. She learned too that the personal income tax was possible only because of the Sixteenth Amendment. And then, it seems, she met Vivien Kellems.[7]

Vivien Kellems was an outspoken feminist and successful entrepreneur just two years younger than Griffith. She credited her fighting spirit and business acumen to the experience of growing up with six brothers in Eugene, Oregon. Her father was a minister, and her mother a lay preacher and suffrage activist. Her youth left her with a commitment to women's rights, a deep knowledge of the Bible, and a talent for oratory. Had she been a man, she might have gone into ministry. Instead, she studied at the University of Oregon and Columbia University, where she stopped just short of earning a Ph.D. in economics.[8] Then she went into business. In 1927, her younger brother Edgar figured out that a woven tube patterned on a Chinese finger trap could be used to grip and install slippery electrical cables. Vivien persuaded him to take out a patent on the "Kellems Cable Grip" and began calling on electric company executives to solicit orders for the new product. Within three years, she was the sole owner of the Kellems Cable Grip Company, with control over "practically all of the business in the United States." She began to travel to Europe and South America in search of new markets for the cable grip.[9]

Kellems was not a born tax fighter. She was an opinionated business executive, and her fame as "the only woman manufacturer in the electrical industry" gave her many opportunities to speak out on issues of the day, but at first she did not use them to advocate tax cuts for the rich. Instead she used them to advocate for her industry and her gender. At a time when the businessmen of the ATA were launching their campaign against the income tax, Kellems was more preoccupied with state taxes on utilities. Her main complaint against the New Deal concerned the creation of the Tennessee Valley Authority, which she saw as unfair competition with private power companies. She also joined the National Woman's Party and spoke in favor of the Equal Rights Amendment (ERA). Throughout the depression, Kellems gave punning speeches to trade associations on "Volts for Women" and earnest speeches to women's clubs on behalf of the ERA.[10]

It was the Second World War that changed her priorities. In the first place, it made her a lot of money. The Kellems Cable Grip Company had always been dependent on government contracts: Streetcars and public utilities were major purchasers of cable grips, and one of her first big federal contracts involved the cables that took power from the Hoover Dam. But the defense buildup on the eve of World War II transformed the business. The Navy discovered a new use for the grips in loading and unloading ordnance. Her employees wove millions of cable grips for the Signal Corps. Kellems soon found that the federal government was her biggest customer.[11]

The war also increased her mistrust of the federal government, for she began to notice similarities between America when mobilized for total war and the totalitarian society she had seen in her 1938 tour of Germany. The New Deal youth programs reminded her of the Hitler Youth, and both made her think of communism. She set sail for Europe again in May 1940 and arrived in Paris just in time to evacuate ahead of the invading German force. Her return voyage via Lisbon and England took her uncomfortably close to air raids and sea battles, and she got a glimpse of the war's destructive impact that remained a distant abstraction to most Americans. On returning home, she learned that one of her closest European business contacts, a German aristocrat named Frederick von Zedlitz, had fallen ill during his detention by the French during the Battle of Belgium.[12] Kellems came to see little difference between militarist governments, and she feared that patriotic mobilization for the war was being used as a pretext to create a totalitarian society in the United States.

Kellems believed that communism was evil. As a preacher's daughter, she knew that the root of all evil was money. And so she set out to strike communism at its root, by depriving the federal government of the income tax.

Toil, Taxes, and Trouble

On January 18, 1944, Vivien Kellems stood before an audience of civic groups in Kansas City, Missouri, and announced that she had refused to make her December income tax payment. "This is a one-woman Westport tea party," she said, "and I cordially invite you to put on your Indian war paint and feathers and join me." Kellems denounced the income tax as a violation of the Fourth and Fifth Amendments. She warned grimly that "small business[es] have been marked for liquidation," and called on "all business, both big and small, to follow my example and put aside postwar reserves out of their taxes" in protest against the law.[13]

Kellems was practicing a tactic of civil disobedience she had learned from the movement for woman suffrage. When an admirer named I. S. Mattingly wrote to Kellems after her speech and likened her to Thoreau, she wrote back to say that she had never heard of Thoreau's essay on civil disobedience.[14] It seems to have been women like Susan B. Anthony and Alice Paul who provided her with examples. Later in life, Kellems described how she had learned about this tactic at the knee of an older suffragist:

> I have a little friend down in Washington—she's like a fragile piece of Dresden china—and I shall never forget the first time she told me how she got ready to go to jail. She knew she was going to jail, so she put her house in apple-pie order, everything was spic and span; the washing and the ironing; everything was laid out for her husband and the children; she baked a lot of pies and she cooked a lot of food; she cleaned everything and had everything ready. Then, she dressed herself in her very best dress and she went down and she stood in front of the White House and she took her banner and it said, "Votes for Women."[15]

This woman's extraordinary courage was rewarded with arrest—but then with victory. It was a potent lesson.

It did not work out that way for the one-woman Westport tea party. Federal officials declined to arrest Kellems. Instead, they responded with a campaign of vilification. Treasury Secretary Morgenthau announced that the refusal to pay taxes in wartime "smacks of disloyalty." Treasury agents began combing through intercepted correspondence between Kellems and Zedlitz, who was now living in Argentina, for evidence of espionage. What they found was not evidence of treason, but rather public relations gold: love letters. Someone leaked excerpts to the press. Radio broadcasters read her letters on the air. The columnist Walter Winchell derided her as a "Swasticutie" in love with an "Argentinazi." Representative John Coffee (D-WA) denounced her on the floor of Congress as a "tool of the Goebbels propaganda machine." While Republicans in Congress began an investigation into how the letters were leaked, Kellems quietly resumed paying taxes.[16]

The experience deepened her sense that totalitarian rule was imminent. She repeatedly warned friends and acquaintances in 1944 that "we are one step removed in this country from the Firing Squad and the Concentration Camp." She likened the Treasury Department to the Gestapo.[17] "I saw this whole thing happen in Germany," she explained to a friend who was baffled by her tax resistance, "and if they put me in prison—which I fully expect them to do—I shall go willingly as my imprisonment could possible crystallize the rebellious sentiment in this country which is ready to break through at any moment."[18] Lyrl Clark van Hyning, a prominent leader of the anti-Semitic and isolationist mothers' movement, wrote to congratulate Kellems and perhaps recruit her; Kellems wrote back politely thanking van Hyning and urging her instead to turn her attention to the income tax. "It is the large sums of money collected by the New Deal under the Income Tax Amendment which have made possible the outrageous extravagance and spending of the present administration and brought us close to communism," she wrote. The solution, she argued, was to repeal the Sixteenth Amendment. And the way to do it, she was convinced, lay in organizing women.[19]

She started small. On April 8, 1947, she organized some seventy-five women, including "society matrons and working girls," to start a shift in her factory at 10 p.m., in violation of a state curfew on night work for women that she described as "an insult to the women of Connecticut."[20] It was her second public civil disobedience. Once again, she was not arrested. And this time, she won. Just weeks later the state legislature voted to end the women's night work law.[21] The experience taught her that civil disobedience actually worked. It also taught her that she could rely on the cooperation of her employees when she broke the law. She decided that she was ready to take on the income tax again.

On February 13, 1948, she announced in a speech before the Los Angeles Rotary Club that she would henceforth refuse to withhold income tax from her employees' paychecks. She asked her employees to remit payment of their income taxes on their own, and then dared the federal government to take her to court. When the Treasury simply impounded her bank account, she sued. She hoped to test the constitutionality of income tax withholding, which she regarded as involuntary servitude in violation of the Thirteenth Amendment. Her suit did not achieve the effect she wanted, but in early 1951, she did get a favorable jury verdict on the matter of the impounded back taxes. She launched a speaking tour to publicize her trial, in hopes of inspiring a nonpartisan uprising of women against the federal tax machinery.[22]

It worked. In January of 1951, a group of eleven women from Marshall, Texas, inspired by a speech that Kellems gave in their town, decided to follow her example. They wrote to Kellems outlining their plans and asking for advice. On April 30, they took their campaign public, with a letter to Treasury Secretary John W. Snyder announcing that they would not comply with the new law that required them to deduct social security taxes from the wages of their domestic servants and remit them with their income taxes.[23] The "Housewives' Rebellion" made national news, and it appears to have convinced Kellems that the time was finally ripe to organize "a women's crusade for the whole country." The crusade would begin, she told the Marshall housewives, with a campaign for the repeal of "the withholding tax law, the social security law, and ultimately the income tax law."[24] She linked their struggles together in her speeches and proclaimed the beginning of a radical new women's movement against taxation. She returned in triumph to the Los Angeles Rotary Club on June 8, 1951. "We are on the verge of a mass civil disobedience!" she told the Rotarians to thunderous applause.[25]

That summer, Kellems met with a small group of conservative women from New York and Connecticut to plan the crusade. By the fall of 1951, they had agreed on a plan for a new organization called the Liberty Belles that had as its objective the abolition of income taxes. The name, Kellems said, was inspired by a Nebraska women's organization called the Cow Belles. On October 1, 1951, the new organization met to draft incorporation papers.[26] Kellems lent the fledgling organization $2,000 of her own money and began recruiting through personal appearances at conservative groups and women's clubs in Southern California, beginning with Pro America, the County Federation of Women's Clubs, the Ebell Club, and the Bond Club. Many of these were holdovers from the women's club movement of the Progressive Era.[27]

The Liberty Belles had their debut at the Shrine Auditorium in Los Angeles on November 19, 1951. It was by all accounts a raging success. Thousands of women (and some men) braved heavy rains to hear Kellems rail against the income tax and the socialists in Washington. Perhaps inspired by the weather, Kellems based her remarks on Matthew 7:25 ("and the rain fell, and the floods came, and the winds blew and beat upon that house, but it did not fall, because it had been founded upon the rock...."). She likened the federal government to a house built "on the sands of socialism" and called for a nonpartisan movement to tear it down and rebuild it on the rock of the Constitution. "We pulled out the bad pillar of [P]rohibition when we found it would not support what it was supposed to support," she told the assembled women. "We can pull out by the same method of repeal the amendment which gave us the income tax through which we can be taxed until the government can own everything we have." The rally was the conservative political event of the season. The *Los Angeles Times* detailed the editor of the women's page, Bess Wilson, to cover it.[28]

Membership continued to grow even after the meeting, as those who were there spread the word through their clubs, neighborhoods, and discussion groups. The activists who joined the Liberty Belles pledged themselves to three broad purposes:

1. The eradication of all socialism, communism, and corruption from our American life.
2. The revision and reduction of all taxes and of all government spending.
3. The return to Congress of the right to declare war so that never again, on the whim of the President, can American boys be sent to foreign lands to be shot.[29]

The women who took the pledge also put their names on a mailing list and agreed to pay annual dues of two dollars. Kellems and her friends on the executive board encouraged the Liberty Belles to recruit their friends and neighbors to local chapters or "units." They likened these units to the secret cells of the early Christians, or to sparks that would start a grass fire. Local chapters were expected to act independently of each other; a list of suggested actions included talking about taxes at every opportunity, writing to their newspapers and elected representatives, denouncing communism, and mobilizing local "telephone brigades" to recruit more Liberty Belles and sound the alarm about socialistic legislation. Kellems had Liberty Bell lapel pins manufactured and distributed to all new members so that they could recognize each other. (Men who joined were sent a slightly smaller pin and relegated to the "Liberty Boys" auxiliary—so that they would know what it was like, Kellems said.) By September 1952, financial records indicate that $20,398 in dues had been collected in California.[30]

Women's Wealth and Men's Tax Policy

Kellems had dreamed for years of a women's movement against the income tax, and now for the first time large numbers of women were ready to join her. Part of the reason, as Kellems recognized, was a historic increase in wealth held by women, and white women in particular. "Approximately 70 to 80 percent of the wealth of the United States is in our little, lily white hands," she wrote in 1952, "and if you dear, sweet men don't start taking care of yourselves, we'll soon own it all." The statistic was guesswork or fiction—the best available data from probate inventories and estate tax returns suggest that women owned less than a third of all wealth in the mid-twentieth-century United States—but the precise number was not the point. More women were wealthy than ever before. Their wealth, moreover, was more likely than men's to come from inheritance, a fact, Kellems argued, that made women "freer to act than men," whose business interests made them vulnerable to government coercion.[31]

For the most part, the policy threats that inspired these wealthy women to act were the same as those that spurred wealthy men. Particularly important was the Korean War and Revenue Act, which restored high wartime rates (including a maximum effective tax rate of 87.2 percent). But there were other tax changes that affected high-income *women* in particular. One was the amendment to the Social Security Act that extended coverage to farm workers and domestic servants, and required the employers of household labor to collect and remit payroll tax on behalf of their employees. Wealthy housewives, as managers of the household's domestic affairs, were now to act as tax assessors and collectors for their servants.[32]

There were also new income tax inequities between married men and married women. The Revenue Act of 1948 created a system of "joint filing" that dramatically increased the effective individual income tax rates on married women. Joint filing nominally created a separate schedule of *lower* tax rates for married couples who pooled their incomes for tax purposes, but in practice the new law affected husbands and wives differently, and it increased taxes on women.

It did so by design. This was a frankly traditionalist law that was intended to stop states from granting married women new property rights—or, in the words of the Senate Finance Committee, to curb the "impetuous enactment of community-property legislation by States that have long used the common law."[33] In most states, the precedent established by English common law held that women had few rights to property acquired in marriage. But a handful of states had community-property laws that treated such property as owned by spouses in equal shares. Prior to the 1930s, these laws were seen as historical curiosities, legacies of the Napoleonic Code in states that were former French or Spanish colonies. In the context of World War II tax policy, with its heavy tax burden and steeply progressive rates, however, these community-property states suddenly discovered that their marital property laws gave them a new importance as tax havens for rich married men. A husband with a high-bracket income could avoid heavy taxes by splitting his income with his spouse, thereby dividing it into two smaller incomes that were taxed at lower rates. By 1947, this tax dodge was well known, and legislators in common law states were starting to adopt community-property laws as a way to prevent their rich residents from decamping to take advantage of it. Congress passed joint filing in 1948 to extend the same tax break to married men in *all* states, and thereby remove the incentive for state legislators to change their marital property regimes.[34]

The effect of joint filing was to drive a wedge between the economic interests of married men and married women. The new system provided a tax cut to a single person upon marriage, if that person married a non-earner. But by the same token, it created a substantial tax penalty on a secondary earner—that spouse in a dual-earner couple whose earnings the couple treated as more optional. The secondary earner was generally the second spouse to enter the labor force or the lower-income spouse, if both were already in the labor force; in the context of a gender-stratified labor market, that meant that the secondary earner was almost always the wife. In other words, joint filing worked just like an individual income surtax on married women. A banker with a $300,000 income who married his secretary could thereby expect to move into a lower tax bracket. But the secretary who married the banker could expect now to have every dollar of her meager wages taxed at 90 percent or 91 percent, the highest marginal rates in the tax code. Perhaps unsurprisingly, the law incentivized married women to leave the paid labor force. Joint filing reduced the tax burden of married men, but it increased the implicit tax burden on their wives.[35]

By 1952, sympathy for the cause of income tax limitation was widespread, especially among married women. In 1952, the Gallup organization polled a random sample of adults on their support for the constitutional tax limitation proposed by the ATA: "It has been suggested that a law be passed so the Federal government could not take more than 25 per cent, or one- fourth, of any person's income in taxes except in wartime. Would you favor or oppose this 25 per cent top limit?" This wording—which understated the radicalism of the millionaire's amendment by incorrectly describing it as a statutory limit on the average tax rate, instead of a constitutional limit on the marginal tax rate—produced a large majority in favor of tax limitation among virtually every socio-demographic group. It also produced a substantial gender gap in sympathy, especially among married adults, with 75 percent of married women, compared to 68 percent of married men, favoring the cause of income tax limitation. The gender gap was statistically significant, and it was substantially greater than the gap between Democrats and Republicans or the gap between the rich and the poor (see table 5.1).[36]

To some extent, this gender gap may have reflected differences in access to information, rather than differences of economic interest. Other economically disadvantaged groups, such as people of color and high school dropouts, were also overrepresented among supporters of the tax limitation, despite the fact that they rarely paid much income tax. Women and men belonging to these other disadvantaged groups may have been more supportive of tax limitation simply because they were less well-informed about the distribution of the tax burden, for the understandable reason that they were less likely than others to have the time, resources, or education to follow politics closely.[37] There is some evidence that people who paid less attention to the news were more likely to support income tax limitation, and a logistic regression analysis suggests that controlling

Table 5.1. **Observed and predicted support for a "25 percent top limit" on income taxes in 1952, by socio-demographic group**

	Observed percent in favor (95 percent confidence interval)	Predicted percent in favor, controlling for other characteristics (95 percent confidence interval)
Gender and Marital Status		
Married men	68 (65 to 71)	69 (64 to 75)
Married women	75 (72 to 79)	77 (73 to 82)
Unmarried men	75 (69 to 81)	76 (68 to 83)
Unmarried women	74 (69 to 80)	73 (66 to 80)
Race		
White people	72 (70 to 74)	73 (68 to 79)
People of color	83 (75 to 91)	82 (74 to 91)
Party		
Democrats	72 (69 to 75)	73 (68 to 79)
Republicans	73 (70 to 76)	75 (70 to 81)
Independents	70 (63 to 77)	70 (61 to 79)
Gallup SES category		
Wealthy	79 (66 to 92)	76 (60 to 91)
Average Plus	64 (57 to 71)	64 (54 to 73)
Average	69 (65 to 73)	67 (61 to 74)
Poor	76 (73 to 79)	73 (68 to 79)
On relief (including OAA)	78 (49 to 100)	64 (27 to 100)
Education		
No schooling	88 (74 to 100)	73 (66 to 81)
Grammar school	74 (70 to 78)	73 (67 to 79)
High school, incomplete	74 (70 to 78)	73 (68 to 79)
High school, grad	72 (68 to 76)	73 (67 to 80)
College, incomplete	71 (65 to 77)	73 (67 to 80)
College, grad	61 (53 to 69)	73 (66 to 81)

for education and political engagement can explain away many of the observed group differences in support for the tax limit proposal (see table 5.2).

But it is likely that even many married women who understood the tax law supported income tax limitation. The regression results show that gender remained a significant predictor of support for tax limitation among married adults. The results summarized in the second column of table 5.1 show that the gender gap in support for tax limitation among otherwise-average adults—unlike the race gap or the education gap—remained even after controlling for socioeconomic status, news consumption, political knowledge, and political engagement. The system of joint filing meant that most married women implicitly faced a higher marginal tax rate than their husbands, and the pattern of political opinion suggests that they resented it. Married women, regardless of socioeconomic status, education, or political engagement, were the largest pool of sympathizers for income tax limitation.

Married women were also the core activist cadre of the new campaign to repeal the Sixteenth Amendment. Detailed membership records for the Liberty Belles and Liberty Boys are available only for the twenty-two months from June 1952 to March 1954, and they exclude members who joined through the California chapter, which jealously guarded its dues base and mailing list. These records show that Kellems recruited 1,326 members by mail and television solicitations over this period, and probably again as many through mass meetings in other cities as distant as Chicago, New York, Washington, Omaha, Indianapolis, Fort Wayne, and Cincinnati.[38] Inspection of the 1,326 names on the membership list permits the inference that somewhere between 76 and 80 percent of these Liberty Belles were women, and by counting those who styled themselves as "Mrs." or joined together with husbands, we can infer that at least 63 percent of those women were married.[39]

It is difficult to infer anything about the socioeconomic status of individual Liberty Belles because Kellems deliberately established a low dues rate that would be affordable to almost any woman. What can be said is that chapters arose chiefly in states where wealthy women were comparatively numerous and where Kellems had extensive personal networks. Internal financial reports and Kellems's private correspondence imply that California—a community-property state with many wealthy people—had the vast majority of the members, although Kellems never had a precise count of the California membership.[40] Members were otherwise concentrated in the Northeast, particularly in Connecticut. The membership lists that Kellems had on file indicated that many members joined through house parties and other forms of direct one-on-one outreach by activists.[41]

Table 5.2. **Logistic regression analysis of support for a "25 percent top limit" on personal income tax in 1952, as expressed in Gallup poll #489 (March 27–April 1, 1952)**

	Logit (standard error)	Sample mean
Intercept	0.95 (0.33**)	...
Gender, marital status, age, race, and education		
Woman =1	−0.13 (0.23)	.50
Married =1	−0.31 (0.2)	.77
Interaction term: Woman =1 and Married =1	0.54 (0.26*)	.36
Age in years	0.010 (0.004*)	44
Non-white = 1	0.53 (0.29)	.05
Education in years	0.0007 (0.02)	9.7
Political party identification		
Republican =1	0.11 (0.12)	.44
Independent =1	−0.16 (0.19)	.10
Gallup socio-economic code (reference category = "Poor")		
Wealthy =1	0.13 (0.42)	.02
Average Plus = 1	−0.46 (0.19*)	.10
Average =1	−0.29 (0.13*)	.32
On relief (incl. OAA or other relief) =1	−0.22 (0.82)	.01
Political knowledge:		
=1 if R correctly identifies Adlai Stevenson	−0.08 (0.12)	.33
News consumption:		
=1 if R has "heard or read anything about the Arnold Schuster killing in Brooklyn"	−0.37 (0.13**)	.69
Political engagement:		
=1 if R voted in 1948	0.11 (0.13)	.73
N	1,812	
McKelvey and Zavoina's pseudo-R^2	.05	
Adjusted count R^2	.00	

*$p < .05$

**$p < .01$

The Liberty Belles were only the beginning of a fundamental shift in the social base of the movement against the income tax. Women acquired new influence through a process of organizational succession as the older all-male anti-tax organizations ceded the field, and the new organizations that took their place made a greater place for women in positions of leadership. Table 5.3 illustrates the shift by reporting the gender composition of selected national organizations that led the campaign against the income tax. The organizations include all of those that were active in lobbying Congress and state legislatures for limitation of income taxes, abolishment of estate taxes, and repeal of the Sixteenth Amendment from the 1920s through the 1960s, except the Western Tax Council, for which no data are available. The data are available only for selected years, but these approximate the years of peak mobilization, and they make clear that the millionaire's amendment was a men's cause until the Liberty Belles arrived on the scene. As late as 1950, the ATA had no women in positions of leadership, and the CCG had only two, neither of whom was an active public spokesperson. The table also shows that within a few years, these older conservative organizations had ceded leadership to new social movement organizations—not only the Liberty Belles, but also co-gendered organizations such as the Organization to Repeal Federal Income Taxes and the Liberty Amendment Committee—that recruited many more women as officers and directors. And these new female board members were activists like Kellems and Griffith, not figureheads, like Mrs. Warren G. Harding, who had been recruited to lend their husbands' names and little else to the older conservative organizations.[42]

In addition to these new anti-tax organizations, Kellems, Griffith, and their sisters-in-arms also enlisted the support of older women's organizations, including women's patriotic societies, Republican women's clubs, and upper-class associations of women who claimed descent from the early English colonists. The Liberty Belles fundraising lists show that Kellems found women's clubs to be particularly good places to recruit. By the mid-1950s, many such conservative women's organizations had become an important and independent voice against the income tax.[43]

The Power of Women

These activist women did not just join the movement; they transformed it. Kellems, and the networks of women that she helped to activate, brought into the movement a new and more militant repertoire of tactics, rhetorical frames, and policy demands.

One manifestation of this repertoire was the increasing use of civil disobedience. After Kellems transposed the tactic of civil disobedience from the

Table 5.3. **The gender composition of formal leadership bodies in three waves of anti-tax mobilization**

Year	Organization	Leadership body	N		%	
			Men	Women	Men	Women
Campaign to repeal estate tax and limit top rate of income tax by statute						
1924	American Bankers' League	Vice-Presidents	6	0	100	0
1927	American Taxpayers' League (formerly American Bankers' League)	Vice-Presidents	15	0	100	0
		State Directors	82	0	100	0
Campaign to repeal Sixteenth Amendment and limit top rate of income and estate tax by constitutional amendment						
1937	National Committee to Uphold Constitutional Government	Prominent founding members	46	2	96	4
1943	Committee for Constitutional Government (formerly National Committee to Uphold Constitutional Government)	Officers and advisory board	30	3	91	9
1943	American Taxpayers' Association (formerly American Taxpayers' League)	Officers and executive committee	14	0	100	0
1944	State Legislators for the XXII Amendment	Directors and officers	33	0	100	0
1949	Committee for Constitutional Government	Officers and advisory board	29	2	94	6
1950	American Taxpayers' Association	Officers and executive committee	18	0	100	0

Table 5.3. (Continued)

Year	Organization	Leadership body	N		%	
			Men	Women	Men	Women
Campaign to repeal Sixteenth Amendment and ban income and estate tax by constitutional amendment						
1951	The Liberty Belles and Liberty Boys	Founding directors and officers	0	5	0	100
1956	The Organization to Repeal Federal Income Taxes	Founding directors and officers	8	2	80	20
		Founding sponsors	16	5	76	24
1963	Liberty Amendment Committee of the U.S.A.	Executive committee	16	1	94	6
		National Board of Directors	61	9	87	13

movement for women's equality to the movement against the income tax, other anti-tax activists took it up. It was not just the Marshall housewives. In 1952, the Mississippi newspaper publisher Mary Dawson Cain, after consulting with Kellems, announced that she would no longer pay social security taxes or deduct them from her employees' wages. When Treasury agents seized her property and padlocked the door of her newspaper office, she sawed the padlock off, thereby earning herself the sobriquet "Hacksaw Mary." A handful of male small business owners in Florida and Ohio announced that they too would not pay the social security payroll tax. Businessmen and women continued to follow suit through the decade, and even when there is not direct evidence that they were imitating Kellems, it is hard not to hear echoes of her in their arguments against the income tax and the social security tax.[44]

Another element of the new tactical repertoire was a framing of the income tax that treated it as a violation of civil rights. This way of framing the income tax implied a moral absolutism inconsistent with the utilitarian arguments put forward by spokesmen for previous waves of anti-income tax mobilization. In the 1920s, for example, spokesmen for the tax club movement had made a consequentialist argument for cutting income taxes on the rich, asserting that such tax cuts were good because they would encourage "progress and growth."[45] In the 1940s, the ATA and the CCG had echoed this argument: A constitutional income tax limit was good because it would increase economic growth.[46] Kellems, Griffith, Cain, and many other women activists in the early 1950s rejected that argument as an unacceptable compromise with expediency. It should not matter whether repealing the Sixteenth Amendment would increase or decrease economic growth. It was the right thing to do.

The problem with the income tax according to these women activists was not that it was bad for the economy but that it violated taxpayers' civil rights—especially, but not only, the civil rights of women. The Sixteenth Amendment, Griffith pointed out, was ratified by an all-male electorate at a time when women were denied the right to vote.[47] Requiring an employer to withhold employees' income taxes, Kellems thought, was a violation of the Thirteenth Amendment's prohibition on involuntary servitude. The income tax itself, she said, violated the Fourth and Fifth Amendments and infringed on the fundamental right to private property—"our right to own something." As Kellems saw it, much as J. A. Arnold had argued before her, the right to own private property was a natural right, and the basis for all civil rights, because only someone who owned property could afford to stand up to abusive and tyrannical authority without fear of losing her livelihood.[48]

Unlike J. A. Arnold, Kellems followed this line of argument to its logical conclusion: The income tax should be not merely limited but abolished. There was no sense tinkering with the Constitution to calibrate by fine degrees just how much of your property the government could legitimately seize. Either private property was an inviolable right or it was not; and if it was an inviolable right, then no income tax rate, however low, could be justified. Kellems therefore rejected the demand for a constitutional limit on the top rate of income tax: "A limitation of even one percent would still mean corruption." Rights were absolute or they were nothing. As if to underscore the distance between her views and those of previous anti-tax activists, Kellems explicitly rejected the view that untaxing the rich would help the economy. She predicted dire economic consequences from even a gradual phase-out of the income tax— and argued that it should be abolished anyway. "[O]ur economy is geared to the income tax," she wrote, "and even though the shift is accomplished over a period of years, it will tend to collapse when the tax is stopped." But economic collapse was worth it, if that was the price of abolishing the income tax.[49]

Such rights rhetoric had many sources in the American political tradition, but its proximate source in this case was Kellems's experience of the women's movement. She sometimes told stories about the political lessons she had learned from older activists in the National Woman's Party. One of these lessons was that the problem with gender inequality was not a matter of degree (there is a little too much inequality) but a matter of absolute rights (there is a violation of the right to equality), and the solution was therefore not piecemeal remedial legislation, but instead a constitutional amendment to protect women's rights. In September 1952, Kellems presented this argument in a radio broadcast called "The Power of Women" that was financed by the Liberty Belles. She described it as a hard-won lesson passed down from one social movement to the next. Activists for woman suffrage, she said, had learned it from the struggle for abolition of slavery: "When it came time to free the negroes and to make them free and equal with the rest of us, which is certainly the thing that should have been done long before it was, we passed an amendment to our Constitution." The lesson that Susan B. Anthony drew, Kellems said, was that constitutional amendment was the path to political rights for women too.[50] And the further lesson that Kellems drew was that women should fight the income tax the same way that they fought their exclusion from the polity: as a violation of their rights, to be remedied by amending the Constitution (or, as she wrote in her outline for the broadcast, "No problem that confronts us today ... can't be solved through the framework of the Constitution").[51]

The new repertoire outlived the Liberty Belles. The organization itself collapsed almost as quickly as it grew. The same quality that made Kellems such a determined activist—her reluctance to submit to anyone's authority but her own—also made her a hard person to work with, even for her closest political allies. The five-woman governing board of the Liberty Belles had an extraordinarily high rate of turnover, and within sixteen months of the organization's incorporation, Kellems was the only original director left.[52] Meanwhile, a conflict over autonomy had also erupted between Kellems and the California unit led by Genevieve Blaisdell. In the spring of 1952, while Kellems was distracted by her own ill-starred campaign to secure the Senate nomination of the Connecticut Republican Party, Blaisdell was using the Liberty Belles' name, resources, and mailing lists to campaign for a conservative challenger named Thomas Werdel in the Republican presidential primary in California. Blaisdell's actions led to an exodus of Eisenhower supporters from the California leadership. Kellems, who favored Robert Taft, dithered at first and then responded too late by attempting to reassert control over policy of the California chapter; she succeeded only in driving out the Blaisdell faction. That left no one. By the spring of 1953, there was a leadership vacuum in the largest state chapter, the membership lists were scattered, and the Liberty Belles were in such disarray that Kellems couldn't even coordinate a letter-writing campaign.[53]

By then, however, others had picked up the tactical repertoire. In the spring of 1952, Corinne Griffith and several other conservative Republicans from Los Angeles began to organize a new co-gendered association for repeal of the Sixteenth Amendment.[54] In February 1954, the conservative Devin-Adair Publishing Company printed a screed by the radical individualist Frank Chodorov entitled *The Income Tax: Root of All Evil* that echoed Kellems's arguments and characterized the income tax as a violation of natural rights. By 1955, many of these activists had come together as the Organization to Repeal Federal Income Taxes (ORFIT). The new organization also welcomed many activists who had previously supported income tax limitation, and who were now, under the influence of Kellems's arguments, coming around to the cause of total repeal. Griffith, as the honorary president of ORFIT, spoke on behalf of income tax repeal in mass meetings and on the air. Kellems signed on as a sponsor and lent her name and considerable notoriety to the organization's fundraising appeals. She also recorded a radio broadcast that passed the baton from the Liberty Belles to ORFIT. "We repealed the 18th Amendment. We can repeal this 16th Amendment," she said. "And certainly with as progressive and as determined an organization as ORFIT and its patriotic members pushing this thing, I have every belief that we are going to repeal this income tax amendment and with it we will get back the right to our money and we'll get back our freedom and privacy."[55]

By the mid-1950s, the movement to repeal the Sixteenth Amendment had radicalized. The men of the ATA and the CCG were still arguing for a constitutional limitation on the top marginal rate of income tax. But congressional hearings on their proposals reveal that they were now being outflanked on the right by women's groups. Table 5.4 illustrates the shift with data on organizations presenting testimony at subcommittee hearings of the Senate Judiciary Committee.[56] As the table shows, in 1954, no women submitted testimony. In 1956, when the committee held hearings again on the same proposed amendment, seven of the fifteen organizations submitting written or oral testimony in favor of repealing the Sixteenth Amendment were represented by women; six were women's organizations, and one was Corinne Griffith on behalf of ORFIT. Moreover, many of these women were there to repudiate constitutional tax limitation in favor of a more radical program. "We the Mothers Mobilized for America protest against a constitutional amendment to limit Federal income tax to 25 percent," wrote Emma Grab. "We stand unequivocally on the Constitution. We demand the repeal of the 16th amendment en toto." Corinne Griffith testified in person to the same effect: "I am not with the 25-percent ceiling limit. Our theory is to repeal it completely and revert it to our original Constitution that our States tax us." These women activists introduced a new and radical note into the proceedings. Their campaign for income tax repeal marked a decisive break with the postwar movement for income tax limitation.[57]

The new radicalism also created the potential for mobilizing a broader constituency. The goal was no longer a millionaire's amendment: Thanks to women like Vivien Kellems and Corinne Griffith, it was now a proposal to abolish

Table 5.4. **Organizations presenting testimony in favor of limiting or abolishing the income tax, 1954 and 1956, by the gender of spokesperson**

Organizations represented by men	*Organizations represented by women*

Senate Judiciary Subcommittee Hearings of April 27, 1954

In favor of limitation: 11	*In favor of limitation: 0*
American Legion	*In favor of abolition: 0*
Committee for Constitutional Government	
Life Insurance Policy Holders' Protective Association	
National Association of Manufacturers	
National Economic Council, Inc.	
National Small Businessmen's Association	
Ohio Chamber of Commerce	
Special Committee of the American Bar Association	
Steuben Society of America	
Taxation Committee, Ohio State Bar Association	
Western Tax Council	
In favor of abolition: 0	

Senate Judiciary Subcommittee Hearings of April 24, 1956

In favor of limitation: 7	*In favor of limitation: 4*
American Coalition of Patriotic Societies	30th Women's Patriotic Conference on National Defense
Associated Industries of Rhode Island	Dames of the Loyal Legion of the United States of America
Committee for Constitutional Government	National Society of the Daughters of the American Colonists
National Economic Council, Inc.	National Society Women Descendants of the Ancient and Honorable Artillery Company
National Small Businessmen's Association	
Special Committee of the American Bar Association	*In favor of abolition: 3*
We, the People	Hollywood Women's Republican Club
Western Tax Council	Organization to Repeal Federal Income Taxes
In favor of abolition: 1	We, The Mothers Mobilized for America
Association for the Balance of Political Power	

income taxes across the board, for rich and middle-income people alike. The goals of the movement and also its means were transformed. The rights-based rhetoric that Kellems and Griffith employed was easily accessible to people without economic expertise; the validity of their arguments did not hinge on technical assumptions about the elasticity of revenues with respect to marginal tax rates. The new tactical repertoire promulgated by the Liberty Belles also invited participation by providing many options for political action along a continuum from low-commitment exercises like wearing Liberty Bell pins all the way to high-commitment activities like practicing civil disobedience against the tax authorities. None of these tactics required great fundraising prowess or lobbying expertise. The turn to civil disobedience put a weapon in the hands of anyone who owed taxes.

Although the form of the protest was populist, the symbolism of the movement remained anything but. At a time when even conservative candidates treated traditional insignia of wealth as symbols of corruption, Kellems and Griffith stood against the tide and insisted on the moral worthiness of the rich. The Republican vice presidential candidate Richard Nixon, in a televised appearance in September 1952, famously pointed to his wife's modest "Republican cloth coat" as evidence of his incorruptibility; but Kellems and Griffith wore their mink coats with pride. Corinne Griffith published her speeches with publicity photos of herself wrapped in an expensive fur. When Kellems reached for a folksy anecdote to illustrate the virtues of economic competition, she hit on a story her furrier told her about the quality difference between coats made from farmed mink and ones made from wild mink: "You see the little wild mink has to fend for itself. It has to protect itself from the bitter cold in the winter; that's why it grows such a beautiful coat." This was the voice of someone who had no idea how her arguments might sound to people who were not rich. But the cultural repertoire that she and other rich women brought into the campaign against the Sixteenth Amendment nevertheless paved the way for the anti-tax populism of the late twentieth century.[58]

CHAPTER 6

The Radical Rich

The collapse of the Liberty Belles did not deter Vivien Kellems. She was optimistic that the end of 1953 or the beginning of 1954 would see another "all-out crusade" to eliminate the income tax once and for all.[1] Many conditions seemed to favor her view. If the promise of an immediate tax cut was enough to draw people into the movement, then most of the American people were now potential recruits to the cause of income tax repeal: The country was richer than ever, and there were more people paying income taxes than at any time in history. The end of the Korean War left many people hoping for a peace dividend. At the same time, the ongoing Cold War led many Americans to fear that some parts of the federal government harbored communist agents who were secretly striving to undermine American capitalism from within. The Bureau of Internal Revenue (BIR) in particular might have been expected to arouse popular suspicion, because the progressive income tax was specifically endorsed in the *Communist Manifesto*.

Political opportunities were favorable too. There was a Republican president, with Republican majorities in the House and the Senate. The chair of the Ways and Means Committee was Daniel Reed, a conservative Republican from upstate New York whom Kellems saw as a stalwart ally in the struggle against the income tax.[2] The movement had allies in the tax bureaucracy as well, including the head of the BIR, Thomas Coleman Andrews, who secretly—and, beginning in 1955, openly—favored repeal of the income tax. Within a few years, the movement's demands would even briefly become a matter for one-upmanship between the Cold War powers, when the Soviet premier Nikita Khrushchev boasted on American television in September 1959 that the Soviet Union was on the verge of abolishing its own income taxes. (He "evidently considered this to be a telling sales point for heavily taxed Americans," wrote the editors of the *Wall Street Journal*.) According to prevailing theories of social movements, any one of these conditions might have made it a propitious time to mobilize protesters against the federal income tax.[3]

Instead, the movement dwindled. No pollster tried to measure the depth of public support for abolishing the income tax, but, as we will see, indirect inferences from the available public opinion polls show that sympathizers cannot have been more than a small fraction of the public. The most influential movement organization, the Liberty Amendment Committee, peaked at 17,200 dues-paying members in the early 1960s, more than the Liberty Belles or ORFIT, but few compared to the supporters claimed by the ATA or the CCG at their peaks.[4] Activists for income tax repeal struggled on without much popular support.

The crux of the problem, oddly enough, was prosperity. Americans were indeed getting richer, but this did not translate into support for a rich people's movement. To the contrary: Because of the graduated schedule of income tax rates, rising incomes produced large increases in tax revenues automatically, without any new act of legislation—and therefore without any explicit policy threat that could provide a focal target for protest.[5] If your income tax liability increased in these years, it was not because Congress had changed the law, but instead because you had received a raise that pushed you into a higher tax bracket. Your tax rate might be higher, but you still had more disposable income than you had before, which tended to take away the sting. It was hard to mobilize a critical mass of protesters against the income tax when there was no act of tax policy threatening their customary standard of living.

The fate of the campaign to repeal federal income taxes in this period illustrates the power of strategic policy crafting. Activists kept their organizations and their campaigns afloat by packaging income tax repeal together with other policy proposals, and thereby attracted constituencies that were concerned with other policy threats. One such threat was the increasingly restrictive regulation of federal lands, which was resented and feared by ranchers in Western states. The other was federal integration policy. In May 1954, the Supreme Court decided *Brown v. Board of Education of Topeka et al.*, 347 U.S. 483, and declared de jure racial segregation of schools unconstitutional, thereby inflaming hostility toward the federal government in white communities throughout the South. There was little obvious connection between either policy threat and the income tax—the federal government was not spending tax revenues to buy up Western lands, civil rights enforcement in the South was comparatively cheap, and African Americans at the time received a disproportionately small share of the benefits from federal social programs—but the advocates of income tax repeal wrote and rewrote their proposed constitutional amendment to persuade Western ranchers and Southern segregationists that income tax repeal was the key to the more general restraint of federal power. By the end of 1964, they had succeeded in getting resolutions of support passed by six state legislatures, all in states where the income tax burden was comparatively low, but where either federal land policy or federal integration policy was particularly unpopular.

The failure of the campaign also illustrates the limits of what activists could accomplish by strategic policy crafting. Policy packaging worked when the stakes were low. Activists were able to win the support of many state legislators because state legislators did not have to weigh the policy tradeoffs involved in repealing the income tax. The decision to pass a resolution at the state level calling for an amendment to the federal Constitution was a decision with few real policy consequences. There was little chance that abolishment of the income tax would actually come to fruition, let alone that any given state legislator could be held accountable for the consequences if it did. But the calculation was different in Congress. Although the advocates of income tax repeal found a few conservative champions who were willing to introduce their amendment in Congress, they failed to have any substantive impact on tax policy. Even otherwise-sympathetic conservatives in Congress had to weigh income tax repeal against competing priorities such as funding national defense or balancing the federal budget. The advocates of income tax repeal could not sway large numbers of votes, and they had little influence in the Republican Party. The movement for income tax repeal had no direct impact on policy outcomes in the 1960s.

The Single Tax Movement and the Radical Rich

The influx of radicals led by Vivien Kellems had made the movement to repeal the Sixteenth Amendment less socioeconomically exclusive than previous campaigns to limit taxation of the rich. But the very radicalism of their demands made the movement even more *ideologically* exclusive. Now some radical conservatives of the middle-income brackets joined the campaign, but more moderate rich people increasingly stayed away. Even the ultra-conservative Robert Dresser found the demand for abolishing the income tax too extreme. The net result was that the movement actually shrank.

The changing character of the movement's social base was exemplified by Frank Chodorov. Born in 1887 to Russian Jewish immigrant parents in New York City, he was the youngest of eleven children who grew up in a subdivided factory loft on the lower west side of Manhattan. His father ran a grocery on the ground floor, and his mother ran a lunch counter serving the factory workers who came downstairs to eat on break. Frank spent his childhood attending public school, running errands for the family business, and doing janitorial work for the landlord to help his family pay the rent.[6]

His first experience with social movements came through his exposure to working-class socialism. Running an errand for his father when he was about twelve years old, he found himself in a "coffee saloon" on Grand Street where socialists were debating the finer points of Marxist doctrine. He was fascinated.

Over the years he returned frequently to Grand Street. He became intimately familiar with the internecine squabbles of the European immigrant left—this coffee shop was for the orthodox Marxists, that coffee shop was for the revisionists—and he found himself drawn to their bookish culture of debate. It was not long before he joined in. He enrolled at Columbia College, where he spent hours poring over *Das Kapital* and immersed himself in the writings of the anarchist communists Kropotkin and Proudhon in order to participate in debates with socialists and other radical students on campus. He later described this period of his life as a "violent love affair with anarchism." His own later essays denouncing the state and calling for a revolution—with titles like "Taxation is Robbery," "Misguided Patriotism," and "About Revolutions"—suggest that he never quite got over his early fling with the revolutionary anarchist and socialist milieu.[7]

His most formative activist experiences, however, came after college, when he joined the single tax movement. Chodorov was working as a copy writer for a mail order catalog company in Chicago when he picked up a copy of Henry George's *Progress and Poverty* that was sitting on a friend's bookshelf.[8] It was an old-fashioned book at the time—indeed, according to Mark Blaug, the distinguished historian of economics, it was "thirty years out of date the day it was published"—but in 1909, a series of major philanthropic grants from the wealthy industrialist Joseph Fels revived the long-dormant single tax movement.[9] The cause found a growing base of support among urban professionals and businesspeople, and single tax leagues launched grassroots campaigns for George-influenced land tax reforms at the state level. Chodorov had no personal contact with these single taxers, but he read and reread *Progress and Poverty* with growing conviction. "I found myself without a cause," he wrote; "yet, though I was not conscious of the need, I must have been ready for one, and the single tax filled the gap."[10]

When Chodorov returned to New York in 1917, he crossed paths with some pamphleteers for the Single Tax Party and promptly signed up. He spent the next two years as a committed activist on behalf of the party. "The work consisted mostly of handing out tracts on street corners and of soapboxing," he wrote. The latter—literally standing on an upturned wooden crate to deliver impromptu political speeches to passersby—"was great fun, developed skill at debating, and accomplished nothing in the way of education," he wrote, because soapboxers attracted hecklers, and most people in the audience stayed only to be entertained by the back-and-forth. Chorodov found the experience "exhilarating," but it left him with a lifelong skepticism about political arguments ever changing anyone's mind.[11] He spent the next two decades bouncing from job to job, first becoming manager of a textile plant, then leaving to start a clothing business of his own, before losing it in the depression and going to work as a traveling salesman, in which capacity he treated his customers to "impromptu lectures" on the economics and politics of Henry George. Finally Chodorov saw a job opening for head of the Henry George School of Social Science in 1937. He applied and got the job. For five years he taught courses and recruited volunteers to spread the gospel of the single tax movement, until the trustees fired him for an antiwar editorial he published in the school paper in 1942. With the encouragement of his friend Albert Jay Nock, he went into business as an independent publisher of a journal called *analysis*, which consisted of his own topical essays. It was not lucrative. He wrote his screeds in favor of competitive individualism while relying on altruistic friends to pay his rent and sometimes buy him meals.[12]

In the coming years, Chodorov elevated his experience in the single tax movement into a general theory of social change. Movements do not grow by persuasion, because people do not change their minds. "Socialists are born, not made," he said, and he thought the same was true of radical individualists like himself. The purpose of his writing screeds and publishing manifestos was therefore not to "teach individualism," he wrote in 1944, but "to find individualists."[13] Historians of conservative thought have seen in this idea the influence of Nock, who likened his Jewish friend to the prophet Isaiah. According to Nock, the job of a prophet was not to recruit the masses, but instead to find the scattered minority of exceptionally virtuous people that he called "the Remnant."[14] But Chodorov's views also had roots in his lived experiences of social movements. The lesson that allies were found, not converted, was not a lesson he had to learn from Nock. It was the lesson that he already had drawn from his years in the Single Tax Party. Soapboxing never converted anyone, but it made the party visible, and thereby allowed like-minded people to find each other, just as a chance encounter with a Single Tax Party pamphleteer had allowed Chodorov to find fellow Georgists in New York City. His publishing enterprise was nothing but soapboxing in print.

By 1951, the single tax movement was moribund, but Chodorov heard an echo of Henry George in the movement for repeal of the federal income tax. He wrote a manifesto for the income tax repealers in 1951. When the CCG declined to publish it, Chodorov helped to found the more radical ORFIT the following year. The other founders included Corinne Griffith and other Hollywood conservatives, including a former member of the CCG named Charles Coburn.[15] Chodorov's book became the organization's manifesto and its calling card. Titled *The Income Tax: Root of All Evil*, it echoed many of the arguments made earlier by Vivien Kellems, and in similarly biblical language. The Sixteenth Amendment was an affront to "Judeo-Christian" values. It violated the natural right of property, weakened the "moral fiber" of the citizenry, and undermined the basis of republican government.[16] But whereas Kellems had sought to recruit a mass movement of women to overturn the income tax, Chodorov explicitly rejected the idea of recruiting or mobilizing a mass movement of any kind. Instead, he asserted, the revolutionary abolition of income taxes would have to await the advent of a critical mass of born individualists. "There is no accounting for the emergence of these superior men, these 'sports of nature,' who sporadically shape the course of mankind," he wrote. "When in her own time and her own pleasure Nature deems America ready for and worthy of them, she will give us the men who will make the good fight. It seems reasonable to assume that their first objective will be—Repeal of the Sixteenth Amendment."[17] In the meantime, until enough of these brave individualists arrived on the scene, there was nothing to do but stand on a soapbox and declaim.

That became the organizational strategy of ORFIT. For the first two years after it was incorporated in 1953, the organization recruited no more than fifty-two members. It began to expand a little bit when the board hired a new executive director named Paul Morgenthaler, who inaugurated a new direct mail recruitment strategy in 1955. Morgenthaler impressed other right-wing activists as a scam artist, and his recruitment strategy looked something like a pyramid scheme: Every person who received a fundraising appeal was asked to submit six more names for the mailing list; all of the revenues were plowed back into fundraising, except for the salaries that Morgenthaler siphoned off for himself and his office staff. He treated the organization as a personal fiefdom and told one activist that the board of directors of ORFIT was "a bunch of dummies" who did whatever he told them. By October 1956, he had recruited only 2,435 members.[18]

The recruiting campaign was probably helped by the media attention given to two high-profile critics of income taxation. The first was J. Bracken Lee, the pugnacious Republican governor of Utah, who in 1954 began criticizing the Eisenhower administration from the right. Lee was a business conservative who objected to income taxation on the grounds that it funded federal programs that he regarded as socialistic; he was also an isolationist who was particularly incensed by the use of the income tax to pay for foreign aid. In 1954, he wrote a foreword to *The Income Tax: Root of All Evil*. On February 17, 1955, he gave a speech declaring that "[w]e have in Washington today what to my mind amounts to a dictatorship" no different in principle from Soviet Russia, because the income tax was a violation of basic property rights.[19] On October 7, he announced that he would not pay his income tax. He said he hoped thereby to test the constitutionality of "the Federal right to tax the American people to support foreign governments."[20] Instead of taking him to court, the BIR simply filed a lien on his bank accounts, and the bank turned over the unpaid taxes.[21] So Lee tried to file a suit against the Treasury secretary. This skirmish with the federal government won him accolades on the far right, including a telegram of congratulations from Vivien Kellems, but it alienated Utah voters and the mainstream Republican Party establishment and effectively ended his career in politics. Lee was up for reelection in 1956. Despite his incumbency, he lost the Republican primary in September, and when he contested the general election as an independent, he lost that too. A week after the election, the Supreme Court denied his petition to sue the Treasury.[22]

The other high-profile income tax rebel was none other than the commissioner of the BIR. T. Coleman Andrews was a conservative accountant from Virginia who in 1953 accepted a presidential appointment to head the BIR. His tenure as commissioner was marked by a pro-taxpayer and pro-business orientation. For example, he instructed agents to accept businessmen's representations of their depreciation schedules with minimal scrutiny, introduced simplified tax forms to ease the paperwork burden on taxpayers, and renamed the bureau the Internal Revenue *Service* to emphasize a new and deferential attitude toward the taxpayer. "There is no excuse whatsoever for any person in the Bureau of Internal Revenue to take any attitude toward the taxpayer other than one that emanates from the sincere desire to be helpful," he said in an interview shortly after his appointment.[23] Andrews also reorganized the service and standardized auditing practices. But his new plans were thrown into turmoil by the Internal Revenue Code of 1954, which completely rewrote the federal income tax law. The experience soured Andrews on the income tax. He observed that the congressional representatives who wrote the law "do not themselves know what they mean." On October 17, 1955, he announced in a radio interview that the new law was "virtually impossible to administer," and on October 31, he resigned. He spent the next six months speaking and writing about the need for Congress to find alternatives to the federal income tax.[24]

Andrews's resignation was a publicity bonanza for the movement to repeal federal income taxes. He began writing and speaking publicly on the need to replace the federal income tax with something better. He wrote an article for a syndicated newspaper supplement called the *American Weekly* in April 1956, titled "Let's Get Rid of the Income Tax!" In August, a small group of conservative activists including Frank Chodorov met with Andrews to try to persuade him to run for president as an independent. He had no hope of winning outright, but the talk radio host and conservative movement entrepreneur Clarence Manion thought that Andrews might draw enough conservative voters away from the Democratic and Republican Parties to deadlock the electoral college and thereby throw the decision into the House of Representatives, where a coalition of conservative Southern Democrats and Northern Republicans could decide the outcome. Andrews remained noncommittal. He stayed away from the "nominating convention" of the States' Rights Party that drew a coalition of segregationist White Citizens' Councils, isolationists, and income tax repealers, including Vivien Kellems, to Memphis on September 14 to endorse his candidacy. But when a *Richmond Times Dispatch* poll two days later showed Andrews winning 29 percent of the popular vote in his home state, he finally decided to announce his candidacy. He began speaking at campaign rallies in Massachusetts, New Jersey, Wisconsin, Iowa, and many Southern states. At each stop he gave a standard stump speech decrying the income tax as an infringement on personal liberty and states' rights. His campaign slogan was "The Income Tax Is Bad."[25]

The publicity given these high-profile income tax repealers helped the movement grow, but only up to a point. In the absence of a policy threat related to the income tax, the activists of ORFIT had trouble persuading people that repealing the income tax was an urgent priority—much less a viable policy option. The personal income tax was 44 percent of the federal budget by 1956. Even otherwise-likely allies who thought the income tax was evil thought it was a *necessary* evil. It provided the largest single source of funding for programs as varied, and as popular, as national defense, school lunches, and veterans' benefits.[26] The proposal to abolish income taxes was also a proposal to pull the support out from under these and most other federal programs—or else fund them from another, unspecified new tax, the incidence of which was uncertain and therefore potentially even worse. Liberals liked the income tax, but conservatives worried about the consequences of eliminating it. How else could they balance the budget? How else could they pay for their national defense? What other taxes would the federal government introduce if it did not have income taxes? Many people might have preferred to live without the income tax; the problem was persuading them that it was possible.[27]

The leaders of ORFIT recognized that they needed answers to these questions. Kellems commented in March 1956 that T. Coleman Andrews was an ineffective advocate because he "lacks a program for raising taxes." Andrews said the same thing about ORFIT. Morgenthaler too thought that ORFIT needed an answer to the question "What will we do without income taxes?" But he did not seem to grasp just how serious the policy problem was; with unintentional irony, he described it as the "$64,000 question" (it was really a $29 billion question). Griffith, who was ORFIT's honorary president, regularly fielded the same question from the conservatives who attended her speaking engagements. "I am sure that those who ask that question are asking it in all honesty," she said. "But my answer is: we have no substitute for *waste, graft,* and *corruption.*" In testimony before a House subcommittee in March 1956, Griffith simply tried to change the subject, by reassuring Congress that repealing the income tax could have no bad consequences if it was done with good intentions: "As far as hurting the Federal Government is concerned, I don't think anyone is thinking about that," she said.[28] The only one who openly acknowledged the scale of the policy tradeoffs involved, and offered a specific solution, was Chodorov, but his solution was cold comfort to conservatives. The way to balance the budget, he said, was not to retain the income tax but instead to cut defense spending to zero. If U.S. soil was invaded, Americans would voluntarily defend themselves with no need for taxes or a draft. Let other countries fend for themselves likewise. All taxation was robbery. Better the rest of the world should fall to the Communists than America should slide further into dictatorship. Chodorov's contrarian position seemed like just more soapboxing—a provocation designed to attract attention rather than to persuade.[29]

Those few Americans who sympathized with the movement for income tax repeal were disproportionately Southern and conservative. Beyond this, little can be said about their social profile. What little information is available about the sympathizers with income tax repeal must be inferred indirectly from data on voters who supported T. Coleman Andrews in the 1956 presidential contest. Despite national publicity for the Andrews campaign, his candidacy was so marginal that only one national opinion poll bothered to ask about support for it, and supporters were so few that the Gallup organization did not bother to code their responses.[30] It is possible to infer an upper bound on support for the Andrews campaign from the pattern of missing codes in the Gallup data file from that poll, however, and table 6.1 reports the maximum percentage of respondents in various social and demographic categories who may have supported or leaned toward the Andrews candidacy. The sample of those who were asked about Andrews included only 352 adults in just a handful of Southern states where Andrews was on the ballot. The upper bound on Andrews's overall vote share in this sample was 9 percent. No data on the wealth or income of these respondents are available, but support for Andrews appears to have been uncorrelated with occupation or education. The only statistically significant group differences were, perhaps unsurprisingly, those based on party identification, with perhaps as many as 3 percent of Democrats, 8 percent of Republicans, and 71 percent of third-party adherents in these states supporting the single-issue Andrews candidacy. When election day came, many of these potential supporters evaporated. His vote share was 0.17 percent nationwide, and in most states he did not qualify for the ballot or garner a single vote. His greatest support came from the South, especially his home state of Virginia, presumably because of his advocacy of states' rights. The movement had become less economically exclusive, but more ideologically exclusive; its social base was confined to a vanishingly small minority of relatively extreme conservatives and libertarians.[31]

The active supporters of the movement were probably somewhat more affluent than the sympathizers, but otherwise not much different. This conclusion is conjectural, because there were no surveys of a representative sample of activists, and no surviving organizational membership lists permit inferences about the socioeconomic background of the movement's active supporters. The best available evidence comes from two interview studies of people who wrote letters to the editors of Oregon newspapers in support of income tax repeal in the

Table 6.1. **Social characteristics of Americans who supported income tax repeal in 1956. Upper bound on the percentage reporting the intention to vote for T. Coleman Andrews in eight Southern states**

	Support for Andrews
Gender	
Men	10%
Women	9%
Race	
White people	9%
People of color	16%
Party	
Democrats	3%
Republicans	8%
Other party	71%
No party	42%
Education	
College graduate	19%
Some college	12%
High school graduate	5%
High school dropout	5%
Elementary school only	11%
No formal schooling	25%
Occupation of household head (selected)	
Farmers	11%
Business	19%
Clerical	8%
Sales	10%
Skilled worker	6%
Unskilled worker	9%
Service	15%
Farm laborers	0%
Laborers, other	7%
Professional	3%
Not in labor force	7%

mid-1960s. The activists in these samples were disproportionately middle- to upper-income businesspeople, professionals, and retirees. But neither study was a probability sample, and both studies lumped income tax repealers together with supporters of other issues endorsed by the far-right anticommunist John Birch Society. The extent to which these findings might generalize to the population at large is a matter of guesswork. The most certain conclusion is that the movement was small and its activists ideologically extreme.[32]

The officers and leaders of the movement organizations certainly included a disproportionate number of rich people, including Corinne Griffith, Vivien Kellems, Charles Coburn, and the millionaire dog-food magnate D. B. Lewis. Frank Chodorov liked to call them the radical rich. "The arguers for a revolution, the theoreticians and the intellectuals, may come from the class called poor," he wrote, perhaps thinking of himself or perhaps thinking of Henry George, "but until rich men get hold of it the proposed change never gets off the ground."[33]

But even if some of these radicals were rich, how could they hope to win legislative support? The answer was policy crafting. And the person who would prove it was another movement entrepreneur named Willis Emerson Stone.

The Legacy of Veterans and Fraternal Organizations

Willis Stone (Bill, to his friends) was not one of the radical rich. He was a struggling business owner who blamed the federal government for his troubles. Stone graduated from a Denver public high school in 1918. The government promptly drafted him into the Army—less than two weeks before the armistice—and discharged him a year later without much to show for his trouble except a bad case of the flu. After his discharge, he moved to Los Angeles and became a salesman. For the next fifteen years he scrambled, never holding a job longer than two years at a stretch and changing jobs sometimes as often as twice a year. He would start out selling, say, blueprints, first on commission, and then jumping to a salaried sales position when he saw an opening, and then jumping again to start his own business—only to see his business go under and go back to selling on commission again. At least twice during the Great Depression, Stone tried to find a more secure income by applying for government jobs, but it seemed like everyone else had the same idea; the competition was fierce, and he never rose to the top of the applicant pool. Stone struggled on without a safety net.[34]

When Stone reflected on his economic insecurity, he concluded that government was the problem, not the solution. Federal relief legislation—whether in the form of agricultural subsidies, business loans, or spending on public works—made life easier for those who got a piece of the action. But for most small business owners, Stone thought, it made life harder: Suddenly they were competing against the government too. Government was "invading the sacred realm of private enterprise," he wrote in early 1932. "Already direct and indirect competition is being encountered by no less than 260 different classifications of business, including banks, railroads, printing, shipping, farming, creameries, hotels, paints, clothing, etc."[35] He blamed President Herbert Hoover, "the father and sponsor of the bureaucratic or commission form of government, which is a full and complete manifestation of the most vicious form of despotism ever developed." Stone voted Democratic in 1932 hoping for less bureaucracy. He got the New Deal instead.[36]

The New Deal seemed to Stone like a disaster. Hoover had opened a faucet of federal relief; Roosevelt opened the floodgates. The Works Progress Administration, the National Labor Relations Act, the Social Security Act, the Fair Labor Standards Act—none of the new programs provided any more security for a self-employed small business owner. And the Second World War only made things worse. Under the cover of a wartime emergency, as Stone saw it, the Roosevelt administration began interfering directly in the management of business: telling businessmen what to produce, how to produce it, who they could hire, even what price they had to accept. The last straw was the seizure of the Montgomery Ward retail company by federal troops on April 26, 1944, to enforce an order of the National War Labor Board. Now Roosevelt was mobilizing the army to seize private property. To Stone, it seemed like exactly the sort of tyranny that the Constitution was supposed to guard against—but the attorney general was insisting that it was perfectly constitutional.[37]

The solution, he decided, was to amend the Constitution. On June 2, 1944, Stone published an op-ed in the weekly *Sherman Oaks Citizen-Tribune* proposing a one-sentence constitutional amendment: "The government of the United States of America shall not engage in any business, commercial, or industrial enterprise in competition with its citizens."[38] For the next several years, he filled his weekly column with examples of federal overreaching. The longer he looked, the more he found. Virtually the entire executive apparatus, Stone thought, ought to be auctioned off, because the Constitution did not specifically authorize any executive agency other than the post office and the armed forces. In the spring of 1946, Stone began circulating a petition in support of his amendment on behalf of a group he named the Committee for Economic Freedom. Progress was slow, but after two years, he had collected enough names and contributions to convene the founding meeting of a new organization called the American Progress Foundation (APF). In 1949, Stone quit his consulting business to devote all his time to the APF and campaigning for his amendment.[39]

His campaign strategy relied on his connections in veterans' and fraternal organizations. Stone was a local officer in the American Legion and the Lions

Club, and an active member of the Los Angeles Chamber of Commerce and the Laguna-Bandini Manufacturers' Association.[40] His initial strategy was to distribute his proposal to similar veterans' clubs, fraternal organizations, and business associations around the country to ask for their endorsement. He borrowed letterhead and mailing lists from local Lions, Kiwanis, and Optimist Clubs, and mailed an appeal to all of their sister organizations around the country. By his estimate, about 10 percent of the groups he contacted passed resolutions.[41] Their efforts snowballed. By 1951, he claimed to have received 6,000 local organizational endorsements, and he persuaded Representative Ralph Gwinn (R-NY) to introduce his one-sentence amendment in Congress the following year.[42]

The crux of his plan was policy crafting. Stone sought to win support by tinkering with the wording of the amendment to broaden its appeal. In practice this meant packaging his privatization amendment together with other policy issues. In 1953, for example, he finalized a three-sentence version that would prevent the government from engaging in "any business, professional, commercial, financial or industrial enterprise" not specifically authorized in the Constitution, and that would privatize most executive functions by requiring the liquidation and sale of any such "enterprises" within three years after ratification of the amendment. The new version also added a clause that would annul any foreign treaties that "abrogated" the amendment. The purpose of this clause baffled the lawyer Robert Dresser, who pointed out that the Constitution superseded any treaty. The main importance of the clause was symbolic, as Stone explained: In particular, it was supposed to attract the supporters of the Bricker Amendment, a cause célèbre that briefly united American conservatives and that came within one vote of passage in the Senate.[43] Representative Gwinn introduced the three-sentence version of Stone's amendment in 1953, 1955, and 1957, and each time it died in committee.[44]

The movement began to attract more grassroots support when Stone rewrote his proposed amendment to attract advocates of income tax repeal. Stone had met ORFIT activists at a Chicago conservative gathering in 1952 or 1953.[45] Two years later, he founded a magazine called *American Progress*, and he dropped a complimentary mention of ORFIT into an early issue. In response, Morgenthaler wrote to thank him, and "Hacksaw" Mary Dawson Cain, who was another ORFIT board member, invited him to join.[46] By the summer of 1956, Stone was having conversations with several ORFIT board members about the possibility of closer cooperation between their organizations.[47] The informal negotiations provoked a split on the ORFIT board: Several of the radical rich were already embarrassed by Morgenthaler's crass manners, and they drew the line at Stone. Griffith and a handful of others departed in August, paving the way for an alliance between ORFIT and APF.[48]

The key to the nascent alliance was packaging their policies together—by writing the constitutional amendment to earmark the savings from privatization (a source of funds) for income tax repeal (a use of funds). Stone first put the two issues together in a spring 1956 op-ed on the T. Coleman Andrews presidential campaign. The argument was simple. Andrews had a problem: "The big government advocates demand that Mr. Andrews identify the sources of revenue government can tap if it should lose the power to tax income." Without some source of savings to make up for the lost income taxes, Stone pointed out, the government might simply compensate by raising other taxes. He had the solution: "[T]he key to repealing individual income taxes is a 'Proposed 23rd Amendment' to the Constitution which would outlaw bureaucratic competition with private enterprise." The savings from privatization of federal assets could pay for income tax repeal.[49]

The argument required some creative arithmetic. Stone inflated his count of illegitimate federal enterprises: As recently as 1955, he claimed they numbered 200, but by 1957, he had tripled the total to "more than 700 federal corporate activities."[50] In 1951, he had claimed only that the savings from selling off these enterprises would be $156 per individual income taxpayer, which worked out to less than one-third of the total individual income tax burden; but by 1957, he decreed that the savings would be sufficient to abolish income tax altogether "and still come out in the black $674 million."[51] He made the numbers work by inventing unbelievable market values for federal assets and then adding some further fanciful assumptions, most notably that the revenue windfall from privatization would somehow inspire the Treasury to buy back all of its outstanding bonds, reducing federal debt service to zero, even though this was not, in fact, mandated by his proposed amendment.[52]

Fantastical or not, this inspired piece of policy packaging made it possible for the advocates of radical privatization and the advocates of income tax repeal to make common cause. The treaty was concretized in a joint operating agreement between APF and ORFIT. In April 1957, the APF board endorsed the cause of income tax repeal and authorized Stone to conduct negotiations toward an eventual merger of the two organizations. The agreement was sealed by August. Each organization kept its own president and board of directors, but both organizations handed their finances and operational control over to a joint operating committee.[53] The benefits of the alliance were summarized by D. B. Lewis, a John Birch Society member who sat on the boards of both organizations. According to the minutes from the April APF board meeting, "Mr. Lewis pointed out that the repeal of the 16th Amendment lack[s] full attractiveness unless we can explain why and how it can be done with profit to both the citizen and government. He also pointed out that the 'Proposed 23rd Amendment' did not hold full attraction value unless we explain the rewards attainable through it in terms of ability to reduce the need for taxes equal to the income taxes now paid."[54] Stone put it more plainly: "I think such close cooperation will strength[en] both sides of the coin, as we have come to think of it, one being our desire (repeal) and the other the method—one deals with our wants and the other the 'how.' "[55] In other words, privatization finally answered the perennial question of how America could afford to abolish its income tax.

Liberty for Me

The offspring of the union between ORFIT and APF was a new proposal for how to amend to the Constitution. The new "Proposed 23rd Amendment" retained Stone's original language privatizing federal enterprises. But it also added a fourth sentence: "Three years after the ratification of this amendment the six-teenth article of amendments [sic] to the Constitution of the United States shall stand repealed and thereafter Congress shall not levy taxes on personal incomes, estates, and/or gifts." The association between income tax repeal and privatiza-tion was purely symbolic. Nothing in the wording of the amendment guaranteed that the funds from privatization would be adequate to substitute for the income tax. Nor did the proposed amendment establish a special privatization-financed "trust fund" for income tax repeal. It did not even explicitly rule out other tax increases to make up for the lost income tax. But the mere juxtaposition implied a causal linkage. Sell off enough federal assets, it appeared to promise, and you could get rid of the income tax forever.

The symbolic alliance lasted longer than the organizational alliance. Morgenthaler and Stone were both self-employed, and neither man was used to sharing or delegating authority. Stone disliked Morgenthaler's staffing deci-sions and thought that he was squandering all the organization's resources on direct mail fundraising. Morgenthaler questioned Stone's use of the joint Diner's Club account and attempted to assert control over *American Progress*, which Stone regarded as his personal property. Stone responded with an ultimatum to the joint operating committee: Devote at least 45 percent of the organization's resources to "research and programming," remove Morgenthaler's paid staff from the committee, and grant Stone more say in financial decision-making. The com-mittee did not meet his demands. He severed the relationship in April 1959.[56]

The organizational split left Stone with everything that mattered—the *American Progress* mailing list, the research files, and the acknowledged author-ship of the new amendment. Morgenthaler's clique got to keep the letterhead and not much else.[57] Stone's group meanwhile was just gathering momentum. He recruited a new board of his Los Angeles friends and renamed his group the National Committee for Economic Freedom (NCEF). The NCEF renamed its amendment in April 1961, after the ratification of the Twenty-third Amendment, which extended certain voting rights to residents of the District of Columbia, made it impossible to refer to Stone's brainchild any longer as the "Proposed 23rd Amendment." They decided to call it the Liberty Amendment instead, and a year later renamed themselves the Liberty Amendment Committee. *American Progress* became *Freedom Magazine*.[58]

Now that the cause of income tax repeal was coupled with a plan that had at least some pretense of plausibility, it began to take off. By 1961, the NCEF had allies and affiliated chapters in thirty states—comprising, according to the Anti-Defamation League, a "Who's Who of the American far right."[59] For the first time the national committee began encouraging activists to bypass the Lions Club and the like in favor of starting their *own* local organizations, via "home study groups" or via the new organizing method of direct one-on-one meetings.[60] In Southern California, activists organized a year-long course of home study groups that led up to the three "California T (for Tax) Parties" held at the Wilshire Ebell Theatre in Los Angeles that fall. These festive evenings drew hundreds of people together to hear inspiring speeches, watch educational films, and honor Liberty Amendment activists.[61] State and local groups from around the country came together every September for an annual conference to share strategies and conviviality; the "high point" of the 1962 conference was reported to be a sing-along session with "Liberty for Me," the new Liberty Amendment marching song ("You and I cannot relax/We must repeal the income tax!"). As Stone explained in the pages of *American Progress*, "Every movement needs music to rally and inspire its supporters."[62]

How Policy Crafting Worked

By packaging income tax repeal together with privatization, Stone won new adherents on the far right. Observers watched it happen at a meeting of We, the People, a "fusionist" organization with annual conferences that drew hundreds of activists from every far-right cause under the sun together to hammer out common positions on the issues of the day. The founding conference in 1955 agreed on a platform that embraced Stone's privatization plan, but stopped short of endorsing income tax repeal. The platform plank on income taxes endorsed Dresser's 25 percent limitation instead.[63] Then Stone hit on the idea of paying for income tax repeal by earmarking the proceeds from privatization for that purpose. He brought the results of his research to the third annual conference of We, the People in September 1957. His presentation was the talk of the conference. The classics professor Revilo P. Oliver reported in the *National Review* that most of those present began as skeptics, but Stone's presentations won them over to near-unanimous support.[64]

There were skeptics even among the Sixteenth Amendment repealers. Robert Dresser was unconvinced by Stone's arithmetic and thought him a terrible legislative draftsman.[65] J. Bracken Lee argued with Stone that it would be better to stick with a "single issue" focus on the income tax. Support, he said, would come from appealing to the self-interest of state officials. Governors and state legislators should oppose the federal income tax because it "dried up" the resources available for state income tax, so that states "had less and less for the social services a government should provide."[66] Lee also suggested that state legislatures would be responsive as long as they had not yet been "bribe[d] into submission" by federal aid.[67]

But Stone's policy crafting paid off with favorable legislative outcomes. He had been toiling for thirteen years with his old privatization amendment, and in that time exactly one state legislature had voted support.[68] Corinne Griffith had been publicly campaigning for income tax repeal since 1951, with no success.[69] Within two years after packaging these proposals into a single amendment, however, Stone had resolutions in support of the amendment from two state legislatures; within five years, six (see table 6.2). Several more states came within one or two votes of passing resolutions.[70]

The pattern of *which* states supported repeal also suggests that Stone's strategy of policy packaging worked. J. Bracken Lee's strategy of a single-issue appeal to state officials' fiscal interests showed little success: States that competed with the federal government to tax income were less likely to support repeal, not more

Table 6.2. **State legislatures calling for a constitutional amendment to repeal the income tax**

State	Year
Wyoming	1959
Texas	1959
Nevada	1960
Louisiana	1960
Georgia	1962
South Carolina	1962
Mississippi	1964
Arizona	1982
Indiana	1982

likely, and indeed the states that supported repeal included a disproportionate number that levied no state income tax at all. States with budgets that were most dependent on federal aid were not bribed into submission. Instead, they were more likely to support income tax repeal, probably because such aid was perceived to come at a cost in states' rights. As Mary Dawson Cain promised the Mississippi legislature, the Liberty Amendment would "eventually give us use of our own moneys—without federal strings!"[71]

The appeal to state legislators was not the promise of tax cuts for the rich, but instead the promise that repealing the Sixteenth Amendment would strip the federal government of assets and power. Activists could therefore sell the Liberty Amendment to potential allies as the solution to diverse policy threats. In the West, the privatization of federal lands was the prime issue. The Bureau of Land Management had gradually reduced the issuance of grazing leases in the 1950s, and livestock owners were furious. Land was the only category of federal assets the abolition of which merited a cover story and a special issue of *Freedom Magazine*.[72] Stone stressed the privatization of federal lands when he wrote to a Wyoming rancher named Dan Hanson in 1959 to encourage his efforts on behalf of the amendment. "I think it is very necessary that the Western States take an active lead in this project," he wrote. "Wyoming, particularly, can be a very great beneficiary under the terms of the 'Proposed 23rd Amendment' because enormous quantities of land and facilities will go back on the State and local tax rolls as a result of it. Because of this, I think the state Legislature has a very real interest in adopting the resolution we suggest."[73] In January, Wyoming indeed became the first state legislature to pass a resolution in favor of the Liberty Amendment. The grassroots support came from ranchers and realtors—investors in land, for whom the proposed privatization of federal land was a potential boon.[74]

In the South, income tax repealers argued that defunding the federal government was the way to preserve racial segregation. Winifred Furrh, the leader of the Marshall housewives, explained this line of argument to Vivien Kellems on June 1, 1954: "This Supreme Court decision on Segregation may be the thing that will unite us all. The Southern governors will organize for States Rights— we own and maintain our own schools. Now—how can we get our States' Rights back—repeal the 16th Amendment. We are going to put that bee in every bonnet we can."[75] Kellems agreed. Her views on segregation are not clear, but she certainly recognized that the enemy of her enemy was her friend. Others, including Mary Dawson Cain and Corinne Griffith, were open segregationists who gladly played up the states' rights angle.[76] Willis Stone's rhetorical appeals on this point were indirect but unmistakable. He did not identify the Department of Justice by name on his lists of illegitimate federal businesses,[77] nor did he openly embrace the cause of racial segregation or denounce *Brown v. Board of Education*. But he appealed directly to Southern conservatives when he described the

Liberty Amendment as the best way to restore "States' Rights" that had been trampled by the federal government.[78]

The defense of states' rights against federal authority was a major theme in campaign literature. According to the Liberty Amendment Committee members Lloyd G. Herbstreith and Gordon van B. King, the authors of the 1963 campaign bible *Action for Americans: The Liberty Amendment,* "The rebirth of State and local sovereignty will be the most important effect of the Liberty Amendment on our fifty State governments, 51,887 local governments and 50,454 school districts."[79] Mary Dawson Cain wrote an open letter to the Mississippi legislature appealing to state legislators to stand up to the federal government by passing the Liberty Amendment: "Won't you Mississippians, representatives of people long noted for love of freedom, for belief in state sovereignty, in states' rights, as well as sovereignty of the individual citizen, raise your voices in a vote to make our beloved nation once again a land of free people, and our equally beloved Mississippi a State governed by its own elected leadership?"[80] Radio stations in South Carolina broadcast editorials in favor of the Liberty Amendment that echoed old populist rhetoric, decrying "the ever-growing octopus of Federal control" and promising that "the Sovereign State of South Carolina, with other states of the union, can by Constitutional Convention, take back from the Federal government, the power that it has abrogated [*sic*] to itself."[81] The issue for these Southern activists was not income taxation at all, but the perception that a fiscally well-provided federal government was more likely to infringe on state sovereignty.

The lobbying campaigns at the state level were run by local grassroots committees without any centralized coordination. Stone's Los Angeles office served as an information clearinghouse and a one-man speakers' bureau, but he had no directing or managing role. Sometimes local committees acted without even consulting him. As of 1961, for example, there was no organization in Georgia, and Stone had written the state off until some grassroots pressure developed.[82] His patience was rewarded in December 1961, when a Mrs. Lent wrote to Stone out of the blue, announcing that a local club called The Conservatives of Savannah had decided to sponsor a state resolution in favor of the Liberty Amendment. Stone wrote back to offer his assistance and was rebuffed: "I have asked whether it would be helpful for either any of us or even you to appear at the State of the Republic Committee hearing," Mrs. Lent's husband wrote to Stone in February 1962, "but they just feel that it is not going to encounter that much opposition." Mr. Lent was right; the Liberty Amendment resolution sailed through the Georgia House of Representatives five days after he wrote the letter and the Senate two days after that.[83]

Agenda Access without Impact

The campaign for the Liberty Amendment illustrates the power of policy crafting to get movement demands on the public agenda, but it also illustrates that policy crafting alone is not sufficient to affect policy outcomes. Getting their demands on the agenda did not guarantee that activists would have an impact on tax policy. It was one thing for a state legislator to take a symbolic stand for abolition of federal income taxes. This was cheap talk: There was little risk that it would actually happen. It was a different thing entirely for a member of Congress to endorse income tax repeal. Such an endorsement carried greater risk that it would pass, and that Congress would have to deal with the consequences. Unsurprisingly, then, almost no one in Congress was willing to entertain the movement's demands, no matter how creatively they were packaged. Leaders of the tax policy committees in Congress dismissed the proposal peremptorily. "Instead of childishly radical proposals for scrapping the income tax or severely restricting it," said Ways and Means Chairman Wilbur Mills (D-AR) in a 1956 interview, "we should lend our mature efforts to conserving its desirable features and in so doing transform it into a more effective instrument for promoting sound and stead economic growth."[84]

Some people in the movement argued that getting their demands on the agenda would influence federal tax policy even without getting the Liberty Amendment passed. On February 4, 1957, for example, Clarence Manion wrote to Representative Clare Hoffman (R-MI) to discuss the progress of various Republican plans for tax reduction, including the 25 percent tax limitation amendment. His argument was simple: "As things stand now, none of these commendable measures has a chance for adoption *unless the spenders are seriously threatened with something a great deal worse*, namely, outright repeal of the Federal Income Tax .... As I have said, we will never get the bramble bush trimmed until we threaten to cut it down." As a former law professor and critic of the New Deal, Manion presumably knew the story of how the Revenue Act of 1935 had been passed in order to steal the thunder of a more radical challenger from the left. He hoped that thunder on the right would provoke an analogous response. Manion offered Hoffman a constitutional amendment of his own design that, he thought, struck an appropriately threatening posture: "Five years after the ratification of this Amendment by the Legislatures in three-fourths of the States, the Sixteenth Amendment to this Constitution shall be for all purposes repealed," it read, "and, thereafter, it will be unlawful for Congress to levy taxes upon incomes derived from any source whatever." Hoffman took a look at Manion's proposal and introduced it less than two weeks later.[85]

Hoffman's colleagues in Congress, however, saw little advantage in supporting him. His amendment was referred to the House Judiciary Committee, now chaired by Emanuel Celler, who had recanted his youthful support for repealing the Sixteenth Amendment. The committee buried the amendment. Representative James Utt (R-CA) introduced Willis Stone's version of the amendment in 1959, with the same result.[86]

When the opportunity for tax cuts for the rich finally came, the movement could claim no credit. In the aftermath of the mild recession that ended in early 1961, President John F. Kennedy proposed what he called an "across the board, top to bottom cut in both corporate and personal income taxes." The purpose, he said, was to stimulate investment. As the political scientist John Witte later remarked, Kennedy's rhetoric "could almost have been written by Andrew Mellon."[87] This historic income tax cut took place during the peak years of mobilization for the Liberty Amendment, and it is tempting to think that the campaign for income tax repeal might have influenced Congress to pass this measure. The evidence suggests otherwise. The Liberty Amendment campaign had no influence on the outcome.

The administration completely ignored the campaign in formulating its plans for income tax cuts. The economist Walter Heller, who was chairman of the Council of Economic Advisors, prepared much of the administration's case for income tax cuts. In this capacity he canvassed interest group opinion and wrote background memos for the president outlining the political case for cutting taxes while the window of opportunity was open. "Congress may be lukewarm, but powerful groups throughout the country are *ready for action*," he wrote. But the arguments that Heller marshaled and the lists of relevant interest groups that he prepared made no reference to the challenge from the radical right. Heller was probably well aware of the campaign to repeal the Sixteenth Amendment; he was one of few commentators who remembered this campaign well enough to connect the dots almost two decades later, when former Liberty Amendment activists emerged from obscurity to play a leading role in the "tax revolt" of the late 1970s. But in the early 1960s, Heller simply did not think the movement for income tax repeal was particularly important.[88]

Nor did congressmen take the Liberty Amendment campaign into account when deciding on what would prove to be the biggest tax cut since the Mellon plan. State resolutions in favor of the Liberty Amendment might have been taken as a signal that the voters demanded big tax cuts. But states with such resolutions were no more likely than other states to vote for the Kennedy tax cuts in 1962. When the administration followed the Revenue Act of 1962 with proposals for additional tax cuts, it was political party and ideology (not grassroots pressure) that determined how legislators voted. Liberal Democrats embraced the income tax cuts, and Republicans and a handful of conservative Southern Democrats opposed them. A logistic regression analysis confirms that senators from states that supported the Liberty Amendment were no more likely than others to support the tax cut bill (see table 6.3). To the contrary: When the bill finally came to a vote in 1964, senators from states that supported the Liberty Amendment were especially likely to vote *against* tax cuts, because such senators were especially likely to be conservative and opposed to the administration.[89]

In short, although the Liberty Amendment campaign coincided with one of the biggest across-the-board income tax cuts in history, there is no evidence that any of the political decision-makers involved were attempting to steal the thunder of the radical income tax repealers. The Liberty Amendment Committee could get its policy proposals heard in a few state houses, but it could not move large numbers of votes. There was no thunder to steal.

The Collapse of the Campaign

Ever since the tax clubs of the 1920s, rich people's movements had been a recurring feature of the American political landscape. But the growth of liberalism in the 1960s sucked the wind from the sails of these movements. The Kennedy-Johnson tax cuts seemed to realize the promise of the Mellon plan: Tax cuts, economic growth, and increased spending all went together, and a rising tide lifted all boats. In the absence of any tax rate increase or major policy threat to business, there was no further influx of grassroots militants into the campaign to repeal the Sixteenth Amendment.

The Liberty Amendment Committee gradually wound down. On September 8, 1971, Willis Stone convened his board of directors in the Ramada Inn at the Detroit Metropolitan Airport to dissolve the Liberty Amendment Committee. He was seventy-two years old. Many of the assembled were no younger.

Table 6.3. **The Liberty Amendment and the Kennedy-Johnson tax cuts. Coefficients from a logistic regression of the vote in favor of the Revenue Act of 1964 in the Senate (N = 93)**

	Model 1	*Model 2*
	Coefficient (standard error)	*Coefficient (standard error)*
Intercept	2.01 (.41)	.85 (.52)
Republican? 1 = yes	−1.05 (.56)	2.24 (.99)
From a state whose legislature has endorsed the Liberty Amendment? 1 = yes	−1.50 (.69)	−.46 (.89)
Economic conservatism	...	−7.16 (1.76)

Their meeting began with a moment of silence for elderly comrades who had died since their last meeting, including Stone's wife. Then they heard Stone's resignation.

"I have over half a million miles on United Airlines alone traveling to your states to help to organize, to hold meetings, to recruit, to do all of these things," Stone told the assembled committee members. Now, he said, the committee was losing members, it had less than $1,000 in the bank, it owed back taxes, and it was embroiled in an ongoing lawsuit against the IRS over an application for tax-exempt status. "I am old, I am tired, and I just can't carry this workload," he said. "And there isn't anybody in our group that's going to." He proposed to keep the committee going only as long as was necessary to wind up the lawsuit. In the meantime, he would turn over all responsibility for the campaign to the ultraconservative John Birch Society. The latter plan had been in the works since January, when Stone had met with the Birch Society chairman Robert Welch to hammer out an agreement, but this was the first time that the full committee had a chance to debate it. Several state chairmen chafed at the idea of associating with the conspiratorial Birchers, and there was a vocal faction in favor of remaining an independent single-issue organization focused on the income tax. The contentious debate ran an hour over time. But after several rounds of procedural haggling, the ayes had it by a vote of twenty to five. As the chair moved to adjourn, he tried to restore levity and goodwill by comparing the meeting to the "caucus race" from *Alice in Wonderland*. Despite all of the furious struggle, he pointed out, everyone won in the end.[90]

It was not a comforting analogy. Anyone who remembered the book knew that the caucus race was futile, and that its chairman was a dodo. The campaign to repeal the Sixteenth Amendment seemed finished.

Appendix 6.1

The evolution of the Liberty Amendment through successive versions, with additions in *italics*.

1944 Version[91]

The Government of the United States of America shall not engage in any business, commercial, or industrial enterprise in competition with its citizens.

1953 Version[92]

Section 1. The Government of the United States of America shall not engage in any business, commercial, *financial* or industrial enterprise *except as specified in the Constitution.*

Section 2. *The constitution or laws of any State, or the laws of the United States shall not be subject to the terms of any foreign or domestic agreement which would abrogate this amendment.*

Section 3. *The activities of the United States Government which violate the intent and purposes of this amendment shall, within a period of three years from the date of the ratification of this amendment, be liquidated and the properties and facilities affected shall be sold.*

1957 Version[93]

Section 1. The Government of the United States of America shall not engage in any business, commercial, financial or industrial enterprise except as specified in the Constitution.

Section 2. The constitution or laws of any State, or the laws of the United States shall not be subject to the terms of any foreign or domestic agreement which would abrogate this amendment.

Section 3. The activities of the United States Government which violate the intent and purposes of this amendment shall, within a period of three years from the date of the ratification of this amendment, be liquidated and the properties and facilities affected shall be sold.

Section 4. *Three years after the ratification of this amendment the sixteenth article of amendments to the Constitution of the United States shall stand repealed and thereafter Congress shall not levy taxes on personal incomes, estates, and/ or gifts.*

CHAPTER 7

Strange Bedfellows

By 1975, the Sixteenth Amendment repealers were thoroughly demobilized. There did not seem to be any prospect of reviving their movement. Democrats controlled Congress; Richard Nixon, the first conservative Republican president since Herbert Hoover, had resigned; and, after a generation of heavy taxes and transfer spending, the income distribution was as equal as it had ever been. By any customary measure of the political opportunity for protest, it seemed like a poor time for a movement on behalf of the rich.[1]

The surviving activists responded by disengaging from direct policy struggles and turning inward to develop institutions that would preserve their movement in abeyance. Their movement survived as a subculture. At its center was the John Birch Society. The candy manufacturer Robert Welch founded the society in 1958 to promulgate his belief that the American republic was in imminent danger from a communist conspiracy at the highest levels of power. He began by circulating a newsletter to a small circle of his trusted associates. Then members of the inner circle began to open chapters of their own. By the mid-1960s, the John Birch Society comprised a network of hundreds of American Opinion bookstores, conservative study groups, speakers' bureaus, and dues-paying associations held together by a staff of full-time organizers. Welch encouraged members to see communist influence everywhere—he even called President Eisenhower "a dedicated, conscious agent of the communist conspiracy"—and the consensus of respectable opinion leaders was that the Birchers were paranoid extremists. "Introducing yourself to other skittish first-timers at a Birch meeting is a touchy thing," wrote Gerald Schomp, a former organizer for the society. "You can never be sure your boss, or a neighbor, or a school chum won't be there or, worse yet, a business competitor.... You can visualize how it will be at the office next day when the word gets around that you're one of those extremist hate-mongers in that organization they're always talking about on TV." Those skittish first-timers who stayed often felt the thrill of being welcomed into an exclusive group. The society demanded secrecy, loyalty, and substantial commitments of time and volunteer labor from its members. In return, it provided them with a feeling of belonging and a social milieu in which their unpopular political views made sense to others.[2]

The John Birch Society provided a particular refuge for many of the Sixteenth Amendment repealers. Its network of bookstores and chapters was particularly dense in Southern California, which had also been the core geographic base for the most influential organizations in the movement for income tax repeal, including the Liberty Belles, ORFIT, and the Liberty Amendment Committee. Many of the activists in these organizations found their way into the John Birch Society. In 1966, when D. B. Lewis, the president of ORFIT, died, he left the name and goodwill of ORFIT to the society. In 1971, when Willis Stone resigned from the executive directorship of the Liberty Amendment Committee, he persuaded the rest of his board to turn its operations and its mailing list over to the John Birch Society too. Robert Welch welcomed the income tax repealers into the society and made their cause a part of society lore. His bulletin regularly reminded Birchers that the *Communist Manifesto* endorsed a progressive income tax, and every issue contained a reminder to support the Liberty Amendment. American Opinion bookstores sold books about the evils of the Sixteenth Amendment and bumper stickers that said, "Repeal the Income Tax." (Schomp, who had one of these stickers on his car, wrote that it reliably drew both chuckles of sympathy and "the comment, which I learned to lip-read at a great distance, 'What are you, some kind of a nut?'"). Support for income tax repeal was an unpopular opinion. For those who joined the John Birch Society, however, it was also a way that members could recognize each other, and a badge of sub-cultural belonging.[3]

Even Robert Dresser retreated into the shadow world of the Birchers. Now well into his eighties, he continued to show up at the office every day in a three-piece suit and take his lunches at the Turks Head Club with the rest of the old Providence establishment; but he was no longer a power in the state Republican Party, and the collapse of the tax limitation movement had left him without national influence. He spent his days alone in his office tracking the progress of the global communist conspiracy and writing anticommunist and pro-Bircher screeds that he paid the *Providence Journal* to run as advertisements. (Typical titles were "Disarmament—A Grave Menace to the U.S.A.," "Russia Is Winning the Arms Race," and "Peaceniks are Nutniks.") "I sincerely believe that the United States is facing a very serious crisis within, involving no less than the issue of whether it will survive as a free and independent nation," he told a reporter in 1967. "But, you know, people are not really interested."[4]

Within a few years, however, a new group of activists would take a renewed interest in Dresser's tax limitation amendment and, by repackaging it, bring federal tax limitation back onto the congressional policy agenda. The leaders of this revival included a disproportionate number of former Birchers and activists from the Southern California conservative milieu. Like the earlier Sixteenth Amendment repealers, they drew on tactics and social networks that they had developed in other movements. These movement entrepreneurs would not have found any takers, however, if not for a series of policy threats—in the form of a wave of state and local property tax increases—that motivated large numbers of people to protest against taxes on the rich.

From the John Birch Society to the Balanced Budget Campaign

One of the first activists to revive Dresser's dream of a constitutional tax limitation amendment was James Dale Davidson. They made an odd couple: Davidson was a libertarian student activist who had nothing against peaceniks (or nutniks). As the publisher of *The Individualist*, the magazine of the Society for Individual Liberty, he even wrote essays condemning militarism and proclaiming that "[t]he very idea of 'sanity and insanity' is a legal fiction which has no place in a free society." Davidson was not exactly countercultural, but he was a far cry from the straitlaced Dresser. He valued individualism above all, and "eccentric" was his highest word of praise. When he left graduate school to found the National Taxpayers' Union (NTU), his principal concession to the dress code of Washington lobbyists was what one journalist called his "trademark polka-dot bow tie." The contrast between Dresser's top-floor law office, with its view of downtown Providence, and the NTU's headquarters in a basement apartment in Washington was emblematic of the social and cultural distance that separated Davidson from the earlier generation of Sixteenth Amendment repealers.[5]

In the early 1970s, however, Davidson recruited Robert Dresser to the board of the NTU. He also recruited a former Pentagon whistleblower named Arthur E. Fitzgerald to be the chairman, and he put former senator and celebrated peacenik Eugene McCarthy in charge of the allied National Taxpayers Legal Fund. This recruitment strategy was a calculated attempt to forge what Fitzgerald called a "strange-bedfellows alliance" between antiwar liberals and fiscal conservatives. One of the NTU's signature issues was criticizing expensive military projects such as the B-1 bomber. Perhaps its most famous publicity stunt involved publishing the names of prominent veterans—including Senator Barry Goldwater (R-AZ)—who were "double-dipping" by holding down federal government jobs while drawing military pensions. This was hardly the hawkish John Birch Society.[6]

The NTU was hardly a lobbying group either. Davidson and his friends were student activists. They had no organizational experience moving a positive legislative agenda. They *had* no legislative agenda, except to hold the line against government spending by lobbying against each new program as it arose. The way to stop the growth of spending, in the view of the idealistic founders, was to expose and ridicule wasteful programs one by one—or, in the words of the NTU's treasurer, a high school friend of Davidson's named William Bonner, to "just spill the beans and tell the story of government waste." They issued press releases and held press conferences. They developed a mailing list of a few thousand like-minded activists and contributors. They shamed some congressmen, including Senator Goldwater, into returning their veterans' pensions or donating them to charity. They did not, however, achieve any major legislative victories. They hardly could have: The NTU did not actually lobby *for* anything.[7]

That changed in 1975, when a Democratic state senator from Maryland named James Clark showed up at the NTU's office with a plan to amend the Constitution. Clark had drafted an amendment that would require Congress to balance the budget every year, except in the event of a national emergency. His plan was to persuade two-thirds of the state legislatures to petition Congress for a constitutional convention. Clark reasoned, much as Robert Dresser had reasoned in 1938, that the threat of a convention would probably force Congress to act before the threshold was crossed.

The idea of a balanced budget amendment was not original. Mississippi State Representative David Halbrook also claimed credit for coming up with it; he said he had the idea while he was sitting around with Senator Ollie Mohamed in the back of Mohamed's dry-goods store in Belzoni, Mississippi, one evening in 1974. And even before that, several other states had approved similar resolutions, including Indiana (1957), Wyoming (1961), and Virginia (1973). Both Clark and Halbrook had introduced balanced budget convention resolutions in their respective state legislatures. Halbrook had also traveled to neighboring states to pitch the idea to his peers in other state legislatures.[8]

It was easy to see why the idea might have occurred independently to many state legislators in 1974. The country was in the grip of the most rapid inflation since 1947. Politicians at all levels of government were hearing from anxious constituents who were concerned that runaway inflation was eroding the value of their life savings. For the first time in the history of public opinion research, a majority of Gallup poll respondents—and an overwhelming majority of 80 percent at that—named "inflation" as "the most important problem facing this country." Politicians were eager to be seen doing something about inflation. Particularly for state officials, Congress was a convenient place to lay the blame. Deficit spending by the federal government did not cause inflation, exactly; but everyone agreed that it did not help matters, and many politicians found it convenient to define the deficit as the problem.[9]

Once state legislators agreed that the federal deficit was a problem, it was not surprising that they should have hit on the idea of a federal balanced budget requirement as the solution, because this requirement was a straightforward extrapolation from state constitutions. The operative language in Clark's proposed amendment ("The total of all Federal appropriations made by the Congress for any fiscal year may not exceed the total of the estimated Federal revenues....") was copied almost word for word from Maryland's constitution ("[T]he figure for total proposed appropriations shall not exceed the figure for total estimated revenues"). Halbrook prepped for his meetings with other state legislators by having the Mississippi state attorney general compile a list of all states that had such provisions. "Thirty-seven States require of themselves that they, as States, live within a balanced budget," he testified before a Senate subcommittee in October 1975. "Certainly, if the States can do it, and if the Federal Government has done it, it is not an impossible task."[10]

Until now, however, no one had tried to organize a national campaign to *force* the federal government to live within a balanced budget. Persuading two-thirds of the state legislatures to call for a convention would be no easy task. Clark went out looking for a nonpartisan grassroots membership organization that could coordinate a national campaign. His first stop was Common Cause, a liberal public-interest group founded in 1970 by John Gardner, former secretary of health, education and welfare in the Johnson administration. It was only after the liberals of Common Cause turned him away that Clark went to the group that William Bonner once jokingly called "the tightwad's Common Cause"— the NTU. "When he came to us I just leapt up out of my chair," Davidson later told a *Wall Street Journal* reporter: "We were in favor of this sort of thing, but hadn't known how to go about it." Clark explained how to go about it. In return, Davidson agreed to put the NTU's resources and contacts with local taxpayer groups at the service of a campaign for the balanced budget amendment.[11]

They convened interested state legislators and grassroots taxpayers' organizations for a campaign planning meeting in Kansas City, Missouri, in December 1975. Then they began lobbying. Clark and Halbrook set to work contacting legislators in other states, peer to peer, in order to make the pitch for a constitutional convention, while the NTU used its contacts with state and local taxpayer groups to generate outside pressure on those legislators in the form of petitions, letters, and personal visits. The campaign drew little publicity and encountered little resistance. In 1975, five states signed on to the call for a constitutional convention; in 1976, another six; in 1977, six again (see table 7.1).[12] In 1978, the NTU hired the first full-time staff for the campaign, including a young man named Grover Norquist.[13]

The grassroots mobilization for the balanced budget amendment was not at first a rich people's movement. Campaign leaders made no specific claims about

Table 7.1. **States petitioning Congress for a balanced budget amendment, by year**

Year	States (postal abbreviation)
1973	VA
1974	
1975	AL, DE, LA, MD, MS, ND, OK, **VA**
1976	FL, GA, NE, NM, PA, SC, **AL, VA**
1977	AZ, NV, OR, TN, TX, **WY**
1978	CO, KS, **IA, SC, TX**
1979	AR, ID, IA, NH, NC, SD, UT, **AZ, IA, NV, IN**
1980	
1981	
1982	AK
1983	MO
1984	
1985	MI

the moral worthiness of the wealthy or the distributional effects of balancing the budget. Nor did their policy itself promise to cut taxes on the rich. Indeed, the early versions of the proposed amendment contemplated balancing the budget by *increasing* taxes. The resolution that Clark shepherded through the Maryland state legislature specifically allowed the president to meet the balanced budget requirement by proposing new tax revenues as a part of the budget package, a provision that seems to have been critical to getting some liberal legislators on board. A version of the amendment endorsed by NTU in 1975 went further and specifically required that the tax increases come in the form of a proportional surtax on income.[14] This form of taxation appears to have been chosen deliberately to uncouple the balanced budget amendment from the question of income redistribution.

There is also no evidence that the idea of a balanced budget amendment held any special appeal for the affluent. To the contrary: It seemed to appeal to everyone. A 1974 *Time Magazine* poll showed that 65 percent of adults agreed fully or partially with a proposal to "balance the government's budget even if it results in some unemployment," with no measurable differences among income groups.[15] National polls that asked specifically about amending the Constitution to balance the budget also found widespread support at all income levels. The earliest such poll, conducted by the Gallup organization in September 1978, found that 70 percent of adults said they favored "a constitutional amendment requiring a balanced federal budget except in times of emergency." These sympathizers included a disproportionate number of young people—80 percent of eighteen-to-twenty-nine-year-olds said they favored the amendment (which was significantly more than in any other age group)—but the proposal enjoyed majority support even among the elderly. There were no measurable differences in sympathy between Republicans and Democrats, men and women, blacks and whites, or high-income and low-income people (see table 7.2).[16] Most of the supporters were not interested in tax cuts for the rich. When they were asked to choose between cutting taxes first or cutting spending first, most supporters of the balanced budget amendment, consistent with their preference for balanced budgets, favored the latter (75 percent gave this answer, compared to 60 percent of people who did not support the balanced budget amendment). Supporters of the amendment, in other words, were especially *unlikely* to support tax cuts for the rich.[17]

The Property Tax Rebels

At the same time, however, a rich people's movement was brewing in response to a new policy threat. One of the first movement entrepreneurs to act was a Los Angeles retiree named Howard Jarvis. He had come to social movement activism late in life. Born in 1903, he was too young to have participated in any of the great social movements of the Progressive Era, or to have fought in the Great War and the struggle for veterans' benefits that followed it. He spent his earliest years on a farm in small-town Utah, and worked as a miner and a boxer before graduating from the University of Utah in 1925. After graduation he bought a small-town newspaper. His role as an editor gave him a good vantage from which to observe the turbulent politics of taxation in depression-era Utah, and he later mused that the events of this period may have awakened his interest in taxation. There is no evidence that he did much about it, however, and some of the claims about his youthful taxpayer activism that appear in his memoir appear to be completely fictitious.[18]

His first real experience of tax protest politics seems to have been the campaign for the Liberty Amendment. In 1935, Jarvis moved to Los Angeles, sold his newspaper business, and invested the proceeds in real estate. He also started a series of industrial ventures, from a new process for demagnetizing warships to a new method for manufacturing soundproof padding. And he became active in the Los Angeles County Republican Party organization. The latter would become a hotbed of anticommunist and right-wing militancy in the 1950s, and

Table 7.2. **Social characteristics of Americans who supported a
balanced budget amendment, 1978**

	Observed percent in favor (95 percent confidence interval)
Age	
18–29	80 (76 to 84)
30–44	67 (62 to 72)
44–64	68 (64 to 72)
65 and up	61 (54 to 67)
Gender	
Men	72 (68 to 75)
Women	69 (66 to 72)
Race	
White	70 (68 to 72)
Black	69 (62 to 76)
Other	74 (62 to 86)
Party	
Republican	74 (69 to 79)
Democratic	70 (66 to 74)
Independent	70 (66 to 74)
Income category	
under $10,000	65 (60 to 70)
$10,000 to $14,999	72 (67 to 76)
$15,000 to $19,999	71 (66 to 77)
$20,000 to $24,999	72 (65 to 78)
$25,000 and up	73 (66 to 79)

it seems to be here that Jarvis crossed paths with some of Southern California's
many income tax repealers. In February of 1961, he announced his plans to
run against incumbent U.S. Senator Thomas Kuchel in the state Republican
Party primary the following year. Jarvis was not himself a Bircher, he said, but
he shared many of their views, and he wanted their votes. So he staked out a
position as the most militantly anticommunist candidate—he even red-baited
Ronald Reagan, who was at the time a well-known anticommunist motivational
speaker—and he came out in favor of the Liberty Amendment. At a meeting of

the North Orange County Young Republican Club, Jarvis pronounced federal income taxation "un-American and illegal" and pledged to support its repeal.[19]

His bold stand for income tax repeal got him less than 10 percent of the vote in the Republican primary. He continued to campaign in the general election as a write-in candidate—the only candidate, he said, who stood for conservative and constitutional principles—and this time he got less than one-fifth of 1 percent of the vote. The promise to root out Communists from the federal government and repeal the income tax was not enough to rouse many voters even in the ultra-conservative enclaves of Southern California.[20]

A more immediate policy threat, however, proved more provoking to many of Jarvis's friends and neighbors. This was the reform of the local property tax. In 1964, the Los Angeles County assessor announced that he would begin updating the assessment rolls consistently to reflect increases in the market value of taxable property. The result, as Willis Stone noted, was that "in many cities and counties, 1964 property taxes zoomed skyward." Many Southern California homeowners who had bought homes expecting low taxes for the rest of their lives now watched with alarm as the rising price of real estate began to inflate their tax bills. Some feared that they might be forced to sell their homes. To the delight of old Sixteenth Amendment repealers like Jarvis and Stone, many of these homeowners began to get organized. Stone observed with obvious relish that the skyrocketing property tax bills of 1964 "resulted in considerable spontaneous action via the formation of taxpayers' protest associations which will be giving local officials headaches with their new budgets." In 1965, dozens of these associations in the San Fernando Valley formed a coalition called the United Organizations of Taxpayers and elected Howard Jarvis as their president.[21]

Some Liberty Amendment activists, like Stone, were unduly optimistic that the property tax protesters would prove to be natural allies in the struggle for federal income tax repeal. "Where there is awareness of the Liberty Amendment within these newly formed groups, it is expected that interest will also be shown in federal expenditures and taxes," Stone wrote in the January 1965 issue of *Freedom Magazine*. This was wishful thinking. There was no necessary progression from protesting local taxes to protesting federal taxes; people who were upset about their property tax bills were upset about their property tax bills, and that did not make them any more ready to sign on for the abolition of the Sixteenth Amendment. While Stone patiently spread the word about the Liberty Amendment to his Los Angeles neighbors, membership in the Liberty Amendment Committee continued to slip. By 1967, he was forced to acknowledge that his political project was failing. He opened the meeting of his executive board at the Knotts Berry Farm that October with a frank acknowledgment that "we do not have adequate organizational base—nor adequate public support—nor a sufficient educational program to finish the job we have started."[22]

Jarvis was more successful because he took the opposite approach: Instead of trying to persuade people who were upset about their property taxes to focus instead on the Liberty Amendment, he decided to rewrite the Liberty Amendment to focus on the local property tax. In the fall of 1967, while Stone was attempting to restart the Liberty Amendment Committee from scratch, Jarvis busied himself crafting a state constitutional amendment that would repeal all state and local property taxes in California. Then he set about building a network of local volunteers for his campaign to repeal the property tax. The United Organizations of Taxpayers circulated the Jarvis amendment as a petition, and in five months the volunteers collected some 55,000 signatures in the Los Angeles area.[23] By the standards of California electoral politics, this was a dismal failure—they needed almost nine times that many signatures to put their proposal before the voters—but measured against his prior experience in the Liberty Amendment campaign, it was an encouraging success. More than five times as many people signed the petition than had written in Jarvis's name as a senate candidate.[24]

The movement against property taxes continued to grow as long as the policy threat of rising property tax bills persisted; and as long as the movement grew, Jarvis continued to write and rewrite his policy to attract support. In 1972, he drafted a new petition, this time for a limitation on the assessed value of real estate. By moderating his demands, he learned, he could attract more supporters: This time he collected 489,000 signatures. California Governor Ronald Reagan and the state legislature sought unsuccessfully to appease the protesters by limiting local property tax rates. The trouble with this solution was that the threat of property tax increases had little to do with rising tax rates; it was driven instead by the new policy of recording rising property values. The property tax protesters did not let up. Their ranks grew to include several of the state's major labor unions and liberal community organizations, which were backing a package of progressive property tax reforms. Jarvis meanwhile teamed up with a more conservative coalition of realtors, apartment owners, and a northern California community organization led by a former used-car salesman named Paul Gann to push for a new constitutional amendment to limit future property tax increases. "It was important to have signatures from every county so that it didn't appear that this was something all those crazies and Birchers who, some think, make up 100 [percent] of the population of Southern California, were trying to put over on the rest of the state," he later said.[25]

The Jarvis-Gann amendment promised to cut property taxes. It would impose a limit on future property tax increases. And, to prevent the state legislature from simply finding another way to impose the same burden, it would require a supermajority of the state legislature to approve *any* tax increase. By the end of 1977, more than a million registered voters signed the Jarvis-Gann petition—an all-time record for ballot initiative petitions in California, and easily double the number needed to qualify the proposed amendment for the ballot. In early 1978, the California secretary of state named the proposed amendment "Proposition 13," in keeping with the bureaucratic practice of numbering ballot measures in the order in which they were approved for submission to the voters. The fate of the initiative was uncertain until a last-minute reassessment by the Los Angeles County assessor in May 1978 revealed that many homeowners were about to see their property taxes double. Suddenly, support for Jarvis-Gann surged—especially in Los Angeles County, and most especially among individual homeowners whose property taxes were increasing most rapidly. On Tuesday, June 6, 1978, California voters approved Proposition 13 by a majority of 65 percent to 35 percent.[26]

And on Wednesday, James Davidson announced that the NTU was taking up the banner of Proposition 13 in a national campaign to limit federal income taxes.[27]

Proposition 13 and Its Sequels

Davidson was not the only one to have this idea. The taxpayer revolt in California was the lead story on the nightly news and a front-page story in every major national newspaper. State legislators meeting in Denver for the annual conference of the National Conference of State Legislatures a month after the California election could talk of nothing else. Colorado State Senator Fred Anderson, the president of the council, told a *New York Times* reporter, "If I've heard the words 'Jarvis-Gann' or 'Proposition 13' mentioned once, it's been 8,000 times." Activists converged on St. Louis on July 29 for a "National Tax Limitation Conference" to discuss how they might replicate the success of Proposition 13 in other states and at the federal level. They interpreted the amendment of the California constitution as a sign that the American public was eager for tax cuts. Many veterans of previous rich people's movements decided the time was right to amend the federal Constitution to limit the taxes of the richest Americans.[28]

The leaders of the NTU had a head start because their balanced budget campaign in the states had given them a national network of activists, contacts with state legislators, and experience pushing for a federal constitutional amendment. In the wake of Proposition 13, they began considering new proposals to cap federal taxes or federal spending as a percentage of GDP. "No wonder Proposition 13 is so popular. The American taxpayer is fed up," wrote the NTU's research director, Sid Taylor, three weeks after the California vote. "We now need a Proposition 14—on spending limitations—at the federal level." The NTU sent out brochures that associated it directly with Proposition 13. One such brochure depicted NTU activists shaking hands with Howard Jarvis and Paul Gann, and asserted that "[t]he recent taxpayer victory in California proves how powerful the taxpayers' movement can be." Another included an endorsement from Paul Gann, who called the NTU's grassroots campaign "an effort to bring the promise of Proposition 13 to you and all Americans."[29]

In Davidson's eyes, bringing the promise of Proposition 13 to all Americans meant applying the principle of constitutional tax limitation to the federal income tax. The NTU quietly reversed its support for balancing the budget with an income surtax. Instead, the NTU began calling openly for repeal of the Sixteenth Amendment. Its fundraising solicitations quoted Willis Stone's old speeches against the income tax. Davidson also announced that the NTU specifically planned to revive Robert Dresser's amendment to limit the marginal tax rate to 25 percent. "This amendment was originally introduced in Congress during the 1930s and came close to passage," Davidson wrote. "It was a good idea then, and it is a better idea now."[30]

He realized, however, that it was hard to campaign for tax cuts and a balanced budget at the same time. A balanced budget amendment was, he said, "a necessary preliminary step," and any tax limitation would come only after a balanced budget amendment was ratified. Bonner also told reporters that the NTU's plan was to postpone the 25 percent tax limitation until after the balanced budget amendment had passed. He did not think it would take long. Seven more state legislatures signed on to the balanced budget amendment in early 1979, and more were poised to join them. The leadership of the NTU expected to succeed within the year. In February, even the *New York Times* reporter Adam Clymer judged it "more likely than not that this year the necessary 34th state will call for a convention."[31]

Other former Sixteenth Amendment repealers sought to transition immediately from property tax limits to federal tax limitation. Howard Jarvis celebrated his California victory by announcing the formation of a national organization called the American Tax Reduction Movement (ATRM). Its first objective, he said, was to cut federal income taxes, particularly income taxes on capital gains. His arguments echoed the rhetoric of the early-twentieth-century tax clubs: Income taxes were so high that rich people were diverting their capital to unproductive uses. "We've gotten to a situation where people are so afraid of capital gains taxes that they're taking money that should go into the productive capacity of the country and putting it into tax shelters instead," he said. The solution Jarvis favored, like the tax clubs before him, was not to eliminate the tax shelters, but instead to cut the top marginal tax rates affecting rich investors. Although Jarvis said he would have liked to abolish all taxes on capital gains— and although he may indeed still have wished he could abolish all taxes on incomes from whatever source derived—he had learned from his experiences that the Liberty Amendment was not a political winner. In its place he proposed a statute that would cut personal income tax rates by 25 percent across the board. It would further index income tax brackets for inflation, thereby limiting future inflation-induced growth in income taxes. The proposal bore an obvious resemblance to a tax cut plan put forward by Representative Jack Kemp (R-NY) and Senator William Roth (R-DE); but it is unclear whether Jarvis was copying Kemp-Roth or just extrapolating the basic logic of Proposition 13, which analogously had cut property tax rates across the board and limited inflation-induced growth in property taxes. He purchased a half-hour spot on national television in September 1978 to advertise the ATRM's tax reduction program, which he portrayed as the logical continuation of Proposition 13. He also spent hundreds of thousands of dollars on direct mail advertising to businesspeople ("Would you like to reduce the taxes on your business by 2/3? That is precisely what businessmen in California did when they joined 4.2 million angry taxpayers in voting for Proposition 13") and on lobbying Congress for his tax cut program. Representatives Robert Dornan (R-CA) and Tom Luken (D-OH) introduced his American Tax Reduction Act in January 1979.[32]

Still other activists took Proposition 13 as a sign that it was time to revive the Liberty Amendment. The California congressman and former John Birch Society publicity director, John Rousselot, reintroduced the Liberty Amendment in Congress on January 15, 1979. Many other Liberty Amendment activists also took heart from Jarvis's example—and took pages from Jarvis's playbook. The most dedicated copycat was a veteran navy pilot and San Diego tax lawyer named Armin Moths. For years, Moths had been seeking with little success to organize taxpayers into a "U.S. Taxpayers Union." Now he changed his tactics: Confronted with an example of success, he decided to revive the grassroots campaign for the Liberty Amendment by imitating the Jarvis-Gann campaign down to even the most superficial particulars. If the California state legislature could not be persuaded to pass a resolution in favor of the Liberty Amendment, then it would be done by ballot initiative. And if everyone was excited about Proposition 13, then perhaps the way to sell the Liberty Amendment was to give it a number too. Moths picked 23, because Rousselot had introduced the amendment as House Joint Resolution 23. So Moths announced the formation of a "Yes on 23 Committee"—named after the "Yes on 13 Committee" that Jarvis had established to finance the campaign for Proposition 13—and he began soliciting donations, circulating newsletters, and setting up card tables in public places to petition for the Liberty Amendment. He even had "Yes on 23" signs printed up in a style that mimicked the "Yes on 13" campaign signs that dotted the suburban lawns of Southern California in the spring of 1978.[33]

Activists in other states were less punctilious about copying every last detail of Jarvis's operation, but they too tried to win adherents by presenting the Liberty Amendment as the sequel to Proposition 13. Sometimes it even worked. In 1982, the legislatures of Arizona and Indiana, both of which had recently passed Jarvis-like property tax limits, followed up by passing resolutions calling for a constitutional convention to pass the Liberty Amendment.[34]

Yet another group of sometime Sixteenth Amendment repealers launched a new campaign for a federal tax limitation amendment. This group was the National Tax Limitation Committee (NTLC), led by a one-time Bircher (and former aide to Rousselot) named Lewis K. Uhler. Prior to founding the NTLC, Uhler had served in the cabinet of California Governor Ronald Reagan, where he had been tasked with drafting a constitutional limitation on the growth of state spending. Uhler recruited an all-star group of libertarian economists to his legislative drafting team, including Milton Friedman, William Niskanen, Gordon Tullock, James Buchanan, and Buchanan's student Craig Stubblebine. Like Howard Jarvis, these men learned the hard way that Californians in the early 1970s were angry about their local property taxes in particular, not about taxation in general. Voters rejected their amendment in 1973. Liberal Democrats campaigned successfully against it by arguing that it would hurt the state's ability to provide property tax relief.[35]

Uhler continued to try to start a new movement for federal tax limitation. In 1973, his task force persuaded Representative Kemp to introduce a federal version of the spending limitation amendment to Congress. Uhler also carried the campaign to other states. In July 1976, he formally announced the founding of the NTLC, consisting mainly of Governor Reagan's old spending limitation task force, plus a small number of well-known conservative public figures (such as the celebrity heir William Rickenbacker, former representative Clare Booth Luce, and retired general Albert Wedemeyer) and corporate backers (such as George Champion, former chairman of Chase Manhattan Bank, and James M. Hall, senior vice president of the Title Insurance Corporation). The purpose of the committee was to serve as a clearing-house for state and local taxpayer organizations. As Rickenbacker put it in an interview on Dean Manion's radio show, such groups "exist like little flowers in their own garden—sort of independently, and without any communication amongst each other." To get the communication started, the NTLC began convening meetings of local taxpayer groups from around the country. It also began distributing a manual of campaign advice, titled *A Taxpayer's Guide to Survival*, in which Uhler and Rickenbacker attempted to distill lessons from their failures. They concluded the manual optimistically with a chapter on "How to Win Campaigns," although they had not yet won any.[36]

In the spring of 1978, their luck began to turn. In March, a Tennessee state legislator named David Copeland persuaded his colleagues to include an NTLC-style limitation in the state constitution. In May, members of the NTLC met with NTU's Clark to discuss the idea of packaging a federal tax limitation with the proposed federal balanced budget amendment. In June, Californians passed Proposition 13. The NTLC promptly called a meeting of state and local groups to a tax limitation conference in Nashville to talk about how they could build momentum for state and federal tax limitation in other states.[37]

The key to getting a tax limitation amendment passed, Uhler told his friends, was crafting the policy in a way that would make it "politically sexy." At the state level, he explained, this meant packaging state limitations together with property tax relief, in order to "ride the political momentum occasioned by the property tax revolt."[38] At the federal level, he concluded, any limitation on the federal income tax should be packaged together with the NTU's balanced budget amendment.

The Packaging of the Balanced Budget/Tax Limitation Amendment

By the spring of 1979, thirty states had called for a constitutional convention to adopt a balanced budget amendment. None of the resolutions said anything about tax limitation. The tax limitation activists nevertheless hoped to seize the day. A convention was a once-in-a-lifetime opportunity to write tax limits into the Constitution. If activists could package balanced budget and tax limitation language together in one amendment, they might finally achieve the goal that had eluded them since the 1920s.

Former Birchers led the way. On March 22, Representative Rousselot introduced the Taxpayer's Protection Amendment (H. J. Res. 278). Much like Clark's proposal, his amendment required a supermajority vote in Congress to approve any deficit spending. Rousselot and his Senate co-sponsor Bill Armstrong (R-CO) echoed the NTU. They identified inflation as "the number one problem facing our country," and pinned the blame for inflation on federal deficits. They also justified their proposed amendment by noting its resemblance to the balanced budget requirements in state constitutions. "[M]ost State and city governments are under constitutional restraints not to spend more than they take in," Rousselot said, "and I see no reason, except for the two exceptions I had included in our bill and allow for that escape valve, we shouldn't [sic] do any differently." In one crucial respect, however, their bill differed from the NTU's proposal, and resembled Proposition 13: It also required a supermajority vote in both houses of Congress to approve any increase in taxes, even if that tax increase would help to balance the budget. "Obviously in light of the positive effects tax cuts can have on the economy, we must not undermine the tax cutting movement by forcing the Congress to raise taxes to balance the budget," Rousselot said. When budget balance and tax limitation were in conflict, in other words, tax limitation won.[39]

Uhler had the same idea but took a different approach. Instead of packaging an explicit balanced budget requirement with an explicit tax limitation, he brazenly redefined budget balance to mean a freeze on the growth of government spending. In January 1979, the NTLC unveiled its new spending limitation amendment, which decreed that "[t]otal outlays of the Government of the United States during any fiscal year shall not increase by a percentage greater than the percentage increase in the nominal gross national product during the last calendar year ending prior to the beginning of such fiscal year." This language said nothing about balancing the budget, the ostensible purpose for which states had called for a constitutional convention.[40] Uhler nevertheless declared that the NTLC's new spending limitation amendment was wholly in keeping with the spirit of the convention call, as long as Congress construed the meaning of a balanced budget in very broad terms. "What has happened is that people's focus has shifted from explicit reductions of taxes to an increasing concern over limitation on spending by Government, an increasing demand that 'budgets be balanced,' in that generic sense," he told a Senate subcommittee in the fall of 1979. Stubblebine also argued that the NTLC spending limit proposal would comply with the state balanced budget amendment petitions and satisfy the public. "Because the words 'balanced budget' roll off the tongue with greater facility than 'spending limit' is not to suggest that the balanced budget approach is preferable functionally or for that matter politically," he said.[41] The NTLC was successful at presenting its amendment as a substitute for the balanced budget amendment. The press characterized it as a more "sophisticated" alternative to the NTU's proposal and reported that conservatives in Congress looked on it more favorably.[42]

In reality the NTLC's proposal was not a more sophisticated version of the NTU's amendment: It was a different policy entirely, one that had less to do with shrinking the deficit than with limiting the progressivity of the income tax. The amendment would do nothing, strictly speaking, to prevent the federal government from running a deficit. What it *would* do, implicitly, was limit the graduation of income tax rates. As long as marginal income tax rates were graduated according to income, rising incomes would continue to drive more people into higher brackets—and thereby increase tax revenues faster than GNP. By fixing the federal budget as a share of GNP, the amendment therefore implicitly required that the graduated feature of the income tax rate structure be abandoned.[43]

This implicit limitation on tax progressivity was deliberate. Indeed, as the name of the NTLC implied, a limit on taxes was the whole point of their proposal. Uhler and the other leaders of the NTLC made no secret of their dislike for progressive income taxation or their belief that income tax rates in the top brackets were too high. In Uhler's words, the purpose of a limit on the growth of federal spending was to "reduce the share of our earnings and wealth flowing to the Federal Government." Stubblebine, in his own congressional testimony, described the NTLC's proposed amendment as a direct response to the Sixteenth Amendment, which, he said, had "removed from the Constitution the severe restraint on Federal revenue provided by the Founding Fathers."[44] The NTLC's *Taxpayer's Survival Guide* instructed local taxpayer groups around the country that limits on the growth of government budgets were necessary because the progressive income tax, if left unchecked, could ultimately lead to a policy of confiscation. "The danger is that *there's no law on the books to stop government from taking 100 per cent of your income,*" it said. Or, as another tax limitation activist liked to say, "The only alternative to tax limitation is unlimited taxation."[45]

The Rich People's Movement Revived

The NTLC's proposal attracted new adherents to the campaign for a constitutional amendment. A Roper Center poll from May 1979 found that a bare majority of adults (52 percent) favored an amendment to "require that the budget be balanced in any given year either by raising taxes or lowering spending, or both." This was the original form of the balanced budget amendment proposed by NTU and endorsed by a majority of state legislatures. Fully 60 percent of adults, however, said they favored a constitutional amendment that would "limit federal spending to a certain fraction of the gross national product," which was the NTLC's proposed amendment in a nutshell. The NTLC version had the support of significantly more people than the NTU version. The sympathizers were a clear majority in virtually every socio-demographic group except for African Americans, among whom support fell just short of a majority (46 percent favored it, compared to 62 percent of white respondents and 68 percent of other respondents). The NTLC's proposed amendment was especially popular among high-income respondents, but the differences among income groups were not statistically significant, so this may have been a quirk of the sample, rather than a reflection of any pattern in the population at large (see table 7.3).[46] Most of those who sympathized with the spending limitation amendment were neither rich nor desirous of cutting taxes on the rich, but were middle-income people eager to cut *their own* income taxes. The same poll from May 1979 asked

Table 7.3. **Social characteristics of Americans who supported two different federal spending limitations, 1979**

	Observed percent in favor of a constitutional amendment...	
	... limiting spending as a share of GNP (95 percent confidence interval)	*... requiring the budget to be balanced annually (95 percent confidence interval)*
Total	60 (57 to 62)	52 (50 to 55)
Age		
18–29	64 (59 to 68)	52 (48 to 57)
30–44	59 (54 to 64)	49 (44 to 54)
44–64	58 (53 to 63)	54 (49 to 58)
65 and up	54 (57 to 60)	54 (47 to 61)
Gender		
Men	63 (59 to 66)	56 (52 to 60)
Women	57 (53 to 60)	49 (45 to 52)
Race		
White	62 (58 to 64)	53 (50 to 55)
Black	46 (38 to 53)	48 (40 to 55)
Other	68 (48 to 88)	55 (33 to 76)
Education		
Less than H.S.	54 (49 to 59)	49 (44 to 53)
H.S. graduate	62 (57 to 66)	58 (54 to 62)
Some college	65 (59 to 71)	53 (47 to 59)
College graduate	59 (53 to 65)	46 (39 to 52)
Income category		
under $9,000	56 (51 to 62)	55 (49 to 60)
$9,000 to $14,999	58 (52 to 64)	57 (51 to 62)
$15,000 to $19,999	64 (57 to 70)	55 (48 to 61)
$20,000 to $24,999	64 (58 to 71)	56 (49 to 63)
$25,000 and up	66 (60 to 72)	50 (43 to 56)
... subcategory: $75,000 and up	72 (35 to 100)	57 (18 to 97)

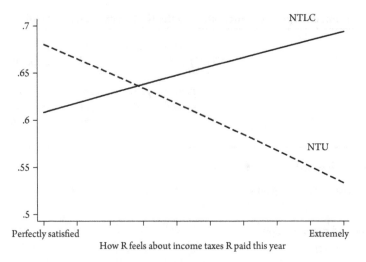

Figure 7.1 The predicted probability that respondents would favor constitutional amendments backed by the NTLC and the NTU, by respondents' feelings toward their own income tax burden. *Source:* Calculated from Roper/H&R Block Study No. 1979-0673, May 5–12, 1979 and regression models reported in Table 7.6.

each respondent to rate "how you feel about the income taxes you paid this year" on a scale from one ("feeling perfectly satisfied") to ten ("extreme anger"), and the results show that the angrier the taxpayer, the more likely he or she was to support the NTLC's proposed limitation on federal spending. The expected probability of supporting the NTLC version of the amendment rose from 61 percent among those who were most satisfied with their taxes to 69 percent among those who were most angry (see figure 7.1). In contrast, the angrier the respondents were about their income taxes, the *less* likely they were to support the NTU's proposed balanced budget amendment. The expected probability of favoring such an amendment was 68 percent among otherwise-average respondents who were most satisfied with their taxes, and it was only 54 percent among those who were most angry about their income taxes.[47]

Active participants who donated time and money to the campaign were almost certainly more affluent than the sympathizers. The only available data concern those who donated money. The NTLC reported a large number of corporate contributors. A partial list of corporate donors that the committee published in a 1986 brochure suggests that manufacturers and oil companies predominated. The majority of the corporate donors named on the list (53 percent) were manufacturing firms, which were overrepresented by a factor of six relative to their sector's share of corporate firms in the economy. Oil companies, despite being a small minority of all named contributors (9 percent), were also

Table 7.4. **Named corporate contributors to the NTLC, by industry, 1986**

Industry	Contributors named in NTLC publications			All workers	All corporations
	N	percent of total	percent of those classified	percent of labor force	percent of corporation income tax returns
Could not be classified	39	15	...	...	...
Agriculture, forestry, fishing and hunting	0	0	0	3	3
Mining, oil and gas extraction, utilities, construction	21	8	9	1	1
Construction	6	2	3	7	10
Manufacturing	116	44	53	20	8
Transportation, communications, electric, gas, and primary services	16	6	7	7	4
Wholesale and retail trade	25	10	11	22	28
Finance, insurance, and real estate	24	9	11	7	16
Services	14	6	6	32	30
Total	261	100	100	99	100

dramatically overrepresented relative to their small numbers in the economy. Firms in other sectors were underrepresented, but only agricultural employers were completely absent from the list (see table 7.4).[48] The NTLC seems to have been supported by a sectorally diverse group of business owners and corporate managers. Nevertheless, the NTLC relied most heavily on small contributions raised by direct mail. They told the press in 1982 that they had 125,000 contributors, and a budget that implied an average contribution of about $20.[49]

The NTU's funders seem to have been slightly less affluent, or at least they made smaller donations on average; but they too seem to have been mostly business owners. Davidson described them as "eccentric industrialists." They included at least some rich individuals, notably the libertarian billionaire Charles Koch, but the NTU did not have many contacts among the very rich. Press reports from 1982 imply that the NTU expected to raise less than half as much money as the NTLC from the same number of donors. When Davidson set out to solicit big donations from multimillionaire donors a few years later, he had to look them up in *Forbes* magazine like anyone else would. (Figuring he had nothing to lose, he sent everyone on the *Forbes 400* a form letter asking for a million dollar dona- tion. This fundraising strategy produced exactly one $500 check and some free publicity in the form of a *Wall Street Journal* story about how cheeky it was.) It was not riches, but a particular social milieu, that distinguished the contributors; Davidson told a reporter that two-thirds of them were from California. If this is correct, it suggests that the single greatest predictor of whether someone would contribute to the NTU was geography—and in particular, proximity to the heart- land of prior movements to repeal the Sixteenth Amendment.[50]

Policy Impact

Presidential politics transformed the campaign by bringing media scrutiny and partisan polarization. The first candidate to endorse the balanced budget amendment was a liberal Democrat, California Governor Jerry Brown, who had declared himself "reborn to the spirit of tax cut and austerity" after the passage of Proposition 13. Brown hoped to challenge President Carter for the Democratic nomination for the presidency. He seems to have calculated that the balanced budget amendment was a bold way to distinguish himself from the incumbent and from Senator Ted Kennedy (D-MA), who was contemplating a challenge from the left. Brown's speedy implementation of Proposition 13 had already won over Howard Jarvis. ("It would be really interesting if he and Reagan are the nominees for president in 1980," Jarvis wrote in 1979. "I don't know what I'd do—I'd have a hard time opposing either of them.") Brown's endorsement of a constitutional convention polarized the Democratic Party. State legislators now began to line up for or against the proposal depending on whether they were for or against Carter.[51]

The leading Republican candidate, Ronald Reagan, meanwhile executed a delicate political maneuver, endorsing most of the activists' substantive demands for balanced budgets and lower income taxes while declining to endorse their call for a constitutional convention. He probably knew he could count on their support anyway. Reagan was a well-known critic of the progressive income tax who had called for its replacement by a flat-rate income tax since the 1970s. He was cozy with many former Birchers; he enjoyed a good relationship with Howard Jarvis; and he even retained some members of the NTLC as his eco- nomic advisors. A promise to cut personal income tax rates was a centerpiece of his presidential campaign. He also promised to cut spending and balance the budget.[52]

The presidential campaign brought media attention to the campaign for a balanced budget amendment, and with scrutiny came opposition. The White House set up a working group to study ways to defeat the amendment. The speaker of the House of Representatives, Thomas P. "Tip" O'Neill (D-MA), began organizing a coalition of liberal lobbying groups, including the United Auto Workers, the League of Women Voters, the NAACP, the American Civil Liberties Union (ACLU), and Common Cause, to campaign against a constitutional convention. Representative David Obey (D-WI) wrote a stern letter to state governors warning that federal government would cut off state aid if any such amendment passed. State legislators who had not yet had a chance to weigh in on the merits of a constitutional convention suddenly found themselves in the media spotlight. The experience led some of them to reconsider the symbolic politics of coming out in favor of a convention. "It was one thing when you could just pass the thing and send it off to Washington with nobody looking," Ohio State Senator William F. Bowen told the *Washington Post*. "But now the newspapers are watching, you've got to have hearings. Everybody's more careful when this comes up in the legislature now." No state legislature passed resolutions in favor of the amendment in 1980.[53]

The looming threat of a convention was sufficient to get the balanced budget amendment on the congressional agenda. Members of the ninety-sixth Congress introduced more than fifty constitutional amendments to require a balanced budget or limit the growth of government revenues or expenditures. The Subcommittee on the Constitution of the Senate Judiciary Committee held a year-long series of hearings. Conservatives on the subcommittee ultimately synthesized these proposals into a combined balanced budget/tax limitation amendment of their own design that embraced features of the NTU and the NTLC amendments. The proposed amendment required a supermajority of three-fifths to approve any deficit spending. It further prohibited any increase in federal revenues as a percentage of national income, unless a majority of members of Congress specifically put themselves on record in favor of such increase with a roll-call vote. Senator Orrin Hatch (R-UT), an author and co-sponsor of the new proposal, acknowledged that it was an "obvious response to the popular call for a balanced budget amendment, reflected in part by the applications of 30 state legislatures for a constitutional convention on this subject." The subcommittee approved it by a vote of five to two in December 1979. The full Judiciary Committee voted it down by the narrowest of margins, nine to eight, the following March.[54]

The amendment came back stronger the following year. Reagan's landslide victory in the November presidential election, and the election of a new Republican majority in the Senate, gave the campaign another boost. Members of the ninety-seventh Congress introduced more than sixty different balanced budget amendments. In March, the Senate Judiciary Committee—now under the chairmanship of Hatch—voted to revive the "balanced budget and tax limitation" amendment that had narrowly failed the previous year. This proposal did not exactly correspond to either the NTU or the NTLC model, but activists in both camps supported it, because neither wanted to be left out of claiming credit for victory. Despite the fact that Davidson and Uhler did not get along—they were, according to reporters, jealous of leadership and barely on speaking terms—they worked out an informal division of labor. The NTLC solicited postcards to Congress via direct mail targeted to constituents in key congressional districts. The NTU, meanwhile, counseled against this tactic—"Avoid sending pre-printed postcards unless you don't have any time to write your own letter," said its *Taxpayer's Action Guide*—and advised local activists instead to set up telephone trees, get their neighbors to turn out for mass meetings, and make personal contact with their legislators. NTU staff continued to convene meetings of state and local taxpayer groups, and took to the field to help organize such groups where they did not exist. Davidson traveled around the country pressuring state legislators to support the convention call, in hopes that the continuing threat of a convention would force Congress to act.[55]

Policy Impact without Success

The activists came close to getting their amendment through Congress. The Senate approved the balanced budget/tax limitation amendment in 1982. On October 1, 1982, a majority of the House also voted in favor, 236 "ayes" to 187 "noes," with nine abstentions. They were fifty-two votes short of the two-thirds required for a constitutional amendment. Had the proposed bill been a statute, rather than a constitutional amendment, it would have passed.[56]

Although the activists did not get the amendment they wanted, there is reason to think that their movement had a substantial impact on tax policy. The mere threat of a constitutional amendment put substantial pressure on members of Congress. Even many of those who opposed the amendment felt that their best strategy was to embrace statutory limitations on tax and budget policy in order to show that the activists' goals could be achieved *without* a constitutional amendment.[57] The Reagan administration proposed deep income tax cuts. Members of Congress moved quickly to pass tax cuts that went far beyond what even the administration requested. The Economic Recovery Tax Act (ERTA) of 1981 ultimately cut tax revenues more deeply than any other previous piece of legislation in American history and, in the words of the historian W. Elliot Brownlee, "reduced the role of the income tax in the nation's revenue system for the first time since the Great Depression."[58] It cut the top marginal rate of personal income tax from 70 percent to 50 percent, and introduced deep rate cuts and exemptions for corporations. Some of the specifics had little to do directly with grassroots mobilization. The most costly provisions of ERTA, for example, included hundreds of particularistic tax breaks introduced into the corporate income tax at the behest of trade and industry groups; this sort of pork-barrel politicking was nothing new, though ERTA was somewhat extreme in the number of such special tax breaks. The largest change that ERTA wrought to the individual income tax, however—the provision that, in the long run, produced by far the largest revenue losses and did the most to constrain future tax increases—had little corporate support and everything to do with grassroots pressure for tax limitation. This was the provision that indexed personal income tax brackets for inflation.[59]

The indexation of income tax brackets had been on the wish list of tax experts for years, but it became law only after the revival of the movement for constitutional tax limitation. Congress had rejected similar proposals for indexing by wide margins in 1975, 1976, 1977, and 1978. As a staff memo prepared for the Republican tax study committee in the House of Representatives in June 1978 noted, however, "The success of Proposition 13 and the 'tax revolt' should encourage added interest in 'indexing.'" It did. In 1979, a Senate vote on an indexing bill failed by only six votes.[60] The growing mobilization for a constitutional convention had convinced many members of Congress to reverse themselves.

Comparisons among members of Congress also support the view that the mobilization for a tax limitation amendment had a substantial impact on the politics of indexation. The champions of indexation in Congress were the same as the champions of constitutional tax limitation. In the Senate, the income tax indexing bill was introduced by Senator Armstrong, who had introduced balanced budget/tax limitation amendments in 1979 and 1981. In the House, the main sponsor of the bill to index the income tax was Representative Barber Conable (R-NY), who was also the sponsor of the House version of the balanced budget/tax limitation amendment. Senators and representatives from states that had endorsed the call for a constitutional convention—and who therefore may have felt particular pressure to show their support for limiting taxes—were especially likely to favor indexation of the income tax. Table 7.5 illustrates the pattern with data from the House roll-call vote on the Conable amendment to the administration's tax bill. This amendment included provisions to index the income tax (alongside other provisions), and it was crucial to the passage of ERTA in the Democratic House. The representatives most likely to vote for it were those from states that had endorsed a balanced budget amendment.[61]

Table 7.5. **Percent voting in favor of indexing income tax brackets, by party and exposure to the campaign for a constitutional amendment**

Party and region	From a state whose legislature had endorsed the balanced budget amendment?	
	Yes	No
Republican	100% (42 of 42)	99% (149 of 150)
Southern Democrat	67% (16 of 24)	35% (16 of 46)
Northern Democrat	16% (3 of 19)	8% (12 of 152)

Robert Dresser died before the passage of ERTA, but had he lived to see it become law, he might have recognized it as a descendant of his own 1938 proposal to limit the income tax. By cutting income tax rates and indexing tax brackets for inflation, it limited the growth of income tax revenues.

The Plains of Hesitation

President Reagan was not above claiming credit for the movement's successes. After waffling between neutrality and opposition to the balanced budget amendment, his cabinet finally came out in favor of it in 1982, and promptly set about organizing a new political action committee called "the American Lobby for President Reagan's Balanced Budget Amendment."[62] When it came to the indexation of income tax brackets, however, Reagan gave credit where credit was due. "Your organization's support for the across-the-board tax rate reduction and income tax indexing helped pave the way for congressional adoption of these important reforms during the first years of this Administration," he wrote to NTU's Davidson in 1982.[63]

Reagan was right: The individual rate cuts and the indexation of income tax brackets were responses to a rich people's movement—kept alive in the Southern California subculture of Birchers and fellow travelers during the long decade of the 1960s, revived by the threat of property tax increases, and channeled by movement entrepreneurs who crafted their policy proposals strategically to win allies and demobilize opponents.

The movement lasted only as long as the policy threat. By 1982, the mobilization for tax limits had already begun to wane. This was not because the activists had achieved their stated goals; to the contrary, ERTA increased the deficit. Nor was it because political elites had turned against the movement; to the contrary, the Reagan administration embraced the balanced budget amendment. The

Table 7.6. **Characteristics of respondents who supported constitutional amendments backed by the NTLC and the NTU, respectively. Results from logistic regression models**

	NTLC	NTU
	Logit (SE)	Logit (SE)
Intercept	.70 (.34)*	.59 (.34)+
Female = 1	.0033 (.13)	−.36 (.13)**
Black = 1	−.79 (.24)**	−.21 (.24)
Age in years	−.0051 (.0044)	.0085 (.0042)*
Education, years completed	−.011 (.015)	.0024 (.015)
Income, in $000s	.0019 (.0051)	−.0066 (.0048)
Anger about R's own income taxes, 1 = feeling perfectly satisfied to 10 = extreme anger	.042 (.024)+	−.069 (.24)**
N	1024	1018

+ p < .10
* p < .05
** p < .01

movement declined because it proved hard to sustain mobilized pressure without the urgent threat of tax increases to motivate the activists. Inflation abated; moreover, the movement's partial policy victories, including property tax limitations and the indexing of personal income tax brackets, had broken the link between rising prices and rising taxes. As the policy threat ebbed, the activists drifted away.

The movement also suffered defections of some loyal conservatives, as many groups on the right came to fear what would happen if the NTU actually succeeded in calling a constitutional convention. The antifeminist crusader Phyllis Schlafly, who had spent years trying to block the Equal Rights Amendment, feared that a convention would open the window of opportunity for liberals to amend the Constitution. Schlafly helped to organize a strange-bedfellows coalition called Citizens to Protect the Constitution that included her Eagle Forum and the Gun Owners Clubs of America, but also such liberal groups as the ACLU and the National Organization for Women. Even the John Birch Society joined. The most stalwart of Sixteenth Amendment repealers had cold feet.[64]

And so the movement lapsed into abeyance again (see table 7.6).[65] The NTU finally gave up the grassroots campaign after convention resolutions failed in New Jersey, Kentucky, Michigan, and Montana. It resorted to selling tax advice as a selective incentive to recruit and keep members. The NTLC, meanwhile, struggled to keep the movement alive with books and conferences devoted to the idea of constitutional tax limitation, even as board members drifted away and donations slowed to a trickle. It was painful to lose after coming so close. "On the plains of hesitation bleach the bones of countless millions who, at the dawn of victory, sat down to rest and, resting, died," Uhler wrote in 1989, misquoting a scrap of half-remembered poetry; "God forbid that we should rest on the 'plains of hesitation'".[66]

Even as he saw victory slipping from his grasp, however, Uhler expressed confidence that a constitutional limitation on the income tax would eventually return to the congressional agenda. After all, this was not the first time a movement for a constitutional limit on the income tax had been defeated. It always came back.

CHAPTER 8

The Temporary Triumph of Estate Tax Repeal

By 1991, the prospects for a rich people's movement looked dimmer than ever, and the prospects for a protest movement against the estate tax looked dimmest of all. There was not much to protest. The total burden of the tax had always been small in proportion to national income. Now it was minuscule. After decades of elite families' lobbying for special treatment, the tax was so riddled with exemptions and deductions that some legal scholars described it as "a voluntary tax"—anyone sufficiently motivated to avoid it, in other words, could do so legally, and with less expense and uncertainty than would be involved in an effort to overturn the entire tax.[1] The ERTA of 1981 had lowered the top marginal rate of estate tax from 70 percent to 55 percent, and raised the exemption in steps from $175,000 to $600,000, in consequence of which the tax yielded less revenue than at any time since the Great Depression. The share of Americans who owed any tax on their estates—approximately 1 percent of all decedents—was also at a historic low. With the end of the Cold War, even the John Birch Society had stopped harping on the threat that progressive taxes would lead to communism.[2] Few people felt any reason to protest the federal taxation of inherited wealth.

Even if anyone had felt like protesting the estate tax, the window of political opportunity seemed to be closing. Elected officials were abandoning the cause of tax cuts for the rich. President George H. W. Bush favored a balanced budget amendment, but only in a form that anti-tax activists regarded as toothless.[3] He had campaigned as an anti-tax hardliner—"The Congress will push me to raise taxes, and I'll say no, and they'll push, and I'll say no, and they'll push again, and I'll say to them 'Read my lips: no new taxes,'" he said at the Republican National Convention—but in the course of budget negotiations in 1990, he gave in after just one push and acknowledged the necessity of tax increases to balance the federal budget.[4] The Democrats who controlled both houses of Congress sent him a long list of tax increases that specifically targeted the rich by raising the top marginal rates of personal income tax and by increasing excise taxes on "furs, jewelry, private jets, expensive cars, and especially boats"; and on November 5, the president signed the tax bill into law.[5] It did not make him popular, but it did not seem to hurt him. Just a few weeks later, his approval rating reached the highest level yet recorded for an American president. If getting a movement off the ground required allies in high office, then the proponents of estate tax repeal were out of luck. [6]

Within two years, however, an unlikely coalition of advocacy groups launched a new campaign to repeal the estate tax. They founded special purpose associations, independent of the Republican Party, and recruited members and activists far outside of Washington, D.C. They circulated petitions and solicited public testimonials in order to arouse public opinion, to increase the salience of the issue, and to persuade Congress that a large and morally worthy constituency was committed to the cause of estate tax repeal. Within a decade, they put estate tax repeal up for a congressional vote—and won.

Where did this campaign come from? Commentators have credited savvy framing by think tanks, but the rhetorical frame that has received the most attention—the framing of the estate tax as a "death tax"—cannot be the explanation for the emergence of a movement, because this name for the tax was nothing new at the time that the movement emerged. This way of describing the tax was, in fact, older than the tax itself, and it was much more prevalent in the mid-twentieth-century discourse about the estate tax than it was at the century's end.[7] Scholars have also drawn attention to the unified government, with the presidency and both houses of Congress under the Republican Party. This truly was an important condition, but it had happened before under Eisenhower without a similar victory for rich people's movements. To explain the success of this movement, it is necessary to note that the Republican Party of 2001 was not the same as the Republican Party of, say, 1952. In the intervening decades, the party had been captured by anti-tax campaigners. And that capture can only be explained by the legacy of rich people's movements.

The War of Attrition

The movement entrepreneur who would do the most to shape the tactics of the estate tax repeal campaign in the 1990s was Grover Norquist. He was born in 1956 in the wealthy suburb of Weston, Massachusetts; his mother was a schoolteacher, and his father was an executive at Polaroid. Although he had conservative views as an adolescent, he was also an ordinary teenager who, in his own words, "always had long hair and thought that Janis Joplin was the high point of

Western civilization." In 1972, he was nearly ejected from a Nixon-for-President fundraiser because he looked like a hippie. Norquist did not fit into the conservative milieu.[8]

He found his niche at Harvard. His political views were out of step with most of his college peers—to his great amusement, the students who ran the *Harvard Crimson* even editorialized in favor of armed socialist revolution in third-world countries—but there were enough like-minded economic conservatives on campus to keep him company.[9] By his senior year, they were numerous enough to found the Harvard Libertarian Association and launch a libertarian newspaper of their own called the *Harvard Chronicle*. The debut issue featured a story by Norquist about a successful petition drive to put a tax limitation initiative before the Massachusetts legislature. "No one wore war paint or carried tomahawks, but on December 7 [1977], Massachusetts began another taxpayers' revolt," he wrote.[10] Norquist graduated two days after Proposition 13 made national headlines. The commencement speaker was the Russian dissident Alexander Solzhenitsyn, who delivered a bracing address deploring the spiritual surrender of Western civilization in the face of the global communist threat. It must have been an exciting time and place to be a young conservative.[11]

Norquist went to work immediately as an organizer for the NTU. It was an education in movement-building. His activism hitherto had consisted mainly of publishing newspapers. Now his job was to run the field campaign for a balanced budget amendment to the Constitution. In practice, this meant traveling around the country helping NTU members set up local affiliates and statewide organizations in order to press for a constitutional convention. He advised local affiliates on how to recruit ("Discuss taxpayer issues with the merchants and businessmen you know"), coached them on how to run meetings, and offered advice on tactics from letter-writing campaigns to press conferences, demonstrations, and ballot initiatives. Three months in, he was promoted to executive director.[12]

The experience gave him a taste for political organizing. Within a year he went back to Harvard for a degree in business administration, but his main purpose in returning to university seems to have been masterminding a conservative takeover of the College Republicans. After graduation and brief stint as a speechwriter for the U.S. Chamber of Commerce, he took a job with another grassroots lobbying organization. This was Citizens for America, funded by the Rite Aid drugstore tycoon Lewis Lehrman at the behest of President Reagan. The mission of the organization was to promote the president's agenda "on everything from Reagan's budget cuts to the landing of U.S. troops in Grenada," in the words of one reporter.[13] Lehrman, a sometime candidate for office, may have hoped it also would become an electoral vehicle. Norquist set to work once again organizing grassroots committees in congressional districts throughout the country.

He also used the opportunity to acquire training in revolutionary warfare. For all Norquist's mockery of the Ivy League rebels at the *Harvard Crimson*, some of their romantic third-worldism seems to have rubbed off on him. He was enchanted by the image of the mujahideen in Afghanistan, the contras in Nicaragua, and the guerrillas in Mozambique, Angola, and Laos who took up arms against Soviet-backed regimes. Somehow he persuaded Lehrman to sponsor a worldwide summit meeting of anticommunist guerrillas at a rebel base in Angola in June 1985. The summit meeting was an expensive flop—Lehrman eventually fired Norquist for squandering virtually the entire budget bringing people to Angola—but it won Norquist a lasting ally in Jonas Savimbi, the charismatic leader of the National Union for the Total Independence of Angola (UNITA). Norquist set to work learning from Savimbi.[14]

It is hard to imagine an unlikelier partnership. Norquist, with his suburban upbringing, his Harvard M.B.A., and his business-friendly résumé, was the very picture of an apologist for American capitalism. (A *Washington Post* reporter, noting the "gray suit and matching tie" that Norquist sported in his late twenties, described his look as that of a "60-year-old Rotarian.")[15] Savimbi, by contrast, was the picture of a third-world Marxist revolutionary. He had been forced out of medical school in Lisbon for consorting with Communist party militants. He had gone on to study revolutionary strategy in China, and he boasted Che Guevara, Mao Tse-tung, and Vo Nguyen Giap—whom he called "the greatest theoreticians, practitioners, martyrs, and heroes of revolution"—as personal acquaintances.[16] The motto of UNITA was "Socialism, Negritude, Democracy, and Nonalignment." But in 1975, a rival guerrilla organization called the Popular Movement for the Liberation of Angola (MPLA)—also nominally socialist, pan-African, democratic, and nonaligned—had seized the capital city Luanda; and now UNITA was engaged in a civil war against a Marxist regime that had the backing of Cuba and the Soviet Union. Savimbi did not mind taking aid from the CIA, and some American conservatives, who otherwise might not have felt favorably disposed toward socialism or negritude, figured that the enemy of their enemy was their friend. When Congress voted to block all funds for aid to UNITA, a handful of wealthy American conservatives began to remit private donations to Savimbi's organization. Norquist became a sort of courier between UNITA and the American right.[17]

In exchange, he received a crash course in how to organize an insurgent movement. Norquist returned to Angola again and again over the next few years. He led classes for the UNITA troops on political philosophy. He also engaged in long dialogues with Savimbi, who regaled him with the tactical lore he had learned from Che, Giap, and Mao. In late 1985, Norquist distilled some of their discussions into an article for the Heritage Foundation's *Policy Review* under Savimbi's byline. Norquist, channeling Savimbi, expounded "the five central

principles of guerrilla warfare": win the trust of the people; have a clear political program; maintain a unified command; live among the people; and forge
international alliances. He also described other lessons he had learned in the
struggle. Welcome allies who do not agree with you 100 percent. ("Yes, UNITA
receives aid from the Republic of South Africa.") Treat religious leaders as allies,
even if you are not particularly religious yourself, for the greatest organizational
resources of the revolutionary are "the religious faith and institutions of his
country's people." And evaluate particular campaigns as positional moves in a
larger strategy. The question is not whether a particular objective conforms to
your ideology, but whether it will strengthen your position for the next encounter with the enemy.[18]

This last lesson may have been the most important one that Norquist took
home. Savimbi played a long game; UNITA planned for a struggle that might
take decades. The revolution was a war of attrition in which the only goal was
to outlast the enemy. Savimbi told Norquist that "a central element" of his strategy was to "deny the colonial forces the revenues that finance their occupation."
Substitute "the welfare state" for "the colonial forces," and this could have been
a description of Norquist's strategy too. He took seriously the idea that he and
Savimbi were fighting on different fronts in the same war. He ditched the gray
suit and started wearing combat fatigues to his meetings in Washington, D.C.[19]

He also started applying some of Savimbi's principles to what he called the
"taxpayers' movement" in the United States.[20] He took a job in another Reagan-
inspired organization, this one called Americans for Tax Reform (ATR), and
quietly set about turning it from a short-term lobbying project focused on the
administration's priorities into an independent cadre of "revolutionaries" who
would wage a war of attrition against the American welfare state. He sought to
"defund the left" by cutting those federal programs that supported pro-welfare-
state constituencies. "We may be a minority in outlook," he said in 1991, "but a
lot of movements have started as minorities."[21] He was particularly keen to unite
the taxpayers' movement and the organized religious right. Observation of the
African American Civil Rights movement had convinced him of what he called
"the power of movements organized through churches." Weekly Sunday wor-
ship reinforced the cohesion of a movement. It also gave the movement leadership a regular channel for communication directly to the grassroots. In contrast,
he pointed out, "[T]here's no special place where the taxpayers meet on, say,
Wednesday."[22]

So he decided to create one. He convened the first Wednesday meeting in
the offices of ATR in early 1993. At first there were barely a dozen regulars. An
early participant described the meetings as more like a weekly sitcom than a serious forum: "a conservative version of *Seinfeld*, with people double-dipping into
the bagels and cream cheese." Journalists reported that it was "a fairly eccentric

affair" attended by "unhygienic libertarian types." The meeting matured as it grew. Norquist did not require adherence to his ideology, and did not limit the attendance list to taxpayer activists or eccentrics. He invited gun activists and anti-abortion activists as well. They referred others. Before long the Wednesday meeting became, in the words of David Brock, a conservative activist who attended in this period, "a who's who of conservative activists in town, representing about seventy interest groups, each with an effective grassroots operation."[23]

Estate tax repeal was not at first a priority. The focus was instead on targeting those aspects of the welfare state that funded constituencies of the left. "At the Wednesday Group sessions," Brock later recalled, "Grover announced that in dismantling the 'liberal welfare state,' we would target 'the weakest parts of the empire'—legal services for the poor and government support for the arts—just as the Cold War had been fought in remote villages in Mozambique."[24] The estate tax seemed ideologically odious to Norquist, but it was not a particularly strategic target. Abolishing this tax would not do much to defund the left. Nor, it first seemed, would it mobilize a large constituency on the right.

That was about to change.

The Death Tax and the Politics of Long-Term Care Insurance

The spur to mobilization was a proposal for national long-term care insurance. By the late 1980s, health policy experts were pointing out a looming crisis of care for America's elderly. The aging American population created more need than ever for long-term nursing care, and the rising cost of medical care meant that few seniors could afford it. Private insurers were not filling the gap. A 1992 study for the Health Insurance Association of America estimated that fewer than half of all seniors would qualify for private long-term care insurance by ordinary underwriting criteria. Advocates for the elderly, most notably the American Association of Retired Persons (AARP), had begun looking for ways to socialize the cost of long-term care. A national system of long-term care insurance, financed by tax revenues, fit the bill. The idea gained additional legitimacy when a bipartisan commission jointly appointed by Congress and the Bush administration—the so-called Pepper Commission—endorsed the idea in September 1990.[25]

Estate and gift taxes had particular appeal as a way to pay for long-term care. They were progressive taxes that very few voters would feel. The taxation of estates also had a kind of insurance logic: Because most people spend down their wealth at the end of life, an estate tax falls most heavily on those who die at the threshold of retirement and provides the rest of the wealthy with an implicit annuity that one economist has described as "Social Security for the rich."

Earmarking the tax revenues for long-term care would simply distribute the benefit more widely. There was also a symbolic symmetry in pairing death duties with end-of-life care. The two were often linked in policy discussions for no better reason than that they both seemed somehow to pertain to old people. In 1989, for example, the Brookings Institution economist Alice Rivlin mentioned "estate tax increases to finance long-term care expenses of the elderly" alongside "tobacco and alcohol taxes to finance health programs" and "energy-use fees to finance conservation and pollution" as earmarked taxes that might be acceptable to voters.[26] The logic of each pairing was not economic but rather cultural and political; voters might understand and accept a tax increase to pay for the care of the elderly if the tax were levied on the estates of the elderly.

Estate and gift taxes also polled well, probably because so few people paid them. One poll commissioned by the AARP in October 1989 presented respondents with various options for how to finance federal long-term care insurance, and found that "increasing estate and gift taxes" was a popular option (62 percent found it at least "somewhat acceptable"). The other options that cleared the majority threshold were increasing social security payroll taxes (59 percent found this acceptable, 78 percent if the increase was restricted to "those who earn over $48,000 a year") and increasing the federal income tax (51 percent).[27] On April 9, 1992, Representatives Henry Waxman (D-CA) and Richard Gephardt (D-MO) introduced a long-term care insurance bill (H. R. 4848) that included all three options. The bill would have expanded the Medicare program to create a new entitlement to long-term care. It was to be financed by an increase in payroll taxes, supplemented by a "long-term care tax" on unearned income, and an increase in estate tax.

It might have been done without incident but for a tactical error in the drafting of the bill. Rather than increase estate tax rates on the small minority of people who paid the tax, the authors of the bill proposed to increase estate tax revenues by expanding the tax to cover more people. The proposal would lower the exemption from $600,000 to $200,000. This provision would merely have restored the exemption to pre-ERTA levels, and Gephardt called it "a small price to pay" for long-term care insurance.[28] But it also would have been first time Congress had reduced the estate tax exemption since the depths of the Great Depression. It was received as an announcement that a historic bargain was about to be undone.

The backlash was nearly instantaneous. Gephardt's office was swamped with letters and phone calls. He responded by backing away from the proposal—he had not written the estate tax portion of the bill, he said, he did not support it, it was provisional, and anyway the bill was tabled. He also acknowledged that the protests had changed his mind. "I have received many comments pointing out problems with the estate tax provision that was included as one of these funding options," he said; "While this measure exempted 86 percent of seniors, these comments have convinced me that reducing the estate tax exemptions was not a good funding source."[29]

No systematic data on individual protesters are available, but they seem at first to have been property owners who were over the proposed threshold. Gephardt described them as family farmers and people with "larger estates." In other areas of the country, suburban homeowners joined in. The outcry was particularly strong in the Southern California suburbs of Orange County. This was the social milieu that had nurtured the greatest density of activists in prior rich people's movements, where many die-hard anticommunists still regarded any taxation of wealth with suspicion—and where housing values put the majority of homeowners at risk for the tax. "Under the Democratic leadership's definition of 'rich' for death-tax purposes, practically every homeowner in Orange County is 'rich,' because the average home value here is well over $200,000," editorialized the *Orange County Register*. "So the estate of nearly every homeowner hereabouts would be taxed heavily."[30]

The tabling of the long-term care bill did not quell the protests, however, because its immediate costs were not the only issue: Protesters saw it as a signal of policy changes yet to come. Many financial advisers and estate planning professionals assumed the estate tax expansion had been shelved only temporarily until after the November election, and advised their clients accordingly.[31] Conservative Republicans also sought to stoke these fears as the election approached. Gephardt's opponent in the 1992 election, Mack Holecamp, said the estate tax provision showed that Gepardt was "no friend of middle-class voters." Phyllis Schlafly called it an "estate tax time bomb." An op-ed in the conservative *Washington Times* warned of a Democratic "plot" to revive the bill after the election.[32] The Clinton campaign denied this allegation, but one of President Clinton's first actions after his inauguration was to appoint a task force on health care reform that, it was widely assumed, would take the recommendations of the Pepper Commission seriously. And in August 1993, the president signed a tax bill that increased estate tax rates by retroactively restoring a temporary top tax rate that had expired in December.[33]

Taxpayer activists began to mobilize. The NTU sued on behalf of its members to block the increase. It enlisted the help of the Landmark Legal Foundation, a conservative public- interest law firm, and hastily put together an argument that the estate tax increase violated the Fifth Amendment to the Constitution. "If the government succeeds in imposing these retroactive tax increases, one wonders what limits will remain on Washington's taxing powers," said a spokesperson for the legal team.[34]

Others began to mobilize in the legislative arena. The grassroots lobbying campaign was led by James L. Martin, a former congressional aide and small-time

Republican political consultant. In 1990, Martin had founded a membership organization of senior citizens called the 60 Plus Association to serve as "the conservative alternative to the American Association of Retired Persons." He saw the nominally nonpartisan AARP as a stalking horse for liberal Democrats and thought that conservative Republicans needed a nonpartisan seniors' organization of their own. "It's time seniors were no longer used as political pawns," he said. He quickly discovered what the AARP had long known: It was hard to mobilize seniors in the absence of a pressing policy threat. The 60 Plus Association thus lay dormant until 1992, when the estate tax finally presented a threat to which seniors responded. Martin rapidly began recruiting members by direct mail, and soon he claimed to have 425,000 members dedicated to the cause of estate tax repeal.[35]

Outside of the capital, estate planners played an important role in organizing the opposition. One leader was Harold Apolinsky, an Alabama estate-planning attorney. By most accounts, however, the central organizer was Patricia Soldano, a lifelong resident of Orange County who had a small business managing the finances of a handful of wealthy families. Prompted by the threat of estate tax increases in the Gephardt-Waxman long-term care bill, she began recruiting her clients and other wealthy families to support a campaign for repeal of the estate tax. She founded an organization called the Policy and Taxation Group to lobby for repeal, and another called the Center for the Study of Taxation to sponsor studies of the issue and to distribute research and talking points to support the case for repeal. She also began to recruit professional and trade associations to join the campaign for estate tax repeal.[36]

The activists who organized the movement do not appear to have been especially wealthy or powerful. Soldano was by all accounts an outsider to Washington.[37] The 60 Plus Association was at first a shoestring operation consisting of little more than Jim Martin and his mailing list. No one would mistake his typo-filled newsletters for the slick mass mailings of a professional grassroots lobbying organization like the AARP. ("For every 'Rockerfeller' [sic] being hit by this double tax there are thousands of mom and pop businesses and small farms in 50 states who are literally 'run out of business' by this unjust tax," read a typical mailer. Another warned grimly that "this particular tax is the third tenant [sic] of the *Communist Manifesto*.") What activists like Martin and Soldano had in common was not great personal wealth or Machiavellian political sophistication or even tremendous organizational resources. The resources would come with time, as more and more wealthy donors got on board. What they had in common at the beginning was simply the fact they had professional reasons for paying attention to the obscure politics of estate taxation and mailing lists that they could use to begin recruiting a movement.[38]

And in every case, the impetus to protest was the perceived threat that the cost of national health insurance would increase the taxation of wealth. Even Norquist credited the "sheer terror of Clinton's health care plan" with swelling the ranks of his Wednesday meetings.[39] It would soon contribute to the movement for estate tax repeal.

Making Political Opportunities

The first stand-alone bill to repeal the estate tax emerged from Orange County. Representative Christopher Cox (R-CA) introduced the Family Heritage Preservation Act on July 23, 1993. He had no cosponsors, and the bill was referred to the House Committee on Ways and Means, where it was shelved. The grassroots campaign gradually persuaded other congressmen to sign on as cosponsors of the bill. Norquist appears to have been particularly influential. As the midterm elections approached, he busied himself soliciting candidates to sign a "Taxpayer Protection Pledge," which obligated them to oppose income tax increases and also put them on record as tax fighters. Of the twenty-nine additional sponsors who ultimately signed on to the Cox bill between June and October 1994, twenty-six were also signers of ATR's pledge; ATR pledgers were almost ten times as likely as non-pledgers to sign on as cosponsors of estate tax repeal.[40]

The midterm elections of 1994 appeared to open a window of political opportunity, but the activists were not yet organized to take advantage of it. Republicans gained seats in the House and Senate, capturing the majorities of both. Almost all of the House Republicans had campaigned on the strength of the Contract with America, a pledge to support a long list of conservative legislative priorities that was reportedly drafted with Norquist's assistance. Insiders spoke confidently of a "Republican Revolution." When it came to the estate tax, however, the revolution fizzled. The contract included a commitment to increase the estate tax exemption from $600,000 to $750,000 and index it for inflation thereafter. This was a modest reform. The Congressional Research Service estimated that it "would increase the proportion of decedents exempt from taxation from about 97.5 percent to about 98 percent." To Norquist, who once said of the estate tax that he "would not cross the street" for anything short of repeal, it may have looked like a step backward.[41]

In the long run, however, grassroots organizing paid off. In 1995, the 60 Plus Association sponsored an "estate tax summit" to get business and taxpayer organizations on the same page. Trade associations and business groups began to coalesce. Martin began speaking on behalf of a "Kill the Death Tax Coalition" that claimed some forty-two member organizations. Soldano, who had a better ear for publicity, convened what she called the Family Business Estate Tax Coalition, led by the National Federation of Independent Businesses, but also including the National Association of Manufacturers, the American Farm Bureau, the National Cattlemen's Beef Association, the Food Marketing Institute, the Newspaper Association of America, and some three dozen more business and professional organizations.[42] These coalitions overlapped with the informal coalition at the Wednesday meetings of ATR. Norquist finally began calling for repeal of the estate tax. The members of the Family Business Estate Tax Coalition meanwhile began recruiting small businesspeople to write letters, lobby, and testify before Congress in favor of repeal.[43]

These organizations also began organizing taxpayers outside of Washington, D.C. By December 1995, a spokesman for the NTU estimated that there were 1,000 state and local think tanks and advocacy organizations in the conservative taxpayers' movement, most of them founded in the 1990s.[44] The rapid spread of such groups partly reflected a concerted effort of the ATR. "We want to have 13,000 taxpayer groups," Norquist said. "The goal is to have indigenous groups, with real local strength."[45] He also began helping conservative activists to set up state-level copies of the Wednesday meeting in dozens of states. Much like the Washington meeting, these were intended to create a regular forum where business conservatives and movement activists could share resources and work out a common program.[46] The loose coalitions that resulted did not resemble the inside lobbying organizations characteristic of elite tax politics. "The corporate guys in every state—the Chamber of Commerce—think the taxpayer groups are nutty," Norquist told activists.[47] But Norquist welcomed the nutty activists. They reminded him of the populist taxpayers' revolt that he had helped to organize in 1978. "Now the tax revolt is gathering momentum again," he wrote in the fall of 1997. "Republicans and taxpayer activists are now establishing coordinating committees in each congressional district dedicated to abolishing the estate and capital gains tax[es]."[48]

Estate tax repeal gradually gained momentum in Congress. There were three bills that called for estate tax repeal in the 103rd Congress, seven in the 104th Congress, and eighteen in the 105th. The growing influence of the estate tax repeal campaign can also be seen in the record of Cox's Family Heritage Preservation Act. At the time he introduced the bill in 1993, he found no cosponsors. Over the summer of 1994, he acquired twenty-nine. In 1995, he reintroduced the bill with 108 cosponsors. In 1997, he had 207. In February 1999, Representative Jennifer Dunn (R-WA) introduced a revised version of the bill called the Death Tax Elimination Act, this time with 244 cosponsors—indicating that it had more than enough votes to pass. Both houses voted to pass the bill; only a presidential veto stopped it. A House vote to override the veto in September 2000 fell just fourteen votes shy of the necessary two-thirds majority.

By that time, the promise to repeal the estate tax had become a core campaign plank of the Republican presidential candidate, George Bush. Campaign workers told Michael Graetz and Ian Shapiro that this issue "would garner Bush the greatest applause from the audiences during his campaign stump speeches."[49]

The election of George Bush appeared to open the door for repeal, and the advocates of estate tax repeal redoubled their outside lobbying. In early 2001, the American Conservative Union, the 60 Plus Association, and the NTLC held an outdoor press conference to present Congress with thousands of petition signatures and display the public testimony of "estate tax victims."[50] The ATR mobilized its network of state affiliates to demand that state legislators go on record in support of repeal. Norquist personally traveled around the country to help lobby state legislatures for resolutions of support. The goal, he explained to a reporter, was to have state legislators deliver these resolutions to reluctant members of Congress. The campaign won resolutions in Georgia, Michigan, North Dakota, and, perhaps most important, Montana, the home of Senate Finance Committee member Max Baucus (D), who had opposed the Death Tax Repeal Act of 1999, but who would reverse himself and vote for estate tax repeal in 2001.[51]

This campaign detour through the states was an unusual move for a Washington tax lobbyist. But it would have been familiar to activists in earlier rich people's movements. The most parsimonious explanation for why a well-funded, media-savvy organization like ATR would resort to this tactic is simply that activists had learned it in prior campaigns. It was the tactic that Norquist had first employed as a young activist in 1978, when his job was to organize the grassroots tax revolt to lobby state legislators for resolutions in favor of a constitutional convention.

A Century of Rich People's Movements

The passage of estate tax repeal as part of the Economic Growth and Tax Relief Reconciliation Act (EGTRRA) of 2001 surprised many social scientists who were schooled in democratic theory. How could democratically elected officials so publicly pass a law to benefit so few people at such great expense to so many? Thanks to a decade of research, we have several good answers, and the passage of this legislation is no longer especially mysterious. The repeal of the estate tax provided concentrated benefits to wealthy constituents and imposed only diffuse costs. Few interest groups bothered to mobilize against it. Nor did voters provide a counterweight. Members of Congress could and did craft the policy strategically to obfuscate its costs. Voters who might have opposed repeal possessed little information about the tax. Many voters also had inconsistent preferences—simultaneously for tax cuts, spending increases, and deficit reduction, or simultaneously for more expansive private property rights and less economic inequality—thereby creating an opportunity for elites to manipulate opinion by framing repeal in the most advantageous way. And many voters simply believed inheritance taxation to be morally wrong. Once members of Congress had made up their minds to pursue estate tax repeal, in short, there was little standing in their way.[52]

In light of this research, the question that remains is not why Congress voted for repeal. It is how repeal of the estate tax came to the attention of Congress in the first place—and especially why it did so as part of a public campaign involving collective petitions, testimony, press conferences, and grassroots organization far from Washington, D.C. This tactical repertoire was invented in the democratizing societies of the nineteenth century by people who wished to demonstrate their "worthiness, unity, numbers, and commitment" because they had few political resources *other* than their worthiness, unity, numbers, and commitment.[53] It is a surprise to find the movement repertoire used at the beginning of the twenty-first century in the service of the wealthiest 1 percent of Americans, who have teams of lobbyists, legal advisors, and think tanks to do their bidding—and whose chief political resource is surely not their numbers or their moral worthiness, but rather their ability to donate lots and lots of money.

Why did this campaign happen? The answer is illuminated by the broader history of campaigns to untax America's wealthy few. As with previous campaigns to repeal the estate tax, affluent protesters were thrown back on the social movement repertoire when a policy threat signaled the failure of politics as usual to protect their interests, and they picked up such tactics when entrepreneurs with experience in previous social movements taught them how. At the beginning of the twentieth century, those movement entrepreneurs were former Populists and Progressives. At the beginning of the twenty-first century, they were activists who drew on a movement tradition of their own. The twenty-first-century activists who repealed the estate tax were the inheritors of a century of rich people's movements.

CONCLUSION: THE CENTURY OF RICH PEOPLE'S MOVEMENTS

On election day, November 2, 2010, more than eight million Americans voted for congressional candidates who claimed to represent the Tea Party and its grassroots insurgency against the federal government.[1] Most of the Tea Party candidates won. Their victory marked a sea change in American government. Even before the winners were sworn in, reporters began to refer to the 112th Congress as "the Tea Party Congress." On the day of the swearing-in, the prominent Tea Party backer David Koch likened the electoral success of the Tea Party to the American Revolution. "It's probably the best grassroots uprising since 1776 in my opinion," he said.[2]

The proposals of the new Congress had little in common with the revolutionary slogans of 1776, but many of them would be familiar to activists who had participated in the grassroots uprisings on behalf of the rich in the twentieth century.

On January 5, for example, House Republicans introduced a "balanced budget amendment" that was really a tax limitation amendment—modeled on the precedents that the NTU and the NTLC had furnished in the 1970s. A flurry of other balanced budget amendment bills followed. On January 23, Senate Republicans, led by Orrin Hatch, introduced a tax limitation/balanced budget amendment bill of their own that was even more restrictive.[3]

The next day, Representatives Steve King (R-IA) and Rob Woodall (R-GA) introduced a one-sentence proposal to repeal the Sixteenth Amendment. On March 15, 2011, Representative Ron Paul (R-TX) introduced the Liberty Amendment, precisely as Willis Stone drafted it in 1956.[4]

And throughout the session, Republicans introduced bill after bill to cut top income tax rates and make estate tax repeal permanent. Many of these tax proposals were regressive enough that they might have made even an Andrew

Mellon blush. But they would have warmed the heart of J. A. Arnold if he could have lived to see them. They could almost have been copied from the 1927 program of the American Taxpayers' League.[5]

Thanks in part to proposals like these, the Tea Party Congress is likely to be remembered as one of the most conservative Congresses in American history. Scholars have described this rightward turn in Congress as "historic," as "a new phase in the extreme ideological polarization of U.S. politics," and as a "historically unprecedented development."[6] And they have pointed to unprecedented conditions to explain it. The historic segmentation of media markets is said to have allowed voters to surround themselves in closed and ideologically extreme social worlds. The influx of money into politics following the Supreme Court's decision in *Citizens United v. Federal Election Commission*, 558 U.S. 50 (2010), is said to have given an edge to ultraconservative candidates whose policy proposals flatter the pocketbook interests of the very richest Americans.[7]

Some new conditions like these are surely part of the explanation for how such radically inegalitarian tax policy proposals came to dominate the policy agenda of Congress. But these new conditions cannot be the whole story, because so many of the proposals themselves are old: not founding-fathers old, but early-twentieth-century old. They are the harvest of a century of rich people's movements.

Why Rich People's Movements Now?

What can we say about the sources of this new radicalism, and how long it is likely to be with us? The answers depend on a proper understanding of the history of rich people's movements.

Even commentators who recognize that the Tea Party has historical roots might be forgiven for thinking those roots do not go very deep. Social scientists have noticed other movements that share many of the hallmarks of rich people's movements—including the use of protest tactics by relatively affluent people; the fact that the activists were already fully enfranchised participants in the political system; and the fact that these activists seem to demand the preservation of comfortable consumer lifestyles, rather than the realization of some utopian vision of the future—and have argued that these are distinguishing characteristics of late-twentieth-century social movements. An influential body of scholarship on "new social movements" argues that protest movements took on these characteristics in postindustrial economies of the late twentieth century because economic development had made earlier agrarian and industrial class conflicts passé. The rising incomes of even ordinary wage earners made the late-twentieth-century United States into a consumer society. It is small wonder, to this way of thinking, that some protest movements today consist of affluent consumers protesting their taxes, rather than wage earners protesting their poverty.[8] Another body of scholarship argues that the professionalization of social movement organizations in the late twentieth century made possible a mainstreaming of social protest, by taming the more disruptive protesters and by standardizing tactics so that they became easier for ordinary citizens to learn and apply in new contexts. Some scholars have also credited, or blamed, the mass media for the spread of social movements to the middle classes. Television, for example, brought images of the 1960s protest movements to middle-class households around the country, and thereby taught a new style of politics to previously staid suburbanites.[9] All of these scholars describe how the economic and technological transformations of the twentieth century made the social movement repertoire available to ever-more affluent people. It is tempting to see the rich people's movements of our time as the endpoint of these transformations—the newest new social movement, the capstone on the social movement society, or the last ripple in the widening circle of people who have appropriated and repurposed the political techniques of the poor.[10]

Whatever the uses of theories like these for explaining the emergence of new social movements in the late twentieth century, they would miss the mark in accounting for rich people's movements, because rich people's movements are not that new. When the Texas tax clubs under the leadership of J. A. Arnold mobilized for tax cuts in the top brackets, they were not expressing the demands of suburban consumers in a postindustrial economy; they were advocating for the interests of rural bankers in a predominantly agrarian economy. When Edward Rumely and Vivien Kellems first began to commit civil disobedience in protest against the federal income tax, television had not yet brought images of the Civil Rights movement into the homes of millions of Americans. For much of the twentieth century, these movements relied on tactics that were decidedly old-fashioned even for their times. In the 1940s, Rumely used direct mail techniques to bypass existing civic associations and recruit directly, because that was the model that he had learned in the Progressive Party. In the 1950s, Kellems organized through women's clubs, argued on the basis of constitutional rights, and attempted to inspire imitators through civil disobedience, because those were the techniques she had learned from the fight for woman suffrage. In the 1960s, Willis Stone recruited supporters for the Liberty Amendment through fraternal organizations and veterans' organizations, because those were the organizations in which he had acquired his own civic education after the First World War. The tactics of all of these activists hearkened to the early decades of the twentieth century because these social movement entrepreneurs acquired their skills and organizing experience in social movement organizations of that era.

Many activists in rich people's movements know that their movements have deeper roots in the early twentieth century. In particular, they have often portrayed their movements as reactions to the so-called revolution of 1913. The ratification of the Sixteenth Amendment, according to these activists, was a turning point in the history of the United States. It marked the end of limited government and the beginning of a new era of expanding federal power. If any great social change of the twentieth century paved the way for rich people's movements, according to this story, it was not economic growth or the development of the postindustrial economy or the development of new communications technologies, but the growth of the federal budget; and that development, the story goes, was set in motion by the Sixteenth Amendment.[11]

This activist story also gets the causal dynamics wrong. It is true that rich people's movements would not have emerged in the absence of federal taxes on income and wealth. But such movements are not inevitable just because the Constitution authorizes progressive taxes. They did not emerge in direct response to the ratification of the Sixteenth Amendment. To contemporaries, there was no "revolution of 1913." It was not until after World War I that the dramatic consequences of the new federal income tax became clear. Nor did these movements grow in lock-step with the long-term expansion of the federal budget.

By comparing the campaigns described in this book, we can see instead that rich people's movements arose episodically in response to immediate policy threats. The particular policies that provoked protest were heterogeneous. The top statutory tax rates on income and wealth nevertheless give us a crude but serviceable index of policy threats to the rich. Figure 9.1 presents this index: It is a timeline of the founding dates of the campaigns covered in this book, superimposed on the top marginal rate of federal estate tax and the top marginal rate of personal income tax. The timeline includes the dates when major new campaigns were launched, although it does not include the founding date of every social movement organization that participated in these campaigns or every time that policy goals were revised. The multiple revisions of the Dresser amendment are omitted, as are spinoff organizations such as the Western Tax Council (which joined the campaign for tax limitation in 1938) or the Liberty Amendment Committee (which joined the campaign for income tax repeal in 1956). By fixing our attention on the timing of new campaigns, the figure illustrates the simple point that activists started these campaigns in the wake of policy threats. It was not heavy taxes that caused protest. It was rapid tax increases on the rich that did.

Two late-twentieth-century campaigns look like exceptions to the rule, but these exceptions are more apparent than real. The campaign to revive a tax limitation amendment in 1978, for example, began at a time when top rates of federal income and estate tax were stable. As chapter 7 showed, however, activists launched this campaign at that time in order to capitalize on an influential

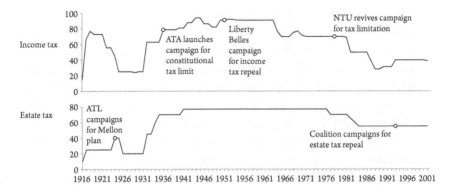

Figure 9.1 Top marginal tax rates and the initiation of rich people's movement campaigns, 1916–2001. *Source:* Top marginal income tax rates from Internal Revenue Service, *SOI Tax Stats*, Historical Table 23, downloaded January 10, 2012, from http://www.irs.gov/uac/SOI-Tax-Stats—Historical-Table-23; top marginal estate tax rates from Darien B. Jacobson, Brian G. Raub, and Barry W. Johnson, "The Estate Tax: Ninety Years and Counting," *SOI Bulletin*, 27, no. 2, 122; for the timeline of important campaign events, see text.

movement for state and local property tax limitation; and *that* movement was triggered by policy changes that produced a rapid increase in local property taxes. The revival of a campaign for estate tax repeal in 1993, at a time when estate tax rates had not changed for almost a decade, also looks like an exception to the rule. As chapter 8 showed, however, the activists who inaugurated that campaign were responding to a *proposed* increase in the estate tax, and their movement gained adherents when a previously scheduled expiration of the top tax rate was revoked. Even these campaigns were triggered by policy threats.

History teaches us that policy threats are necessary conditions for the emergence of rich people's movements. Such threats help to explain not just when people felt aggrieved enough to protest taxes on the rich, but also *who* felt aggrieved enough to support tax cuts for the rich. In every case, the pool of potential recruits extended well below the top tax brackets. The non-rich sympathizers, however, always had particular reasons to see top tax rates as threatening—from the farm mortgage bankers of 1924 who feared that high tax rates advantaged their competitors, to the married women of 1952 who saw that they were subject to higher marginal tax rates than their husbands, to the upper-middle-income taxpayers of 1978 who saw that inflation could push them into higher income tax brackets. Many people like these campaigned for tax cuts in the top brackets because they believed they were also protecting their own economic security.

These movements took advantage of the structure of political opportunities established by the American constitutional order, which may help to explain why they seem so distinctively American. In Western Europe, affluent people who feared taxes on the rich in the twentieth century sometimes started new political parties. But they rarely used the sort of populist tactics employed in the United States, and they never made the sort of constitutional arguments that characterized the American movement.[12] Perhaps it is unsurprising that the American rich and their allies turned to social movement organizing and interest group lobbying instead of third-party politics; the combination of direct presidential elections, single-member districts, and the winner-takes-all electoral system make it difficult for small political parties to achieve anything in the United States. But there is more to the explanation than that. These political institutions merely create obstacles to founding new political parties. They do not dictate which alternative to party politics will be pursued by threatened people.[13]

Why did policy threats to the rich provoke grassroots movements instead of conventional interest-group lobbying? Given the ease with which many rich people have secured selective tax privileges by back-room lobbying, the choice to pursue universalistic benefits for all rich people by means of public grassroots lobbying campaigns is puzzling. The solution to this puzzle is tradition. The rich and their allies joined grassroots social movement campaigns because that is what they were recruited and taught to do by experienced movement entrepreneurs. Those entrepreneurs were passing on tactical skills and lore that they had learned in other movements. To call this set of political practices a tradition is to say that it is more than merely a recurrent phenomenon. It is to say that similar patterns recur because people learn from and imitate the past.

It may be that all social movements rest on a bedrock of tradition. For rich people's movements, however, the existence of a social movement tradition was almost certainly indispensable. Short-term causes such as policy threats were necessary, but not sufficient, conditions to explain mobilization. Social movement tactics have a history; they must be passed down in order to become available to particular people at a particular time. It is doubtful whether rich people's movements would exist at all today if activists did not have a long movement tradition to draw on.

Under What Conditions Do They Win?

The history of rich people's movements may also tell us about their prospects for victory in the future. Even the wildest optimists in the Tea Party Caucus probably did not expect their proposals to become law, at least as long as the Democratic Party retained the presidency and the majority in the Senate. But the comparison of past rich people's movements shows that such radical proposals may influence policies even when they are not enacted. Rich people's movements in the twentieth century made extreme demands that made moderate groups appear comparatively reasonable. Sometimes they also used tactics that threatened public order—for example, by calling on businesses to disobey the Internal Revenue Service, or plausibly threatening to call a constitutional convention that could throw American politics into turmoil—and thereby permitted moderate conservatives to sell their own preferred policies as ways to co-opt an unruly movement and restore order. The Tea Party may have similar effects. Its activists have not won the war against the income tax, nor are they likely to repeal the Sixteenth Amendment. By keeping radical tax proposals on the policy agenda, however, they have positioned a radical flank for battles to come.

The history of rich people's movements shows that the mobilization of a radical flank can indeed influence the shape of federal tax policy. Influential Republican politicians sometimes felt compelled to propose tax cuts in order to obviate the need for more radical proposals to repeal the Sixteenth Amendment. The Republican chairman of the House Ways and Means Committee, Daniel Alden Reed of New York, made this argument explicitly to his collegues in 1944. "[T]he movement to limit federal tax rates by constitutional amendment should be noted," he wrote; "One way to meet this issue is by voluntary Congressional action to establish moderate tax rate levels."[14] So did the presidential candidate Dwight David Eisenhower in 1952, when he wrote that "a prudent and positive administration should be able to approach the goal which the amendment seeks without the difficulty and dangers involved in the adoption or continuing operation of such an amendment to our Constitution."[15] There is no evidence that rich people's movements had any direct influence on legislation under these leaders. But in a handful of other instances, including the Revenue Act of 1926, the ERTA of 1981, and the EGTRRA of 2001, there *is* evidence—in the timing of the laws, in the geographic distribution of legislators' support, and in the statements of some members of Congress—that at least some provisions of the law were intended as responses to movement demands. These acts legislated some of the largest tax cuts in American history. So it is that rich people's movements, through their influence on the ERTA and the EGTRRA, made a small but real contribution to the growing income inequality—the rise of the so-called 1 percent—that is one of the most important social changes of our time.

Sometimes rich people's movements had an impact, but at other times, the radical rich found themselves isolated and powerless. Their failure to influence policy is most evident in the case of the Sixteenth Amendment repealers. The activists of the American Taxpayers' Association and the Committee for Constitutional Government tried for two decades to bend federal tax policy toward greater inequality, with no measurable success. Their peak years of mobilization corresponded to the years when federal income tax rates were highest, and yet there is little evidence that they were able to pull top tax rates down. It is possible that these movements may have exercised a kind of diffuse cultural influence, and thereby helped to restrain policymakers by swaying public opinion against progressive taxation; perhaps federal revenues would have grown even more rapidly in the absence of their grassroots pressure. History does not give us a comparison case that would provide the critical test of this hypothesis. But it is clear that, in many instances, their efforts had no immediate impact. Consider the Liberty Amendment campaign. The peak years of the Liberty Amendment Committee coincided with one of the biggest income tax cuts in American history, but the activists could claim no credit for the Kennedy-Johnson tax cuts. Their radical posture condemned them to stand on the sidelines while liberal technocrats cut rich people's taxes.

Why were these movements sometimes so influential and other times so impotent? The comparison of campaigns shows that geographically dispersed grassroots mobilization made a difference. Activists sometimes had particular influence when they were able to mobilize in congressional swing districts, as when the tax clubs swayed the votes of Representatives Green and Garner in 1926. As the comparisons across states have shown, policy crafting was also crucial for allowing these activists to get tax cuts for the rich on the policy agenda. Some tax cuts for the rich could not get a serious hearing because they were too politically costly. Activists had the greatest impact when they were willing to craft their policy demands to obscure these costs, and package their favored tax cuts with additional policy benefits for new allies.

But to move beyond agenda access to influence legislation required more than clever policy crafting. It also required a critical mass of ideological allies in Congress and the presidency. There were only three presidents in the last century who allied themselves openly with rich people's movements—Calvin Coolidge, Ronald Reagan, and George W. Bush—and it was during their administrations that these movements exercised the greatest sway over legislative outcomes. The late-twentieth-century movement for estate tax repeal provides a critical test of presidential influence. Activists managed to get the Death Tax Elimination Act through both houses of Congress, only to have it vetoed by President Bill Clinton in 2000. Estate tax repeal would become law the following year, when President Bush signed the EGTRRA. The support of the president made the difference.

The program of the party that controlled Congress mattered too. Both the Revenue Act of 1926 and the EGTRRA of 2001 passed Congress when it was united under conservative Republican control. The ERTA of 1981 does not quite fit this pattern. It was passed by a divided Congress, with the help of some Democratic votes in the House. Even in this case, however, it was near-unanimous Republican support that made it possible; and congressional Democrats were under extraordinary pressure from a popular Republican president and an assertive grassroots campaign that nearly called a constitutional convention.

Rich people's movements, in short, may influence policy when their partisan allies have control of elected policymaking bodies. For this reason, the most important legacy of rich people's movements for American politics may be the capture of the Republican Party by veteran activists of these movements in the twenty-first century. This also may be the most important lesson of rich people's movements for students of other American social movements. Sociologists know that activists are most likely to win collective benefits from policymakers when those policymakers are their partisan allies. But our most successful theoretical models of social movements persist in treating the party in power as an external condition, like the weather. The lesson that social movement scholars have drawn from their studies is that a movement may be most influential when its grassroots campaign is timed to match a window of political opportunity opened by its partisan allies in office.[16] The most astute activists in twentieth-century rich people's movements saw the same historical pattern, but they drew a different conclusion. The lesson they drew was not that they should time their actions carefully, or wait for partisan allies to show up and open a window of political opportunity. It was that they should take over a political party.

The Century of Rich People's Movements

The first century of rich people's movements is over. Rich people's movements emerged in response to big wartime increases in the progressive rates of income tax and estate tax; comparable tax increases are almost unimaginable today. The most influential social movement entrepreneurs who led these movements acquired their skills in social movement organizations of the Progressive Era, and those movements and organizations are mostly long gone too. Rich people's movements have been thoroughly institutionalized and thereby tamed. Many former activists are now well entrenched in the Republican Party and its allied think tanks, and their tactics are now correspondingly oriented toward inside lobbying. Some movement goals remain unrealized only because they are nigh unachievable. The barriers to amending the Constitution are so high, for example, that the Sixteenth Amendment will almost certainly remain unrepealed. For all of these reasons, it is tempting to think that the story told in this book is at an end.

I think it is much more likely that the story of rich people's movements is just beginning. The Tea Party may prove to have been a flash in the pan. The long-term trends, however, suggest that something like it will be back. The population of the United States is growing older. The cost of caring for our elders and our sick loved ones continues to rise. For these reasons, the pressure on the federal budget is unlikely to abate. Pressure on the budget means that pressure for tax increases is unlikely to go away; and the threat of tax increases, in turn, is likely to stimulate more protest. Even when a tax increase can be targeted to a narrow segment of the richest Americans, it is likely to provoke a broader backlash, if people lower in the income distribution believe that this policy change signals further tax increases to come. People need not be dupes in order to protest on behalf of others who are richer than they are. The activists and supporters of rich people's movements were defending their own real interests, as they saw them. A tax increase on the richest 1 percent may be perceived by many upper-middle-income property owners as the first step in a broader assault on property rights. When it is so perceived, we can expect a movement in defense of the rich.

Knowledge of the history of rich people's movements will not allow us to predict the date when these movements will arise, or who exactly will join them. Such movements do not arrive like clockwork, any more than tax increases do. What we can predict is that some people will be ready to protest when policy threats come. We can also predict that some skilled movement entrepreneurs will be ready to help them organize. The proliferation of professional tax protest organizations since the 1970s has given rise to a generation of skilled movement entrepreneurs whose experience in rich people's movements equips them for future campaigns. When policy threats make people ready to protest, there will be no shortage of movement entrepreneurs who have the skills and the mailing lists to recruit them.

No doubt the rich people's movements of the future will also surprise us. They will exploit new technologies and organizing techniques. They will draw on some very old arguments and policy ideas, but they will recombine them and thereby invent some new ones. They will craft their policy proposals to recruit strange-bedfellows coalitions, just as their predecessors did. We can be confident that they will also continue to have all of the characteristics that so baffled observers of rich people's movements in the twentieth century. They will use the traditional tactics of the poor on behalf of tax cuts for the rich. They will behave like outsiders, but demand policies designed to benefit people who are consummate insiders in American politics. They will include many protesters who look unusually well heeled, and who will demand collective benefits for people even better off than themselves.

Rich people's movements have a permanent place in the American political bestiary. As long as one of our great political parties is programmatically allied with the radical rich, it is safe to predict that rich people's movements will continue to influence public policy in ways that preserve—and perhaps even increase—the extremes of inequality in America.

NOTES

Front Matter

1. Kate Zernike, "With Tax Day as Theme, Tea Party Groups Demonstrate," *New York Times*, April 15, 2010; "Tea Party Rallies Across the Country," *Sacramento Bee*, April 15, 2010, http://www.sacbee.com/2010/04/15/2681967/tea-party-rallies-across-the-country.html; Amy Gardner and Mark Ruane, " 'Tea Party' Protesters Gather in Washington to Rally against Taxes, Spending," *Washington Post*, April 16, 2010, http://www.washingtonpost.com/wp-dyn/content/article/2010/04/15/AR2010041503344.html; Teddy Davis, "Tea Party Activists Unveil 'Contract from America,' " *ABC News*, April 15, 2010, http://abcnews.go.com/Politics/tea-party-activists-unveil-contract-america/story?id=10376437.
2. Edward Ashbee, "Bewitched—The Tea Party Movement: Ideas, Interests, and Institutions," *The Political Quarterly*, 82, no. 2 (2011), 159; Skocpol and Williamson write of Tea Party activists that "it was the progressive policy agenda of Barack Obama that triggered their mobilization." Theda Skocpol and Vanessa Williamson, *The Tea Party and the Remaking of Republican Conservatism* (Oxford, UK, and New York: Oxford University Press, 2012), 31. See also Kate Zernike, *Boiling Mad: Inside Tea Party America* (New York: Times Books, 2010).
3. Brad DeLong, "In Which Mr. Deling Responds to Someone Who Might Be Professor Todd Henderson," 2010, http://delong.typepad.com/sdj/2010/09/in-which-mr-deling-responds-to-someone-who-might-be-professor-todd-henderson.html. On the income distribution of the protesters, see Zernike, *Boiling Mad*, 227; on recent income trends in the U.S., see Jacob S. Hacker and Paul Pierson, "Winner-Take-All Politics: Public Policy, Political Organization, and the Precipitous Rise of Top Incomes in the United States," *Politics and Society* 38, no. 2 (2010): 152–204.
4. Kevin Arcenaux and Stephen P. Nicholson, "Who Wants to Have a Tea Party? The Who, What, and Why of the Tea Party Movement," *PS: Political Science and Politics* 45, no. 4 (2012): 707; Christopher Parker, "2010 Multi-state Survey on Race and Politics," University of Washington Institute for the Study of Ethnicity, Race, and Sexuality, 2010, http://depts.washington.edu/uwiser/racepolitics.html; Skocpol and Williamson, *Tea Party*, 68–9. David Koch, a major donor to organizations affiliated with the Tea Party, has attributed the president's policy agenda in part to his Kenyan ancestry; see Matthew Continetti, "The Paranoid Style in Liberal Politics: The Left's Obsession with the Koch Brothers," *The Weekly Standard* 16, no. 28 (April 4, 2011), http://www.weeklystandard.

com/articles/paranoid-style-liberal-politics_555525.html. On this point Koch appears to be echoing Dinesh D'Souza, "How Obama Thinks," *Forbes Magazine*, September 27, 2010, http://www.forbes.com/forbes/2010/0927/politics-socialism-capitalism-private-enterprises-obama-business-problem.html.

5. See Jonathan Rauch, "How Tea Party Organizes without Leaders," *National Journal*, September 11, 2010, http://www.nationaljournal.com/njmagazine/cs_20100911_8855. php; Ben McGrath, "The Movement: The Rise of Tea Party Activism," *The New Yorker*, February 1, 2010, http://www.newyorker.com/reporting/2010/02/01/100201fa_fact_ mcgrath?currentPage=all. Zernike, *Boiling Mad*, 13–23, presents evidence that some people who became Tea Party activists were already protesting prior to Santelli's famous rant; but she argues that the broadcast contributed to the spread of the movement.

6. Mark Lilla, "The Tea Party Jacobins," *New York Review of Books*, May 27, 2010, http://www. nybooks.com/articles/archives/2010/may/27/tea-party-jacobins/; see also Anthony DiMaggio, *The Rise of the Tea Party: Political Discontent and Corporate Media in the Age of Obama* (New York: Monthly Review Press, 2011).

7. Many commentators have noticed other parallels between the Tea Party and earlier political phenomena. Zernike, *Boiling Mad*, 57–8, likens the Tea Partiers to the middle-class populist protests of the 1970s; Skocpol and Williamson, *Tea Party*, 81–2, argue that the Tea Party represents a rebirth of the Republican conservative movement of the 1960s; Charles Postel, "The Tea Party in Historical Perspective: A Conservative Response to a Crisis of Political Economy," in *Steep: The Precipitous Rise of the Tea Party*, eds. Lawrence Rosenthal and Christine Trost (Berkeley and Los Angeles: University of California Press), 29–31, emphasizes parallels with the Liberty League and the John Birch Society; Chip Berlet, "Reframing Populist Resentments in the Tea Party Movement," in *Steep*, eds. Rosenthal and Trost, identifies similarities between the rhetoric of the Tea Party and that of various other movements that have been called "populist"; and Ronald P. Formisano, *The Tea Party: A Brief History* (Baltimore: Johns Hopkins University Press, 2012), 17, less plausibly links the Tea Party to a "third party/independent tradition" in American politics stretching back to the early nineteenth century. None of these accounts notes the continuity between the Tea Party and the long prior history of protest movements against progressive taxation.

8. Frances Fox Piven and Richard Cloward, *Poor People's Movements: Why They Succeed, How They Fail* (New York: Vintage, 1978). Their most provocative argument was that attempts to create formal membership organizations of the poor are invariably demobilizing: Because poor people are poor, their organizations must depend for resources and legitimacy on external constituencies that discourage mass mobilization and tactical militancy. Subsequent scholarship has documented exceptions to this generalization. Some poor people's organizations are apparently able to sustain an orientation toward militant mass mobilization over considerable spans of time, in part because some external patrons are more supportive of such mobilization than Piven and Cloward assumed. A few highlights of the empirical literature are Daniel M. Cress and David A. Snow, "Mobilization at the Margins: Resources, Benefactors, and the Viability of Homeless Social Movement Organizations," *American Sociological Review* 61, no. 6 (1996): 1089–1109; Debra Minkoff, "Bending with the Wind: Strategic Change and Adaptation by Women's and Racial Minority Organizations," *American Journal of Sociology* 104, no. 6 (1999): 1666–1703; Edward T. Walker and John D. McCarthy, "Legitimacy, Strategy, and Resources in the Survival of Community-based Organizations," *Social Problems* 57, no. 3 (2010) : 315–40; Kim Voss and Rachel Sherman, "Breaking the Iron Law of Oligarchy," *American Journal of Sociology*, 106, no. 2 (2000): 303–49.

9. A typical rich person is no doubt more likely to feel popular than a typical poor person, because he or she is more likely to be surrounded by flattering admirers, but rich people are even more unpopular than poor people in the abstract. The American National Election Study, for example, asks voters to rate their warmth of feeling toward various groups on a "feeling thermometer" that runs from 0 to 100. In 2008, "rich people" received an average

rating of 58, indicating that they were substantially less popular than "middle-class people" (77), "poor people" (74), and "black people" (72), though more popular than such despised groups as "Congress" (54), "big business" (54), "Muslims" (52), "gay men and lesbians" (51), "illegal immigrants" (44), and "atheists" (39). These are my own calculations from the ANES 2008 Time Series Study; see Arthur Lupia, Jon A. Krosnick, Pat Luevano, Matthew DeBell, and Darrell Donakowski, *User's Guide to the ANES 2008 Time Series Study* (Ann Arbor, MI, and Palo Alto, CA: University of Michigan and Stanford University, 2009).

10. For example, as Charles Tilly observed, etymological evidence strongly suggests that wage earners invented the tactic of the strike independently on multiple occasions; Charles Tilly, *From Mobilization to Revolution* (New York: Random House, 1978), 159.

11. Lipset and Raab's concept of "cultural baggage" (1970: 90, 487–92) is in fact somewhat narrower than my concept of tradition, insofar as their concept refers only to "manners and morals," or the symbols and ritual practices of private life, and not to learned strategies, skills, or organizational styles. They use the metaphor of baggage in order to make the point that such cultural legacies as Protestantism do not cause right-wing behavior; they are "less the motivation than the excuse for nativist bigotry—its 'cultural baggage' rather than its engine": Seymour Martin Lipset and Earl Raab, *The Politics of Unreason: Right-Wing Extremism in America, 1790-1970* (Chicago: University of Chicago Press, 1970), 90, 487–92. My thinking on the role of tradition in social movements was more influenced by Charles Payne, *I've Got the Light of Freedom: The Organizing Tradition and the Mississippi Freedom Struggle* (Berkeley, CA: University of California Press, 2007), who documents an "organizing tradition" consisting of specific interactional skills and organizational styles that was handed down through generations of activism. I am also influenced by Edward Shils, *Tradition* (Chicago: University of Chicago Press, 1980), and by more recent theories that depict political culture as a repertoire or toolkit from which activists select skills, styles, and strategies; see Charles Tilly, *Contentious Performances* (Cambridge, UK, and New York: Cambridge University Press, 2008); Ann Swidler, "Culture in Action: Symbols and Strategies," *American Sociological Review* 51, no. 2 (1986): 273–86.

Introduction

1. "California T Parties Score Hit," *American Progress* 7, no. 5 (November–December 1962), 6.

2. In fact, at least in the late-twentieth-century United States, it is the picture of poor people marching in the street that is the exception; see Doug McAdam, Robert J. Sampson, Simon Weffer, and Heather MacIndoe, "'There Will Be Fighting in the Streets': The Distorting Lens of Social Movement Theory," *Mobilization* 10, no. 1 (2005): 1–18.

3. My inventory of state resolutions comes from a variety of sources including U.S. Senate and House of Representatives Joint Economic Committee, *The Proposed 23rd Amendment to the Constitution to Repeal the 16th Amendment to the Constitution Which Provides That Congress Shall Have Power to Collect Taxes on Incomes* (Washington, D.C.: Government Printing Office, 1961); and James V. Saturno, *A Balanced Budget Constitutional Amendment: Background and Congressional Options*, Congressional Research Service Report No. 97-379 (Washington, D.C.: Congressional Research Service, 1997). These sources were supplemented by reference to archival sources including Peter Knight to Andrew Mellon, September 13, 1927 (RG 56, Entry 191, Box 165), and to *American Progress Magazine*, *Freedom Magazine*, and *Break Free with 23 News*. I calculated the number of *New York Times* articles from a full-text search of the ProQuest *Historical New York Times* database for articles mentioning any social movement organizations on this list: American Bankers' League, the American Taxpayers' League, the American Taxpayers' Association, the Committee for Constitutional Government, the Western Tax Council, the Liberty Belles,

the Organization to Repeal Federal Income Taxes, the Liberty Amendment, the National Taxpayers Union, the National Tax Limitation Committee, Americans for Tax Reform, the 60 Plus Association, and the Family Business Estate Tax Coalition.

4. See Leonard L. Richards, *Gentlemen of Property and Standing: Anti-Abolition Mobs in Jacksonian America* (New York and Oxford, UK: Oxford University Press, 1970); Susan E. Marshall, *Splintered Sisterhood: Gender and Class in the Campaign against Woman Suffrage* (Madison, WI: University of Wisconsin Press, 1997).

5. See, e.g., Anthony Oberschall, *Social Conflict and Social Movements* (New York: Prentice-Hall, 1973); Herbert H. Haines, "Black Radicalization and the Funding of Civil Rights: 1957-1970," *Social Problems* 32, no. 1 (1984): 31–43.

6. In other words, I define rich people's movements in terms of the relative socioeconomic status of their intended beneficiaries, *not* in terms of the socioeconomic status of their participants. It is an empirical finding of this study that the participants in rich people's movements, so defined, were, on average, relatively high in socioeconomic status, though not as high in status as their intended beneficiaries.

7. Edward Bellamy, *Looking Backward: 2000-1887* (Boston: Ticknor and Company, 1888), 341. Bellamy did not make a very specific quantitative prediction, but he imagined that the increase in per capita wealth from 1887 to 2000 would be "not greater, for example, than that between the poverty of this country during the earliest colonial period of the seventeenth century and the relatively great wealth it had attained at the close of the nineteenth" (385). This prediction was too conservative: With the benefit of hindsight, we can state with reasonable confidence that it *was* greater. The estimates published by the economic historian Angus Maddison, for example, imply that real GDP per capita in the territory now occupied by the United States increased eightfold from 1600 to 1887, and ninefold from 1887 to 2000: see Angus Maddison, *The World Economy, vol. 2: Historical Statistics* (Paris: Organisation for Economic Co-operation and Development, 2006), 465–7.

8. Alexis de Tocqueville, *Democracy in America*, trans. Henry Reeve (New York: Edward Walker, 1850), 249, 259. The British politician James Bryce, for example, noted in 1888 that "Europeans, already prepared to expect to find the tyranny of the majority a characteristic sin of democratic nations, have been accustomed to think of the United States as disgraced by it"; he devoted a chapter of his popular book on American politics to refuting this charge. James Bryce, *The American Commonwealth, Volume II*, Second Edition (New York: Macmillan, 1891), 337.

9. Tocqueville, *Democracy in America*, 226. See Thomas Manson Norwood, *Plutocracy, or, American White Slavery: A Politico-Social Novel* (New York: Metropolitan, 1888); Leslie Chase, *Plutocracy* (New York: Grafton, 1910); Milford Wriarson Howard, *The American Plutocracy* (New York: Holland, 1895); John Calvin Reed, *The New Plutocracy* (New York: Abbey, 1903).

10. Thomas Paine, *The Rights of Man, Part the Second: Combining Principle and Practice*, third edition (London: J. S. Jordan, 1792), 142, 146.

11. Simon Kuznets, "Economic Growth and Income Inequality," *American Economic Review* 45, no. 1 (1955): 9.

12. Examples of studies that use absolute thresholds include Pitirim Sorokin, "American Millionaires and Multi-Millionaires: A Comparative Statistical Study," *Journal of Social Forces* 3, no. 4 (1925): 627–40; Lisa Keister, *Getting Rich: America's New Rich and How They Got That Way* (New York: Cambridge University Press, 2005). This method is useful for some purposes, but it is ill suited for a study of political struggles over income and wealth shares in the economy, and especially for a study that compares the politics of distribution over a long span of time, because the meaning of a million dollars has changed dramatically with changes in the wealth distribution over the twentieth century. Examples of studies that use relative thresholds include most studies of the power elite (see C. Wright Mills, *The Power Elite*, Oxford, UK, and New York: Oxford University Press, 1956; G. William Domhoff, *Who Rules America? Power and Politics in the Year 2000*, Mountain View, CA:

Mayfield, 1998) and many recent studies of the politics of economic inequality (see esp. Hacker and Pierson, "Winner-Take-All Politics").

13. "Potential beneficiaries" include those income tax units or individual decedents, respectively, who would enjoy the direct benefit of a tax cut if the movement's demands became law. I do not here evaluate any claims about indirect benefits or costs of such tax cuts, such as the claim that they might benefit the poor by stimulating economic growth.

The next to last column reports the number of tax returns above the threshold targeted for cuts (from Internal Revenue Service, *Statistics of Income*, various years) as a percentage of all income tax units in the United States, including individuals and couples who did not file tax returns (from Atkinson, Piketty, and Saez, "Top Incomes," table A.3). When the exact number of returns in the bracket targeted for cuts cannot be calculated from published aggregate statistics, the number here is an upper bound. Calculations reflect movement demands as of the first year of the campaign; both the policy content of the demands and their distributional implications often shifted over the course of a single campaign.

The last column reports taxable estate tax returns as a percentage of all adult deaths. When the estates targeted for tax cuts did not include all taxable decedents, the number reported here is an upper bound. The figures for 1938 to 2000 are from Internal Revenue Service, *Statistics of Income Bulletin*, Historical Table 17. The figures for 1925 are from the Bureau of Internal Revenue, *Statistics of Income, 1925*, p. 78, table 2, and *Statistical Abstract of the United States, 1973*, p. 51, table 65. The denominator for 1925 reflects all deaths, not all adult deaths. Calculations reflect movement demands as of the first year of the campaign; both the policy content of the demands and their distributional implications may have shifted somewhat over the course of a single campaign.

14. The list excludes twenty-first-century phenomena such as the Tea Party and the campaign for the so-called Fair Tax. It also excludes the grassroots "Flat Tax" lobby that emerged in conjunction with the presidential campaign of Steve Forbes in 1996. Sources that proved most instructive included W. Elliot Brownlee, *Federal Taxation in America: A Short History* (Cambridge, UK, and Washington, D.C.: Cambridge University Press and Woodrow Wilson Center Press, 1996); id., "Historical Perspective on U.S. Tax Policy toward the Rich" in *Does Atlas Shrug? The Economic Consequences of Taxing the Rich, ed. Joel B. Slemrod* (Cambridge, MA: Harvard University Press, 2000), 29–73; Sidney Ratner, *Taxation and Democracy in America* (New York: Octagon Books, 1980); Mark H. Leff, *The Limits of Symbolic Reform: The New Deal and Taxation, 1933-1939* (New York: Cambridge University Press, 1984); John Witte, *The Politics and Development of the Federal Income Tax* (Madison, WI: University of Wisconsin Press, 1985); Sara Diamond, *Roads to Dominion: Right-Wing Movements and Political Power in the United States* (New York: Guilford, 1995); Lipset and Raab, *Politics of Unreason*; Jerome Himmelstein, *To the Right: The Transformation of American Conservatism* (Berkeley, CA: University of California Press, 1992); Lisa McGirr, *Suburban Warriors: The Origins of the New American Right* (Princeton, NJ: Princeton University Press, 2001); George Nash, *The Conservative Intellectual Movement in America since 1945* (New York: Basic Books, 1976); Michael Graetz and Ian Shapiro, *Death by a Thousand Cuts: The Fight over Taxing Inherited Wealth* (Princeton, NJ: Princeton University Press, 2005).

15. As of 1951, when Vivien Kellems and Corinne Griffith announced the beginning of a campaign to repeal the income tax, over 66 percent of the financial benefit from repeal would have accrued to the highest-income 16 percent of all tax units in the country (including non-filers). The income tax data for this calculation come from Internal Revenue Service, *Statistics of Income: Individual Income Tax Returns for 1954* (Washington, D.C.: Author), 80; and the denominator (all tax units in the U.S.) comes from Anthony B. Atkinson, Thomas Piketty, and Emmanuel Saez, "Top Incomes in the Long Run of History: Data Appendix," http://www.econ.berkeley.edu/~saez/atkinson-piketty-saezJEL09series.xls, accessed October 2, 2010, table A.3.

16. These quotations concerning the "rich" or "rich men" are from Vivien Kellems, *Toil, Taxes, and Trouble* (New York: E. P. Dutton, 1954), 58; Robert B. Dresser, *Brief in Support of Proposed Constitutional Amendment Limiting the Power of Congress to Impose Taxes on Incomes, Inheritances and Gifts to a Maximum Rate of 25%* (New York: Committee for Constitutional Government, Inc., 1943), 10; and American Bankers' League, "Iowa Tax Clubs Before House Ways and Means Committee," October 25, 1925, RG 56, Entry 191, Box 163. For more implicit praise of the wealthy, see J. A. Arnold, *The Desire to Own* (Washington, D.C.: American Taxpayers' Association, 1983); Lewis K. Uhler, *Setting Limits: Constitutional Control of Government* (Washington, D.C.: Regnery Gateway, 1989).

17. It is widely accepted among social movement scholars that activists tend to be more socio-economically advantaged than their intended beneficiaries. Well-known examples include participants in the black Southern sit-in movement, who had very high education and occupational status relative to most Southern black people; rank-and-file feminist activists of the 1980s, who reported more education and labor market experience than most women; and labor activists in most times and places, who have included a disproportionate number of relatively privileged craft workers. Maurice Pinard, Jerome Kirk, and Donald von Eschen, "Processes of Recruitment in the Sit-In Movement," *Public Opinion Quarterly* 33, no. 3 (1969): 355–69; Pat Dewey Dauphinais, Steven E. Barkan, and Steven F. Cohn, "Predictors of Rank-and-File Feminist Activism: Evidence from the 1983 General Social Survey," *Social Problems* 39, no. 4 (1992): 332–44; Roger Gould, "Historical Sociology and Collective Action," *Remaking Modernity: Politics, History, and Sociology*, eds. Julia Adams, Elisabeth S. Clemens, and Ann Shola Orloff (Durham, NC: Duke University Press, 2005), 286–99.

18. On new versus old money, see Lipset and Raab, *Politics of Unreason*, 210; on domestic versus multinational firms, see Thomas Ferguson, "From Normalcy to New Deal: Industrial Structure, Party Competition, and American Public Policy in the Great Depression," *Industrial Organization* 38, no. 1 (1984): 41–94; on cowboys and Yankees, see Val Burris, "The Political Partisanship of American Business: A Study of Corporate Political Action Committees," *American Sociological Review* 52, no. 6 (1987): 732–44. For other classifications of capitalists based on industry, see, e.g., Ferguson, "From Normalcy to New Deal," who also distinguishes the political strategies of investors in labor-intensive and capital-intensive industries; and Peter Swenson, *Capitalists against Markets: The Making of Labor Markets and Welfare States* (Oxford, UK, and New York: Oxford University Press, 2002), who argues that the political interests of investors depend on the firm's labor market strategy.

19. Quoted in Melinda Burns, "K Street and the Status Quo," *Miller-McCune* (September–October 2010), 68.

20. On the insulating effect of high incomes with respect to environmental and status shocks, see, e.g., Gary W. Evans and Elyse Kantrowitz, "Socioeconomic Status and Health: The Potential Role of Environmental Risk Exposure," *Annual Review of Public Health* 23 (2002): 303–31; Ronald C. Kessler, Kristen D. Mickelson, and David R. Williams, "The Prevalence, Distribution, and Mental Health Correlates of Perceived Discrimination in the United States," *Journal of Health and Social Behavior* 40, no. 3 (1999): 208–30.

21. We know this because comparative survey evidence shows that it is income relative to others (not absolute purchasing power) that matters for happiness. See Richard Ball and Kateryna Chernova, "Absolute Income, Relative Income, and Happiness," *Social Indicators Research* 88, no. 3 (2008): 497–529; Andrew E. Clark, Paul Frijters, and Michael A. Shields, "Relative Income, Happiness, and Utility: An Explanation for the Easterlin Paradox and Other Puzzles," *Journal of Economic Literature* 46, no. 1 (2008): 95–144; Richard A. Easterlin, "Will Raising the Incomes of All Increase the Happiness of All?" *Journal of Economic Behavior and Organization* 27, no. 1 (1995): 35–47; Bruno S. Frey and Alois Stutzer, "What Can Economists Learn from Happiness Research?" *Journal of Economic Literature*, 40, no. 2 (2002): 402–35.

22. See Paul K. Piff, Michael W. Kraus, Stéphane Côté, Bonnie Hayden Cheng, and Dacher Keltner, "Having Less, Giving More: The Influence of Social Class on Prosocial Behavior," *Journal of Personality and Social Psychology* 99, no. 5 (2010): 771–84.

23. This is, of course, the classic problem of the "free rider." For an application of this argument to social protest, see Mancur Olson, *The Logic of Collective Action: Public Goods and the Theory of Groups* (Cambridge, MA: Harvard University Press, 1965); see also Gerald Marwell and Pamela Oliver, *The Critical Mass in Collective Action: A Micro-Social Theory* (Cambridge, UK, and New York: Cambridge University Press, 1993).

24. Robert H. Frank points out that policies to increase the incomes of the rich across the board may actually produce little or no increase in happiness even for the rich, because many of the things that great riches are thought to secure are positional goods; for example, "when 30,000 square-foot mansions grow ten percent larger, the primary effect is just to raise the bar that defines 'adequate' housing in elite circles." Robert H. Frank, "Why the Rich Have an Interest in Paying Higher Taxes," *Scholars Strategy Network Basic Facts*, 2012, http://www.scholarsstrategynetwork.org/sites/default/files/ssn_basic_facts_frank_on_interests_of_rich_0.pdf.

25. See Paul D. Almeida, "Opportunity Organizations and Threat-Induced Contention: Protest Waves in Authoritarian Settings," *American Journal of Sociology* 109, no. 2 (2003): 346-400; Rachel L. Einwohner, "Opportunity, Honor, and Action in the Warsaw Ghetto Uprising of 1943," *American Journal of Sociology* 109, no. 3 (2003): 650–75; Jack A. Goldstone and Charles Tilly, "Threat (and Opportunity): Popular Action and State Response in the Dynamics of Contentious Action," in *Silence and Voice in the Study of Contentious Politics*, eds. R. R. Aminzade, J. A. Goldstone, D. McAdam, E. J. Perry, W. H. J. Sewell, S. Tarrow, and C. Tilly (New York: Cambridge University Press), 179-94; Isaac William Martin, *The Permanent Tax Revolt: How the Property Tax Transformed American Politics* (Stanford, CA: Stanford University Press, 2008); Nella Van Dyke and Sarah A. Soule, "Structural Social Change and the Mobilizing Effect of Threat: Explaining Levels of Patriot and Militia Mobilizing in the United States," *Social Problems* 49, no. 4 (2002): 497–520. In addition to these studies, other sociologists who study right-wing movements have often advanced similar hypotheses under different names. Where I refer to threats, Rory McVeigh refers to "power devaluation," and Lipset and Raab refer to "status displacement": Rory McVeigh, *The Rise of the Ku Klux Klan: Right-Wing Movements and National Politics* (Minneapolis: University of Minnesota Press, 2009); Lipset and Raab, *Politics of Unreason*. These concepts are not exactly equivalent, but they correspond to the same basic intuition: People with relatively high status protest when they are threatened with its loss.

26. Goldstone and Tilly, "Threat (and Opportunity)," provide a formal version of this argument consistent with rational choice theory.

27. See Daniel Kahneman, Jack L. Knetsch, and Richard H. Thaler, "Anomalies: The Endowment Effect, Loss Aversion, and Status Quo Bias," *Journal of Economic Perspectives*, 5, no. 1 (1991): 193–206.

28. On intragenerational income mobility of the rich, see Maury Gittleman and Mary Joyce, "Have Family Income Mobility Patterns Changed?" *Demography* 36, no. 3 (1999): 299–314; Peter Gottschalk, "Inequality, Income Growth, and Mobility: the Basic Facts," *Journal of Economic Perspectives* 11, no. 2(1997): 21-40; U.S. Department of the Treasury, *Income Mobility in the U.S. from 1996 to 2005* (Washington, D.C.: Author, 2008), http://www.treasury.gov/resource-center/tax-policy/Documents/incomemobilitystudy03-08revise.pdf; Jonathan A. Parker and Annette Vissing-Jorgensen, "The Increase in Income Cyclicality of High-Income Households and Its Relation to the Rise in Top Income Shares," *Brookings Papers on Economic Activity* 41, no. 2 (2010): 1–70; Faith Guvenen, Serdar Ozkan, and Jae Song, "The Nature of Countercyclical Income Risk" (National Bureau of Economic Research, working paper 18035, 2012). Data on wealth mobility are scarce, but see Keister, *Getting Rich*, 46.

29. See Andrea Louise Campbell, "Participatory Reactions to Policy Threats: Senior Citizens and the Defense of Social Security and Medicare," *Political Behavior* 25, no. 1 (2003):

29–49; id., *How Policies Make Citizens: Senior Activism and the American Welfare State* (Princeton, NJ: Princeton University Press, 2005); Ellen Reese, "Policy Threats and Social Movement Coalitions: California's Campaign to Restore Legal Immigrants' Rights to Welfare," in *Routing the Opposition: Social Movements, Public Policy, and Democracy*, eds. David S. Meyer, Valerie Jenness, and Helen Ingram (Minneapolis: University of Minnesota Press, 2005), 259–87; Martin, *Permanent Tax Revolt*, 17–19.

30. Marwell and Oliver, *Theory of the Critical Mass*; Debra Javeline, "The Role of Blame in Collective Action: Evidence from Russia," *American Political Science Review* 97, no. 1 (2003): 107–21.

31. Javeline, "The Role of Blame"; cf. David A. Snow, E. Burke Rochford Jr., Steven K. Worden, and Robert D. Benford, "Frame Alignment Processes, Micromobilization, and Movement Participation," *American Sociological Review* 51, no. 4 (1986): 464–81.

32. Both political process theory and resource mobilization theory, in their classic forms, were limited in scope to protest by resource-deprived and politically excluded people. McAdam, for example, argued that political opportunities matter for protest because "under ordinary circumstances excluded groups or challengers face enormous obstacles in their efforts to advance group interests," and thereby implicitly restricted the scope of his theory to excluded groups or challengers; Doug McAdam, *Political Process and the Development of Black Insurgency, 1930-1970* (Chicago: University of Chicago Press, 1999), ix. Classic statements of resource mobilization theory argued that fluctuations in the available resources should matter more for protest than fluctuations in grievances because they assumed that "grievances are relatively constant and pervasive"—as indeed they are among the poor; J. Craig Jenkins and Charles Perrow, "Insurgency of the Powerless: Farmworker Movements (1946-1972)," *American Sociological Review* 42, no. 2 (1977), 266.

33. Charles Tilly, *Social Movements, 1768-2004* (Boulder, CO: Paradigm, 2004), 3; see also Tilly, *Contentious Performances*. As this list of tactics implies, movements have conventions of their own. They are "unconventional" only in the sense that they take place substantially outside of the officially scheduled and sanctioned routines of the political system.

34. See, e.g., William Gamson, *The Strategy of Social Protest* (Belmont, CA: Wadsworth, 1990); Sidney Tarrow, *Power in Movement: Social Movements and Contentious Politics* (New York: Cambridge University Press, 1998); Tilly, *From Mobilization to Revolution*; McAdam, *Political Process*; Piven and Cloward, *Poor People's Movements*.

35. The literature on campaign contributions is large. For a review, see Stephen Ansolabehere, John M. de Figueiredo, and James M. Snyder, "Why Is There So Little Money in U.S. Politics?" *Journal of Economic Perspectives* 17, no. 1 (2003): 105–30. For an overview of the effects on unequal access, see Larry Bartels, Hugh Heclo, Rodney E. Hero, and Lawrence R. Jacobs, "Inequality and American Governance," in *Inequality and American Democracy: What We Know and What We Need to Learn*, eds. Lawrence R. Jacobs and Theda Skocpol (New York: Russell Sage Foundation, 2005), 88–155; Domhoff, *Who Rules America?*; Dan Clawson, Alan Neustadtl, and Mark Weller, *Dollars and Votes: How Business Campaign Contributions Subvert Democracy* (Philadelphia: Temple University Press, 1998).

36. Bartels et al., "Inequality and American Governance"; Larry Bartels, *Unequal Democracy: The Political Economy of the New Gilded Age* (New York and Princeton, NJ: Russell Sage Foundation and Princeton University Press, 2008); Martin Gilens, "Inequality and Democratic Responsiveness," *Public Opinion Quarterly* 69, no. 5 (2005): 778–96.

37. On various alternative modes of collective action, see Neil Fligstein, *The Transformation of Corporate Control* (Cambridge, MA: Harvard University Press, 1993); Jeffrey Haydu, *Citizen Employers: Business Communities and Labor in Cincinnati and San Francisco, 1870-1916* (Ithaca, NY: Cornell University Press, 2009); Patrick J. Akard, "Corporate Mobilization and Political Power: The Transformation of American Economic Policy in the 1970s," *American Sociological Review* 57, no. 5 (1992): 597–615; Key Lehman Schlozman, Benjamin I. Page, Sidney Verba, and Morris P. Fiorina, "Inequalities of Political Voice," in *Inequality and American Democracy*, eds. Jacobs and Skocpol (New York: Russell Sage

Foundation, 2005), 19-87; Edward Walker, "Privatizing Participation: Civic Change and Organizational Dynamics of Grassroots Lobbying Firms," *American Sociological Review* 74, no. 1 (2009): 83–105.

38. Analysis of recent polling data by Schlozman, Verba, and Brady, e.g., shows that the likelihood of contributing money relative to other forms of political participation rises dramatically with income; in contrast, attending a protest is a form of political participation that the rich are no more likely to engage in than the poor. Kay Lehman Schlozman, Sidney Verba, and Henry E. Brady, *The Unheavenly Chorus: Unequal Political Voice and the Broken Promise of Democracy in America* (Princeton, NJ: Princeton University Press, 2012), 124–5. See also Benjamin Page, Fay Lomax Cook, and Rachel Moskowitz, "Wealthy Americans, Philanthropy, and the Common Good," Russell Sage Foundation, working paper, September 25, 2011. For evidence that there is little or no socioeconomic inequality in rates of protest, in contrast to other forms of participation, see Rory McVeigh and Christian Smith, "Who Protests in America: An Analysis of Three Political Alternatives—Inaction, Institutionalized Politics, or Protest." *Sociological Forum* 14, no. 4 (1999): 693–4; Catherine Corrigall-Brown, *Patterns of Protest: Trajectories of Participation in Social Movements* (Stanford, CA: Stanford University Press, 2012), 32.

39. See Domhoff, *Who Rules America*; Mills, *Power Elite*.

40. On the role of exogenous crises in imposing new burdens on the rich, see Brownlee, "Historical Perspective"; Robert Higgs, *Crisis and Leviathan: Critical Episodes in the Growth of American Government* (Oxford, UK, and New York: Oxford University Press, 1989); Sheldon D. Pollack, *War, Revenue, and State Building: Financing the Development of the American State* (Ithaca, NY: Cornell University Press, 2009).

41. The work of Charles Tilly masterfully documents the evolution of protest repertoires. For highlights, see Charles Tilly, "Repertoires of Contention in America and Britain, 1750-1830," in *The Dynamics of Social Movements*, eds. Mayer N. Zald and John D. McCarthy (Cambridge, MA: Winthrop, 1979), 126-55; id., *The Contentious French: Four Centuries of Popular Struggle* (Cambridge, MA: Harvard University Press, 1986); id., *Social Movements*; id., *Contentious Performances*.

42. The definition is from Suzanne Staggenborg, "The Consequences of Professionalization and Formalization in the Pro-Choice Movement," *American Sociological Review* 53, no. 4 (1988): 587. The concept of the movement entrepreneur has a family resemblance with the concepts of "political entrepreneur," "policy entrepreneur," and "issue entrepreneur"; see Mark Schneider and Paul Teske, "Toward a Theory of the Political Entrepreneur: Evidence from Local Government," *American Political Science Review* 86, no. 3 (1992): 737-47; Steven Teles, *The Rise of the Conservative Legal Movement: The Battle for Control of the Law* (Princeton, NJ: Princeton University Press, 2008); Michael Mintrom, "Policy Entrepreneurs and the Diffusion of Innovation," *American Journal of Political Science* 41, no. 3 (1997): 738-70; John D. McCarthy and Mayer Zald, "Resource Mobilization and Social Movements: A Partial Theory," *American Journal of Sociology* 82, no. 6 (1977): 1211-41. All of these categories refer to individuals who attempt to influence politics by defining the issues on the public agenda, and all of them refer to individuals who attempt to manipulate what symbolic interactionists called "the definition of the situation" in order to solve collective action problems. In contrast to policy entrepreneurs and political entrepreneurs as they are defined in the literature, however, movement entrepreneurs as I conceptualize them do not typically operate within established public bureaucracies or political parties. In contrast to "issue entrepreneurs" described by early resource mobilization theorists, I conceive of movement entrepreneurs as engaged in entrepreneurial activity that goes well beyond the rhetorical work of framing movement goals "for specific and general audiences" to include also the material work of soliciting contributions, forging relationships, founding organizations, and the like: cf. id., "The Enduring Vitality of the Resource Mobilization Theory of Social Movements," in *Handbook of Sociological Theory*, ed. Jonathan H. Turner (New York: Kluwer), 536.

43. My conception of general social skill, and insight into its importance for entrepreneurs in movements and other fields, comes from Neil Fligstein, "Social Skill and the Theory of Fields," *Sociological Theory* 19, no. 2 (2001): 105-25.

44. Staggenborg, "Consequences," 590

45. See Elizabeth S. Clemens, *The People's Lobby: Organizational Innovation and the Rise of Interest Group Politics in the United States, 1890-1925* (Chicago: University of Chicago Press, 1997); Haydu, *Citizen Employers*; Marshall Ganz, "Resources and Resourcefulness: Strategic Capacity in the Unionization of California Agriculture, 1959-1966," *American Journal of Sociology* 105, no. 4 (2000): 1003-62.

46. The scope of this argument is limited to rich people's movements. I expect that aggrieved people who are not rich have fewer effective options to secure redress of their grievances, and therefore might be more likely to reinvent some aspects of the social movement repertoire out of necessity, even if they do not have previous movement experience. Cress and Snow, however, present some evidence that the availability of skilled actors with movement-specific "know-how" may also be a necessary condition for the emergence of viable social protest organizations among the very poor; id., "Mobilization at the Margins," 1097.

47. This finding is consistent with most scholarship on the subject, which finds that one of the most important predictors of social movement participation, as with other forms of political participation, is simply whether an individual was asked to participate. See, e.g., Bert Klandermans and Dirk Oegema, "Potentials, Networks, Motivations and Barriers: Steps toward Participation in Social Movements," *American Sociological Review* 52, no. 4 (1987): 519-31; Sidney Verba, Kay Lehman Schlozman, and Henry E. Brady, *Voice and Equality: Civic Voluntarism in American Politics* (Cambridge, MA: Harvard University Press, 1995). For an overview of the literature on social networks and recruitment to social protest, see Mario Diani, "Networks and Participation," in *The Blackwell Companion to Social Movements*, eds. David A. Snow, Sarah A. Soule, and Hanspeter Kriesi (Malden, MA: Blackwell, 2005), 339-59.

48. E. E. Schattschneider, *The Semi-Sovereign People: A Realist's View of Democracy in America* (Belmont, CA: Wadsworth, 1975); Bartels, *Unequal Democracy*; Schlozman, Verba, and Brady, *The Unheavenly Chorus.*

49. Jack L. Walker, *Mobilizing Interest Groups in America: Patrons, Professions, and Social Movements* (Ann Arbor, MI: University of Michigan Press, 1991), 106. See Pepper Culpepper, *Quiet Politics and Business Power: Corporate Control in Europe and Japan* (Cambridge, UK: Cambridge University Press, 2011); Schattschneider, *The Semisovereign People.*

50. For this picture of ordinary American tax politics, see Ronald F. King, *Money, Time, and Politics: Investment Tax Subsidies and American Democracy* (New Haven, CT: Yale University Press, 1993); Cathie Jo Martin, *Shifting the Burden: The Struggle over Growth and Corporate Taxation* (Chicago: University of Chicago Press, 1991); Sven Steinmo, *Taxation and Democracy: Swedish, British, and American Approaches to Financing the Modern State* (New Haven, CT: Yale University Press, 1993); Witte, *Politics and Development.* On the importance of concealment in tax politics, see R. Douglas Arnold, *The Logic of Congressional Action* (New Haven, CT: Yale University Press, 1990); Christopher Howard, *The Hidden Welfare State: Tax Expenditures and Social Policy in the United States* (Princeton, NJ: Princeton University Press, 1997).

51. For an insightful discussion of the distinction between "success" and "having an impact," see Edwin Amenta and Michael P. Young, "Making an Impact: Conceptual and Methodological Implications of the Collective Benefits Criterion," in *How Social Movements Matter: Theoretical and Comparative Studies on the Consequences of Social Movements*, eds. Marco Giugni, Doug McAdam, and Charles Tilly (Minneapolis: University of Minnesota Press, 1999), 22-42.

52. For evidence of continuity in the Republican Party program over this period, see Sheldon D. Pollack, *Refinancing America: The Republican Antitax Agenda* (Albany, NY: State

University of New York Press, 2003); John Gerring, *Party Ideologies in America, 1828-1996* (Cambridge, UK, and New York: Cambridge University Press, 2001), ch. 4.

53. See, e.g., Edwin Amenta and Drew Halfmann, "Wage Wars: Institutional politics, WPA wages, and the struggle for U.S. Social Policy," *American Sociological Review* 65, no. 4 (2000): 506-28; Edwin Amenta and Jane D. Poulsen, "Social Politics in Context: Institutional Politics Theory and Social Spending at the End of the New Deal," *Social Forces* 75, no. 1 (1996): 33-61; Nancy K. Cauthen and Edwin Amenta, "Not for Widows Only: Institutional Politics and the Formative Years of Aid to Dependent Children," *American Sociological Review* 61, no. 3 (1996): 427-48; Robert C. Lieberman, *Shifting the Color Line: Race and the American Welfare State* (Cambridge, MA: Harvard University Press, 1998); Anthony S. Chen, *The Fifth Freedom: Jobs, Politics, and Civil Rights in the United States, 1941-1972* (Princeton, NJ: Princeton University Press, 2009).

54. David A. Snow and Robert D. Benford, "Ideology, Frame Resonance, and Participant Mobilization," *International Social Movement Research* 1 (1988), 198; see more generally Robert D. Benford and David A. Snow, "Framing Processes and Social Movements: An Overview and Assessment," *Annual Review of Sociology* 26 (2000): 611-39; Robert D. Benford, "An Insider's Critique of the Social Movement Framing Perspective," *Sociological Inquiry* 67 (1997): 409-30.

55. For any given regulation, there is an equivalent tax that would achieve the same distributional outcomes, and any desired pattern of tax incidence could be achieved equivalently by a lump sum tax combined with transfer spending. For an interesting empirical example from social policy, see Howard, *Hidden Welfare State*. On "policy packaging," see Margaret Weir, *Politics and Jobs: Boundaries of Employment Policy in the United States* (Princeton, NJ: Princeton University Press, 1993).

56. "Crafted talk" is from Lawrence R. Jacobs and Robert Y. Shapiro, *Politicians Don't Pander: Political Manipulation and the Loss of Democratic Responsiveness* (Chicago: University of Chicago Press, 2000), 7. For highlights of the literature on the framing of fiscal policy, see Edward J. McCaffery and Joel Slemrod, eds., *Behavioral Public Finance* (New York: Russell Sage Foundation, 2006); William G. Jacoby, "Issue Framing and Public Opinion on Government Spending," *American Journal of Political Science* 44 (2000): 750-67; Edward J. McCaffery and Jonathan Baron, "Framing and Taxation: Evaluation of Tax Policies Involving Household Composition," *Journal of Economic Psychology* 25 (2004): 679-705; id., "The political psychology of redistribution," *UCLA Law Review* 52 (2005): 1745-92; id., "Thinking about tax," *Psychology Public Policy and Law* 12 (2006): 106-35; Edward J. McCaffery, "Cognitive Theory and Tax," *UCLA Law Review* 41 (1994): 1861-1947; Brian Steensland, "Why Do Policy Frames Change? Actor-Idea Coevolution in Debates over Welfare Reform," *Social Forces* 86 (2008): 1027-54.

57. This argument builds on several recent social movement studies that argue policy-oriented social movement organizations can expect the most success when they tailor their tactics to their institutional environment: Edwin Amenta, *When Movements Matter: The Townsend Plan and the Rise of Social Security* (Princeton, NJ: Princeton University Press, 2005); Edwin Amenta, Drew Halfmann, and Michael P. Young, "The Strategies and Contexts of Social Protest: Political Mediation and the Impact of the Townsend Movement in California," *Mobilization* 4 (1999): 1-23; Melissa Wilde, "How Culture Mattered at Vatican II: Collegiality Trumps Authority in the Council's Social Movement Organizations," *American Sociological Review* 69, no. 4 (2004): 576-602; Holly J. McCammon, *The U.S. Women's Jury Movements and Strategic Adaptation: A More Just Verdict* (New York and Cambridge, UK: Cambridge University Press, 2012). I add that the tactical decisions may go beyond the choice of lobbying tactics to include the drafting of the policy text itself. This argument also draws on several recent studies that argue advocacy groups succeed by tailoring their proposals to the discursive opportunity structure, the cultural assumptions of their milieu, or the perceptions of policy elites: Myra Marx Ferree, "Resonance and Radicalism: Feminist Framing in the Abortion Debates of the United States and Germany,"

American Journal of Sociology 109, no. 2 (2003): 304-44; Brian Steensland, "Cultural Categories and the American Welfare State: The Case of Guaranteed Income Policy," *American Journal of Sociology* 111, no. 5 (2006): 1273-1326; John D. Skrentny, "Policy-Elite Perceptions and Social Movement Success: Understanding Variations in Group Inclusion in Affirmative Action," *American Journal of Sociology* 111, no. 6 (2006): 1762-1815. Much of this research, however, characterizes the relevant cultural context as a set of inarticulate, taken-for-granted, or "background" assumptions. I conceptualize the proximate cultural context instead as a limited set of other policies and policy proposals that are salient, or readily available to the foreground of policymakers' attention.

58. For an inventory of ways to affect tax opinion by framing, see, e.g., McCaffery and Baron, "Framing and Taxation"; id., "Thinking about Tax."

59. On the idea of a "radical flank" effect, see Haines, "Black Radicalization," who applied the term to the effect of radical protesters on the decisions of the philanthropic sector about whether to fund more moderate movement organizations. For evidence that protesters making radically egalitarian tax policy demands encouraged more moderate egalitarian redistribution in 1935, see Edwin Amenta, Kathleen Dunleavy, and Mary Bernstein, "Stolen Thunder? Huey Long's 'Share Our Wealth,' Political Mediation, and the Second New Deal," *American Sociological Review* 59, no. 5 (1994): 678-702. For evidence that militant protest by the black poor influenced decisions about how progressive to make tax legislation, see David Jacobs and Ronald Helms, "Racial Politics and Redistribution: Isolating the Contingent Influence of Civil Rights, Riots, and Crime on Tax Progressivity," *Social Forces* 80, no. 1 (2001): 91-121. The evidence that protest by the poor has sometimes influenced redistribution on the spending side of the budget is copious. For reviews, see Frances Fox Piven and Richard Cloward, *Regulating the Poor: The Functions of Public Welfare*, 2nd ed. (New York: Vintage, 1993); Eric Swank, "Welfare Reform and the Power of Protest: Quantitative Tests of Piven and Cloward's 'Turmoil-Relief' Hypothesis," in *The Promise of Welfare Reform: Political Rhetoric and the Reality of Poverty in the Twenty-First Century*, eds. Keith M. Kilty and Elizabeth Segal (New York: Haworth Press, 2006), 287–300.

60. See, e.g., Bartels, *Unequal Democracy*; Graetz and Shapiro, *Death*; Jacob S. Hacker and Paul Pierson, *Off Center: The Republican Revolution and the Erosion of American Democracy* (New Haven, CT: Yale University Press, 2005); Monica Prasad, "Starving the Beast: the Bush Tax Cuts and the Role of Public Opinion" (Paper presented at the Annual Meetings of the Social Science History Association, Portland, OR, 2005); Arthur Lupia, Adam Seth Levine, Jessie O. Menning, and Gisela Sin, "Were Bush Tax Cut Supporters 'Simply Ignorant'? A Second Look at Conservatives and Liberals in 'Homer Gets a Tax Cut,' " *Perspectives on Politics* 5 (2007): 773-84; Bryan D. Jones and Walter Williams, *The Politics of Bad Ideas: The Great Tax Cut Delusion and the Decline of Good Government in America* (New York: Longman, 2008).

61. The identification of economic conservatism as a "libertarian" strand within the American conservative tradition follows Nash, *Conservative Intellectual Movement*, 3-35. Notable recent contributions to the intellectual history of libertarianism and business conservatism more generally include Brian Doherty, *Radicals for Capitalism: A Freewheeling History of the Modern American Libertarian Movement* (New York: Public Affairs, 2007); Jennifer Burns, *Goddess of the Market: Ayn Rand and the American Right* (Oxford, UK, and New York: Oxford University Press, 2009) Kim Phillips-Fein, *Invisible Hands: The Businessmen's Crusade against the New Deal* (New York: W. W. Norton, 2009). For a recent review of scholarship on conservative intellectuals, see Neil Gross, Thomas Medvetz, and Rupert Russell, "The Contemporary American Conservative Movement," *Annual Review of Sociology* 37 (2011): 325–54. An excellent but lonely exception to the generalization in this paragraph is David Beito, *Taxpayers in Revolt: Tax Resistance during the Great Depression* (Chapel Hill, NC: University of North Carolina Press, 1989), which treats grassroots tax protest by property owners in the Great Depression as a chapter in social history, not intellectual history. I tried to do the same for property tax payers of the 1970s in Martin, *Permanent Tax Revolt*.

62. Classic studies in this vein include Joseph R. Gusfield, *Symbolic Crusade: Status Politics and the American Temperance Movement* (Urbana, IL: University of Illinois Press, 1966) and Lipset and Raab, *Politics of Unreason.* For a review of the recent sociological literature on conservative movements and right-wing extremism, see Kathleen Blee and Kimberly Creasap, "Conservative and Right-Wing Movements," *Annual Review of Sociology* 36 (2010): 287–307.
63. Influential works include McGirr, *Suburban Warriors*; Matthew Lassiter, *The Silent Majority: Suburban Politics in the Sunbelt South* (Princeton, NJ, Princeton University Press, 2007); Robert O. Self, *American Babylon: Race and the Struggle for Postwar Oakland* (Princeton, NJ: Princeton University Press, 2003).
64. E.g., Phillips-Fein, *Invisible Hands*; Bethany Moreton, *To Serve God and Wal-Mart: The Making of Christian Free Enterprise* (Cambridge, MA: Harvard University Press, 2009).
65. Donald T. Critchlow, *The Conservative Ascendancy: How the GOP Right Made Political History* (Cambridge, MA: Harvard University Press, 2007); Sean Wilentz, *The Age of Reagan: A History, 1974-2008* (New York: HarperCollins, 2009); Rick Perlstein, *Before the Storm: Barry Goldwater and the Unmaking of the American Consensus* (New York: Hill and Wang, 2001); id., *Nixonland: The Rise of a President and the Fracturing of America* (New York: Scribner, 2008).
66. Cf. Peter Hedström, Rickard Sandell, and Charlotta Stern, "Mesolevel Networks and the Diffusion of Social Movements: the Case of the Swedish Social Democratic Party," *American Journal of Sociology* 106, no. 1 (2000): 145–72. For other recent contributions that take a broadly similar approach to the history of other conservative movements in the late-twentieth-century U.S., see Teles, *Rise of the Conservative Legal Movement*; Donald T. Critchlow, *Phyllis Schlafly and Grassroots Conservatism: A Woman's Crusade* (Princeton, NJ: Princeton University Press, 2005).

Chapter 1

1. Arnold, *Desire to Own*, 14; Chodorov, *Income Tax*, ch. 5; Robert Charlton, "The Tragic Year," *Freedom Magazine* (Spring 1974), 10; Uhler, *Setting Limits*, 26; Larry Arnn and Grover Norquist, "New Approaches to Tax Reform: Repeal the 16th Amendment," *Wall Street Journal* (April 15, 1997), A18.
2. On Mellon's daily round in this period, see David Cannadine, *Mellon: An American Life* (New York: Vintage, 2006), 245–6. Mellon's dour, workaholic attitude made him something of a throwback; the younger rich of the Progressive Era had begun to acquire a sense that pleasure in luxury was justified. See Michael McGerr, *A Fierce Discontent: The Rise and Fall of the Progressive Movement* (Oxford, UK, and New York: Oxford University Press, 2003), 11–2.
3. Despite a determined program of sewer construction begun by reformers in the Bureau of Public Health in 1907, experts estimated that there were still some 8,000 to 10,000 unsanitary "privy vaults" in the working-class wards of Pittsburgh in 1914. See Emily Wayland Dinwiddie and F. Elisabeth Crowell, "Housing Pittsburgh's Workers," in *The Pittsburgh District: Civic Frontage*, ed. Paul W. Kellogg (New York: Survey Associates, Inc. and the Russell Sage Foundation, 1914), 93.
4. Any individual worker's share of the city's property tax would have been small, but his share of the city's income generally would have been even smaller. On property tax inequalities in Pittsburgh, see Shelby M. Harrison, "The Disproportion of Taxation in Pittsburgh," in *The Pittsburgh District: Civic Frontage*, ed. Paul W. Kellogg (New York: Survey Associates, Inc. and the Russell Sage Foundation, 1914), 182–8. Pennsylvania's precocious taxes on income had been repealed in the 1870s: William J. McKenna, "The Income Tax in Pennsylvania," *Pennsylvania History* 27, no. 3 (1960): 291–310.

5. On the wealthy of that era, see McGerr, *A Fierce Discontent*, ch. 1. A list of the very richest is in Bertie Charles Forbes, *Men Who Are Making America* (New York: B. C. Forbes, Co.,1918), 635. We may infer Mellon's approximate position in the wealth distribution by comparing the 1913 estimate from Cannadine, *Mellon*, 230, to the 1916 threshold reported in Wojciech Kopczuk and Emmanuel Saez, "Top Wealth Shares in the United States, 1916-2000: Evidence from Estate Tax Returns" (NBER, working paper no. 10339, 2004), table B2. I estimate the share of Americans who held 50 percent of the nation's wealth on the eve of the Great War at 2.49 percent, or about 1.5 million, by extrapolation from the wealth distribution for 1916 reported by Kopczuk and Saez, on the assumptions that (i) the wealth distribution in 1913 was identical to that in 1916, and (ii) the wealth distribution followed a Pareto distribution with parameter $\alpha = 1.42$ (calculated from the reported wealth shares of the top 1 percent and the top.01 percent). At the time, Chicago had more than two million people. On perceptions of the United States in the Gilded Age and the Progressive Era, see, e.g., Walter Helbich, "Different, but not Out of this World: German Images of the United States between Two Wars, 1871-1914," in *Transatlantic Images and Perceptions: Germany and America since 1776*, eds. David E. Barclay and Elisabeth Glaser-Schmidt (Cambridge, UK, and New York: Cambridge University Press, 1997), 109-30; Birgitta Steene, "The Swedish Image of America," in *Images of America in Scandinavia*, eds. Poul Houe and Sven Hakon Rossel (Amsterdam: Rodopi, 1998), 156–8; Steffen Elmer Jørgensen, "Ideal or Counterimage? Aspects of the American Cultural Impact on Denmark," in *Images of America in Scandinavia*, eds. Poul Houe and Sven Hakon Rossel (Amsterdam: Rodopi, 1998), 59–61; Robert Perry Frankel, *Observing America: the Commentary of British Visitors to the United States* (Madison, WI: University of Wisconsin Press, 2007).

6. For a polemical overview of the Gilded Age focused on the politics of rising inequality, see Jack Beatty, *The Age of Betrayal: The Triumph of Money in America, 1865-1900* (New York: Vintage Books, 2008). For data on trends in wealth inequality, see Wojciech Kopczuk and Emmanuel Saez, "Top Wealth Shares in the United States, 1916-2000: Evidence from Estate Tax Returns," *National Tax Journal* 57, no. 2 (2004): 483; Peter Lindert, "When Did Inequality Rise in Britain and America?" *Journal of Income Distribution* 9, no. 1 (2000): 11-25. On the accumulation of wealth by black Southern farmers after the Civil War, see Robert Higgs, "The Accumulation of Property by Southern Blacks before World War I," *American Economic Review* 72, no. 4 (1982): 725-37; Roger L. Ransom and Richard Sutch, "Growth and Welfare in the American South of the Nineteenth Century," *Explorations in Economic History* 16, no. 2 (1979): 207–36. "Debt peonage" is the term Ransom and Sutch used to describe the situation of sharecroppers, both black and white, who had to borrow to feed their families, and who were forced to plant cotton instead of food crops in order to secure credit, thereby insuring that their farms would continue to be unable to feed their families. Because debt peonage was an informal relation, there are no precise statistics on its extent, and the prevalence of this relation in the period is an unsettled question of economic history. Ransom and Sutch estimate that between 30 percent and 40 percent of their sample of small family farms in the South were in debt peonage in 1880. Roger L. Ransom and Richard Sutch, "One Kind of Freedom: Reconsidered (and Turbo Charged)," *Explorations in Economic History* 38, no. 1 (2001): 28.

7. For top income shares, see Anthony Atkinson, Thomas Piketty, and Emmanuel Saez, "Top Incomes in the Long Run of History," *Journal of Economic Literature* 49, no. 1 (2011): 3-71. Cannadine, *Mellon*, 231, estimates Mellon's income at $1 million in current dollars; compare table 6 in Thomas Piketty and Emmanuel Saez, "Income Inequality in the United States, 1913-2002," in *Top Incomes over the Twentieth Century*, eds. Anthony B. Atkinson and Thomas Piketty (Oxford, UK: Oxford University Press, 2007), 141–225.

8. On laborers' wages, see John R. Commons and William M. Leiserson, "Wage-Earners of Pittsburgh," *Wage-Earning Pittsburgh*, ed. Paul U. Kellogg (New York: Russell Sage Foundation, 1914), 119–20; on sharecroppers' wages, see James R. Irwin and Anthony Patrick O'Brien, "Where Have All the Sharecroppers Gone? Black Occupations in

Postbellum Mississippi," *Agricultural History* 72, no. 2 (2001): 177. The calculation of sharecroppers' income is sensitive to the decision about what to count. The figure of $333 is Irwin and O'Brien's estimate of the cash equivalent of the wage paid in crop shares, which is probably the income definition that is most comparable to an urban cash wage, or to Cannadine's estimate of Mellon's income. Including the value of tools and other in-kind income provided by the owner, but excluding imputed income from household labor, would yield an annual income of $435. For an overview of wages in this era, see McGerr, *A Fierce Discontent*, 16–8. On Mellon's art-buying habits, see Cannadine, *Mellon*, 183, 192.

9. Robert Hunter, *Poverty* (New York: Macmillan, 1904), 52–3; cf. Linda Barrington and Gordon M. Fisher, "Poverty," in *Historical Statistics of the United States: Millennial Edition*, vol. 2, eds. Susan B. Carter, Scott Sigmund Gartner, Michael R. Haines, Alan L. Olmstead, Richard Sutch, and Gavin Wright (Cambridge, UK, and New York: Cambridge University Press, 2006): 637–40. Hunter's estimate for the North would have corresponded to about $500 in 1913, adjusted for inflation. On the rise of poverty measurement in this period, see Morton Keller, *Regulating a New Society: Public Policy and Social Change in America, 1900-1933* (Cambridge, MA: Harvard University Press, 1998), 182–7; Alice O'Connor, *Poverty Knowledge: Social Science, Social Policy, and the Poor in Twentieth-Century U.S. History* (Princeton, NJ: Princeton University Press, 2001); and James T. Patterson, *America's Struggle Against Poverty in the Twentieth Century* (Cambridge, MA: Harvard University Press, 2000), 3-36. For critical attempts to apply the current federal poverty measure—the so-called Orshansky measure—to data from the Progressive Era, see Patterson, *America's Struggle against Poverty*, 11; Robert D. Plotnick, Eugene Smolensky, Eirik Evenhoues, and Siobhan Reilly, "The Twentieth Century Record of Poverty and Inequality in the United States" (University of Wisconsin Institute for Research on Poverty, discussion paper no. 1166-98, 1998), 25; Barrington and Fisher, "Poverty," 630. All of these scholars tried it and judged it futile because of the income elasticity of definitions of poverty.

10. On the Southern state income taxes, see Edwin Robert Anderson Seligman, *The Income Tax: A Study of the History, Theory, and Practice of Income Taxation at Home and Abroad*, 2nd ed. (New York: Macmillan, 1914), 414–8; on Wisconsin, see id., 421–8; W. Elliot Brownlee, *Progressivism and Economic Growth: The Wisconsin Income Tax, 1911-1929* (Port Washington, NY: Kennikat Press, 1974).

11. F. W. Taussig, "The Taxation of Securities in the United States," *Political Science Quarterly* 14 (1899): 104; Mabel Newcomer, *Separation of State and Local Revenues in the United States* (Ph.D. dissertation, Columbia University Department of Political Science, 1917), 71. See also Edwin Robert Anderson Seligman, "The General Property Tax," in *Essays on Taxation*, 5th ed. (New York: Macmillan, 1905).

12. Michael B. Katz, *Improving Poor People: The Welfare State, the "Underclass," and Urban Schools as History* (Princeton, NJ: Princeton University Press, 1995); Stephen T. Ziliak with Joan Underhill Hannon, "Public Assistance: Colonial Times to the 1920s," in *Historical Statistics of the United States: Millennial Edition*, vol. 2, eds. Susan B. Carter, Scott Sigmund Gartner, Michael R. Haines, Alan L. Olmstead, Richard Sutch, and Gavin Wright (Cambridge, UK, and New York: Cambridge University Press, 2006), 693–700.

13. Kathleen Gorman, "Confederate Pensions as Southern Social Welfare," in *Before the New Deal: Social Welfare in the South, 1830-1930*, ed. Elna C. Green (Athens, GA: University of Georgia Press, 1999), 27; Theda Skocpol, *Protecting Soldiers and Mothers: The Political Origins of Social Policy in the United States* (Cambridge, MA: Harvard University Press, 1992), 139–40; James R. Young, "Confederate Pensions in Georgia, 1886-1929," *Georgia Historical Quarterly* 66, no. 1 (1982): 47–52.

14. Much of the benefit probably went to employers of domestic servants who were thereby spared the need to pay a living wage. On the Chicago program, see Joanne L. Goodwin, "An American Experiment in Paid Motherhood: The Implementation of Mothers' Pensions in Early Twentieth-Century Chicago," *Gender and History* 4, no. 3 (1992): 330–2; on the administration of early mothers' pensions more generally, see Theda Skocpol,

Marjorie Abend-Wein, Christopher Howard, and Susan Goodrich Lehmann, "Women's Associations and the Enactment of Mothers' Pensions in the United States," *American Political Science Review* 87, no. 3 (1993): 686; Mark H. Leff, "Consensus for Reform: The Mothers' Pension Movement in the Progressive Era," *Social Service Review* 47, no. 3 (1973): 397-417.

15. Isaac Max Rubinow, *Social Insurance: With Special Reference to American Conditions* (New York: Henry Holt and Co., 1913), 404, 408; see also Laura Jensen, *Patriots, Settlers, and the Origins of American Social Policy* (Cambridge, UK, and New York: Cambridge University Press, 2003), 213–4; Skocpol, *Protecting Soldiers and Mothers*. On the incomes of the elderly in this period, see Brian Gratton, "The Poverty of Impoverishment Theory: The Economic Well-Being of the Elderly, 1890-1950," *Journal of Economic History* 56, no. 1 (1996): 39–61.

16. Douglas A. Irwin, "Tariff Incidence in America's Gilded Age," *Journal of Economic History* 67, no. 3 (2007): 582–607.

17. For a description of tariff legislation in force from 1897 to 1913, see Taussig, *Tariff History*, 321–408. On the incidence of the tariff, see John Mark Hansen, "Taxation and the Political Economy of the Tariff," *International Organization* 44, no. 4 (1990): 527–51; Irwin, "Tariff Incidence."

18. Charles Edward Russell, *Lawless Wealth: The Origin of Some Great American Fortunes* (New York: B. W. Dodge and Co., 1908), 1; see also John Calvin Reed, *The New Plutocracy* (New York: Abbey Press, 1903); Gustavus Myers, *History of the Great American Fortunes*, 3 vols. (Chicago: Charles H. Kerr & Co, 1909); Walter Weyl, *The New Democracy* (New York: Macmillan, 1912); Anna Pritchitt Youngman, *The Economic Causes of Great Fortunes* (New York: Bankers Publishing Co., 1909).

19. The remainder of this section draws on the general sociological literature that is ably summarized by Kathryn M. Neckerman and Florencia Torche, "Inequality: Causes and Consequences," *Annual Review of Sociology* 33 (2007): 335–57; Richard G. Wilkinson and Kate E. Pickett, "Income Inequality and Social Dysfunction," *Annual Review of Sociology* 35 (2009): 493-511; Richard G. Wilkinson and Kate E. Pickett, *The Spirit Level: Why More Equal Societies Almost Always Do Better* (London: Allen Lane, 2009).

20. Cannadine, *Mellon*, 50–5, 142, 216; W. E. B. DuBois, *The Philadelphia Negro: A Social Study* (Philadelphia: University of Philadelphia Press, 1899), 172. On the income tax as an automatic stabilizer, see Alan Auerbach and Daniel J. Feenberg, "The Significance of Federal Taxes as Automatic Stabilizers," *Journal of Economic Perspectives* 14, no. 3 (2000): 37–56.

21. Quoted in Francis G. Couvares, *The Remaking of Pittsburgh: Class and Culture in an Industrializing City, 1877-1919* (Albany, NY: State University of New York Press, 1984), 99, 104; Paul Mellon, *Reflections in a Silver Spoon: A Memoir* (New York: William Morrow and Co., 1992), 70. On the general relationship between inequality and economic segregation, see Wilkinson and Pickett, "Income Inequality and Social Dysfunction."

22. Cannadine, *Mellon*, 218–9; Paul Kellogg, "Community and Workshop," in *Wage-Earning Pittsburgh*, ed. Paul Underwood Kellogg (New York: Survey Associates, Inc., 1914), 20. A short-lived reform administration that came to power in Pittsburgh in 1906 succeeded in creating a Bureau of Public Health, only to watch it be captured by the Republican Party machine as a patronage operation. By 1914, two-thirds of the health department budget was simply handed over to garbage removal contractors toward whom the department "followed an extreme go-as-you-please policy" (Kellogg, "Community and Workshop," 16, 14).

23. Kellogg, "Community and Workshop," 11, 14; Cannadine, *Mellon*, 236. This paragraph is also indebted to I. Kawachi, B. P. Kennedy, K. Lochner, and D. Prothrow-Stith, "Social Capital, Income Inequality, and Mortality," *American Journal of Public Health* 87, no. 9 (1997): 1491–8; S. V. Subramanian and Ichiro Kawachi, "Income Inequality and Health: What Have We Learned So Far?" *Epidemiologic Reviews* 26 (2004): 78–91; and Wilkinson and Pickett, "Income Inequality."

24. Cannadine, *Mellon*, 168–76, 248. The qualitative evidence of mistrust between rich and poor in the Progressive Era is consistent with quantitative studies of the late twentieth

century that show a general association, both over time and across places, between unequal societies and societies in which people mistrust strangers: see Dora L. Costa and Matthew E. Kahn, "Understanding the American Decline in Social Capital, 1952-1998," *Kyklos* 56, no. 1 (2003): 17-46; Markus Freitag and Marc Bühlmann, "Crafting Trust: The Role of Political Institutions in Comparative Perspective," *Comparative Political Studies* 42, no. 12 (2009): 1537-66; Kawachi et al., "Social Capital"; Eric M. Uslaner, *The Moral Foundations of Trust* (New York: Cambridge University Press, 2002); Eric M. Uslaner and Mitchell Brown, "Inequality, Trust, and Civic Engagement," *American Politics Research* 33, no. 6 (2005): 868–94; Wilkinson and Pickett, *The Spirit Level*. For a cautionary note on these studies, however, see Malcolm Fairbrother and Isaac William Martin, "Does Inequality Erode Social Trust? Results from Multilevel Models of U.S. States and Counties," *Social Science Research* 42, no. 2 (2013), 347–60, who argue that there is insufficient evidence to conclude that rising inequality is responsible for the rise in mistrust in the U.S. since the 1970s.

25. Alexander Berkman, *Prison Memoirs of an Anarchist* (New York: Mother Earth, 1912), 32; Mellon, *Reflections*, 79. We do not know the motive of the stranger who pushed Mellon in front of the train, but the story of the apparently unprovoked assault was interpreted and retold within the Mellon family as a story about class resentment. On Czolgosz, see Eric Rauchway, *Murdering McKinley: The Making of Theodore Roosevelt's America* (New York: Hill and Wang, 2003), 42.

26. Rauchway, *Murdering McKinley*, 196–7. I reproduce the speech as quoted from a transcript in Roosevelt's papers by Sidney M. Milkis, *Theodore Roosevelt, the Progressive Party, and the Transformation of American Democracy* (Lawrence, KS: University of Kansas Press, 2009), 247. Rauchway has "recognized creeds" in place of "organized greeds" (*Murdering McKinley*, 192). It is not clear which Roosevelt actually said on that occasion; both alternatives are plausible enough in the context of his remarks, which concerned not only the evils of inequality but also the evils of intemperate partisan rhetoric on the left and the right.

27. They may have been right to do so. Roosevelt was a former police commissioner for New York City and probably knew that homicide rates were on the rise. Some commentators even spoke of a "murder wave" in Progressive-Era American cities. In part, the perception of a wave may have been a statistical artifact; this was the era in which crusading reformers in municipal administration learned to standardize statistical reporting of violent deaths, and gradually trained coroners and police to classify an increasing share of preventable deaths as murders. But the best estimates suggest that there was a real increase underneath the statistical noise, and studies of other times and places suggest that rising inequality may have something to do with the rising tide of violence. On rising homicide rates in the first decade of the 20th century, see Eric Monkkonen, "New York City Homicides: A Research Note," *Social Science History* 19, no. 2 (1995), 210; cf. Eric Monkkonen, "Homicide in Los Angeles, 1827-2002," *Journal of Interdisciplinary History* 36, no. 2 (2005): 167–83; Eric Monkkonnen, "Homicide: Explaining America's Exceptionalism," *American Historical Review* 111, no. 1 (2006): 76–94. For cautionary notes on the quality of the data, see Jeffrey S. Adler, " 'Halting the Slaughter of the Innocents': The Civilizing Process and the Surge in Violence in Turn-of-the-Century Chicago," *Social Science History* 25, no. 1 (2001): 29–52; Douglas Lee Eckberg, "Estimates of Early Twentieth-Century U.S. Homicide Rates: An Econometric Forecasting Approach," *Demography* 32, no. 1 (1995): 9. Scholars have found in dozens of cross-sectional studies that inequality is associated with higher rates of homicide. Conclusive evidence for a causal relationship is elusive, however, and some historical periods—most notably, the U.S. at the end of the 1960s, when American society was about as equal as it has ever been, yet becoming more violent—tell against the simple linear hypothesis that any increase in income inequality causes a proportional increase in murder rates.

28. In Mellon's circle of the top 0.01 percent, fully three-quarters were men in 1916. There are no data on the average age of the super-rich before 1919, but in that year, the average age of the wealthiest 0.01 percent of Americans was 58 (Kopcuk and Saez, "Top Wealth Shares," table B4). There are no systematic data on the race of the wealthiest Americans

in this period, but it is safe to assume that the top wealth holders in Mellon's stratum were white. A handful of black people were reputed to be millionaires in the Progressive Era, including the hair-care entrepreneur Madame C. J. Walker; but Madame Walker's income in 1913 was just over $30,000, and her wealth was approximately $20,000; Beverly Lowry, *Her Dream of Dreams: the Rise and Triumph of Madam C. J. Walker* (New York: Vintage, 2003), 304. For evidence that a determined researcher failed to uncover any actual black millionaires in this period, see Booker T. Washington, *The Story of the Negro: the Rise of the Race from Slavery*, vol. 2 (New York: Doubleday, 1909), 209–10.

29. There must have been considerable overlap between the people with the greatest fortunes and the people drawing the largest incomes, because the top incomes consisted mainly of interest and dividends from invested wealth. Still, the overlap between the wealthy and those with high income was not total: Although almost all very high-income people were wealthy, the converse was not always true. Far below Mellon in the wealth distribution— among those men and women whose wealth was merely above average—there must have been many struggling small business owners whose incomes were not very great at all.

30. On "millionaire," see Mellon, *Reflections*, 79; Andrew Mellon sometimes denied he was "rich" because others, he said, were richer in happiness (Cannadine, *Mellon*, 241). On manliness and the ideology of "character," see Jerome Karabel, *The Chosen: The Hidden History of Admission and Exclusion at Harvard, Yale, and Princeton* (New York: Houghton Mifflin, 2005), 29–38; E. Digby Baltzell, *The Protestant Establishment: Aristocracy and Caste in America* (New Haven, CT: Yale University Press, 1964). For studies of how elites drew social boundaries in the Progressive Era, see Jeffrey Haydu, *Citizen Employers: Business Communities and Labor in Cincinnati and San Francisco* (Ithaca, NY: Cornell University Press, 2009); Nicola Beisel, *Imperiled Innocents: Anthony Comstock and Family Reproduction in Victorian America* (Princeton, NJ: Princeton University Press, 1997); William G. Roy, "The Organization of the Corporate Class Segment of the U.S. Capitalist Class at the Turn of This Century," in *Bringing Class Back In: Contemporary and Historical Perspectives*, eds. Scott G. McNall, Rhonda F. Levine, and Rick Fantasia (Boulder, CO: Westview Press, 1991), 139-63. Other historians emphasize the gradual, harmonious integration of old families of proprietary capitalists and the new corporate rich into a common upper class. "Frictions and irritations there were of the snobbery and bigotry kind," writes Martin Sklar, "but not such as to obstruct the process as a whole"; Martin J. Sklar, *The Corporate Reconstruction of American Capitalism, 1880-1916* (New York: Cambridge University Press, 1988), 29. See also Olivier Zunz, *Making America Corporate, 1870-1920* (Chicago: University of Chicago Press, 1990), 14.

31. On the Southern rich, see Bryan Burroughs, *The Big Rich: The Rise and Fall of the Greatest Texas Oil Fortunes* (New York: Penguin, 2009). The pattern of business vote-buying had begun to change in the decade before 1913, as big business lobbying became professional- ized and increasingly focused on administrative agencies, rather than on suborning indi- vidual legislators. See Richard McCormick, *The Party Period and Public Policy: American Politics from the Age of Jackson to the Progressive Era* (Oxford, UK, and New York: Oxford University Press, 1986); Robert H. Wiebe, *The Search for Order, 1877-1920* (New York: Hill and Wang, 1967), 181–3.

32. On Mellon's streetcar lines, see Cannadine, *Mellon* 140–1. On the divorce legislation, see 205–6.

33. Cannadine, *Mellon*, 176.

34. Robert H. Wiebe, "Business Disunity and the Progressive Movement, 1901-1914," *Mississippi Valley Historical Review* 44, no. 4 (1958): 664-85; Samuel P. Hays, "The Politics of Reform in Municipal Government in the Progressive Era," *Pacific Northwest Quarterly* 55, no. 4 (1964): 157-64; Clifton K. Yearley, *The Money Machines: The Breakdown and Reform of Governmental and Party Finance in the North, 1860-1920* (Albany, NY: State University of New York Press, 1969), 121–34; McCormick, *Party Period*; Roy, "Organization of the Corporate Class Segment."

35. On the wave of business consolidation in this period, see Gabriel Kolko, *The Triumph of Conservatism: A Reinterpretation of American History, 1900-1916* (New York: Quadrangle, 1967). On Mellon's holdings, see Harvey O'Connor, *Mellon's Millions: The Biography of a Fortune* (New York: John Day Co., 1933), 400–1; Cannadine, *Mellon*, 229.

36. See, e.g., Kim Voss, *The Making of American Exceptionalism: The Knights of Labor and Class Formation in the Nineteenth Century* (Ithaca, NY: Cornell University Press, 1993); Haydu, *Citizen Employers*, 49–51, 71–8.

37. Christopher Capozzola, "The Only Badge Needed Is Your Patriotic Fervor: Vigilance, Coercion and the Law in World War I America," *Journal of American History* 88, no. 4 (2002): 1354-82; Larry Isaac, "To Counter 'The Very Devil' and More: The Making of Independent Capitalist Militia in the Gilded Age," *American Journal of Sociology* 108, no. 2 (2002): 353-405; Jason Kaufman, *For the Common Good? American Civic Life and the Golden Age of Fraternity* (Oxford, UK, and New York: Oxford University Press, 2002).

38. William D. Carrigan, "The Lynching of Persons of Mexican Origin or Descent in the United States, 1848 to 1928," *Journal of Social History* 37, no. 2 (2003), 411–3; Clive Webb, "The Lynching of Sicilian Immigrants in the American South, 1886-1910," *American Nineteenth-Century History* 3, no. 1 (2002): 45–76; W. Fitzhugh Brundage, *Lynching in the New South: Georgia and Virginia, 1880-1930* (Urbana, IL: University of Illinois Press, 1993), 17–48. That is not to say that vigilantism was identical to lynch-mob rule, or that businessmen had a monopoly on either. Michael J. Pfeifer, *Rough Justice: Lynching and American Society, 1874-1947* (Urbana, IL: University of Illinois Press, 2004), 38–44, emphasizes the socio-economic diversity of lynch mobs, and Philip Dray, *At the Hands of Persons Unknown: The Lynching of Black America* (New York: Modern Library, 2002), 229, describes an instance in Abbeville, South Carolina, in 1916, when the local business elite formed an informal militia to *prevent* lynchings.

39. Emma Goldman, *Living My Life*, vol. 1 (New York: Dover, 1970), 500; Roger Bruns, *The Damndest Radical: The Life and World of Ben Reitman, Chicago's Celebrated Social Reformer, Hobo King, and Whorehouse Physician* (Chicago: University of Chicago Press, 2001), 122–4. We have this detailed description because Reitman lived to tell the story, and because he was a doctor who was able and willing to provide a detailed clinical description of what had happened to him.

40. The San Diego businessmen who assaulted Reitman, for example, appear to have acted with the connivance of local police; Bruns, *Damndest Radical*, 122.

41. Even in the nineteenth century, the term was sometimes used in a more general sense (see Tilly, *Social Movements*, ch. 1), but such usage did not yet predominate. For an example of the usage of "social movement" to mean the labor movement, see Werner Sombart, *Socialism and the Social Movement in the Nineteenth Century*, trans. Anson P. Atterbury (New York: G. P. Putnam's Sons, 1898).

42. On lobbying, see, e.g., Wiebe, *Search for Order*, 183; Elizabeth S. Clemens, *The People's Lobby: Organizational Innovation and the Rise of Interest Group Politics in the United States, 1890-1925* (Chicago: University of Chicago Press, 1997). On national, candidate-centered political campaign organizations, see Milkis, *Theodore Roosevelt*, 75–122. This discussion of social movements in the Progressive Era is indebted to Alan Dawley, *Struggles for Justice: Social Responsibility and the Liberal State* (Cambridge, MA: Harvard University Press, 1991); Nell Irvin Painter, *Standing at Armageddon: The United States, 1877-1919* (New York: W. W. Norton, 1987); McGerr, *A Fierce Discontent*, and most especially Clemens, *The People's Lobby*.

43. "Grass roots" is obviously an agrarian metaphor. The first usage of this metaphor to describe non-elite civic participation that I have been able to find is a reference to the Progressive-Era farmers' movement in C. A. McNabb, "Monthly Meetings," in *Proceedings of the Twelfth Annual Meeting of the American Association of Farmers' Institute Workers*, Washington, D.C., October 23–24, 1907 (U.S. Department of Agriculture Office of Experiment Stations, Bulletin 199): 73–4.

44. Patrick H. Mooney and Theo J. Majka, *Farmers' and Farm Workers' Movements: Social Protest in American Agriculture* (New York: Twayne, 1995), 52–60; Elizabeth Sanders, *Roots of Reform: Farmers, Workers, and the American State, 1877-1917* (Chicago: University of Chicago Press, 1999), 149–51; Robert Lee Hunt, *A History of the Farmers' Union in Texas* (Ph.D. thesis, Department of Economics, University of Wisconsin, 1934).

45. "Whereasing and resolving" is from Carl C. Plehn, "Tax Reform in California," *The American Review of Reviews* 43 (1911): 86. On the Farmers' Union, see Charles Simon Barrett, *The Mission, History and Times of the Farmers' Union: A Narrative of the Greatest Industrial-Agricultural Organization in History and Its Makers* (Nashville, TN: Marshall and Bruce Co., 1909), 253–414.

46. Lawrence Glickman, *A Living Wage: American Workers and the Making of Consumer Society* (Ithaca, NY: Cornell University Press, 1997); Max Morris, "Our Living Wage Movement," *Retail Clerks International Advocate* 15, no. 10 (1908): 13-18; Sanders, *Roots of Reform*, 39; David Montgomery, *The Fall of the House of Labor: the Workplace, the State, and American Labor Activism 1865-1920* (New York and Cambridge, UK: Cambridge University Press, 1987), 289.

47. Joseph R. Gusfield, "Social Structure and Moral Reform: A Study of the Women's Christian Temperance Union," *American Journal of Sociology* 61, no. 3 (1955): 222.

48. Daniel Okrent, *Last Call: The Rise and Fall of Prohibition* (New York: Scribner, 2010), 14–9.

49. Michael Kazin, *The Populist Persuasion: An American History* (Ithaca, NY: Cornell University Press, 1995), 82–93.

50. Carry Amelia Nation, *The Use and Need of the Life of Carry A. Nation* (Topeka, KS: F. M. Steves and Sons, 1908), 69–70; Fran Grace, *Carry A. Nation: Retelling the Life* (Bloomington, IN: University of Indiana Press, 2001) 240, 145–7; Kazin, *Populist Persuasion*, 87.

51. For the background of suffrage activism, see Okrent, *Last Call*; Clemens, *People's Lobby*, 222. On the club movement, see Mary I. Wood, *The History of the General Federation of Women's Clubs for the First Twenty-Two Years of Its Organization* (New York: General Federation of Women's Clubs, 1912), 310; Clemens, *People's Lobby*, 94, 196–7.

52. Kloppenberg has called the graduated income tax "the central doctrine of progressivism"; James T. Kloppenberg, *The Uncertain Victory: Social Democracy and Progressivism in European and American Thought, 1870-1920* (Oxford, UK, and New York: Oxford University Press, 1986), 300. For some of the debates over "progressivism," see Peter G. Filene, "An Obituary for 'The Progressive Movement,' " *American Quarterly* 22, no. 1 (1970): 20-34; Daniel T. Rodgers, "In Search of Progressivism," *Reviews in American History* 10, no. 4 (1982): 113–32; Arthur Stanley Link and Richard L. McCormick, *Progressivism* (Arlington Heights, IL: Harlan Davidson, Inc., 1983). I am following some more recent works that have rehabilitated the term to refer to the heterogeneous but overlapping social movements of what are sometimes called "social progressives," in particular those who came together in 1912 to form the Progressive Party. See esp. Painter, *Standing at Armageddon*; Daniel T. Rodgers, *Atlantic Crossings: Social Politics in a Progressive Age* (Cambridge, MA: Harvard University Press, 1998); McGerr, *A Fierce Discontent*; Eldon Eisenach, "Introduction," in *The Social and Political Thought of American Progressivism*, ed. Eldon Eisenach (Indianapolis, IN: Hackett, 2006), vii-xx; Milkis, *Theodore Roosevelt*.

53. See Yearley, *Money Machines*; Plehn, "Tax Reform in California"; R. Rudy Higgens-Evenson, *The Price of Progress: Public Services, Taxation, and the American Corporate State, 1877 to 1929* (Baltimore, MD: Johns Hopkins University Press, 2003).

54. Ajay Mehrotra, "More Mighty than the Waves of the Sea: Toilers, Tariffs and the Income Tax Movement, 1880-1913," *Labor History* 45, no. 2 (2004): 182. The AFL endorsed a progressive income tax at its 26th annual convention. See "Report of Federation Delegates," *Typographical Journal* 31 (1907): 122.

55. Okrent, *Last Call*, 57; on temperance and the income tax, see 55–8.

56. Carrie Chapman Catt, "Reading for Clubs," *National Suffrage Bulletin* 4, no. 2 (1898): 1–2; see also Belle Case La Folette and Caroline L. Hunt, "Women's Views on Some Political

Questions," *La Follette's* 4, no. 5 (1912): 11; Elizabeth Williams, "A Woman Tells Why Women Are Free Traders," *American Economist* 11, no. 10 (1893): 1-2.

57. Marshall, *Splintered Sisterhood*, 110.

58. On tax resistance by post-Civil-War suffragists, see Carolyn C. Jones, "Dollars and Selves: Women's Tax Criticism and Resistance in the 1870s," *University of Illinois Law Review* 1994, no. 2 (1994): 265-310; Linda Kerber, *No Constitutional Right to Be Ladies: Women and the Obligations of Citizenship* (New York: Hill and Wang, 1998), 81–123.

59. The Connecticut suffrage activist Julia Smith, who had most of her cows seized for her refusal to pay property tax after the Civil War, made this point in an 1878 speech to other suffragists in Washington, D.C. "There are but two of our cows left at present, Taxey and Votey," she said. "It is something a little peculiar that Taxey is very obtrusive; why, I can scarcely step out of doors without being confronted by her, while Votey is quiet and shy, but... it is my opinion that in a very short time, wherever you find Taxey there Votey will be also" (quoted in Kerber, *No Constitutional Right*, 112).

60. On voting rights in the states, see Alexander Keyssar, *The Right to Vote: the Contested History of Democracy in the United States* (Philadelphia: Basic Books, 2000), table A.18. On the Tax Resistance League, see Hilary Frances, " 'Pay the Piper, Call the Tune!': the Women's Tax Resistance League," in *The Women's Suffrage Movement: New Feminist Perspectives*, eds. Maroula Joannou and June Purvis (Manchester, UK: Manchester University Press, 1998), 65-76. After 1913, some leading American suffragists would follow the lead of their British comrades by refusing to report their incomes to the federal government; see Anna Howard Shaw, "Women and the Income Tax," *Labor Digest* 7, no. 1 (1914): 32.

61. On the background of the lawsuit, see Richard J. Joseph, *The Origins of the American Income Tax: The Revenue Act of 1894 and Its Aftermath* (Syracuse, NY: Syracuse University Press, 2004), 106–7; *Pollock v. Farmers' Loan and Trust Company*, 157 U.S. 429; and *Pollock v. Farmers' Loan and Trust Company (Rehearing)*, 158 U.S. 601. The decision in the rehearing hinged on the treatment of rental income from land, and the court's reasoning on this matter was unusually tortuous; most interpreters have found it to be both logically inconsistent and historically incorrect in its interpretation of the direct tax clause of the Constitution. Lawrence Friedman, in his magisterial *History of American Law*, describes the judgment as "bad law, bad politics, and bad form"; Lawrence Friedman, *A History of American Law* (New York: Simon and Schuster, 1985), 430.

62. John D. Buenker, *The Income Tax and the Progressive Era* (New York: Garland, 1985), 104; Robert Stanley, *Dimensions of Law in the Service of Order: Origins of the Federal Income Tax, 1861–1913* (New York: Oxford University Press, 1993), 180; Steven R. Weisman, *The Great Tax Wars: Lincoln to Wilson—the Fierce Battles over Money and Power that Transformed the Nation* (New York: Simon and Schuster, 2002), 226; Ratner, *Taxation and Democracy*, 280–6.

63. Weisman, *Great Tax Wars*, 226–7. The actual amendment was introduced by conservatives on the Senate Finance Committee, but it was a revision of a text first drafted by Nebraska Senator Norris Brown, whom the progressive historian Sidney Ratner described as "a halfway insurgent" (*Taxation and Democracy*, 298). Brown seems to have genuinely favored an income tax, but he also seems to have been acting in this instance on Taft's instructions; see Buenker, *Income Tax*, 126.

64. Milkis, *Theodore Roosevelt*, 125–9, 156–64; Allen F. Davis, "The Social Workers and the Progressive Party, 1912-1916," *The American Historical Review* 69 no. 3 (1964): 671-88. On the role of former Populists in the Bull Moose Party, see Samuel L. Webb, "From Independents to Populists to Progressive Republicans: The Case of Chilton County, Alabama, 1880-1920," *The Journal of Southern History* 59, no. 4 (1993): 707-36.

65. Buenker, *Income Tax*, 138–56. On the election of 1912, see Painter, *Standing at Armageddon*, 269; Milkis, *Theodore Roosevelt*.

66. Buenker, *Income Tax*, 157–8, 377; Brownlee, *Federal Taxation*, 43–6.

67. Ratner, *Taxation and Democracy*, 392; see David M. Kennedy, *Over Here: The First World War and American Society* (Oxford, UK, and New York: Oxford University Press,

1980), 107–12; Steven A. Bank, Kirk J. Stark, and Joseph J. Thorndike, *War and Taxes* (Washington, D.C.: Urban Institute, 2008), 52–7.

68. O'Connor, *Mellon's Millions*, 119, 123.

69. O'Connor, *Mellon's Millions*, 134. The story of Mellon's appointment is told in Cannadine, *Mellon*, 267–71.

70. O'Connor, *Mellon's Millions*, 143–4; Cannadine, *Mellon*, 287–8; on the business agitation for tax reform, see Ajay Mehrotra, "The Paradox of Retrenchment: Post-World War I Republican Ascendancy and the Consolidation of the Modern American Fiscal State" (paper presented at the Annual Meetings of the Midwest Political Science Association, Chicago, April 14, 2007); Ratner, *Taxation and Democracy*, 403–6.

Chapter 2

1. Jack Pfeiffer to Andrew W. Mellon, May 7, 1925, National Archives and Records Administration, RG 56, Entry 191, Box 163, Binder: Tax (General): April–June, 1925.

2. Paul Dickson and Thomas B. Allen, *The Bonus Army: An American Epic* (New York: Walker and Co., 2004), 28–9.

3. On the veterans' bonus movement and the 1924 confrontation with Mellon, see Dicksen and Allen, *Bonus Army*, 25–38; Cannadine, *Mellon*, 315; Andrew W. Mellon, *Taxation: The People's Business* (New York: Macmillan, 1924), 188–9. The publicity campaign is described in M. Susan Murnane, "Selling Scientific Taxation: The Treasury Department's Campaign for Tax Reform in the 1920s," *Law and Social Inquiry* 29, no. 3 (2004): 834–6.

4. Arnold's date of birth is from the U.S. Senate Committee on the Judiciary, *Lobby Investigation: Hearings before a Subcommittee of the Committee on the Judiciary, United States Senate, 71st Congress, 2nd Session, pursuant to S. Res. 20, A resolution to investigate the activities of lobbying associations and lobbyists in and around Washington, District of Columbia, October 15 to November 15, 1929*, Vol. 1. (Washington, D.C.: Government Printing Office, 1929), 696; Chicago *Tribune*, "Obituaries: James Asbury Arnold," July 31, 1948, 4. On the Arnold family in Foster Township, see Marion County Historical Society, *Marion County, Illinois: History and Families* (Salem, IL: Turner Publishing Co., 1995), 12, 33, 37, 40–1.

5. Marion County Historical Society, *Marion County*, 41; Brink, McDonough and Company, *History of Marion and Clinton Counties, Illinois, with Illustrations Descriptive of the Scenery and Biographical Sketches of Some of the Prominent Men and Pioneers* (Evansville, IN: Unigraphic, 1974), 252.

6. Charles Postel, *The Populist Vision* (New York: Oxford University Press, 2007), points out that Populist radicals were also agrarian boosters, in order to make a point that this was a "modern" movement; this paragraph echoes his account.

7. For evidence of a robust ecological correlation between market income volatility and agrarian radicalism, see Robert A. McGuire, "Economic Causes of Late Nineteenth Century Unrest: New Evidence," *Journal of Economic History* 41 (1981): 835-52. For evidence concerning the component of income variability that was due to fluctuating railroad rates, see Robert Higgs, "Railroad Rates and the Populist Uprising," *Agricultural History* 44 (1970): 291-8; and Mark Aldrich, "A Note on Railroad Rates and the Populist Uprising," *Agricultural History* 54, no. 3 (1980): 424–32.

8. Taylor, *Farmer's Movement*, 163–5; "Farmers' Convention of the 6th Congressional District," *Prairie Farmer* 44, no. 10 (March 8, 1983): 75; Roy Vernon Scott, *The Agrarian Movement in Illinois, 1880-1896* (Urbana, IL: University of Illinois Press, 1962), 50. The Farmers' Mutual Benefit Association, one of the founding organizations of the People's Party, held its first convention in Centralia, and Herman Taubeneck, the first chairman of the People's Party, was a farmer from Marshall, Illinois, three counties over from J. A. Arnold's childhood home. Peter H. Argersinger, "Taubeneck's Laws: Third Parties in

American Politics in the Late Nineteenth Century," *American Nineteenth Century History*, 3, no. 2 (2002): 93–116.

9. Hamlin Garland, *A Son of the Middle Border* (Whitefish, MT: Kessinger, 2005 [1917]), 244.

10. Milton L. Ready, *The Southern Tariff Association* (M.A. thesis, Department of History, University of Houston), 10

11. Though not as often as blue-collar workers. See Susan B. Carter and Elizabeth Savoca, "Labor Mobility and Lengthy Jobs in Nineteenth-Century America," *Journal of Economic History* 50, no. 1 (1990): 1–16; Sanford M. Jacoby and Sunil Sharma, "Employment Duration and Industrial Labor Mobility in the United States 1880-1980," *Journal of Economic History* 52, no. 1 (1992): 161–79. On the clerical occupation in the late nineteenth century, see Harry Braverman, *Labor and Monopoly Capital* (New York: Monthly Review Press, 1974), 295; Elyce J. Rotella, "The Transformation of the American Office: Changes in Employment and Technology," *The Journal of Economic History* 41, no. 1 (1981): 51-7; Zunz, *Making America Corporate*.

12. U.S. Senate Committee on the Judiciary, *Lobby Investigation* (1929), 695. The date he moved from Kansas to Missouri is unclear from his testimony, but it was not more than a few years before his move to Texas.

13. See Robert C. McMath, *American Populism: A Social History, 1877-1898* (New York: Hill and Wang, 1993); John Donald Hicks, *The Populist Revolt: A History of the Farmer's Alliance and the People's Party* (Minneapolis: University of Minnesota Press, 1931), 25, 84–7.

14. Hicks, *Populist Revolt*, 275–80.

15. Richard Hofstadter, *The Age of Reform: From Bryan to F.D.R.* (New York: Vintage, 1955), 132; William Allen White, "What's the Matter with Kansas?" *Emporia Gazette*, August 15, 1896, reprinted at http://projects.vassar.edu/1896/whatsthematter.html.

16. On the TFU's early days and demands, see Robert Lee Hunt, *A History of the Farmers' Union in Texas* (Ph.D. thesis, Department of Economics, University of Wisconsin, 1934), xxx, 126–7. On the failure of Texas Populism, see Gregg Cantrell and D. Scott Barton, "Texas Populists and the Failure of Biracial Politics," *Journal of Southern History*, vol. 55, no. 4 (1989): 659-92.

17. On Arnold's mercurial temperament, see Ida Darden to John Henry Kirby, November 17, 1921, JHK, Box 96, Folder 3; John K. Emmerson, *The Japanese Thread: A Life in the Foreign Service* (New York: Holt, Rinehart and Winston, 1978), 19. Congressional investigators concluded that he was destroying documents deliberately, but private correspondence with funders and auditors suggests that his books were always a mess. Cf. U.S. Senate Committee on the Judiciary, *Lobby Investigation* (1929), vol. 1, 698; Ready, *Southern Tariff Association*, 135–6; Fred C. Reimann to J. A. Arnold, February 15, 1921, JHK, Box 92, Folder 15.

18. See John Henry Kirby to John W. Blodgett, March 12, 1928, JHK, Box 96, Folder 20.

19. Quoted in Ready, *Southern Tariff Association*, 137.

20. E. E. Schattschneider, *Politics, Pressure and the Tariff: A Study of Free Private Enterprise in Pressure Politics, as Shown in the 1929-1930 Revision of the Tariff* (New York: Prentice-Hall, 1935), 210–1; Christopher M. Loomis, "The Politics of Uncertainty: Lobbyists and Propaganda in Early Twentieth-Century America," *Journal of Policy History* 21, no. 2 (2009): 187-213; Murnane, "Selling Scientific Taxation," 821.

21. Ready, *Southern Tariff Association*, 11.

22. Ready, *Southern Tariff Association*, 11.

23. Ready, *Southern Tariff Association*, 14; Kevin C. Motl, "Under the Influence: The Texas Business Men's Association and the Campaign against Reform, 1906-1915," *Southwestern Historical Quarterly* 109, no. 4 (2006): 501

24. Ready, *Southern Tariff Association*, 16; U.S. Senate Committee on the Judiciary, *Brewing and Liquor Interests and German and Bolshevik Propaganda. Report and Hearings of the Subcommittee on the Judiciary, United States Senate. Submitted pursuant to S. Res. 307 and 439, Sixty-Fifth Congress, relating to charges made against the United States Brewers' Association and Allied Interests*, vol. 2. (Washington, D.C.: Government Printing Office, 1918), 2525. It

had been the policy of the Texas Farmers' Union to "keep a man at Austin during the sessions of the legislature to look after the farmers' interests" since 1905 (Hunt, *History of the Farmer's Union*, 138).

25. Ready, *Southern Tariff Association*, 17; Elna C. Green, "From Antisuffragism to Anticommunism: The Conservative Career of Ida M. Darden," *Journal of Southern History* 65, no. 2 (1999): 291.

26. Motl, "Under the Influence," 509.

27. U.S. Senate Committee on the Judiciary, *Brewing and Liquor Interests*, 2525.

28. Hunt, *History of the Farmers' Union*, 255; Charles Simon Barrett, *The Mission, History and Times of the Farmers' Union: A Narrative of the Greatest Industrial-Agricultural Organization in History and Its Makers* (Nashville, TN: Marshall and Bruce Co., 1909), 405.

29. Motl, "Under the Influence," 514; U.S. Senate Committee on the Judiciary, *Brewing and Liquor Interests*, 2531.

30. Hofstadter, *Age of Reform*, 102.

31. Motl, "Under the Influence"; U.S. Senate Committee on the Judiciary, *Brewing and Liquor Interests*.

32. Kirby quoted in Ready, *Southern Tariff Association*, 29.

33. Ready, *Southern Tariff Association*, 128–9.

34. Ready, *Southern Tariff Association*, 51.

35. Arnold is quoted in U.S. Senate Committee on the Judiciary, *Lobby Investigation* (1929), vol. 1, 633. On the 1921 Act, see Ready, *Southern Tariff Association*, 69. Ready argues that other farm groups were more influential in getting farm products into the 1922 Act, and that the main effect of the association was to co-opt Southern congressmen into supporting protectionism (*Southern Tariff Association*, 115). See also Schattschneider, *Politics, Pressure and the Tariff*, 134; F. W. Taussig, *The Tariff History of the United States*, 8th ed. (New York: G. P. Putnam's Sons, 1931), 471.

36. J. A. Arnold to John Henry Kirby, January 3, 1923, JHK, Box 96, Folder 18.

37. Arnold to Kirby, December 22, 1923, JHK, Box 96, Folder 10.

38. Arnold to Kirby, December 23, 1922, JHK, Box 96, Folder 6; Arnold to Kirby, September 18, 1922, JHK, Box 96, Folder 7.

39. J. A. Arnold to Andrew W. Mellon, November 1, 1924, National Archives and Records Administration, RG 56, Entry 191, Box 195, Binder Tax-Inheritance, July–December 1924.

40. Arnold to Kirby, December 22, 1923, JHK, Box 96, Folder 10.

41. Arnold to Kirby, January 23, 1924, JHK, Box 96, Folder 18.

42. King, *Money, Time and Politics*, 110; Ratner, *Taxation and Democracy*, 415; see also Murnane, "Selling Scientific Taxation."

43. On the prestige of Mellon, see J. A. Arnold to Garrard B. Winston, December 19, 1924, RG 56, Entry 191, Box 163, Folder: Tax (General)—September–December 1924.

44. Arne Clarence Wiprud, *The Federal Farm-Loan System in Operation* (New York: Harper and Brothers, 1921), 16, 24–5; Stuart W. Shulman, "The Origin of the Federal Farm Loan Act: Issue Emergence and Agenda-Setting in the Progressive Era Print Press," in *Fighting for the Farm: Rural America Transformed*, ed. Jane Adams (Philadelphia: University of Pennsylvania Press, 2003).

45. U.S. Senate Committee on Banking and Currency, *Hearings before the Committee on Banking and Currency of the United States Senate, Sixty-Sixth Congress, Second Session, on S. 3109, A Bill to Amend Section 26 of the Act Approved July 17, 1916 Known as the Federal Farm Loan Act, January 10, 12, and 13, 1920* (Washington, D.C., 1920), 10; Jesse Eliphalet Pope, *The Federal Farm Loan Act* (Washington, D.C., 1917), 11; Charles George, "Validity of Federal Farm Loan Act," *The Lawyer and Banker and Southern Bench and Bar Review* 11, no. 5 (1918): 424; Shulman, "Origin of the Federal Farm Loan Act," 127. On the tax exemption, see Maureen O'Hara, "Tax-Exempt Financing: Some Lessons from History," *Journal of Money, Credit and Banking* 15, no. 4 (1983): 425–41.

46. George E. Putnam, "Recent Developments in the Federal Farm Loan System," *American Economic Review* 11 (1921), 432; Wiprud, *Federal Farm Loan System*, 34–5.

47. Lee J. Alston, "Farm Foreclosures in the United States During the Interwar Period," *Journal of Economic History*, 43, no. 4 (1983), 885–903; Lee J. Alston, Wayne A. Grove, and David C. Wheelock, "Why Do Banks Fail? Evidence from the 1920s," *Explorations in Economic History* 31 (1994): 409–31; David C. Wheelock, "Deposit Insurance and Bank Failure," *Economic Inquiry* 30 (1992): 530–43; Linda M. Hooks and Kenneth J. Robinson, "Deposit Insurance and Moral Hazard: Evidence from Texas Banking in the 1920s," *Journal of Economic History* 62, no. 3 (2002): 833–53.

48. Mellon, *Taxation*, 76–9.

49. G. H. Colvin (chairman, Texas Division, American Bankers' League) to P. P. Langford, November 1, 1924, RG 56, Entry 191, Box 195, Binder: Tax-Inheritance, July–December 1924; Andrew W. Mellon to J. A. Arnold, November 19, 1924, Box 195, Binder: Tax-Inheritance, July–December 1924.

50. This graph omits 21 meetings reported to have taken place in January 1925, the precise dates of which were not recorded. The inventory of meetings comes from Nathan Adams to Andrew Mellon, January 10, 1925; and Nathan Adams to Andrew Mellon, January 27, 1925, both in RG 56, Entry 191, Box 163, Folder: Tax (General) January–April 1925.

51. J. A. Arnold to Garrard B. Winston, January 9, 1925, RG 56, Entry 191, Box 163, Folder: Tax (General) January–March 1925. Contrast Arnold's account of his reception in Virginia: "I spent yesterday in Richmond and was somewhat surprised to find outstanding bankers and businessmen under the impression that there was nothing to do," he wrote on December 19, 1924; "that the Republican party had won the election and all that was necessary was for Secretary Mellon to write a letter to Congress stating what he wanted; that we could get tax revision of any kind at any time the Secretary cared to dictate such a letter, and that any activity on the part of citizens, especially in the South, was unnecessary and might confuse the situation." Arnold to Winston, December 19, 1924, RG 56, Entry 191, Box 163.

52. See U.S. Senate Subcommittee on the Judiciary 1929: 617–630 on the organizational structure and pay structure. For evidence that at least some bankers suspected Arnold of shady dealings, see Melvin Traylor to Garrard B. Winston, December 19, 1924, RG 56, Entry 191, Box 163, Folder: Tax-General (September–December 1924); John Henry Kirby to John W. Blodgett, March 12, 1928, JHK, Box 96, Folder 20.

53. Bankers' Encyclopedia Co., *Polk's Bankers' Encyclopedia (Purple Book)*, 60th ed. (Detroit, 1924). See the inventory of black-owned banks in Abram L. Harris, *The Negro as Capitalist: A Study of Banking and Business among American Negroes* (Gloucester, MA, 1968), 192.

54. Petition of W. C. Stonestreet et al. to Andrew W. Mellon, October 31, 1924, RG 56, Entry 191, Box 195, Binder: Tax-inheritance, July–December 1924.

55. Petition of J. S. Rice et al. to Andrew W. Mellon, November 15, 1924, RG 56, Entry 191, Box 195, Binder: Tax-inheritance, July–December 1924.

56. The characteristics of tax conference conveners in column 1 are inferred from a list of conveners in Nathan Adams to Andrew Mellon, January 10, 1925; and Nathan Adams to Andrew Mellon, January 27, 1925, RG 56, Entry 191, Box 163, Folder: Tax (General) January–April 1925. Occupation and gender were inferred from names listed in *Polk's Bankers' Encyclopedia*. Race and ethnicity were inferred from Harris, *The Negro as Capitalist*, and from the 1990 "Spanish surnames list" of the Census Bureau, available online as Florida Cancer Data System, "Census List of Spanish Surnames," appendix to *Florida Cancer System Data Acquisition Manual*, http://fcds.med.miami.edu/downloads/dam2008/26%20Appendix%20E%20Census%20List%20of%20Spanish%20Surnames.pdf, accessed September 4, 2009. The characteristics of all Texas adults in column 2 were calculated from the 1 percent sample of the 1920 Census: Steven Ruggles, J. Trent Alexander, Katie Genadek, Ronald Goeken, Matthew B. Schroeder, and Matthew Sobek, *Integrated Public Use Microdata Series: Version 5.0* [Machine-readable database] (Minneapolis: University of Minnesota, 2010).

57. "Dallas Citizens Want Taxes Cut," *Dallas Morning News*, Nov. 7, 1924; see also J. A. Arnold to Andrew W. Mellon, November 24, 1924, RG 56, Entry 191, Box 163, Folder: Tax (General)—September–December 1924.

58. Nathan Adams to Hon. Morris Sheppard, January 10, 1925, RG 56, Entry 191, Box 163, Folder: Tax (General): January–March 1925.

59. Author's calculations from data reported in Federal Reserve Board, "Earnings and Expenses of Member Banks," *Federal Reserve Bulletin* (June 1925), 402–5; Federal Reserve Board, "All Member Banks," *Federal Reserve Bulletin* (March 1925), 216.

60. The figure of 188 is my calculation from data in U.S. Office of the Commissioner of Internal Revenue, *Statistics of Income: Individual Income Tax Returns, 1924* (Washington, D.C., 1926), 260–1.

61. Calculated by comparing the conferences listed in Nathan Adams to Andrew Mellon, January 10, 1925, and Nathan Adams to Andrew Mellon, January 27, 1925, RG 56, Entry 191, Box 163, to the enumeration of income tax returns in U.S. Office of the Commissioner of Internal Revenue U.S., *Statistics of Income*, 302, table 17.

62. W. C. Stonestreet et al. to Andrew W. Mellon, October 31, 1924, RG 56, Entry 191, Box 193.

63. J. S. Rice et al. to Andrew W. Mellon, November 15, 1924, RG 56, Entry 191, Box 193.

64. "Dallas Citizens Want Taxes Cut," *Dallas Morning News*, Nov. 7, 1924, attached to J. A. Arnold to Andrew W. Mellon, November 24, 1924, RG 56, Entry 191, Box 193.

65. Nathan Adams to Morris Shepard and Earle B. Mayfield, January 10, 1925, RG 56, Entry 191, Box 163.

66. Arnold to Winston, December 3, 1924, RG 56, Entry 191, Box 163.

67. J. A. Arnold to Andrew W. Mellon, November 24, 1924, RG 56, Entry 191, Box 193 (emphasis added).

68. Mellon, 1924: 82, 92. The petition is included in Nathan Adams to Morris Shepard and Earle B. Mayfield, January 10, 1925, RG 56, Entry 191, Box 163.

69. Many bank officers in larger towns failed to convene tax conferences simply because the role of chairman was already taken by one of the other bankers in town. In order to focus the comparison on bankers who actually had the opportunity to participate as tax conference chairmen, I took a stratified random sample of Texas banks operating in September 1924 from *Polk's Bankers' Encyclopedia*. The sample included all banks whose directors or officers chaired tax conferences, and one randomly selected bank from each Texas town listed in the *Encyclopedia* that did not have a tax conference. The result was a sample of 955 banks, of which 204 had led tax meetings. For each bank in the dataset, I recorded selected financial and organizational information and town characteristics reported in the *Encyclopedia*. I also merged each record geographically with county-level data on 1924 tax returns, election returns, agricultural property relations, and population characteristics. The data sources include U.S. Bureau of Internal Revenue, *Statistics of Income 1924*; Inter-university Consortium for Political and Social Research [ICPSR], United States Historical Election Returns, 1824-1968 [computer file], ICPSR00001-v3 (Ann Arbor, MI, 1999); U.S. Bureau of the Census, *Census of Agriculture* (Washington, D.C., 1925); University of Virginia Library, Historical Census Data Browser, Census Data for Year 1920, http://mapserver.lib.virginia.edu/php/start.php?year=V1920, accessed December 29, 2008. Means in Table 2.2 are weighted to adjust for the stratified sample design.

70. U.S. Senate Judiciary Committee, *Lobby Investigation*, vol. 1 (1929), 697; Harry Haas to Garrard B. Winston, April 6, 1925, RG 56, Entry 191, Box 163, Folder: Tax (General): April–June 1925.

71. For an example of bank-to-bank outreach along these lines, see G. H. Colvin (chairman, Texas Division, American Bankers' League) to P. P. Langford, November 1, 1924, RG 56, Entry 191, Box 195, Binder: Tax-Inheritance, July–December 1924.

72. J. A. Arnold to Bird W. Spencer, February 21, 1925, Folder: Tax (General), January–March 1925, RG 56, Entry 191, Box 163.; American Taxpayers' League, Bulletin No. 1, 1925, Washington, D.C., January 15, 1925, Box 163, RG 56, Entry 191.

73. J. A. Arnold to Garrard B. Winston, August 5, 1925; Arnold to Winston, August 7, 1925, RG 56, Entry 191, Box 164, Folder: Tax (General), July–September, 1925; "Iowa Tax Clubs Before House Ways and Means Committee," October 25, 1925, RG 56, Entry 191, Box 164, Folder: Tax (General), October–December 1925.

74. Alston, "Farm Foreclosures," 890; U.S. Bureau of the Census, *Statistical Abstract of the United States* (Washington, D.C., 1924), 252.

75. American Taxpayers' League, Bulletin No. 1, January 15, 1925, RG 56, Entry 191, Box 193.

76. J. A. Arnold to Garrard B. Winston, August 5, 1925, RG 56, Entry 191, Box 164, Folder: Tax (General), July–September 1925.

77. J. A. Arnold to Garrard B. Winston, August 7, 1925, RG 56, Entry 191, Box 164, Folder: Tax (General), July–September 1925.

78. Arnold to Winston, August 21, 1925; Arnold to Winston, August 27, 1925, RG 56, Entry 191, Box 164, Folder: Tax (General) July–September 1925; Arnold to R. A. Crawford, September 30, 1925, RG 56, Entry 191, Folder: Tax (General), October–December 1925. See Murnane, "Selling Scientific Taxation," 846–7.

79. U.S. House of Representatives Committee on Ways and Means, *Revenue Revision 1925: Hearings before the Committee on Ways and Means, United States House of Representatives, 69th Congress, 1st Session, October 19 to November 3, 1925* (Washington, D.C.: Government Printing Office, 1925), 312–4.

80. *Congressional Record* 67, part 1 (December 10, 1925), 654.

81. See Ratner, *Taxation and Democracy*, 425–8.

82. Darien B. Jacobson, Brian G. Raub, and Barry W. Johnson, "The Estate Tax: Ninety Years and Counting," *Statistics of Income (SOI) Bulletin* 27, no. 1 (2007), 125.

83. U.S. House of Representatives Committee on Ways and Means, *Revenue Revision 1927-28: Hearings before the Committee on Ways and Means, United States House of Representatives, Interim, 69th-70th Congresses, October 31 to November 10, 1927* (Washington, D.C.: Government Printing Office, 1927), 765.

84. Mellon, *Taxation*, 112; American Taxpayers' League, "Socialism in Our Tax System," July 18, 1927, and American Taxpayers' League, "Why We Are Opposed to a Federal Estate (Inheritance) Tax," July 2, 1927, RG 56, Entry 191, Box 196, Folder: Tax-inheritance, 1926-27.

85. U.S. House of Representatives Committee on Ways and Means, *Revenue Revision 1927-28*, 623, 815–20; J. A. Arnold to John Henry Kirby, August 18, 1926, and Arnold to Kirby, June 7, 1926, JHK, Box 96, Folder 15.

86. Peter O. Knight to Andrew W. Mellon, September 13, 1927, RG 56, Entry 191, Box 165, Binder: Tax-inheritance,1925.

87. U.S. House of Representatives Committee on Ways and Means, *Revenue Revision 1927-28*, 592, 604, 615, 617, 666–7, 805.

88. Ratner, *Taxation and Democracy*, 431–2.

89. On this point, I differ with Murnane, who argues that the support of expert opinion and national newsmagazines was the critical distinguishing factor; M. Susan Murnane, "Andrew Mellon's Unsuccessful Attempt to Repeal Estate Taxes," *Tax History Project*, August 22, 2005, http://www.taxhistory.org/thp/readings.nsf/ArtWeb/672746F8E859EA7785257 0900006AC21?OpenDocument, accessed February 14, 2009.

90. *Congressional Record* 67, part 1 (December 1925, 10), 654.

91. Ratner, *Taxation and Democracy*, 432.

92. American Taxpayers' League, "Tax Reduction Program," May 15, 1927, RG 56, Entry 191, Box 165, Folder: Tax (General), January–September 1927.

Chapter 3

1. Cannadine, *Mellon*, 382.
2. In 1936, when Democratic Senator Hugo Black characterized Arnold's mailing list of poten-tial donors as a "sucker list," Arnold protested the characterization from the witness stand, and then told Black tartly that, of all the mailing lists he had submitted in evidence, the wealthy Democratic donors were "the only suckers you have"; U.S. Senate Special Committee to Investigate Lobbying Activities, *Investigation of Lobbying Activities: Hearings before a Special Committee to Investigate Lobbying Activities, United States Senate, 74th Congress, 1st Session, part 5* (Washington, D.C.: Government Printing Office, 1936), 1692. Arnold seems to have been a lifelong Republican; Ready, *Southern Tariff Association*, 11.
3. "Premier Issues Hard Hit," *New York Times*, October 29, 1929: 1.
4. John Kenneth Galbraith, *The Great Crash* (Boston: Houghton Mifflin, 1997 [1954]), 113. See also Maury Klein, *Rainbow's End: the Crash of 1929* (Oxford, UK, and New York: Oxford University Press, 2001), 207–38.
5. This is evidence against a simple "power devaluation" model of elite mobilization (cf. McVeigh, *Rise of the Ku Klux Klan*). Rich people lost political power, economic power, and cultural prestige in the crash, but rich people's movements were not seen until policy threats provoked mobilization. The account of the crash in this paragraph draws most heavily on Christina Romer, "The Great Crash and the Onset of the Great Depression," *Quarterly Journal of Economics* 105 (1990): 597–624; Christina Romer, "The Nation in Depression," *Journal of Economic Perspectives* 7 (1993): 19–39; Milton Friedman and Anna Jacobson Schwartz, *The Great Contraction, 1929-1933* (Princeton, NJ: Princeton University Press, 2008 [1963]), 92–102; Benjamin S. Bernanke, *Essays on the Great Depression* (Princeton, NJ: Princeton University Press, 2004), 41–69.
6. U.S. Senate Committee on the Judiciary, *Lobby Investigation*, 725; Vance Muse, "Making Peace with Grandfather," *Texas Monthly* 14, no. 2 (1986): 142; U.S. Senate Special Committee to Investigate Lobbying Activities, *Investigation of Lobbying Activities*, 1668, 1679; Emmerson, *The Japanese Thread*, 18–9. On the date of Muse's departure, see also Ida Muse Darden, "The Christian American, Inc.: Its Purposes and Accomplishments," *The Southern Conservative* 1, no. 4 (1950): 5; on the reorganization, see "Big Business Reported Behind Tax-Ceiling Plan," *Christian Science Monitor*, January 8, 1952: 11.
7. National Research Institute, *17 States Say—Repeal the Income Tax Amendment* (Washington, D.C.: Author, 1944), 15, WP, Box 108a; See "Phillips, Thomas Wharton, Jr., (1874-1956)," in *Biographical Directory of the United States Congress*, INSERT WEBSITE ADDRESS, accessed August 20, 2012; on the father, see Alfred Russell Crum, *The Romance of American Petroleum and Gas* (n.p., 1911), 329–30.
8. "T. W. Phillips, Jr. Served in Congress," *New York Times*, January 3, 1956: 31; Robert F. Burk, *The Corporate State and the Broker State: The Du Ponts and American National Politics, 1925-1940* (Cambridge, MA: Harvard University Press, 1990), 46.
9. Burk, *Corporate State*, 59–60, 71; George Wolfskill, *The Revolt of the Conservatives: A History of the American Liberty League, 1934-1940* (Boston: Houghton Mifflin, 1962), 47–9. On the draft form letter, see U.S. Senate Committee on the Judiciary, *Lobby Investigation* (1929), 3999.
10. U.S. Senate Committee on the Judiciary, *Lobby Investigation: Hearings before a Subcommittee of the Committee on the Judiciary, 71st Congress, 2nd Session* (Washington, D.C.: Government Printing Office, 1931), 3992. On Phillips's position as a trustee, see "Drive for National Church Will Close," *Washington Post*. October 20, 1928: 10.
11. Burk, *Corporate State*, 72.
12. Okrent, *Last Call*, 143, 333, 353; David E. Kyvig, *Repealing National Prohibition*, 2nd ed. (Kent, OH: Kent State University Press, 2000), 133–6.
13. Leff, *Limits*, 31–48; Witte, *Politics and Development*, 98.

14. National Research Institute, *17 States Say...*, 16.
15. Quoted in Okrent, *Last Call*, 363.
16. Lorraine L. Hopkins, "The Voice from 15 Westminster Street," *Providence Sunday Journal Magazine*, June 25, 1967: 28–31; Lorraine Hopkins, "R. B. Dresser, 95, lawyer, GOP power, dies at home," *Providence Sunday Journal*, September 26, 1976: B19; James Clark Fifield, *The American Bar: Contemporary Lawyers of the United States and Canada* (Minneapolis: The James C. Fifield Co., 1918), 599; Robert Luce and J. Ransom Bridge, *Twenty Thousand Rich New Englanders: A List of Taxpayers Who Were Assessed in 1888 to Pay a Tax of One Hundred Dollars or More* (Boston: Luce & Bridge, 1888), 78; Sibley *v. Maxwell*, 303 Mass. 94 (1909); *Acts and Resolves Passed by the General Assembly of the State of Rhode Island and Providence Plantations*, 1912, 620; John A. Salmond, *The Great Textile Strike of 1934* (Columbia, MO: University of Missouri Press, 2002), 92; "Code for Industry Voted Here to Back Aims of New Deal," *New York Times*, December 11, 1936: 1, 31.
17. Hopkins, "The Voice from 15 Westminster Street," 29; "$40,000,000 Net Value Placed Upon Estate of Late Frank Sayles," *Providence Journal*, June 17, 1921: 4; "Eight-Year Fight Over Sayles Suit Will Be Settled," *Providence Journal*, April 17, 1929: 1, 5.
18. Salmond, *Great Textile Strike*, 91–102; Gary Gerstle, *Working-Class Americanism: The Politics of Labor in a Textile City, 1914-1960* (Cambridge, UK, and New York: Cambridge University Press, 1989), 129; A. J. Gordon, "Rhode Island Legislators Balk Move for U.S. Troops," *New York Times*, September 13, 1934: 1.
19. "President is Urged to Balance Budget," *New York Times*, November 19, 1934: 1; "Code for Industry Voted Here," 1, 31; "Committees on Convention Problems," *New York Times*, June 10, 1936: 15; *Republican Party Platform of 1936*, American Presidency Project, http://www.presidency.ucsb.edu/ws/index.php?pid=29639, accessed August 20, 2012; Charles R. Michaels "Platform Draft is Ready," *New York Times*, June 11, 1936: 1, 16. On the National Economy League, see "Future Taxes," *California and Western Medicine* 37, no. 6 (1932): 425–6; Stephen R. Ortiz, "The 'New Deal' for Veterans: The Economy Act, the Veterans of Foreign Wars, and the Origins of New Deal Dissent," *Journal of Military History* 70, no. 2 (2006): 419; Lisle Abbott Rose, *Explorer: the Life of Richard E. Byrd* (Columbia, MO: University of Missouri Press, 2008), 292. On Dresser's authorship of the original 1938 amendment, see the address of Robert B. Dresser, Houston, Texas, May 14, 1953, CCGE.
20. On the confrontation, see William E. Leuchtenburg, "The Origins of Franklin D. Roosevelt's 'Court-Packing' Plan," *The Supreme Court Review*, 1966; William E. Leuchtenburg, "FDR's Court-Packing Plan: A Second Life, a Second Death," *Duke Law Journal* 1985 (3–4): 673–89; William E. Leuchtenburg, *The Supreme Court Reborn: The Constitutional Revolution in the Age of Roosevelt* (Oxford, UK, and New York: Oxford University Press, 1996); for its impact on jurisprudence, see Bernard Schwartz, *A History of the Supreme Court* (Oxford, UK, and New York: Oxford University Press, 1993), 234–8.
21. See Robert B. Dresser to T. Coleman Andrews, May 6, 1956, TCA, Box 15, Folder: Income tax-Robert B. Dresser.
22. Robert B. Dresser, "Reply to Objections of Tax Research Division of U.S. Treasury," n.d. (1944): 6, CCGE.
23. U.S. Advisory Commission on Intergovernmental Relations, *Tax and Expenditure Limits on Local Governments: An Information Report* (Bloomington, IN: Center for Urban Policy and the Environment, Indiana University, 1995); New York State Tax Commission and Commerce Clearing House, *Tax Systems of the World* (Chicago: Commerce Clearing House, 1940).
24. Dresser, *Brief in Support of Proposed Constitutional Amendment*, 14–16.
25. Burk, *Corporate State*, 265.
26. Arnold had resigned from the Southern Tariff Association in 1929 to devote himself full-time to the taxpayers' association; Mary Lasswell, *John Henry Kirby: Prince of the Pines* (Austin, TX: Encino Press, 1967), 189.

27. U.S. Senate Special Committee to Investigate Lobbying Activities, *Investigation of Lobbying Activities*, 1664. The Supreme Court subsequently struck down the tax in January 1936 (*U.S. v. Butler et al.*, 297 U.S. 1).

28. U.S. Senate Special Committee to Investigate Lobbying Activities, *Investigation of Lobbying Activities*, 1680.

29. On Long, see Edwin Amenta, Kathleen Dunleavy, and Mary Bernstein, "Stolen Thunder? Huey Long's 'Share Our Wealth,' Political Mediation, and the Second New Deal," *American Sociological Review* 59, no. 5 (1994): 678–702.

30. See Joseph J. Thorndike, " 'The Unfair Advantage of the Few': The New Deal Origins of 'Soak the Rich' Taxation," in *The New Fiscal Sociology: Taxation in Comparative and Historical Perspective*, eds. Isaac William Martin, Ajay K. Mehrotra, and Monica Prasad (Cambridge, UK, and New York: Cambridge University Press, 2009), 29–47; Leff, *Limits of Symbolic Reform*, 93–168.

31. Burroughs, *Big Rich*, 143; D. E. Casey, "Merits of Tax Limitation," in *Should There Be a Constitutional Amendment Limiting Federal Income, Estate and Gift Taxes? Forum Pamphlet* 3 (New York: Tax Institute, 1944), 3.

32. Wolfskill, *Revolt of the Conservatives*, 130.

33. T. W. Phillips to "Dear Sir," August 10, 1938, SBP, Box 29, Folder 5, University of Oregon Special Collections.

34. On the donations to the American Taxpayers, Association, see U.S. Senate Special Committee to Investigate Lobbying Activities, *Investigation of Lobbying Activities*, 1702.

35. Wolfskill, *Revolt of the Conservatives*, 22; Burk, *Corporate State*, 138–9; on the Liberty League, see also Frederick Rudolph, "The American Liberty League, 1934-1940," *American Historical Review* 56, no. 1 (1950): 19-33; Phillips-Fein, *Invisible Hands*.

36. See Wolfskill, *Revolt of the Conservatives*, 139, 163–88.

37. "Patriotic Societies," *Chicago Tribune*, February 3, 1936: 12.

38. Thomas W. Phillips, Jr., n.d., "This is a Tax Depression," SBP, Box 29, Folder 5.

39. National Research Institute, *17 States Say...*, 15–6.

40. American Taxpayers' Association, "Labor's Stake in the Tax Battle," TI, No. 3, October 15, 1939; American Taxpayers' Association, "The Woman Pays and Pays," TI, No. 4, November 1, 1939.

41. When Gallup asked, "Do you think that conditions in this country would be more prosperous if taxes on business were reduced," 75 percent of respondents agreed. But most people apparently did not think that tax cuts should be targeted to the rich.

42. The table presents the percent offering positive response to the question, "Do you think that conditions in this country would be improved if taxes on people with high incomes were reduced so that they could put this money into business?" (Gallup Poll #1939-0156, May 4–9, 1939— Roper Center for Public Opinion Research, USAIPO1939-0156). These proportions are calculated using post-stratification weights to compensate for the Gallup non-random quota sampling design; in particular, I used the post-stratification weights calculated by Adam Berinsky and Eric Schickler; see Adam J. Berinsky, "American Public Opinion in the 1930s and 1940s: The Analysis of Quota-Controlled Sample Survey Data," *Public Opinion Quarterly* 70, no. 4 (2006): 499-529; Adam Berinsky and Eric Schickler, "Gallup Data, 1936-1945: Guide to Coding and Weighting," unpublished manuscript, Massachusetts Institute of Technology and University of California–Berkeley, 2011.

43. National Research Institute, *17 States Say...*, 14.

44. *Poor's Register of Corporations, Directors and Executives in the United States and Canada* (New York: Standard and Poor's, 1935).

45. The contributions and contributors were calculated from a list in U.S. Senate Special Committee to Investigate Lobbying Activities, *Investigation of Lobbying Activities*, 1676–8; industry was inferred by comparing contributors to listings in the 1935 edition of *Poor's Register of Corporations, Directors and Executives in the United States and Canada*.

46. U.S. Senate Special Committee to Investigate Lobbying Activities, *Investigation of Lobbying Activities*, 1673, 1679.

47. Totals for each state were calculated from contributions listed in U.S. Senate Special Committee to Investigate Lobbying Activities, *Investigation of Lobbying Activities*, 1676–8.

48. Id., 1657, 1673–4.

49. "Patriotic Societies," 12; *Why the 25 Percent Limit on Federal Taxes* (Washington, D.C.: American Taxpayers' Association, 1944), WP, Box 108A, Folder: Booklets and pamphlets on the tax limitation amendment.

50. Phyllis Cohen, *Representative Emanuel Celler: A Case Study in Legislative Behavior, 1923-1950* (Ph.D. thesis, New York University, 1952), 14, 78, 104–6, EC.

51. National Research Institute, *17 States Say...*, 18; U.S. House of Representatives Committee on the Judiciary, *Amending Constitution Relative to Taxes on Incomes, Inheritances, and Gifts: Hearing before Subcommittee No. 3 of the Committee on the Judiciary, House of Representatives, 85th Congress, 2nd Session* (Washington, D.C.: Government Printing Office, 1958), 6.

52. *Summary of the History of the Adoption of the Sixteenth Amendment and of the Current Efforts of the American Taxpayers Association to Limit the Taxing Powers of the Federal Government* (Washington, D.C.: American Taxpayers' Association, Inc., n.d. [1955?]), 136.

53. U.S. House of Representatives Committee on the Judiciary, *Amending Constitution Relative to Taxes on Incomes*, 6; see also Emanuel Celler, *You Never Leave Brooklyn: The Autobiography of Emanuel Celler* (New York: John Day Co., 1953).

54. Edward H. Collins, "Economics and Finance: A Ceiling on Taxes?" *New York Times*, July 9, 1951: 37.

55. National Research Institute, *17 States Say...*, 22. See also Robert B. Dresser, "Address," Houston, Texas, May 14, 1953: 5, CCGE.

56. Arnold, *Desire to Own*, 7; cf. *Handbook on Taxation* (Washington, D.C.: American Taxpayers' League, 1932).

57. Arnold, *Desire to Own*, 102, 114, 143, 148. On "producerism" in populist rhetoric, see Kazin, *Populist Persuasion*, 13–4.

58. "Big Business Reported behind Tax Ceiling Plan," 11; see U.S. Senate Committee on the Judiciary, *Lobby Investigation* (1929), 739.

59. U.S. Bureau of Internal Revenue, *Statistics of Income 1938* (Washington, D.C.: Government Printing Office); Leonard Arrington, "The New Deal in the West: A Preliminary Statistical Inquiry," *Pacific Historical Review* 38, no. 3 (1969): 311-6; Leonard Arrington, "The Sage Brush Resurrection: New Deal Expenditures in the Western States, 1933-1939," *Pacific Historical Review*, 52, no. 1 (1983): 1–16.

60. T. A. Larson, *History of Wyoming* (Lincoln, NE: University of Nebraska Press, 1978), 462, 468.

61. A. Dudley Gardner, "Continuity and Change: The Great Depression, A Brief Case Study of the New Deal and Wyoming Politics," Western Wyoming Community College, 2008, http://www.wwcc.cc.wy.us/wyo_hist/depression3.htm, accessed August 20, 2012.

62. *Journal of the House of Representatives of the Twenty-Fifth State Legislature of Wyoming* (1939): 200, 296, 327, 329, 358; *Session Laws of the State of Wyoming passed by the Twenty-Fifth State Legislature* (1939): 259–60; *Congressional Record*, 76th Congress, 1st Session (1939): 2509. Party affiliation data are from the *Wyoming Blue Book* (1939), vol. 2, 367–8.

63. Martha H. Swain, *Pat Harrison: The New Deal Years* (Oxford, MS: University of Mississippi Press, 1978), 115–7; Ira Katznelson, Kim Geiger, and Daniel Kryder, "Limiting Liberalism: The Southern Veto in Congress, 1933-1950," *Political Science Quarterly* 108, no. 2 (1993): 283–306.

64. On the New Deal and Mississippi politics, see V. O. Key, *Southern Politics in State and Nation* (New York: Vintage, 1949), 243; more generally on the Southern Democrats and the New Deal, see Robert C. Lieberman, *Shaping Race Policy: The United States in Comparative Perspective* (Princeton, NJ: Princeton University Press, 2005), 38.

65. *General Laws of the State of Mississippi* (1940), 602–3; *Mississippi Senate Journal* (1940), 234, 823–4; *Mississippi House Journal* (1940), 980–1.
66. See, e.g., Robert B. Dresser to Willford I. King, November 13, 1943, WIK, Box 8, Folder 21, University of Oregon Library.
67. Memorandum from Robert B. Dresser to Trustees and Advisors of the Committee for Constitutional Government, Inc., October 26, 1943, WIK, box 8, folder 20.
68. *Journal of the Senate of Rhode Island*, February 16, 1940, 2; *Journal of the House of Rhode Island*, March 15, 1940, 9. Party affiliation data are from Rhode Island Secretary of State, *Manual with Rules and Orders for the Use of the General Assembly of the State of Rhode Island*, 1939-1940 (Providence, RI, 1939).
69. For an overview of where and when the resolution was introduced, see the untitled spreadsheets in folder: Status of States on Millionaires' Amendment, Box 108A, WP.
70. *Congressional Record*, 84th Congress, 1st session (1939), 2509–10.

Chapter 4

1. Mark H. Leff, "The Politics of Sacrifice on the American Home Front in World War II," *Journal of American History* 77, no. 4 (1991): 1296-1318; Carolyn C. Jones, "Mass-Based Income Taxation: Creating a Taxpaying Culture," in *Funding the Modern American State, 1941-1995: The Rise and Fall of the Era of Easy Finance*, ed. W. Elliot Brownlee (Cambridge, UK, and New York: Cambridge University Press, 1996), 107–47; James T. Sparrow, " 'Buying Our Boys Back': The Mass Foundations of Fiscal Citizenship in World War II," *Journal of Policy History* 20, no. 2 (2008): 263-86.
2. This section relies heavily on Rumely's unpublished autobiographical writings, including the "Biographical Statement" prepared for his defense after his 1918 indictment under the Trading with the Enemy Act (EAR, Box 1, Folders 11–14) and the later, much abridged "Autobiography" (EAR, Box 1, Folders 1–3). On his early years, see Rumely, "Biographical Statement," 27–30. Although it is conventional for historians today to see the single tax movement as a "conservative" movement (see Mehrotra, "More Mighty than the Waves of the Sea"), in contrast to more radical challenges to capitalism that labor movements would later come to embrace, it was seen in George's time as pure socialism. The contemporary socialist Richard T. Ely characterized the Single Tax movement as "the beginnings of revolutionary socialism in the United States": see Richard T. Ely, *Recent American Socialism* (Baltimore, MD: John Murphy and Co., 1885), 16.
3. Gary Dean Best, *Peddling Panaceas: Popular Economists in the New Deal Era* (New Brunswick, NJ: Transaction, 2005), 2. On the Notre Dame episode, see Rumely, "Biographical Statement," 27–30. On "laissez faire," see "Biographical Statement," 39; on social insurance, see 54–5, 84, 240. On dress and diet, see "Biographical Statement," 39, and Rumely, "Autobiography," ch. 7. Rumely's autobiographical writings are inconsistent on the question of his drinking; the earlier "Biographical Statement" has him as a teetotaler at the time of his graduation (656), but the later "Autobiography" includes the boast that he once went to the *Kneipe* with the German students and showed them "that a vegetarian American could stand 21 mugs of beer without losing his feet" ("Autobiography," ch. 7, p. 8). On his contacts with socialists, see "Biographical Statement," 45–7, 100. I infer that Rumely may have helped distribute revolutionary propaganda to Russia from the facts that he apparently had inside knowledge of Russian students' plans to smuggle "bible-paper tracts written by Lenin" back home concealed in a coffin ("Autobiography," ch. 8, p. 12) and that another American student recalled that Rumely once recruited him to hide Russian pamphlets in his apartment ("Biographical Statement," 45).
4. "Biographical Statement," 49. On the influence of Dewey on Rumely's school, see Lynne Hamer, "Caging Wild Birds: Making 'Real Boys' into 'Real Men' at the Interlaken School,

1907-1918," *Educational Studies* 29, no. 4 (1998): 365. Dewey in turn held up Rumely's school at Interlaken as an exemplary progressive school; see John Dewey and Evelyn Dewey, *Schools of To-morrow* (New York: E. P. Dutton, 1915), 87–9. On the transatlantic Progressive movement, see Rodgers, *Atlantic Crossings*.

5. Milkis, *Theodore Roosevelt*, 125–9, 156–64; Davis, "Social Workers and the Progressive Party"; Webb, "From Independents to Populists to Progressive Republicans."

6. Rumely, "Autobiography," ch. 22; Milkis, *Theodore Roosevelt*, 154–6, 243–5. Milkis illustrates the Progressive Party's tactical novelty by noting the contrast between Roosevelt and Robert La Follette, another progressive Republican and would-be independent candidate whose candidacy sputtered because he failed "to pay court to the mass media" (*Theodore Roosevelt*, 53).

7. Rumely, "Biographical Statement," 211–8, 222–45; U.S. House of Representatives Committee to Investigate Campaign Expenditures, *Hearings before the Committee to Investigate Campaign Expenditures, House of Representatives, 78th Congress, 2nd Session* (Washington, D.C.: Government Printing Office, 1944), 401–2; for an overview of the case, see *Rumely et al. v. United States*, 293 F. 532 (1923).

8. Arthur Schlesinger, *The Coming of the New Deal, 1933-1935* (Boston: Houghton Mifflin, 1958), 198, attributes the formation of the committee to the efforts of the banker Frank Vanderlip, but it seems to have been Rumely who recruited Vanderlip (Best, *Peddling Panaceas*, 4–5).

9. Rexford Tugwell, "Review of *The Economic Thought of Franklin D. Roosevelt and the Origins of the New Deal* by Daniel R. Fusfield," *Journal of Politics* 19, no. 1 (1957): 141; Rumely, "How Gold Causes Depression" (1938), 9, EAR, Box 3, Folder 8. On the Committee for the Nation, see Herbert M. Bratter, "The Committee for the Nation: A Case History in Monetary Propaganda," *Journal of Political Economy* 49, no. 4 (1941): 531-53; Schlesinger, *Coming of the New Deal*, 198–9. The Committee for the Nation was correct to diagnose the gold standard as a crucial cause of the depression, and the orthodox view today is that going off the gold standard in 1933 was critical to the recovery. See Bernanke, *Essays on the Great Depression*, 70–107.

10. Rumely, "Autobiography," ch. 22, p. 3; on old progressives and the New Deal, see Otis Graham, *An Encore for Reform: The Old Progressives and the New Deal* (Oxford, UK: Oxford University Press, 1967), 24–100.

11. Richard Polenberg, "The National Committee to Uphold Constitutional Government, 1937-1941," *Journal of American History* 52 (1965): 582–3; Frank E. Gannett to E. B. Macrae, July 21, 1943, FEG, Box 4, Folder 15; U.S. House of Representatives Committee to Investigate Campaign Expenditures, *Hearings*, 442.

12. Edward A. Rumely to Willford I. King, January 5, 1957, WIK, Box 85, Folder 8; Rumely to Robert B. Dresser, September 27, 1951, WIK, Box 41, Folder 3.

13. Willford I. King to Robert R. Young, November 14, 1943, WIK, Box 8, Folder 22. On King's earlier role in the campaign *for* the Sixteenth Amendment, see Buenker, *Income Tax*, 28.

14. Ratner, *Taxation and Democracy*, 516–7.

15. Executive Order 9250 Establishing the Office of Economic Stabilization, October 3, 1942, http://www.presidency.ucsb.edu/ws/index.php?pid=16171; W. H. Lawrence, "Roosevelt to Push $25,000 Income Top on Unearned Gains," *New York Times*, December 2, 1942: 1; Leff, "Politics of Sacrifice," 1299–1304. FDR is quoted in Brownlee, *Federal Taxation*, 91. On the UAW's position, see Nelson Lichtenstein, *Walter Reuther: The Most Dangerous Man in Detroit* (Urbana, IL, and Chicago: University of Illinois Press, 1995), 196–7; James B. Atleson, *Labor and the Wartime State: Labor Relations and Law During World War II* (Urbana, IL, and Chicago: University of Illinois Press, 1998), 49–51.

16. Percentages and dollar amounts in the table are calculated from responses to the questions: "Do you think there should be any limit on the amount of income (including wages and salary) that each person should be allowed to keep per year in war time after paying all taxes?"

and "What do you think the limit should be?" (Gallup Poll # 1942-0286, December 17–22, 1942—Roper Center for Public Opinion Research, USAIPO1942-0286F). Answers are calculated using post-stratification weights kindly supplied by Adam Berinsky and Eric Schickler.

17. F. B. Dezendorf, "The New Poor," *Wall Street Journal*, Nov. 11, 1942: 1; John Fisher, "F.D.R. Policies Linked to Reds' 1928 Platform," *Chicago Daily Tribune*, Nov. 21, 1942: 2; "Why Not $1,900?" WIK, Box 84, Folder 3.

18. *Needed Now—Capacity for Leadership, Courage to Lead* (New York: Committee for Constitutional Government, Inc., 1944), 24–5.

19. "82.3% Vote to Limit Federal Income Tax Rates," *Modern Industry* 7, no. 5 (1944): 110.

20. The percentages in favor are calculated from responses to the question: "At present, some people with large incomes have to pay more than half of their income in income taxes. Do you think an income tax limit should be placed on large incomes so that no one would pay more than half of his income in Federal income tax?" (Gallup poll #0363, January 5–10, 1946—Roper Center for Public Opinion Research, USAIPO1946-0363). Gallup respondents are weighted with post-stratification cell weights to approximate their proportions in the population of non-institutionalized adults 21 and over, excluding residents of the District of Columbia. Following Berinsky, "American Public Opinion in the 1930s and 1940s," I calculated these weights from the 1950 Census 1 percent IPUMS to replicate population proportions in cells defined by combinations of race (black vs. white), gender, education (4 categories), and region (4 categories) for white respondents, and by race and gender for black respondents. I report confidence intervals on the assumption that they are heuristically valuable even if they do not have a classical statistical interpretation because the sample is not a probability sample.

21. Thomas W. Phillips Jr. to Col. O. R. McGuire, September 20,1943, WIK, Box 8, Folder 17; U.S. House of Representatives Committee to Investigate Campaign Expenditures, *Hearings*, 418, 446.

22. E. A. Rumely to Mr. Springer, December 8, 1939, FEG, Box 1, Folder 62; Rumely, "Autobiography," ch. 22, p. 5; Polenberg, "National Committee to Uphold Constitutional Government," 590.

23. Dresser, *Brief in Support of Proposed Constitutional Amendment*, 9, 15; Committee for Constitutional Government, "A Ceiling on the Power to Destroy You By Taxation," n.d. [1944?], CCGE.

24. Thomas W. Phillips Jr. to Col. O. R. McGuire, September 20, 1943, WIK, Box 8, Folder 17.

25. American Taxpayers' Association, "Recent action of state legislatures in connection with repeal of 16th amendment: tax information series no. 48," March 10, 1944, TI.

26. *A Proposed Amendment to the Constitution: 25% Tax Rate Limitation, Its Pros and Cons*, Report no. 2-403 (Washington, D.C.: Citizens National Committee, Inc., 1944), 15, WP, Box 108B, Folder: File on American Taxpayers' Association. On the origins of the Citizens' National Committee, see Murnane, "Selling Scientific Taxation," 834.

27. U.S. House of Representatives Committee to Investigate Campaign Expenditures, *Hearings*, 424; see also 405–6.

28. George Norris Green, *The Establishment in Texas Politics: The Primitive Years, 1938-1957* (Westport, CT: Greenwood Press, 1979), 46–7, 52–4.

29. U.S. House of Representatives Committee to Investigate Campaign Expenditures, *Hearings*, 547.

30. U.S. House of Representatives Committee to Investigate Campaign Expenditures, *Hearings*, 507.

31. U.S. House of Representatives Committee to Investigate Campaign Expenditures, *Hearings*, 518; Arthur Temple and M. E. Melton, Memorandum, April 19, 1944, WP, Box 110A, Folder: Texas; Judson to Wright (Patman), n.d. [April 20, 1944?], WP, Box 110A, Folder: Texas.

32. Dickson and Allen, *Bonus Army*, 31; Nancy Beck Young, *Wright Patman: Populism, Liberalism, and the American Dream* (Dallas: Southern Methodist University Press, 2000), 32–40; Cannadine, *Mellon*, 450–3. See Judson to Wright (Patman), n.d. [April 20, 1944?], WP, Box 110A, Folder: Texas.

33. Wright Patman to A. F. Whitney, June 13, 1944; Arthur H. Utt to Wright Patman, July 5, 1944; Stanley Dixon to Wright Patman, July 12, 1944, WP, Box 10B, Folder: 1944 General Correspondence: Requests for information—CCG; Wright Patman, "Millionaire's Amendment to Make the Rich Richer and the Poor Poorer," June 8, 1944, WP, Box 121A, Folder: Income tax; Ed Hart, "Is Congress Doing Its Job?" WINX, October 6, 1946, WP, Box 52B, Folder: Fascism file; *Congressional Record*, 78th Congress, 2nd Session, A2370-A2372, A2665-A2669, A2895-A2899; U.S. House of Representatives Committee to Investigate Campaign Expenditures, *Hearings*, 495.

34. See Frank E. Gannett to E. B. Macrae, July 21, 1943, FEG, Box 4, Folder 15; Thomas W. Phillips Jr. to Col. O. R. McGuire, September 20, 1943, WIK, Box 8, Folder 17.

35. Godfrey N. Nelson, "Ceiling is sought for federal taxes," *New York Times*, October 30, 1943: 7. Daniel Alden Reed, chairman of the Republican Postwar Tax Study Committee, circulated a memorandum that called for a discussion of the appropriate level of taxation: "In this connection, the movement to limit federal tax rates by constitutional amendment should be noted. One way to meet this issue is by voluntary Congressional action to establish moderate tax rate levels." See Daniel Alden Reed, "Some Matters of Policy to be Settled Prior to Planning Tax Revision.," n.d. [1944?], DAR, Box 1, Folder: 1944 Ways and Means. Early memoranda of the Republican Postwar Tax Study Committee called for study of constitutional tax limitation, but the issue was not taken up in subsequent reports. See Daniel Alden Reed, "Republican Postwar Tax Study Committee," n.d.; and Daniel A. Reed to "Dear Sirs," September 22, 1944, DAR, Box 1, Folder: 1944 Ways and Means.

36. U.S. Treasury Department Division of Tax Research, "Proposed Constitutional Amendment to Prohibit Federal Tax Rates Exceeding 25 Percent," May 31, 1944, WP, Folder: T, Box 108D. See Robert B. Dresser, "Reply to Objections of Tax Research Division of U.S. Treasury," n.d. [1944?], 2, CCGE.

37. For a quantitative analysis of rates of passage before and after 1944, see Isaac William Martin, "Redistributing to the Rich: Strategic Policy Crafting in the Campaign to Repeal the Sixteenth Amendment, 1938-1958," *American Journal of Sociology*, 116, no. 1 (2010): 1-52.

38. See, e.g., Sumner Gerard to Willford I. King, n.d. [1945?], WIK, Box 84, Folder 3; Committee for Constitutional Government, "What's the Matter with America?" n.d. [1946?]; Robert B. Dresser, "Congress Can Provide Tax Relief, Balance the Budget and Free Revenue for Business Expansion and More Jobs: Open Letter to the President and Members of Congress," January 14, 1947, WIK, Box 84, Folders 3 and 4.

39. Committee for Constitutional Government, "My Platform as a Fighter for Freedom," n.d. [1949?]; Committee for Constitutional Government, "Intra-Office Memorandum," n.d. [1949?]; Merrill D. Arnold et al. to "500 Knoxville Civic Leaders," October 9, 1949, CCGE. Homer Tomlinson to "Dear Tarrant County Citizen and Fellow American," 1950, WIK, Box 84, Folder 8; Confidential Memorandum from the Committee for Constitutional Government, May 1950, WIK, Box 84, Folder 8.

40. "Big Business Reported Behind Tax-Ceiling Plan," 11.

41. Frank Packard, "The Farmers' Movement in North Dakota and Taxation," in *Proceedings of the Eleventh Annual Conference of the National Tax Association, Held at Atlanta, Georgia, November 13-16, 1917* (New Haven, CT: National Tax Association, 1918), 167, 173; "Packard, Foe of High Taxes, Is Dead at 87," *Chicago Daily Tribune*, Feb. 10, 1961: C8. On WTC lobbying in the states, see Charles Delphenis to Wright Patman, August 21, 1951, WP, Box 108A, Folder: Booklets and pamphlets on the tax limitation amendment. Packard declined to copy another key feature of the Farmers' Nonpartisan League that involved

endorsing candidates, regardless of party, who embraced the league's program. Candidate endorsements would have jeopardized the Western Tax Council's tax-exempt status.

42. American Taxpayers' Association, "The Sixteenth Amendment is on the way out: Tax information series no. 103," Nov. 10, 1950, TI; Ida Muse Darden, "A Report of Activities in Behalf of Sound Principles of Taxation and Regulation of Radical Labor Leaders and Groups Furnished by the Christian American and the Tax Relief Committee of Houston, Tex," *Southern Conservative* 1, no. 4 (1950): 4.

43. Edward A. Rumely to Robert B. Dresser, October 30, 1951, WIK, Box 41, Folder 14; Edward A. Rumely to Robert B. Dresser, August 4, 1951, WIK, Box 40, Folder 1.

44. Edward Collins, "Economics and Finance: A Ceiling on Taxes?" *New York Times*, July 9, 1951: 37; U.S. Senate Committee on the Judiciary, *Hearing before a Subcommittee of the Committee on the Judiciary of the United States Senate, Eighty-Third Congress, Second Session, on S. J. Res. 23, Proposing an Amendment to the Constitution of the United States Relative to Taxes on Incomes, Inheritances and Gifts, 27 April 1954* (Washington, D.C.: Government Printing Office, 1954), 50–1; John D. Morris, "Drive for 25% Limit on Taxes Revived," *New York Times*, January 2, 1952: 18; John D. Morris, "States Push Drive to Curb Tax Power," *New York Times*, May 5, 1952: 18.

45. Robert B. Dresser, "Reply to Objections of Tax Research Division of U.S. Treasury," n.d. [1944?], 6, CCGE.

46. *Why the 25 Percent Limit on Federal Taxes* (Washington, D.C.: American Taxpayers' Association, n.d. [1944?]), 12, 16, WP, Box 108A, Folder: Booklets and leaflets on the Tax Limitation Amendment.

47. Samuel B. Pettengill, "The Grand Strategy of Freedom," address delivered in Chicago, October 12, 1949, Committee for Constitutional Government.

48. State legislators for the XXII Amendment, "An Argument for the XXII Amendment," n.d. [1945?], Committee for Constitutional Government.

49. Robert B. Dresser, *Brief in Support of Proposed Constitutional Amendment Limiting the Power of Congress to Tax Incomes, Inheritances and Gifts*, December 28, 1951, 13, WIK, Box 85, Folder 2.

50. Frank Packard, "Put a Ceiling on Taxes!" *The Kiplinger Magazine* 5, no. 8 (1951): 44; Lammot du Pont to Edward A. Rumely, October 8, 1951, WIK, Box 41, Folder 6.

51. Robert B. Dresser, *Brief in Support of Proposed Constitutional Amendment*, December 28, 1951, WIK, Box 85, Folder 2; Robert B. Dresser to E. A. Rumely, August 15, 1951, WIK, Box 40, Folder 7.

52. Everett Dirksen, "Joint Resolution," 1952, ED, Folder 1111. See also Legislative Reference Service, "Economic Aspects of an Income Tax Rate Limitation of 25 Percent," February 13, 1953, ED, Folder 1112. For evidence of Dresser's direct participation in designing the ultimate versions of the amendment, see Edward A. Rumely to Willford I. King, January 9, 1953, WIK, Box 49, Folder 3; E. A. Rumely to Mr. Sexauer, Mr. Gerard, and Dr. King, January 13, 1953, WIK, Box 49, Folder 4.

53. For the concerns of Rumely and King, see Willford I. King to Everett Dirksen, Dec. 11, 1952, ED, Folder 1111; Robert B. Dresser to E. A. Rumely, August 15, 1951, WIK, Box 40, Folder 7.

54. Iowa, which passed a resolution endorsing the amendment in 1941, rescinded its endorsement in 1945 and approved a later version of the amendment in 1951; Arkansas, which endorsed the amendment in 1943, rescinded its endorsement in 1945 and approved a later version of the amendment in 1957. New Hampshire endorsed the version without the emergency clause in 1943 and the version with the emergency clause in 1953, with no explicit rescission of its earlier resolution. See U.S. Senate and House of Representatives, Joint Economic Committee, *The Proposed 23rd Amendment to the Constitution to Repeal the 16th Amendment to the Constitution which Provides that Congress Shall have Power to Collect Taxes on Incomes: A Study Made by the Staff of the Joint Economic Committee of the*

United States Senate and House of Representatives to Determine the Effects of Its Adoption (Washington, D.C.: Government Printing Office, 1961).

55. See *Congressional Record*, 73rd Congress, 1st Session, 345; 74th Congress, 1st Session, 544, 1006.

56. Howard V. Lee to Committee for Constitutional Government, July 30, 1951, WIK, Box 39, Folder 19.

57. Robert B. Dresser to E. A. Rumely, August 15, 1951, WIK, Box 40, Folder 7.

58. Robert B. Dresser to Edward A. Rumely, October 29, 1951, WIK, Box 41, Folder 13; U.S. House of Representatives Select Committee on Lobbying Activities, *Lobbying, Direct and Indirect: Part 4 of Hearings before the House Select Committee on Lobbying Activities, House of Representatives, 81st Congress, 2nd Session,* part 4 (Washington, D.C., 1950), 17–29; U.S. House of Representatives Select Committee on Lobbying Activities, *Lobbying, Direct and Indirect,* part 5 (Washington, D.C., 1950), 122, 233–50; *United States v. Rumely,* 345 U.S. 41. The definition of lobbying is from *United States v. Rumely,* 197 F.2d 166, at 176.

59. Frank E. Packard, "Constitutional Law: The States and the Amending Process," *ABA Journal* 45 (1959): 161–4, 196–8.

60. U.S. Senate Committee on the Judiciary, *Hearing before a Subcommittee of the Committee on the Judiciary of the United States Senate, Eighty-Third Congress, Second Session, on S. J. Res. 23, Proposing an Amendment to the Constitution of the United States Relative to Taxes on Incomes, Inheritances and Gifts, 27 April 1954* (Washington, D.C.: Government Printing Office, 1954), 55.

61. American Taxpayers' Association, *Summary,* 200; for a list of states passing resolutions, see U.S. Senate and House of Representatives, Joint Economic Committee, *The Proposed 23rd Amendment.*

62. Gladwyn Hill, "Coast Unit Seeks Repeal of U.S. Tax," *New York Times,* March 24, 1957: 57.

63. "Proposed Amendments to the Constitution," ED, working papers, Folder 1111.

64. *Congressional Record,* 73rd Congress, 1st Session, 319.

Chapter 5

1. Charles Delphenis to Wright Patman, September 27, 1951, WP, Box 108A, Folder: Correspondence, 1951.

2. On the women's club movement, see Clemens, *People's Lobby,* 195–202. On the mothers' movement, see Glen Jeansonne, *Women of the Far Right: The Mothers' Movement and World War II* (Chicago: University of Chicago Press, 1996).

3. Corinne Griffith, *My Life with the Redskins* (New York: A. S. Barnes & Co., 1947), 169; Griffith, *Papa's Delicate Condition* (New York: Houghton Mifflin, 1952); Griffith, *Antiques I Have Known* (New York: F. Fell, 1961), 146–7.

4. Griffith, *Antiques,* 151, 154; Mordaunt Hall, "The Screen," *New York Times,* May 31, 1930: 21; Nelson B. Bell, "A Few Kindly Observations upon Three Years of Sound," *Washington Post,* March 23, 1930: A2; "Miss Griffith in Sad Role," *New York Times,* Feb. 22, 1930: 19. "Talks through her nose" is from "Cinema: The New Pictures," *Time Magazine,* March 10, 1930, http://www.time.com/time/magazine/article/0,9171,752385,00.html, accessed August 20, 2012. For invidious comparisons concerning her appearance, see Myrtle Gebhart, "The Most Beautiful Woman in the World," *Los Angeles Times,* December 6, 1931: L3.

5. "Actress Pays Fine for Tax Mistake: Arrears to Uncle Sam Remitted," *Los Angeles Times,* March 1, 1930: A1; Mary Mayer, "Film Dollars Put to Work," *Los Angeles Times,* Feb. 2, 1930: B11. The quotation is from "Corinne Griffith," *Dawn,* vol. 1, no. 13 (Nov. 1956): 1–2, TCA, Box 15, Folder: TAX: Frank Chodorov, 1956. On the marriage proposal, see Griffith, *My Life with the Redskins,* 1–6.

6. Griffith, *My Life with the Redskins*, 200; Griffith, *Antiques*, 156; see Roger W. Lotchin, *Fortress California, 1910-1961: From Warfare to Welfare* (Urbana, IL, and Chicago: University of Illinois Press, 2002), 132.

7. Corinne Griffith, *Abolish the Individual Federal Income Tax* (Beverly Hills, CA: Author, 1960), 23.

8. The best biographical studies of Kellems are Carolyn C. Jones, "Vivien Kellems and the Folkways of Taxation," in *Total War and the Law: The American Home Front in World War II*, eds. Daniel R. Ernst and Victor Jew (Westport, CT: Praeger, 2002), 121-48; and Olivier Burtin, "The 'One-Woman Army': Vivien Kellems and American Conservatism, 1896-1975" (M.A. thesis, Institut d'Etudes Politiques de Paris, Programme doctoral d'histoire, 2011), which became available to me only after I finished the first draft of this chapter. Two incomplete biographies by Polly King Ruhtenberg mix fact and speculation and should be used with caution: "Vivien: Profile in Courage" (n.d.) and "Vivien Kellems: Woman with a Mission" (n.d.), PKR, Box 8, Folder 3. On Kellems's education, see "Doctoral Dissertations," *American Economic Review*, vol. 12, no. 2 (1922): 390. See also Kellems to Julie Shoape Medlock, October 18, 1935, VK, Folder 90, Box 4.

9. Kellems, *Toil, Taxes, and Trouble*, 12; Julie Shoape Medlock, "Modern Home News Feature... Release for Week of November 10th, 1941," VK, Folder 111, Box 9; Vivien Kellems, "Volts for Women," n.d., VK, Folder 90, Box 4; Vivien Kellems to Julie Shoape Medlock, October 18, 1935, VK, Folder 90, Box 4; Julie Shoape Medlock, "Notes for Kellems publicity releases in reference to her October visit to your city," VK, Folder 111, Box 9. On Europe, see Kellems to Clare Yuchtman, September 25, 1938, and unidentified correspondent to Kellems, September 15, 1938, VK, Folder 104, Box 4.

10. Kellems to Medlock, October 18, 1935, VK, Folder 90, Box 4; Kellems, Speech for the Fairfield County Public Forum, Norwalk, CT, June 11, 1937, VK, Folder 90, Box 4; Kellems, "Volts for Women," n.d., VK, Folder 90, Box 4. Kellems, "Let's Join the Ladies," VK, Folder 90, Box 4; Kellems, "We, the Women," VK, Folder 123, Box 4, University of Connecticut Special Collections; "Equal Rights Move Promised in House," *New York Times*, January 6, 1944: 20.

11. Kellems, *Toil, Taxes and Trouble*, 12–13.

12. Kellems to Yuchtman, September 25, 1938, VK, Folder 104, Box 4; Harold H. Corbin to Kellems, n.d. [1944?], VK, Folder 134, Box 5; Medlock, "Notes for Kellems publicity releases in reference to her October visit to your city," VK, Folder 111, Box 9.

13. "Will Not Pay Tax, Miss Kellems Says," *New York Times*, Jan. 19, 1944: 38; Harold Corbin to Vivien Kellems, n.d. [1944?], VK, Box 5, Folder 134.

14. Kellems to I. S. Mattingly, January 31, 1944, VK, Box 5, Folder 134.

15. "DuMont Presents 'The Power of Women' Moderated by Kellems," September 2, 1952, VK, Box 37, Folder: Power of Women scripts, 1952; see also "The Power of Women (Final Program)," September 9, 1952, VK, Box 37, Folder: Power of Women scripts.

16. Jones, "Vivien Kellems," 126–7; Corbin to Kellems, n.d. [1944?], VK, Box 5, Folder 134, University of Connecticut Special Collections.

17. Kellems to Mrs. W. N. Holmes, February 28, 1944, VK, Box 5, Folder 134.

18. Kellems to Robert P. Vanderpoel, February 1, 1944, VK, Folder 134, Box 5.

19. Kellems to Lyrl Clark van Hyning, March 15, 1944, VK, Folder 134, Box 5; Kellems to Mrs. W. N. Holmes, February 28, 1944; Kellems to Mrs. W. N. Holmes, March 20, 1944, VK, Folder 134, Box 5.

20. "100 to Work Tonight in Women's Law Test," *New York Times*, April 8, 1947: 29; "Miss Kellems Tests State's Labor Law," *New York Times*, April 9, 1947: 27.

21. "The Power of Women (Final Program)," September 9, 1952, VK, Box 37, Folder: Power of Women scripts.

22. "Miss Kellems Wins U.S. Court Suit over Defiance on Withholding Tax," *New York Times*, Jan. 25, 1951: 1; and Kellems, *Toil, Taxes and Trouble*. She had long held the view that civil disobedience could inspire mass rebellion, e.g., expressing the view that her

imprisonment might "crystallize the rebellious sentiment in this country" in Kellems to Robert P. Vanderpoel, February 1, 1944, VK, Box 5, Folder 134.

23. Kellems to Winifred Furrh, April 22, 1951; Kellems to Winifred Furrh, May 21, 1951; Ethelda Spangler, Winifred Furrh, Carolyn Abney, Eileen Pelz, Lucille Burnett, Genevieve O'Bannion, Elizabeth Barnes, Frances Abney, Lois Wilver, Kethyln [*sic*] Sheley, Virginia Whelan, Laura Becknagel, Dorothy Martin, and Bessie Smith to John W. Snyder, April 30, 1951, VK, Box 35, Folder: Tax rebels. On the social security amendments, see Julian Zelizer, *Taxing America: Wilbur D. Mills, Congress, and the State, 1945-1975* (Cambridge, UK: Cambridge University Press, 2000), 73–8.

24. Kellems to Winifred Furrh, June 29, 1951 and Kellems to Winifred Furrh, June 1, 1951, VK, Box 35, Folder: Tax rebels. On the Marshall housewives, see also Jones, "Mass-Based Income Taxation," 131.

25. "New Blast Hurled by Kellems," *Los Angeles Times*, June 9, 1951: B1.

26. Ethelda Spangler, R. B. Lothrub, Celeste Clemens, Janis F. Pitts, Eileen Pelz, Virginia Whelan, Carolyn M. Abney, Connie Wood, Dorothy Martin, Moselle Warren, Jennie M. Abney, Rubye Pelz, and Winifred Furrh to Kellems, September 8, 1951, VK, Box 37, Folder: Marshall housewives, 1952-1953; "Liberty Belles Present Miss Kellems," September 15, 1952, VK, Box 37, Folder: Power of Women scripts; Minutes of First Meeting of Incorporators of The Liberty Belles Incorporated, October 1, 1951, VK, Box 37, Folder: Liberty Belles, Inc. Minutebook, University of Connecticut Special Collections; "Miss Kellems Crusading," *New York Times*, September 29, 1951: 16.

27. Minutes of First Meeting of Directors of the Liberty Belles Incorporated, October 18, 1951, VK, Box 37, Folder: Liberty Belles, Inc. Minutebook; Vivien Kellems to Donald MacLean, October 17, 1951, VK, Box 9, Folder 200; "Misses Kellems, Griffith to Address Pro America," *Los Angeles Times*, September 30, 1951: C14; Bess M. Wilson, "Liberty Belles Unit Begins in Southland," *Los Angeles Times*, October 2, 1951: B1; Bess M. Wilson, "Organizations Plan Varied, Busy Week," *Los Angeles Times*, November 11, 1951: B1; "Miss Kellems Calls for People's Revolt," *Los Angeles Times*, November 16, 1951: 2.

28. Bess M. Wilson, "Women: Liberty Belles Launch National Drive for Government Cleanup," *Los Angeles Times*, November 20, 1951: B1. Reports of turnout at this meeting varied from 5,000 to "approximately 7,000," but no one counted heads carefully, and Kellems, like many activists, did not mind exaggerating her turnout numbers for impact. See Hedda Hopper, "Drama: Cake-Baking Suzan Ball Lead in 'Untamed,' " *Los Angeles Times*, November 23, 1951: B6; DuMont Television Network, "Kellems Turns to TV to Point up 'Power of Women' in Politics," July 3, 1952, VK, Box 35, Folder: Power of Women publicity plan; Affidavit of Kellems, September 8, 1953, VK, Box 37, Folder: Application for tax-exempt status. Financial records might give a better clue because Kellems was a careful businesswoman who made a point of knowing her accounts well. She later reported in sworn statements that $3,500 in membership dues were collected at the Shrine meeting. At the annual dues rate of two dollars, this implies that at least 1,750 attended and joined, which seems broadly consistent with substantially higher turnout figures. These figures are also consistent with unaudited financial statements for the California chapter, which recorded $20,398 in membership contributions for the fiscal year ending September 30, 1952. See "Income and distribution sheet," attached to L. Jeanette Walton to Kellems, July 20, 1953, VK, Box 37, Folder: Liberty Belles Inc., California, 1953.

29. Affidavit of Kellems, September 8, 1953, VK, Box 37, Folder: Application for tax- exempt status.

30. "Once again... Liberty Needs You!" VK, Box 37, Folder: Application for tax-exempt status; *Liberty Belles Bulletin*, vol. 1, no. 1 (March 1953), VK, Box 37, Folder: Application for tax-exempt status; Allegra Taylor to Mrs. Fred C. Greisel, April 15, 1952, VK, Box 35, Folder: Minute Women. On men's smaller pins, see Wilson, "Women: Liberty Belles Launch National Drive," B1. For figures, see "Income and distribution sheet," attached to L. Jeanette Walton to Kellems, July 20, 1953. In her public statements, Kellems claimed

as many as 35,000 members, but private correspondence indicated 13,500 (see Burtin, "One Woman Army," 96). The latter is more consistent with the surviving membership and financial records.

31. Kellems, *Toil, Taxes and Trouble,* 27; "Liberty Belles Present Miss Kellems," September 15, 1952, VK, Box 37, Folder: Power of Women scripts. For data on women's wealth ownership, see Carol Shammas, "Re-assessing the Married Women's Property Acts," *Journal of Women's History* 6, no. 1 (1994): 9–30; Ann Tickamyer, "Wealth and Power: A Comparison of Men and Women in the Property Elite," *Social Forces* 60, no. 2 (1981): 463–81; Lena Edlund and Wojciech Kopczuk, "Women, Wealth, and Mobility," *American Economic Review* 99, no. 1 (2009): 146–78.

32. Witte, *Politics and Development,* 137–8; Zelizer, *Taxing America,* 73–8.

33. Carolyn Jones, "Split Income and Separate Spheres: Tax Law and Gender Roles in the 1940s," *Law and History Review* 6, no. 2 (1988): 294.

34. Edward McCaffery, *Taxing Women* (Chicago: University of Chicago Press, 1997), 57; Stephanie Hunter McMahon, "To Save State Residents: States' Use of Community Property for Federal Tax Reduction, 1939-1947," *Law and History Review* 27, no. 3 (2009): 585-627; Jones, "Split Income and Separate Spheres."

35. McCaffery, *Taxing Women,* 56.

36. The first column reports the percent offering favorable responses to the question: "It has been suggested that a law be passed so the Federal government could not take more than 25 per cent, or one- fourth, of any person's income in taxes except in wartime. Would you favor or oppose this 25 per cent top limit?" (Gallup poll #489, March 27-April 1, 1952—Roper Center for Public Opinion Research, USAIPO1952-0489).

The second column reports predicted percentages calculated from the logistic regression model reported in ch. 5, table 5.2, assuming that the respondent is otherwise statistically average. The 95 percent confidence intervals for predicted probabilities are calculated by the delta method.

37. On inequalities of political knowledge and political engagement, see Michael X. Delli Carpini and Scott Keeter, *What Americans Know about Politics and Why It Matters* (New Haven, CT: Yale University Press, 1997); Schlozman, Page, Verba, and Fiorina, "Inequalities of Political Voice."

38. Data compiled from Liberty Belles membership and contributors' lists, VK, Box 37, Folder: Liberty Belles, Inc. membership, 1953.

39. As a point of comparison, approximately 66 percent of all women 15 years of age and older in 1950 were married. U.S. Bureau of the Census, "Table MS-1, Marital Status of the Population 15 years Old and Over, by Sex and Race: 1950 to present," http://www.census.gov/population/socdemo/hh-fam/ms1.xls, accessed October 29, 2010.

40. Affidavit of Kellems, September 8, 1953, VK, Box 37, Folder: Application for tax- exempt status; DuMont Television Network, "Kellems Turns to TV to Point up 'Power of Women' in Politics," July 3, 1952, VK, Box 35, Folder: Power of Women publicity plan.

41. Liberty Belles membership and contributors' lists, VK, Box 37, Folder: Liberty Belles, Inc. membership, 1953.

42. The gender composition of these leadership bodies was inferred from the following lists, in order in which the rows appear in the table: J. A. Arnold to Andrew W. Mellon, November 24, 1924, RG 56, Entry 191, Box 163, Binder: Tax (General), September–December 1924; J. A. Arnold to Ogden L. Mills, July 2, 1927, RG 56, Entry 191, Box 196, Binder: Tax-inheritance, 1926-1927; Committee for Constitutional Government, *Needed Now— Capacity for Leadership, Courage to Lead,* 1944, 3–4, WP, Box 108a, Folder: Booklets and pamphlets on the tax limitation amendment; Norman Vincent Peale, "Stop Confiscatory Federal Taxation," n.d. [1943?], CCGE; American Taxpayers' Association, "Why the 25 Percent Limit on Federal Taxes...," n.d. [1943?], WP, Box 108A, Folder: Booklets and pamphlets on the tax limitation amendment; State Legislators for the XXII Amendment, "An Argument for the XXII Amendment," n.d. [1944?], CCGE; Sumner Gerarrd, "Dear

Friend and Supporter," spring 1949, CCGE; American Taxpayers' Association, "Primary Policies and Program of the American Taxpayers Association," January 1, 1950, WP, Box 108a, Folder: Booklets and pamphlets on the tax limitation amendment; Minutes of First Meeting of Directors of the Liberty Belles Incorporated, October 18, 1951, VK, Box 37, Liberty Belles Minutebook; "Take This First Step To-Day to Do Away with Federal Income Taxes," n.d. [1956?], WES, Box 1, Folder: ORFIT—Reports and releases; Liberty Amendment Committee of the U.S.A., *1963 Annual Report*.

43. Liberty Belles membership and contributors' lists, VK, Box 37, Folder: Liberty Belles, Inc. membership, 1953. See U.S. Senate Committee on the Judiciary, *Hearing before a Subcommittee of the Committee on the Judiciary of the United States Senate, Eighty-Fourth Congress, Second Session, on S. J. Res. 23, Proposing an Amendment to the Constitution of the United States Relative to Taxes on Incomes, Inheritances and Gifts, April 24, 1956* (Washington, D.C.: Government Printing Office, 1956).

44. Lisa Kay Speer, " 'Contrary Mary': The Life of Mary Dawson Cain" (Ph.D. dissertation, Department of History, University of Mississippi, 1988), 155–202; "Florida Man Also Strikes, Urges Test; Unconstitutional, Miss Kellems Says," *Miami Herald*, March 17, 1952; Robert F. Loftus, "Revenue Agents to Check Up On Rebel Woman Editor," *Sturgis (Mich.) Journal*, March 15, 1952, VK, Box 35, Folder: Tax rebels. See also John Hart to Clarence E. Manion, March 30, 1956, CEM, Box 3, Folders 3–7.

45. W. C. Stonestreet et al. to Andrew W. Mellon, October 31, 1924, RG 56, Entry 191, Box 193.

46. Dresser, *Brief in Support of Proposed Constitutional Amendment* (1943); Robert B. Dresser, "Reply to Objections of Tax Research Division of U.S. Treasury" (1944), 2, CCGE. See also "Address of Mr. Robert B. Dresser," Houston, TX, May 14, 1953; Robert B. Dresser, "An Explanation of the Proposals to Limit by Constitutional Amendment the Taxing Power of Congress," *It's Still Your Fight* (1953), CCGE.

47. Norma H. Goodhue, "Real Estate Women Hear of Crusade to Cut Income Tax Power," *Los Angeles Times*, November 12, 1953: B1. Of course, by the logic of this argument, the rest of the Constitution was also illegitimate.

48. Kellems, *Toil, Taxes and Trouble*, 33, 149.

49. Ibid., 155.

50. "The Power of Women (Final Program)," September 9, 1952, VK, Box 37, Folder: Power of Women scripts.

51. Undated outline (August 1952), VK, Box 35, Folder: Power of Women publicity plan.

52. Compare Minutes of First Meeting of Directors of the Liberty Belles Incorporated, October 18, 1951, to Minutes of February 7, 1953, VK, Box 37, Folder: Liberty Belles Minutebook.

53. "Liberty Belles Battle over Primary Backing," *Los Angeles Times*, May 7, 1952: 19; "Liberty Belles' Protest on Werdel Move Grows," *Los Angeles Times*, May 8, 1952: 29; "Leader Quits Liberty Belles in New Dispute," *Los Angeles Times*, May 20, 1952: 9; "Belles Back Republican Candidates," *Los Angeles Times*, Aug. 15, 1952: B1; Minutes of special meeting of the Board of Directors of Liberty Belles Inc., December 2, 1952, VK, Box 37, Folder: Liberty Belle Minutebook; Kellems to Mrs. Paul Blaisdell, July 25, 1952; Lloyd Wright to John Wibel, Jan. 5, 1953; Kellems to Mrs. Ralph L. Cason, March 27, 1953, VK, Box 37, Folder: Liberty Belles Inc.: California, 1953. Kellems to Winifred Furrh, April 7, 1953, VK, Box 32, Folder: tax rebels.

54. Corinne Griffith to Kellems, May 10, 1952, VK, Box 9, Folder 200; Griffith to Kellems, May 1, 1953, VK, Box 9, Folder 200.

55. Frank Chodorov, *The Income Tax: Root of All Evil* (New York: Devin-Adair, 1954); Vivien Kellems, "Radio broadcast for ORFIT"; Corinne Griffith to Kellems, July 6, 1955; Kellems to Griffith, July 11, 1955; Griffith to Kellems, August 16, 1956, VK, Box 11, Folder 250. For evidence that Kellems swayed Charles Coburn, a former member of the Committee for Constitutional Government who later joined ORFIT, see Bertrand W. Gearhart to Kellems, November 29, 1952, VK, Box 9, Folder 200.

56. Organizations listed in the table in *italics* testified in favor of abolishing the income tax altogether. Among those testifying for repeal of the Sixteenth Amendment at the 1956 hearings, women were significantly more likely than men to demand abolition rather than limitation of the income tax (Pearson's $\chi^2 = 7.1$, 1 d.f., p <. 01). List of organizations from U.S. Senate Committee on the Judiciary, *Hearings*, April 27, 1954; U.S. Senate Committee on the Judiciary, *Hearings*, April 24, 1956.

57. U.S. Senate Committee on the Judiciary, *Hearings*, April 24, 1956, 80, 114.

58. Griffith, *Abolish the Individual Federal Income Tax*; Kellems, *Toil, Taxes and Trouble*, 87; on Kellems and her mink, see also ibid., 13. Nixon's "Checkers Speech" is available at http://www.millercenter.org/president/speeches/detail/4638.

Chapter 6

1. Kellems to Mr. and Mrs. Richard Dexter, July 13, 1953, VK, Box 9, Folder 200; Kellems to Winifred Furrh, August 26, 1953, VK, Box 37, Folder: Marshall housewives 1952-1953.

2. "For months I have stood on the side lines cheering you on and admiring every single thing that you have done," Kellems wrote to Reed, who was a former Cornell quarterback; "There isn't a doubt in my mind that the American people expected a tax cut when the Republican administration was elected.... You alone have had the courage to make the fight and millions of people are backing you up" (Kellems to Reed, August 20, 1953, VK, Box 9, Folder 205).

3. "Khrushchev's Inferiority Complex," *Wall Street Journal*, September 29, 1959: 16; "Transcript of Khrushchev's News Conference on His Talks with President," *New York Times*, September 28, 1959: 18; for American responses to Khrushchev's boast, see Arthur Krock, "In the Nation," *New York Times*, September 29, 1959: 38; Franklyn D. Holzman, "Soviet Taxes Defined," *New York Times*, October 6, 1959: 38. On the Soviet abolition of income tax, see "Khrushchev's Congress," *New York Times*, February 7, 1959: 18; Harry Schwartz, "Khrushchev Seen in Bid for Favor," *New York Times*, May 6, 1960: 8; "Russ to Abolish Taxes on Income," *Los Angeles Times*, May 6, 1960: 7.

4. John Birch Society, Tape #2 ("Detroit, September 18, 1971"), JBS, Box 23.

5. See Witte, *Politics and Development*, 150–5.

6. Frank Chodorov, *Out of Step: The Autobiography of an Individualist* (New York: Devin-Adair Co., 1962), 15; other collections of his essays include Chodorov, *Income Tax*; Chodorov, *Fugitive Essays: Selected Writings of Frank Chodorov*, ed. Charles H. Hamilton (Indianapolis, IN: Liberty Fund, 1980). He was an engaging memoirist, and much of the rest of this section draws heavily on his own writings. For biographical sketches, see also Nash, *Conservative Intellectual Movement*, 16–8, 28–30; and Charles H. Hamilton, "Introduction," in Chodorov, *Fugitive Essays*, 11–32.

7. Chodorov, *Out of Step*, 83–4, 88, 104.

8. Ibid., 50, 75.

9. Mark Blaug, *Economic Theory in Retrospect* (Cambridge, UK, and New York: Cambridge University Press, 1997), 83.

10. Chodorov, *Out of Step*, 51. On Fels's role in reviving the single-tax campaign, see Arthur Nichols Young, *The Single Tax Movement in the United States* (Princeton, NJ: Princeton University Press, 1916), 163–83); Arthur Power Dudden, *Joseph Fels and the Single-Tax Movement* (Philadelphia: Temple University Press, 1971).

11. Chodorov, *Out of Step*, 51.

12. Hamilton, "Introduction," 19; Chodorov, *Out of Step*, 78–9.

13. Chodorov quoted in Hamilton, "Introduction," 19.

14. Albert Jay Nock, "Isaiah's Job," *Atlantic Monthly* 157, no. 6 (1936); on the influence of this doctrine, see Nash, *Conservative Intellectual Movement*, 41. Critchlow, *Conservative Ascendancy*, 10, traces the doctrine of the remnant to the architect Ralph Adams Cram.

15. Robert B. Dresser to Edward A. Rumely, August 2, 1951, WIK, Box 39, Folder 21. The preliminary discussions about the founding of ORFIT took place in 1952; see Corinne Griffith to Vivien Kellems, March 10, 1952, VK, Box 9, Folder 200. ORFIT was incorporated in 1953; see Organization to Repeal Federal Income Taxes, Inc., n.d., HH.

16. Chodorov, *Income Tax*, 34, 52.

17. Ibid., 116.

18. For poor first impressions of Morgenthaler, see, e.g., Thomas Coleman Andrews to Corinne Griffith, August 1, 1956, TCA, Box 16, Folder: Corinne Griffith, 1956; Willis Stone to Mary Dawson Cain, August 2, 1956, WES, Box 3, Folder: Cain, Mary Dawson; Willis Stone to Cain, November 18, 1956, WES, Box 16, Folder: Cain, Mary D. On the fundraising scheme, see Gladwyn Hill, "Coast Unit Seeks Repeal of U.S. Tax," *New York Times*, March 24, 1957: 57; Willis Stone to Max Koffman, May 14, 1958, and Stone to Koffman, July 15, 1958, WES, Box 1, Folder: Joint Operating Committee. The "bunch of dummies" is quoted in Mary D. Cain to Paul K. Morgenthaler, May 7, 1956, WES, Box 16, Folder: Cain, Mary D. On membership, see ORFIT, Operating Statement—Month of October 1956, WES, Box 1, Folder: ORFIT Operating Statements.

19. "Governor of Utah Sees Dictatorship," *New York Times*, February 18, 1955: 19. On Lee's opposition to income tax, see George B. Russell, *J. Bracken Lee: The Taxpayer's Champion* (New York: Robert Speller and Sons, 1960), 123–8.

20. "Utah's Governor to Battle Taxes," *New York Times*, January 7, 1956: 15; "Tax Warning Goes to Utah Governor," *New York Times*, October 8, 1955: 28.

21. "Lien Filed on Gov. Lee," *New York Times*, May 2, 1956: 14; "Tax Lien on Gov. Lee is Satisfied by U.S.," *New York Times*, August 11, 1956: 11.

22. "National Affairs: Lee's Defeat," *Time Magazine*, September 24, 1956, http://www.time.com/time/magazine/article/0,9171,867097,00.html, accessed August 21, 2012; *Lee v. Humphrey*, 352 U.S. 904, 77 S. Ct. 144 (1956).

23. "Square Deal for Taxpayer," *U.S. News and World Report*, May 8, 1953: 28.

24. James Corbett Baker, "T. Coleman Andrews: Intellectual Portrait of a Self-Made Man" (M.A. thesis, University of Oregon Department of History, 1968), 42–5, 50–2.

25. Ibid., 68–94; "Why the Income Tax is Bad," *U.S. News and World Report*, May 25, 1956; Perlstein, *Before the Storm*, 11. For the Andrews stump speech, see Dean Clarence E. Manion, "The Income Tax—Unconstitutional Extortion," *Manion Weekly Broadcast* 104 (September 23, 1956), TCA, Box 16, Folder: Dean Manion.

26. *Budget of the United States Government 2012*, Historical Table 2–12, http://www.gpo.gov/fdsys/pkg/BUDGET-2012-TAB/xls/BUDGET-2012-TAB-2-2.xls, accessed August 20, 2012.

27. See, e.g., John W. Blodgett Jr. to B. K. Pattersen, September 20, 1956, CEM, Box 3, Folders 3–8; Clarence E. Manion to Al G. Hill, January 3, 1957, CEM, Box 3, Folders 3–9.

28. Kellems to Griffith, March 15, 1956, VK, Box 11, Folder 250; Baker, "T. Coleman Andrews," 64; Paul K. Morgenthaler to Thomas Coleman Andrews, March 2, 1956, TCA, Box 16, Folder: Organization to Repeal Federal Income Taxes, Inc., 1956. The total take of the personal income tax in 1955 was $29 billion; see *Historical Statistics of the United States* (1970), vol. 2, p. 1105, Series Y343-351; Griffith, *Abolish the Individual Federal Income Tax*, 5; U.S. Senate Committee on the Judiciary, *Hearing*, April 24, 1956, 81.

29. Chodorov, *Income Tax*, 26; Chodorov, "A War to Communize America," *The Freeman* 5 (1954); on the debate that Chodorov unleashed, see Nash, *Conservative Intellectual Movement*, 113–5.

30. See Gallup poll #1956-0573.

31. The data are from Gallup poll #0573, October 18–23, 1956 (Roper Center for Public Opinion Research, USAIPO1956-0573). The Gallup poll on presidential vote intentions included T. Coleman Andrews as an option for respondents in Virginia, South Carolina, Alabama, Mississippi, Louisiana, Texas, Tennessee, and Arkansas, for a total sample size of N = 352. The archived data file does not include specific codes to distinguish respondents who supported or

leaned toward Andrews. I coded all respondents as favoring Andrews if they belonged to the residual category of respondents who were coded as neither supporting nor leaning toward any other candidacy, nor being undecided, nor having refused the question. This yields a total of 33 potential Andrews supporters in the data. The percentages reported here should be understood as upper bounds on the sample proportion of actual Andrews-Werdel supporters. The percentage of potential Andrews supporters differed significantly among political party categories ($p < .05$). No other differences were statistically significant.

32. Lipset and Raab, *Politics of Unreason*, 294–300.

33. Chodorov, *Out of Step*, 191; for the application of the "radical rich" to the income tax repeal movement, see ibid., 195.

34. See *Application for employment in the Classified Civil Service of the City of Los Angeles*, n.d. [1933?], and *United States Civil Service Examination: Selection of Assistant Commissioner of Labor Statistics*, February 26, 1934, WES, Box 1, Folder: Stone, Willis Emerson.

35. Willis Stone, "Legislation Versus Economic Laws," February 1932, WES, Box 1, Folder: Stone, Willis E., Speeches.

36. "Republicans on Pan as Speaker Addresses Group," *Highland Park News-Herald*, March 11, 1932, WES, Box 15, Scrapbook 1 (of 4).

37. Sewell Avery, the chairman of the board of Montgomery Ward, had repeatedly and publicly defied an order of the War Labor Board to extend the terms of a previous contract with the United Retail, Wholesale, and Department Store Employees' Union. He had further-more advertised his defiance with full-page newspaper ads across the country. This appar-ently deliberate provocation led workers in other subsidiaries of the company—including the Hummer manufacturing plant in Springfield, Illinois, which was directly engaged in military production—to strike in sympathy with the Chicago retail workers. Roosevelt ordered the seizure of the company to end the conflict before it spread further. See U.S. House of Representatives Select Committee to Investigate Seizure of Montgomery Ward & Co., *Hearings before the Select Committee to Investigate Seizure of Montgomery Ward & Co., 78th Congress, 2nd Session, May 22-25 and June 6-8, 1944* (Washington, D.C.: Government Printing Office, 1945), 118–9, 189–94; "F.D.R. Authority in Ward Case Hit," *Los Angeles Times*, May 3, 1944: 2. On the evolution of Stone's ideas in this period, including his view of the Montgomery Ward crisis, see Willis E. Stone, "This Curious World," *Sherman Oaks Citizen-Tribune*, June 2, 1944, WES, Box 15, Scrapbook 2 (of 5), University of Oregon Library; Rowena George, "Willis Emerson Stone: Author of the Liberty Amendment," *Freedom Magazine* 6 (1974); Lloyd Herbstreith and Gordon van B. King, *Action for Americans: The Liberty Amendment* (Los Angeles: Operation America, Inc., 1963), 74–5; Willis E. Stone, "Progress Report," *American Progress* (Summer 1958): 67.

38. Willis E. Stone, "This Curious World," *Sherman Oaks Citizen-Tribune*, June 2, 1944, WES, Box 15, Scrapbook 2 (of 5).

39. Contributions to Committee for Economic Freedom, n.d. [1948?]; Committee for Economic Freedom (petition), n.d. [1946–1948?]; and Agenda of the Organization Meeting, American Individual Enterprise Foundation, April 6, 1948, all in WES, Box 15, Scrapbook 5 (of 5).

40. "Who is Willis E. Stone," n.d. [1937?], WES, Box 1, Folder: Stone, Willis Emerson.

41. Stone to Dan Hanson, September 28, 1957, WES, Box 6, Folder: Hanson, Dan.

42. Willis E. Stone, "Organizational Plans Okayed by Executive Committee," *Freedom Magazine*, Sept.–Oct. 1967: 25; George, "Willis Emerson Stone"; Herbstreith and King, *Action for Americans*, 74–5; Stone, "Progress Report," 67.

43. See Robert B. Dresser to Willis Emerson Stone, August 24, 1955; and Stone to Dresser, August 30, 1955, WES, Box 1, Folder: Amendment Revisions. Representative John Bricker's proposed constitutional amendment would have prohibited the federal gov-ernment from implementing any treaties that conflicted with the Constitution. Like many conservatives, Bricker (R-OH) feared that the Constitution's supremacy clause (Article VI, paragraph 2) might otherwise allow the president to sign a treaty that would

override constitutionally protected states' rights. This belief was not wholly unfounded—the Supreme Court had apparently ruled to this effect in *State of Missouri v. Holland*, 1920, 252 U.S. 416, and some liberals, both in and out of the Truman administration, had used similar logic to argue that federal civil rights legislation was constitutional insofar as it fulfilled U.N. treaty obligations. Right-wing groups embraced the Bricker Amendment for a variety of reasons: Southern conservatives liked it because it protected state Jim Crow laws from federal interference, while isolationists liked it because a nonrestrictive clause in some versions (by using the word "which" instead of "that") appeared to imply that *all* treaties abrogated the Constitution and were therefore void. See Duane Tananbaum, *The Bricker Amendment Controversy: A Test of Eisenhower's Political Leadership* (Ithaca, NY: Cornell University Press, 1988), 3–4, 93, 113–21.

44. George, "Willis Emerson Stone"; Herbstreith and King, *Action for Americans*, 74–5; Stone, "Progress Report," 67.

45. Stone referred in correspondence to a first meeting at a conference in 1952 or 1953; Stone to Mary D. Cain, September 20, 1956, WES, Box 3, Folder: Cain, Mary Dawson. It was probably the 1953 Congress of Freedom, on which see Diamond, *Roads to Dominion*, 51.

46. Paul K. Morgenthaler to Willis Stone, July 11, 1955, WES, Box 16, Folder: O; Mary D. Cain to Willis Stone, May 17, 1955, WES, Box 16, Folder: Cain, Mary D.

47. Willis Emerson Stone to Corinne Griffiths [*sic*], March 1, 1956, WES, Box 16, Folder: G, University of Oregon Library; Stone to Mrs. Mary D. Cain, August 2, 1956, WES, Box 3, Folder: Cain, Mary Dawson.

48. In public, Griffith was oblique: She said only that "certain executives and directors of the organization she helped to found had, without her knowledge, aligned themselves with other groups with other purposes." See "Corinne Griffith Quits U.S. Tax Repeal Group," *Los Angeles Times*, August 17, 1956: C2. In private communication to T. Coleman Andrews, she apparently singled out Morgenthaler, Stone, and Dwight Claar as disreputable characters with whom she could not be associated; see T. Coleman Andrews to Corinne Griffith, September 20, 1956, TCA, Box 16, Folder: Corinne Griffith, 1956. For Stone's view of the showdown, see Stone to Mrs. Mary D. Cain, August 2, 1956 and Stone to Cain, Nov 6, 1956, WES, Box 3, Folder: Cain, Mary Dawson.

49. Willis Emerson Stone, "Repealing Income Taxes," April 28, 1956, WES, Box 1, Folder: American Way; see also Willis Emerson Stone to J. Bracken Lee, March 17, 1958, WES, Box 5, Folder: For America.

50. In 1955, the total was 204; Mary D. Cain to John Gregg, September 29, 1955, WES, Box 16, Folder: Cain, Mary D. In 1957, it was "more than 700"; Willis Emerson Stone to "Dear Friend," November 27, 1957, WES, Box 3, Folder: Birch, John (Society). When Stone counted establishments rather than corporations or "corporate activities," he naturally arrived at even greater figures; by 1961, he was counting more than 19,000 illegitimate, federally owned or operated "business, commercial and industrial establishments" in the Defense Department alone. Willis Stone to Dan Hanson, November 2, 1961, WES, Box 13. Folder: Hanson, Dan—Wyoming.

51. Bess M. Wilson, "High Cost of Federal Competition Assailed," *Los Angeles Times*, February 16, 1951: B1; *Congressional Record*, vol. 103, part 23, Aug. 22–Sept. 19, 1957, p. A7520. I calculated the share of the total tax burden from *Historical Statistics of the United States*, vol. 2, Series Y358-373 and Series Y393-401, pp. 1107, 1110.

52. *Congressional Record*, vol. 103, part 23, Aug. 22–Sept. 19, 1957, p. A7520.

53. See Willis E. Stone to Max A. Koffman, July 15, 1958, WES, Box 1, Folder: Joint Operating Committee, APF and ORFIT, Correspondence and Memos.

54. The American Progress Foundation, Minutes of the Regular Meeting of the Board of Directors, March 14, 1957, WES, Box 1, Folder: American Progress Foundation. At Lewis's death, it was discovered that he had left millions to the right-wing broadcaster Dan Smoot and the John Birch Society. See Arnold Forster and Benjamin R. Epstein, *Danger on the Right* (New York: Random House, 1964), 164.

55. Willis E. Stone to Mary D. Cain, September 20, 1956, WES, Box 3, Folder: Cain, Mary Dawson.

56. Willis E. Stone to the Finance Committee, July 5, 1958; "The Resolution by which...," n.d. [August 1958?]; Agenda, Joint Operating Committee, n.d. [June 1958?]; Stone to members of Joint Operating Committee, n.d. [May 1958?]; Stone to Max Koffman, May 14, 1958; Stone to ORFIT, April 13, 1959, WES, Box 1, Folder: Joint Operating Committee, APF and ORFIT, Correspondence and Memos.

57. For the custody of the letterhead, see W. S. (Stuart) McBirnie, "Report to the Field," n.d. [1961?], WES, Box 1, Folder: ORFIT—Reports and Releases. On the relationship between the John Birch Society and ORFIT, see Lipset and Raab, *Politics of Unreason*, 249, 271.

58. Charles W. Caine to Charles S. Martin Jr., April 24, 1961, WES, Box 13, Folder: Caine, Curtis W., MD.

59. Forster and Epstein, *Danger on the Right*, 168; Liberty Amendment Committee of the U.S.A., *Progress Report* (January through August 1963): 1. For the leadership roster circa summer 1961, see "Leadership Conference for the Liberty Amendment," *American Progress* (summer 1961): 12.

60. "Leadership Conference for the Liberty Amendment," *American Progress* (summer 1961): 12–3; "Annual Conference Results Promise Profitable 1963," *American Progress* 7, no. 5 (November–December 1962): 24–5.

61. "California T Parties Score Hit," *American Progress* 7, no. 5 (November–December 1962): 6.

62. Jane Andrews and Mark Andrews, "The Liberty Amendment," *American Progress* 7, no. 5 (November–December 1962): 26; "New Victory Song," *American Progress* 7, no. 5 (November–December 1962): 11. On the first annual conferences, see "Leadership Conference for the Liberty Amendment," *American Progress* (summer 1961): 12–3; "Annual Conference Results Promise Profitable 1963," *American Progress* 7, no 5 (November–December 1962): 11. The song was later recorded under the title "Liberty for Me" (sound recording, Box 15, WES, University of Oregon Library).

63. Robert B. Dresser, *A Program for Americans Who Desire to Retain Freedom* (Berwyn, IL: Berwyn Publishing Co., 1956), Robert B. Dresser papers, package 2 (of 4), Hoover Institution, Stanford University.

64. Oliver also described the income tax as the "taproot of totalitarianism," and intimated darkly that the federal government might defend it with armed force if necessary: Revilo P. Oliver, "Conservative Rally Opposes Bureaucracy," *National Review* (October 5, 1957). Skeptics remained; see Willis A. Carto to Willis E. Stone, April 29, 1959, WES, Box 3, Folder: Carto, Willis A., University of Oregon Library; Willis E. Stone to Robert B. Dresser, November 7, 1957, TCA, Box 16, Folder: S (Sm-Su).

65. See Stone to Dresser, September 10, 1957; Stone to Dresser, July 11, 1957; and Dresser to Edward A. Rumely, February 14, 1958, WES, Box 4, Folder: Dresser.

66. Chodorov, *Income Tax*, vi.

67. Ibid., vi.

68. That state was Illinois, whose legislature voted a resolution in support of the three-sentence version of Stone's amendment on May 6, 1953: see American Progress Foundation, *1953 Annual Report*, WES, Box 1, Folder: American Progress Foundation Annual Reports.

69. The table was compiled with data on state resolutions reported in *American Progress*, 1955–1963; *Freedom Magazine*, 1963–1976; and *Break Free with 23 News*, 1982.

70. Liberty Amendment Committee of the U.S.A., *Progress Report* (January through August 1963): 2.

71. Mary Dawson Cain to Ladies and Gentlemen of the Mississippi legislature, n.d. [May 1960?], WES, Box 3, Folder: Cain, Mary Dawson.

72. *Freedom Magazine* 8, no. 4 (July–August 1963); and *Freedom Magazine* 11, no. 6 (November–December 1966). On the declining availability of leases in the 1950s, see Patrick Culhane, *Public Lands Politics: Interest Group Influence on the Forest Service and the Bureau of Land Management* (Baltimore, MD: Johns Hopkins University Press, 1981), 91–2.

73. Willis E. Stone to Dan Hanson, January 19, 1959, WES, Box 6, Folder: Dan Hanson.

74. On support from realtors, see Dan Hanson, "Letter from Wyoming," *American Progress* (fall 1959): 47. On ranchers, see Hanson to Stone, January 1, 1959, and Stone to Hanson, January 29, 1959, WES, Box 6, Folder: Dan Hanson.

75. Furrh to Kellems, June 1, 1954, VK, Box 10, Folder 236.

76. Kellems to Furrh, June 4, 1954, VK, Box 10, Folder 236; Mary Dawson Cain to Ladies and Gentlemen of the Mississippi legislature, n.d. [1960?], WES, Box 3, Folder: Mary Dawson Cain, University of Oregon Library; Corinne Griffith to T. Coleman Andrews, September 10, 1956, TCA, Box 16, Folder: Corinne Griffith.

77. See Herbstreith and King, *Action for Americans*; Willis Emerson Stone, *Where the Money Went* (Los Angeles: Fact Sheet, 1971).

78. See, e.g., Willis E. Stone, "Address for presentation before the Christian Freedom Foundation," New York City, April 16, 1958, WES, Box 1, Folder: Stone, Willis E., Speeches.

79. Herbstreith and King, *Action for Americans*, 37. Herbstreith would later make white-back-lash history when he put the Wisconsin Liberty Amendment Committee at the disposal of George Wallace's 1964 campaign for the Democratic nomination, thereby enabling the cause of segregation and states' rights to capture a stunning 34 percent of the vote in a northern Democratic primary election. See Perlstein, *Before the Storm*, 318; on the Wallace campaign, see Michael Rogin, "Wallace and the Middle Class: The White Backlash in Wisconsin," *Public Opinion Quarterly* 30, no. 1 (1966).

80. Cain to Ladies and Gentlemen of the Mississippi legislature, n.d. [May 1960?], WES, Box 3, Folder: Cain, Mary Dawson.

81. "Radio plays an important role," *American Progress* 7, no. 2 (May–June 1962): 8.

82. Willis E. Stone to Harry Hart, January 17, 1961, WES, Box 13, Folder: Hart, Harry E.—Georgia.

83. J. Milton Lent to Willis E. Stone, February 9, 1962; Stone to Mrs. J. Milton Lent, December 12, 1961; Mrs. J. Milton Lent to Stone, December 1, 1961, WES, Box 13, Folder: Lent, Mrs. J. Milton—Georgia, University of Oregon Library; "Liberty Wins in Georgia," *American Progress* (spring 1962): 5.

84. Zelizer, *Taxing America*, 113.

85. Clarence E. Manion to Clare E. Hoffman, Feb. 4, 1957, CEM, Box 3, Folders 3–9; *Congressional Record*, 85th Congress, 1st Session, 2062. Hoffman's bill was H.J. Res. 232.

86. *Congressional Record*, 86th Congress, 1st Session, 58. Utt's resolution was H.J. Res. 23.

87. Witte, *Politics and Development*, 158–9; see also Brownlee, *Federal Taxation*, 102–3; Martin Prachowny, *The Kennedy-Johnson Tax Cut: A Revisionist History* (Northampton, MA: Edward Elgar, 2002). The parallels between the regressive Kennedy tax cut and the "supply-side" policy associated with Mellon have been noted by many analysts. See Ronald F. King, "From Redistributive to Hegemonic Logic: The Transformation of American Tax Politics, 1894-1963," *Politics and Society* 12, no. 3 (1983): 46–8; Mary C. Michelmore, "*Taxing State/Welfare State: How the Politics of Aid to Families with Dependent Children and the Federal Income Tax Shaped Modern America, 1960-1980*" (Ph.D. dissertation, University of Michigan, Department of History, 2006); Elizabeth Popp Berman and Nicholas Pagnucco, "Economic Ideas and the Political Process: Debating Tax Cuts in the U.S. House of Representatives, 1962-1981," *Politics and Society* 38, no. 3 (2010).

88. See Walter Heller and Arthur Burns, "The Tax Revolt: The Lady or the Tiger?" *Public Opinion* 1, no. 3 (1978): 3–4; Walter Heller, "Memorandum for the President," December 6, 1962, and "Private Groups and Individuals in Favor of a Tax Cut," JFK Staff Memoranda, brief book on economic matters, December 20, 1962 (JFKPOF-063-021).

89. Table 6.3 presents the results of a logistic regression analysis of senators' support for the Revenue Act of 1964. The dependent variable is a yes vote on the conference report for the act, and the data set includes all senators who cast a vote (N=93). Coefficients indicate the association between a unit increase in a particular variable and the logarithm of the odds of voting in favor of the act. Thus, the negative coefficient of being from a state

whose legislature has endorsed the Liberty Amendment in model 1 implies that senators from such states were *less* likely to favor the act, *ceteris paribus*. This negative association is attenuated in model 2, which controls for the senator's ideology. DW-NOMINATE is a two-dimensional measure of congressional ideology computed by Jeff Lewis, James Lo, Nolan McCarty, Keith Poole, and Howard Rosenthal. The first dimension, used here as a control variable, is a standard measure of economic conservatism, with higher scores indicating greater skepticism about government intervention in the economy. The negative coefficient of this variable indicates that conservative senators, i.e., those who favored less government intervention in the economy, tended to *reject* the Kennedy-Johnson tax cuts. Once we control for economic conservatism, there is no measurable difference in the voting behavior of senators from states that had endorsed the Liberty Amendment. The data are from "DW-NOMINATE Scores with Bootstrapped Standard Errors," updated February 3, 2011, http://www.voteview.com/dwnominate.asp, accessed July 29, 2011; 88th Senate roll-call data, http://www.voteview.com/senate88.htm, accessed July 29, 2011. For more details on the DW-NOMINATE scores, see Keith T. Poole and Howard Rosenthal, *Congress: A Political-Economic History of Roll-Call Voting* (Oxford, UK, and New York: Oxford University Press, 1997).

90. The recording of this meeting is in the John Birch Society, Tape #2 ("Detroit, Sept. 18, 1971"), JBS, Box 23.

91. Willis Emerson Stone, "This Curious World," *Sherman Oaks Citizen-Tribune* (June 2, 1944), WES, Box 15, Scrapbook 2 (of 5).

92. Herbstreith and King, *Action for Americans*, 75–9.

93. Herbstreith and King, *Action for Americans*, 75–9.

Chapter 7

1. Atkinson, Piketty, and Saez, "Top Incomes in the Long Run of History"; Martina Morris and Bruce Western, "Inequality in Earnings at the Close of the Twentieth Century," *Annual Review of Sociology* 25 (1999): 623-57.

2. J. Allen Broyles, *The John Birch Society: Anatomy of a Protest* (Boston: Beacon Press, 1964), 7; Gerald Schomp, *Birchism Was My Business* (New York: Macmillan, 1970), 17. The analysis in this section draws on Verta Taylor's argument that a movement is more likely to reemerge after a period of demobilization and decline if activists have been able during the meantime to "create or find a niche for themselves" in an "abeyance organization" that is durable, centralized, exclusive, demanding of personal commitment, and characterized by an intense and elaborate subculture; Verta Taylor, "Social Movement Continuity: The Women's Movement in Abeyance," *American Sociological Review* 54, no. 5 (1989): 762, 765. See also Traci M. Sawyers and David S. Meyers, "Missed Opportunities: Social Movement Abeyance and Policy," *Social Problems* 46, no. 2 (1999): 187-206. On the John Birch Society, see Forster and Epstein, *Danger on the Right*, 204–7; McGirr, *Suburban Warriors*.

3. Forster and Epstein, *Danger on the Right*, 16, 196–7; Schomp, *Birchism Was My Business*, 64.

4. Hopkins, "The Voice from 15 Westminster Street," 31; Robert B. Dresser, "#17—Disarmament—A Grave Menace to the U.S.A.," August 18, 1961; "#135—Russia is Winning the Arms Race," August 1, 1967; "#133—The Suicide of the U.S.A.—Tenth Article—'Peaceniks are Nutniks,' " May 16, 1967, RBD. See also "#8—The John Birch Society: Letter to the Editor of the Providence Journal from Robert B. Dresser and Norman D. Macleod," April 13, 1961; and "#80—An Answer to the Attack on the John Birch Society and Other So-Called Reactionary Groups," October 14, 1964, RBD.

5. David Lindorff, "The Global Sleaze Trade." *Mother Jones Magazine* 10, no. 4 (1985): 10; James Dale Davidson, "The Dangers of Psychiatry," *Individualist* 3, no. 2 (1971): 18; James Dale Davidson, "Notes on the Politics of D. H. Lawrence." *Individualist* 3, no. 12 (1972):

15-18. Davidson even spared some kind words for communists as long as they were eccentric (and not statist); see James Dale Davidson, *An Eccentric Guide to the United States* (New York: Berkeley Publishing Corp., 1977), 109, 256, 279. On the basement apartment, see Clarence Y. H. Lo, *Small Property Versus Big Government* (Berkeley, CA: University of California Press, 1990), 188.

6. A. Ernest Fitzgerald, *The High Priests of Waste* (Boston: Houghton Mifflin, 1972), 6; A. Ernest Fitzgerald, *The Pentagonists: An Insider's View of Waste, Mismanagement, and Fraud in Defense Spending* (Boston: Houghton Mifflin, 1989), 43, 131, 133; Iwan Morgan, "Unconventional Politics: The Campaign for a Balanced-Budget Amendment Constitutional Convention in the 1970s," *Journal of American Studies* 32, no. 3 (1998): 425; Wendell Rawls Jr., "150,000 Get U.S. Salary as Well as Military Pension," *New York Times*, April 5, 1977: 56; Adam Clymer, "Proposed Convention on Balancing Budget," *New York Times*, February 16, 1979: B7. On the whistle-blower episode, see Fitzgerald, *High Priests of Waste*, 224–82, esp. 270; Fitzgerald, *Pentagonists*, 1–126.

7. Morgan, "Unconventional Politics," 425; "Rep. Rhodes to Return Army Pension to U.S.," *New York Times*, August 31, 1976: 17; Rawls, "150,000 Get U.S. Salary." Lo, *Small Property*, 188, reports that the organization had 6,000 members in 1973.

8. James M. Perry, "Conventional Wisdom: Missouri Reflects Widespread Doubts about Idea of Forcing Congress to Balance the U.S. Budget," *Wall Street Journal*, March 15, 1979: 48; Carrie Johnson, "The Budget and the Constitution," *Washington Post*, February 14, 1979: A23; U.S. Senate Committee on the Judiciary, *Balancing the Budget: Hearing before the Subcommittee on Constitutional Amendments of the Committee on the Judiciary, United States Senate, Ninety-Fourth Congress, First Session*, September 23 and October 7, 1975 (Washington, D.C.: Government Printing Office, 1975), 79. On the chronology of state petitions, see Saturno, *A Balanced Budget Constitutional Amendment*, table 4; Richard L. Madden, "A Balanced U.S. Budget Debated in Connecticut," *New York Times*, March 19, 1985: B4.

9. On public concern over inflation, see Tom W. Smith, "The Polls: America's Most Important Problems Part I: National and International," *Public Opinion Quarterly* 49, no. 2 (1985): 266; Stanley Fischer and John Huizinga, "Inflation, Unemployment, and Public Opinion Polls," *Journal of Money, Credit and Banking* 14, no. 1 (1982): 3. Home owners, middle-aged persons, and high-income persons were most likely to express concern about inflation in the period from 1975 to 1978 (Fischer and Huizinga, "Inflation," 11–5). James D. Savage, *Balanced Budgets and American Politics* (Ithaca, NY: Cornell University Press, 1990), emphasizes that deficits do not cause inflation, and characterizes the concern for budget balancing instead as a cultural constant of American history; but, of course, public concern about deficits comes and goes. For good, general discussions of the political economy of inflation, see Greta Krippner, *Capitalizing on Crisis: The Political Origins of the Rise of Finance* (Cambridge, MA: Harvard University Press, 2011), 17, 63–4; and the essays in Fred Hirsch and John H. Goldthorpe, eds., *The Political Economy of Inflation* (Cambridge, MA: Harvard University Press, 1978).

10. U.S. Senate Committee on the Judiciary, *Balancing the Budget*, 80–1, 173, 181.

11. Ibid., 195; James C. Hyatt, "Taxpayer Revolt: Group's Plan to Force a Balanced Budget Faces a Barrage by Congressional Critics," *Wall Street Journal*, February 8, 1979: 40; Charles Mohr, "Tax Union Playing Chief Role in Drive," *New York Times*, May 15, 1979: D18. See also Johnson, "The Budget and the Constitution," A23. On the origins of Common Cause, see Andrew S. McFarland, *Common Cause: Lobbying in the Public Interest* (Chatham, NY: Chatham House, 1984), 6–8; Lawrence S. Rothenburg, *Linking Citizens to Government: Interest Group Politics at Common Cause* (Cambridge, UK, and New York: Cambridge University Press, 1992), 9–10.

12. States submitting their second and third petitions are indicated in this table by postal abbreviations in boldface. The table omits petitions submitted in 1957 (Indiana) and 1961 (Wyoming). It also omits rescissions. Data are from Saturno, *A Balanced Budget Constitutional Amendment*, table 4; Madden, "A Balanced U.S. Budget Debated in Connecticut," B4.

13. Mohr, "Tax Union Playing Chief Role," D18; see also Johnson, "The Budget and the Constitution," A23

14. U.S. Senate Committee on the Judiciary, *Balancing the Budget*, 3, 180–2; for NTU's endorsement, see 194.

15. The response was significantly more likely among the plurality of voters who named "the government" in response to the question: "Whom do you blame the most for the trouble we're having with the economy—the government, big business, the unions, the Republican party, the Democratic party, or the general public?" It was also more likely among those who said they feared "runaway inflation" more than unemployment. Among those who said they *both* feared inflation *and* blamed the government, support for balancing the budget was 78 percent; among those who gave neither response, it was 51 percent (plus or minus 7 percent with 95 percent confidence). Author's analysis of the Yankelovich, Skelly & White poll, "*Time* Soundings #8422," September 1974 (N=1,023 interviews).

16. Percent responding affirmatively to the question: "Would you favor or oppose a constitutional amendment requiring a balanced national budget except in times of emergency?" CBS News Pre-Congressional Election Poll, September 25–29, 1978 (N = 1,451 adults). All responses are weighted to adjust for sampling probabilities.

17. The wording was "What do you think it is more important for the government in Washington to do first—cut taxes, or cut government spending?"

18. He claimed, for example, that Utah Governor George Dern appointed him to a five-member State Tax Commission, where he served for "about five years"; Howard Jarvis with Robert Pack, *I'm Mad as Hell* (New York: Times Books, 1979), 5. The Utah State Tax Commission, which the legislature created in 1931 to oversee property assessments, had only four members, and Jarvis was never one of them. Nor is there any evidence that he was ever appointed to or even consulted by the Utah Tax Revision Commission, a temporary commission appointed by Dern in 1929 to propose a major overhaul of the state's tax structure. See *Report of the Tax Revision Commission of the State of Utah to Governor George H. Dern* (Salt Lake City, UT: Utah Tax Revision Commission, 1929), 8, 17; *First Biennial Report of the State Tax Commission of Utah for the Years 1931-32* (Salt Lake City, UT: Utah State Tax Commission, 1932); *First Biennial Report of the State Tax Commission of Utah for the Years 1933-34* (Salt Lake City, UT: Utah State Tax Commission, 1934); *Third Biennial Report of the State Tax Commission of Utah for the Years 1935-36* (Salt Lake City, UT: Utah State Tax Commission, 1936). Jarvis also falsely claimed to have been a delegate representing Utah taxpayers at the 1932 meetings of the Western States Taxpayers' Association. In fact, Utah was represented at the Western States Taxpayers' Association meetings by Utah State Tax Commission member R. E. Hammond, Utah Taxpayers' Association Secretary A. C. Rees, and Orval Adams; "Proceedings of the Western States Taxpayers' Association," *Tax Digest* 10, no. 11 (1932): 392, 406, 409.

19. Wayne Stedman, "Countians Hear Senate Candidate Jarvis," *Register (Santa Ana)*, June 29, 1961: C3; McGirr, *Suburban Warriors*, 239; Robert Kuttner, *Revolt of the Haves: Tax Rebellions and Hard Times* (New York: Simon and Schuster, 1980), 39; Jarvis with Pack, *I'm Mad as Hell*, 267; "Howard Jarvis to Oppose Sen. Kuchel," *Los Angeles Times*, February 24, 1961: B7; "Jarvis Claims Effort to Raid His Supporters," *Los Angeles Times*, March 2, 1962: 8; "Wright Assails Jarvis for Attacking Chairman," *Los Angeles Times*, March 3, 1962: 10; "Conservative Party Makes Its Bow Here," *Los Angeles Times*, November 30, 1962: A1

20. *Statement of Vote at Primary Election* (Sacramento, CA: Secretary of State of California, 1962), 14; *Statement of Vote at General Election* (Sacramento, CA: Secretary of State of California, 1962), 10.

21. Willis Stone, "Launch Plans for April Tax Protest," *Freedom Magazine*, 10, no. 1 (1965): 23.

22. Ibid., 23; Willis Stone, "Prospectus: Organizational Plan of Local Liberty Amendment Committees," October 9, 1967, CLM, Box 4, Folder 8.

23. Kuttner, *Revolt of the Haves*, 37; cf. Jarvis with Pack, *I'm Mad as Hell*, 29.

24. Jarvis estimated the UO membership variously between 50,000 and 200,000, but these numbers were sheer invention; Daniel A. Smith infers from UO financial records that it had 4,000 dues-paying members in 1976. Smith, *Tax Crusaders and the Politics of Direct Democracy* (New York: Routledge, 1998), 69, 75; Jarvis with Pack, *I'm Mad as Hell*, 25.

25. Jarvis with Pack, *I'm Mad as Hell*, 51; Lo, *Small Property*, 139; Lou Cannon, *Governor Reagan: His Rise to Power* (New York: PublicAffairs, 2003), 362–6.

26. The secretary of state counted 1.263 million signatures, of which 1 million were valid, an all-time record for California initiative petitions; John Allswang, *The Initiative and Referendum in California, 1898-1998* (Stanford, CA: Stanford University Press, 2000), 105.

27. Adam Clymer, "California Vote Seen as Evidence of U.S. Tax Revolt," *New York Times*, June 8, 1978: A23.

28. Adam Clymer, "Eight States Voting in Primaries Today: Property Tax Issue in California Overshadows Political Contests," *New York Times*, June 6, 1978: A1; James M. Perry and James C. Hyatt, "Stopping the Bucks: While California Votes on Taxes, Other States Mull Spending Limits," *Wall Street Journal*, June 6, 1978: 1; CBS Evening News, "Campaign '78," June 6, 1978; ABC Evening News, "Campaign '78," June 6, 1978; "Tax-Cut Issue Dominates State Legislators' Parley," *New York Times*, July 8, 1978: 6; "Tax-Cut Group, Meeting in St. Louis, Plans Strategy," *New York Times*, July 30, 1978: 18.

29. Sid Taylor, "Charting a Course of Fiscal Sanity," *Washington Post*, July 1, 1978: A14; William Bonner to Milton Friedman, June 20, 1978, MF, Folder 206.3; National Taxpayers' Union, "The Second American 'Taxpayer Revolt,' " n.d. (received October 22, 1978), WC; Paul Gann to "Dear Citizen," n.d. [1981?], HH, Folder: National Taxpayers' Union.

30. Jim Davidson to "Dear Friend," n.d. [1979?], HH, Folder: National Taxpayers' Union. See also Davidson to "Dear Friend," December 1980; and Davidson to Dear Friend, n.d. [1983?], HH, Folder: National Taxpayers' Union. For NTU's endorsement of an amendment that mandated an income surtax, see U.S. House of Representatives Committee on the Judiciary, *Constitutional Amendments to Balance the Federal Budget: Hearings before the Subcommittee on Monopolies and Commercial Law of the Committee on the Judiciary, United States House of Representatives, Ninety-Sixth Congress, First and Second Sessions* (Washington, D.C.: Government Printing Office, 1979), 75.

31. James Dale Davidson to Milton Friedman, May 6, 1977, MF, Folder 206.5; Mohr, "Tax Union Playing Chief Role," D18; Adam Clymer, "Proposed Convention on Balancing Budget," *New York Times*, February 16, 1979: B7.

32. Jarvis also proposed to offset the tax cuts with deep cuts in federal spending, because, he said, "deficit spending is the single most important cause of inflation." Jarvis with Pack, *I'm Mad as Hell*, 173, 172–7. See also American Tax Reduction Movement, "Howard Jarvis' American Tax Reduction Movement," n.d. [1979?]; Howard Jarvis to Colonial Lecture Management, n.d. [1979?]; American Tax Reduction Movement, "Death and Taxes are Inevitable," n.d. [1979?], all in HH, Folder: American Tax Reduction Movement.

33. The symbolic use of number "23" for the Liberty Amendment seems to have begun in the years when Willis Stone still called it the proposed 23rd Amendment. On Moths, see Martin A. Larson, *Tax Revolt: The Battle for the Constitution* (Greenwich, CT: Devin-Adair, 1985), 52, 104. For the "Yes on 23" campaign, see Armin Moths, n.d. [1979?], "Petition to reduce federal spending and taxes: Yes on 23"; Armin Moths to "Dear Supporter," n.d. [1980?]; Yes on 23 Committee, n.d., "Cut Federal Taxes: Yes on 23"; Yes on 23 Committee, n.d. [1980?], "Hundreds of Candidates Say Yes to Liberty Amendment Poll," all in CLM, Box 4, Folder 6; and *Yes on 23/Liberty Amendment News*, various issues, HH, Folder: Yes on 23/Liberty Amendment Committee. On Howard Jarvis's "Yes on 13 Committee," see Smith, *Tax Crusaders*, 76–8; *Congressional Record*, 96th Congress, 1st session, 131.

34. "Arizona Votes to Repeal Fed. Income Tax," *Break Free with 23 News* (April 1982); "Indiana Votes to Repeal Fed. Income Tax," *Break Free with 23 News* (April 1982).

35. Lewis K. Uhler, *History of Proposition #1 Initiative* (Oral History Transcript, Oral History Project, Claremont Graduate School, 1982), 15–6; William Craig Stubblebine, *The*

Development of Proposition #1 (Oral History Transcript, Oral History Program, Claremont Graduate School, 1982); on Uhler's former John Birch Society membership, see Jeff Madrick, *The Age of Greed: The Triumph of Finance and the Decline of America, 1970 to the Present* (New York: Alfred A. Knopf, 2011), 6.

36. Congressman Jack Kemp, news release, November 1, 1973, MF, Folder 207.1; National Tax Limitation Committee, press release, July 9, 1976, MF, Folder 100.6; William F. Rickenbacker, "A Practical Plan to Limit Taxes," *Manion Forum,* weekly broadcast no. 1147, October 3, 1976, MF, Folder 207.4; William F. Rickenbacker and Lewis K. Uhler, *A Taxpayer's Guide to Survival: Constitutional Tax Limitation* (Washington, D.C.: National Tax Limitation Committee, 1976), MF, Folder 100.6.

37. Kuttner, *Revolt of the Haves,* 143; "Tax Convention Urges Limits," *Washington Post,* November 19, 1978: A6; James Clark Jr. to Milton Friedman, January 13, 1984, MF, Folder 206.4; Lew Uhler to Board of Founders and Sponsors, April 26, 1978, MF, Folder 207.6; Lewis K. Uhler to Lawrence P. Mueller, January 24, 1980, MF, Folder 207.2; see also W. C. Stubblebine to Rose and Milton Friedman, December 1, 1986, MF, Folder 207.5; W. C. Stubblebine, Wm. F. Rickenbacker, and Lewis K. Uhler, untitled memo, January 30, 1979, MF, Folder 207.5.

38. Lewis K. Uhler to Milton Friedman, December 16, 1977, MF, Folder 206.7; Lewis K. Uhler to Richard H. Headlee, February 2, 1977, RHH, Box 1, Folder: General correspondence—1977; Lewis K. Uhler to James Barrett, January 17, 1977, RHH, Box 1, Folder: General Correspondence—1977.

39. *Congressional Record,* 96th Congress, 1st session, 5924; U.S. House of Representatives Committee on the Judiciary, *Constitutional Amendments to Balance the Federal Budget,* 338, 340, 372.

40. U.S. House of Representatives Committee on the Judiciary, *Constitutional Amendments to Balance the Federal Budget,* 258–9; U.S. Senate Committee on the Judiciary, *Proposed Constitutional Amendment to Balance the Federal Budget: Hearings before the Subcommittee on the Constitution of the Committee on the Judiciary of the United States Senate,* March 12, May 23, July 25, October 4, 11, and November 1, 1979 (Washington, D.C.: Government Printing Office, 1979), 499.

41. U.S. Senate Committee on the Judiciary, *Proposed Constitutional Amendment to Balance the Federal Budget,* 356, 360–1.

42. Warren Weaver, "A Tax Group Urges Amendment Linking Spending to G.N.P. Gain," *New York Times,* January 31, 1979: A12; William Safire, "Friedman Amendment," *New York Times,* February 5, 1979: A19.

43. U.S. Senate Committee on the Judiciary, *Proposed Constitutional Amendment to Balance the Federal Budget,* 7.

44. Ibid., 353, 355.

45. Rickenbacker and Uhler, *A Taxpayer's Guide to Survival,* 12; Sherry Tvedt, "*Enough is Enough: The Origins of Proposition 2 ½*" (M.A. thesis, MIT Department of City Planning, 1981), 39.

46. The first column of the table reports the percentage within each group responding that they favored "a constitutional amendment to limit government spending" that would "Limit federal spending to a certain fraction of the gross national product—which is the total of all goods and services produced in the nation." The second column of the table reports the percentage within each group indicating that they favored "a constitutional amendment to limit government spending" that would "[r]equire that the budget be balanced in any given year either by raising taxes or lowering spending, or both." Percentages are calculated from Roper/H&R Block Study No. 1979-0673, May 5–12, 1979 (N = 1,459). All responses are weighted to adjust for sampling probabilities.

47. These predicted probabilities are calculated from the logistic regression models reported in table 7.6, this chapter. For illustrative purposes, the calculation assumes that the typical respondent is a 40-year-old white man with 12 years of education and annual family income of $20,618, which is the sample average.

48. Data on contributors are calculated from the list of contributors in National Tax Limitation Committee, "About the National Tax Limitation Committee," HH, Folder: National Tax Limitation Committee; Gale, *Business and Company Resource Center* [machine-readable database]. Labor force and tax return data are from U.S. Census Bureau, *Statistical Abstract of the United States 1988,* 379, and *Statistical Abstract of the United States 1990,* 521.

49. Edward Cowan, "Reagan's Speech Elates Lobbyists," *New York Times,* May 1, 1982: 12.

50. Morgan, "Unconventional Politics," 425; Cowan, "Reagan's Speech Elates Lobbyists"; Fitzgerald, *Pentagonists,* 131; Roger Lowenstein, "The Rich are Indeed Different: Simply Look at Their Junk Mail," *Wall Street Journal,* November 15, 1988: B1.

51. Lester Sobel, *The Great American Tax Revolt* (New York: Facts on File, 1979), 125; Hyatt, "Taxpayer Revolt," 40; Johnson, "The Budget and the Constitution," A23; T. R. Reid, "Constitutional Convention Drive May Not Reach Finish Line," *Washington Post,* February 25, 1979: A13; Jarvis with Pack, *I'm Mad as Hell,* 157; T. R. Reid, "Balanced-Budget Amendment Campaign Falters," *Washington Post,* May 29, 1979: A2.

52. Steven Rattner, "The Candidates' Economists," *New York Times,* November 18, 1979: F1; for the perspective from an NTLC insider in the Reagan camp, see William A. Niskanen, *Reaganomics: An Insider's Account of the Policies and the People* (Oxford, UK, and New York: Oxford University Press, 1988), 4–7.

53. Reid, "Constitutional Convention Drive," A13; Stacey Jolna, "Constitutional Convention's Foes Uniting," *Washington Post,* March 14, 1979: A2; Reid, "Balanced-Budget Amendment Campaign Falters," A2; Mohr, "Tax Union Playing Chief Role," D18.

54. U.S. Senate Committee on the Judiciary, *Proposed Constitutional Amendment to Balance the Federal Budget,* 57, 518; Adam Clymer, "Budget Amendment Backed at Hearing," *New York Times,* March 12, 1981: A14; Daniel P. Strickland, *Balanced Budget and Spending Limitations: Proposed Constitutional Amendments in the 97th Congress,* Congressional Research Service Issue Brief No. IB81056 (1982): 1

55. National Taxpayers' Union, *Taxpayer's Action Guide,* n.d. [1981?], WC; Grover Norquist, "R.I.P. John Berthoud, Friend of Taxpayers (1962-2007)," *Human Events,* October 8, 2007: 18; Cowan, "Reagan's Speech Elates Lobbyists"; Edward Cowan, "Balancing the Budget— By Law," *New York Times,* March 7, 1982: F6.

56. *Congressional Record,* 97th Congress, 2nd session, 27176, 27254; the debate is from 27171-4.

57. Democratic Senator Birch Bayh, who was chairman of the subcommittee on the Constitution of the Senate Judiciary Committee in 1980, introduced a "Spending and Tax Limitation Act" for the express purpose of accomplishing the ends of S. J. Res. 126 via statute. See U.S. Senate Committee on the Judiciary, *Proposed Constitutional Amendment to Balance the Federal Budget,* 520.

58. Brownlee, *Federal Taxation,* 117.

59. Monica Prasad, "The Popular Origins of Neoliberalism in the Reagan Tax Cut of 1981," *Journal of Policy History* 24, no. 3 (2012): 351-83; Akard, "Corporate Mobilization"; Martin, *Shifting the Burden;* King, *Money, Time and Politics.* For evidence that indexing was not of interest to corporate lobbyists, see Monica Prasad, *The Politics of Free Markets: The Rise of Neoliberal Economic Policies in Britain, France, Germany and the United States* (Chicago: University of Chicago Press, 2006), 46–60; On the effects of indexing, see C. Eugene Steuerle, *The Tax Decade: How Taxes Came to Dominate the Public Agenda* (Washington, D.C.: Urban Institute, 1992), 43–4.

60. Donald J. Senese, June 16, 1978, MF, Folder 207.5; see R. Kent Weaver, *Automatic Government: The Politics of Indexation* (Washington, D.C.: Brookings Institution, 1988), 195–6; Witte, *Politics and Development,* 193, 202.

61. Percentages calculated from the July 29, 1981, roll-call vote on Rep. Conable's (R-NY) substitute to H.R. 4242, the Tax Incentive Act of 1981, which provided for a 25 percent individual tax reduction over three years, indexing, and provisions to encourage increased personal savings. I relied on the 97th House roll-call data archived at Keith Poole's Voteview website, http://www.voteview.com/house97.htm, accessed October 11, 2011. States endorsing the balanced budget amendment are listed in table 7.1.

62. President Ronald Reagan to Milton Friedman (telegram), July 9, 1982, MF, Folder 207.4. The leaders of the NTLC were affronted by his attempt to claim credit for their work, and Milton Friedman warned Reagan that putting his name on the amendment would "make it more difficult to keep the drive for the amendment truly bipartisan," Milton Friedman to Ronald Reagan, July 15, 1982, MF, Folder 207.4.

63. National Taxpayers' Union, "This is the Official National Referendum," n.d. [1982?], HH, Folder: National Taxpayers' Union.

64. Critchlow, *Phyllis Schlafly*, 283–5; "To Amend or Not: The Debate Continues," *New York Times*, April 2, 1987: A28; Uhler, *Setting Limits*, 190.

65. Uhler, *Setting Limits*, 209–10. The original of this line, which Uhler attributed to an "unknown poet," was advertising copy penned by George Cecil in 1928; Uhler's version was better. See "Chapter and Verse," *Harvard Magazine* (July–August 2003): 25. On the fate of the movement, see Critchlow, *Phyllis Schlafly*, 285; National Taxpayers' Union, "The Big Loophole," 1987, HH, Folder: National Taxpayers' Union; National Taxpayers' Union to "Dear Taxpayer," June 1985, HH, Folder: National Taxpayers' Union; W. Craig Stubblebine to Rose and Milton Friedman, December 1, 1986, MF, Folder 207.5.

66. In order to determine the correlates of support for NTLC and NTU versions of the balanced budget amendment, I estimated two logistic regression models reported in this table. The data are from Roper/H&R Block Study No. 1979-0673, May 5–12, 1979 (N=1,459). Respondents were asked the following question: "There are several ways that a constitutional amendment to limit government spending could be written. Here are some of those ways. For each one, please tell me if you would be in favor of such an amendment, or not?" The column labeled "NTLC" reports results of a model of a dichotomous measure of support for an amendment that would "Limit federal spending to a certain fraction of the gross national product—which is the total of all goods and services produced in the nation." The column labeled "NTU" reports results of a dichotomous measure of support for an amendment that would "Require that the budget be balanced in any given year either by raising taxes or lowering spending, or both." The resulting coefficients were used to calculate the predicted probabilities reported in figure 7.1, this chapter.

Chapter 8

1. George Cooper, *A Voluntary Tax? New Perspectives on Sophisticated Estate Tax Avoidance* (Washington, D.C.: Brookings Institution, 1979).

2. See Jacobson, Raub, and Johnson, "The Estate Tax." For evidence of the softening line of the John Birch Society after the fall of the Soviet Union, see Gary Benoit, "Less Government, Lower Taxes: T.R.I.M. Puts Pressure on House of Representatives," *The New American* 7, no. 9 (April 23, 1991), 13-15. The society still favored cutting top income tax rates, but no longer supported a constitutional ban on income taxation.

3. President Bush favored H.J. Res. 268, a balanced budget amendment. George Bush, "Letter to Congressional Leaders on the Balanced Budget Amendment," July 16, 1990, http://www.presidency.ucsb.edu/ws/index.php?pid=18684&st=balanced+budget+amendment&st1=#axzz1mmj9mLkT, accessed August 20, 2012; see Lawrence A. Hunter, deputy chief economist, U.S. Chamber of Commerce to Milton Friedman, June 14, 1990, MF, Folder 206.7; Milton Friedman to Lewis K. Uhler, June 26, 1990, MF, Folder 207.7.

4. George H. W. Bush, "Address Accepting the Presidential Nomination at the Republican National Convention in New Orleans," August 18, 1988, http://www.presidency.ucsb.edu/ws/index.php?pid=25955, accessed August 20, 2012. See Wilentz, *Age of Reagan*, 308; Duane Windsor, "The 1990 Deficit Reduction Deal," in *Principle over Politics? The Domestic Policy of the George H. W. Bush Administration*, eds. Richard Himelfarb and Rosanna Perotti (Westport, CT: Greenwood Press, 2004), 28-9; George H. W. Bush, "Statement on the

Federal Budget Negotiations," June 26, 1990, by Gerhard Peters and John T. Woolley, *The American Presidency Project*, http://www.presidency.ucsb.edu/ws/index.php?pid=18635, accessed August 20, 2012.

5. C. Eugene Steuerle, *Contemporary U.S. Tax Policy* (Washington, D.C.: Urban Institute, 2008), 151.

6. Signs of incipient division among the ruling elite are also sometimes said to be a dimension of the "political opportunity structure" that encourages protest—see Doug McAdam, "Political Opportunities: Conceptual Origins, Current Problems, and Future Directions," in *Comparative Perspectives on Social Movements*, eds. Doug McAdam, John D. McCarthy, and Mayer Zald (New York: Cambridge University Press, 1996), 27—and it might be thought that the acrimonious split between Bush and House Republicans over the budget deal represents such a division. But the logic of political process theory suggests that such divisions encourage protest to the extent that they represent elite defections to the side of the protesters. In this instance, the split was triggered by Bush's movement *away* from the anti-tax position—a symptom of a closing, not an opening, window of opportunity. The immediate aftermath also sent discouraging signals to potential tax protesters. It was the Republicans, not the Democrats, who lost seats in the midterm elections that followed immediately on the heels of the budget fight; and within two months, Bush's approval rating was at a record high; Wilentz, *Age of Reagan*, 289. On the politics of the budget deal, see Dennis S. Ippolito, "Governance versus Politics: The Budget Policy Legacy of the Bush Administration," in *Principle over Politics? The Domestic Policy of the George H. W. Bush Administration*, eds. Richard Himelfarb and Rosanna Perotti (Westport, CT: Greenwood Press, 2004), 3-22; Windsor, "The 1990 Deficit Reduction Deal."

7. On the role of framing, see, e.g., Graetz and Shapiro, *Death by a Thousand Cuts*; for evidence that "death tax" rhetoric was more common mid-century, see http://books.google.com/ngrams/graph?content=death+tax&year_start=1800&year_end=2000&corpus=0&smoothing=3.

8. Cathy Areu, "First Person Singular: Grover Norquist," *Washington Post*, August 23, 2009, http://www.washingtonpost.com/wp-dyn/content/article/2009/08/14/AR2009081402035.html, accessed August 20, 2012.

9. Nina J. Easton, *Gang of Five: Leaders at the Center of the Conservative Crusade* (New York: Simon and Schuster, 2002), 73. The rest of this section draws heavily on Easton's *Gang of Five*, which is the indispensable biographical source on Norquist.

10. Quoted in Easton, *Gang of Five*, 72. On the *Harvard Chronicle*, see ibid., 409 n. 72; Nancy A. Tentindo, "Libertarian Group Plans to Publish 'Harvard Chronicle,' " *Harvard Crimson*, February 11, 1978, http://www.thecrimson.com/article/1978/2/11/libertarian-group-plans-to-publish-harvard/, accessed August 20, 2012. On the tax limitation drive, see *Limiting Taxation and Spending by State and Local Governments* (Boston: Massachusetts Legislative Research Council, 1980), 351–70; Tvedt, "Enough is Enough."

11. Alexander Solzhenitsyn, "The Exhausted West," *Harvard Magazine* (July–August 1978): 21–6, http://harvardmagazine.com/sites/default/files/1978_Alexander_Solzhenitsyn.pdf, accessed August 20, 2012.

12. Quotation is from Timothy Condon and Grover Norquist, *Taxpayer's Manual: How to Survive Despite Government* (Washington, D.C.: National Taxpayers' Union, 1979), 83; see also 42, 82–98. Easton, *Gang of Five*, 81; Americans for Tax Reform, "Who is Grover Norquist?" http://www.atr.org/about-grover, accessed August 20, 2012.

13. Walt Harrington, *American Profiles: Somebodies and Nobodies Who Matter* (Columbia, MO: University of Missouri Press, 1992), 244; on Norquist's role, see Easton, *Gang of Five*, 160–1.

14. Alan Cowell, "4 Rebel Units Sign Anti-Soviet Pact," *New York Times*, June 6, 1985: A16; Easton, *Gang of Five*, 166.

15. Quoted in Matthew Continetti, *The K Street Gang: The Rise and Fall of the Republican Machine* (New York: Doubleday, 1997), 33.

16. Jonas Savimbi, "The War against Soviet Colonialism," *Policy Review* 35 (winter 1985–6): 18; on his studies in Europe and China, see Fred Bridgland, *Jonas Savimbi: A Key to Africa* (Edinburgh, UK: Mainstream, 1986), 35–40, 67; for Savimbi's account of his relationship with Guevara, see ibid., 59–61; Savimbi, "War against Soviet Colonialism," 18–20.

17. W. Martin James III, *A Political History of the Civil War in Angola 1974-1990* (New Brunswick, NJ: Transaction Publishers, 1992), 70, 285.

18. Savimbi, "War against Soviet Colonialism," 19–20, 21, 24; on Norquist's authorship, see Easton, *Gang of Five*, 171.

19. Philip Gourevitch, "Fight on the Right," *The New Yorker* 80, no. 8 (April 12, 2004); Savimbi, "War against Soviet Colonialism," 21; on UNITA's strategy, see James, *Political History of the Civil War in Angola*, 286.

20. Condon and Norquist, *Taxpayer's Manual*, 41; John Berlau, "Grover Norquist Takes on the Tyranny of Federal Taxation," *Insight on the News* (January 26, 1998): 21.

21. Fred Barnes and Grover Norquist, "The Politics of Less," *Policy Review* 55 (1991): 70. "Revolutionaries" is Norquist quoted in Rick Henderson and Steven Hayward, "Happy Warrior," *Reason Magazine* 28, no. 9 (1997); "defund the left" is Norquist quoted in Easton, *Gang of Five*, 137; David Brock, *Blinded by the Right: the Conscience of an Ex-Conservative* (New York: Three Rivers Press, 2002), 71.

22. Easton, *Gang of Five*, 216.

23. Brock, *Blinded by the Right*, 70; Michael Scherer, "Grover Norquist: the Soul of the New Machine," *Mother Jones* (January/February 2004), http://motherjones.com/politics/2004/01/grover-norquist-soul-new-machine, accessed August 20, 2012; John Micklethwait and Adrian Wooldridge, *Right Nation: Conservative Power in America* (New York: Penguin, 2004), 16; Easton, *Gang of Five*, 278; on the meeting, see Thomas Medvetz, "The Strength of Weekly Ties: Relations of Material and Symbolic Exchange in the Conservative Movement," *Politics and Society* 34, no. 3 (2006).

24. Brock, *Blinded by the Right*, 71.

25. Marc A. Cohen, Nanda Kumar, Thomas McGuire, and Stanley S. Wallack, "Financing Long-Term Care: A Practical Mix of Public and Private," *Journal of Health Politics, Policy and Law* 17, no. 3 (1992): 411; Lynn Etheredge, "An Aging Society and the Federal Deficit," *The Millbank Quarterly* 62, no. 4 (1984): 521-43; Carroll Estes, "Long-Term Care and Public Policy in an Age of Austerity," *Journal of Public Health Policy* 6, no. 4 (1985): 464-75; U.S. Bipartisan Commission on Comprehensive Health Care, *A Call for Action: Final Report* (Washington, D.C.: Government Printing Office, 1990).

26. Wojciech Kopczuk, "The Trick Is to Live: Is the Estate Tax Social Security for the Rich?" *Journal of Political Economy* 111, no. 6 (2003): 1318-41; Alice Rivlin, "The Continuing Search for a Popular Tax," *American Economics Review* 79, no. 2 (1989): 116; see also Etheredge, "An Aging Society," 541; Michael Graetz, "100 Million Unnecessary Returns: A Fresh Start for the U.S. Tax System," *Yale Law Journal* 112 (2002): 267.

27. The unpopular options were increasing Medicare premiums (35 percent) and "taxing a greater proportion of social security benefits" (29 percent). See Survey by American Association of Retired Persons (AARP), conducted by Daniel Yankelovich Group, October 21–November 29, 1989 [USDYG.89AARP].

28. Thomas O'Neil, "Gephardt Wants Medicare Expanded," *St. Louis Post-Dispatch*, April 28, 1992: 8A.

29. Richard Gephardt, "Democrat's Health Plan Won't Depend on Estate Tax Monies," *Washington Times*, November 3, 1992: B5; Charlotte Grimes, "Gephardt Backs Off on Inheritance Tax Based on Opposition, He Will Offer New Bill," *St. Louis Post-Dispatch*, September 26, 1992: 8A.

30. Grimes, "Gephardt Backs Off"; "Clinton, Death, and Taxes," *Orange County Register*, October 22, 1992: B12.

31. See, e.g., Jan Rosen, "Tax Advisers Say the Time for Substantial Gifts May Be Now," *New York Times*, December 19, 1992: 35; Terry Savage, "How Proposed Estate Tax Changes

Would Affect You," *Chicago Sun-Times*, December 13, 199: 57; Richard Schroeder, "Middle Class Could Be Facing Estate Taxes," *Buffalo News*, December 9, 1992, Your Money, 1.

32. Grimes, "Gephardt Backs Off"; Phyllis Schlafly, "Estate Tax Time Bomb in Works," *Orange County Register*, October 21, 1992: B13; Reed Irvine and Joe Goulden, "Soak the Survivors Taxation," *Washington Times*, October 28, 1992: E3.

33. Donald Lambro, "House Leaders Get Elderly Care Plan Ready for Clinton," *Washington Times*, October 30, 1992: A6; Joshua M. Wiener, Carroll L. Estes, Susan M. Goldenson, and Sheryl C. Goldberg, "What Happened to Long-Term Care in the Health Reform Debate of 1993-1994? Lessons for the Future," *Millbank Quarterly*, 79, no. 2 (2001): 210–2; David Hilzenrath, "Retroactive Rise in Estate Tax is Challenged," *Washington Post*, August 28, 1993: B1; see Steuerle, *Contemporary U.S. Tax Policy*, 163–7.

34. Quoted in Hilzenrath, "Retroactive Rise," B1. The district court judge would later dismiss this case on the grounds that courts generally may not enjoin the government to stop tax collection (see *National Taxpayers' Union v. United States of America*, 862 F. Supp. 531). The Landmark Legal Foundation was a conservative movement law firm best known for property rights litigation on behalf of "clients, including African-Americans, who were not typically associated with conservatives" (Teles, *Rise of the Conservative Legal Movement*, 85).

35. 60 Plus Association, *News Releases*, http://web.archive.org/web/19970327041004/ http://www.60plus.org/NewsReleases/, accessed March 3, 2012; Derk Arend Wilcox, "60 Plus Association," in *The Right Guide* (Ann Arbor, MI: Economics America, Inc., 2000): 30; James L. Martin, "Testimony by James L. Martin, House Ways and Means Committee," *60 Plus Association Legislative Alerts* (April 24, 1996), http://web.archive. org/web/19970327040915/http://www.60plus.org/LegislativeAlert/, accessed March 3, 2012; James L. Martin, " 'Mediscare' Tactics for Political Advantage," *60 Plus Association Legislative Alerts* (February 1, 1996), http://web.archive.org/web/19970327040915/ http://www.60plus.org/LegislativeAlert/, accessed March 3, 2012. On the difficulty of mobilizing seniors absent a policy threat, see Campbell, *How Policies Make Citizens*.

36. David Cay Johnston, *Perfectly Legal: The Covert Campaign to Rig Our Tax System to Benefit the Super-Rich and Cheat Everybody Else* (New York: Penguin, 2005), 81–93; Graetz and Shapiro, *Death by a Thousand Cuts*, 17–23, 100.

37. Michelle Jordan, "Broadly Speaking: Getting under the Skin of Orange County's Leading Women," *Orange Coast: The Magazine of Orange County* (February 2004): 229; cf. Graetz and Shapiro, *Death by a Thousand Cuts*, 19.

38. 60 Plus Association, *News Releases*; James L. Martin, "Prepared Testimony of James L. Martin, President, the 60 Plus Association, before the House Small Business Committee Subcommittee on Tax, Finance and Exports," Federal News Service (June 12, 1997).

39. Henderson and Hayward, "Happy Warrior."

40. Calculated from data reported for the 104th Congress. ATR reported 210 pledge signers in the House, 26 of whom appear on the list of cosponsors of Cox's bill, in contrast to 3 of the 225 non-signers. Americans for Tax Reform, "The Pledge Takers for the 104th Congress: as of Thursday, September 19, 1996," http://web.archive.org/web/19970209055434/ http://www.atr.org/atr/pledge/pled926b.html, accessed August 20, 2012.

41. Salvatore Lazzari, "The Estate Tax Exemption and the House Republican Contract" (Congressional Research Service Report 95-167, January 13, 1995), 18; Norquist quoted in Graetz and Shapiro, *Death by a Thousand Cuts*, 30. On the reform, see U.S. House of Representatives, "The Job Creation and Wage Enhancement Act of 1995," http://www. house.gov/house/Contract/cre8jobsb.txt, accessed March 3, 2012.

42. Martin, "Prepared Testimony"; Graetz and Shapiro, *Death by a Thousand Cuts*, 14, 21.

43. Grover Norquist, "Americans for Tax Reform," *National Review* 48, no. 1 (1996); Alyssa Rubin, "Congressmen Say Cut in Estate Tax Would Aid Small Businesses, Farmers," *Dallas Morning News*, March 30, 1997: 5H; Roger K. Lowe, "Business Groups Search for Estate Tax Compromise," *Crain's Cleveland Business*, April 14, 1997: 6.

44. Rich Lowry, "How the Right Rose," *National Review*, December 11, 1995: 70.

45. Quoted in Steve Rubin, "Americans for Tax Reform: Grover Norquist," *Human Events* 52, no. 22 (June 14, 1996): 17.

46. Berlau, "Grover Norquist," 21; Graetz and Shapiro, *Death by a Thousand Cuts*, 29; Medvetz, "Strength of Weekly Ties," 345–6.

47. Norquist quoted in Henderson and Hayward, "Happy Warrior."

48. William Niskanen and Grover Norquist, "CPR for Tax Reform," *Policy Review* 85 (1997): 42.

49. See Graetz and Shapiro, *Death by a Thousand Cuts*, 135.

50. "American Conservative Union Presents Real Victims of the Death Tax," *U.S. Newswire*, March 19, 2001.

51. Steven Thomma, "Real Fight over Tax Cuts Is Being Waged Outside Washington," *Knight Ridder News Wire*, March 8, 2001. See Georgia Senate Resolution 11 (February 1, 2001); Michigan Senate Resolution 15 (February 15, 2001); Michigan House Resolution 33 (February 22, 2001); Montana, Senate Joint Resolution 18 (April 9, 2001); North Dakota, S.C.R. 4002 (April 2, 2001). Campaigns were reportedly also underway "in Florida, South Carolina, Ohio, Kansas, Indiana, Hawaii, Iowa, Montana, New Jersey, Oregon and Washington state" (Thomma, "Real Fight"). Steven Thomma also reports a resolution in Kentucky, but no such resolution appears in the journal of the state legislature.

52. Graetz and Shapiro, *Death by a Thousand Cuts*; Jacob S. Hacker and Paul Pierson, "Abandoning the Middle: The Bush Tax Cuts and the Limits of Democratic Control," *Perspectives on Politics* 3 (2005): 33-53; Bartels, *Unequal Democracy*; Joel Slemrod, "The Role of Misconceptions in Support for Regressive Tax Reform," *National Tax Journal* 59, no. 1 (2006): 57-75; John Sides, "Stories, Science, and Public Opinion about the Estate Tax" (George Washington University Department of Political Science, 2011), http://home.gwu.edu/~jsides/estatetax.pdf, accessed August 21, 2012.

53. Tilly, *Contentious Performances*, 121.

Conclusion

1. Many of them were incumbent Republicans. I calculated the votes cast in the 2010 election for winning candidates who identified as members of the Tea Party caucus. Caucus membership is from Michele Bachmann, "Members of the Tea Party Caucus," February 28, 2011, http://bachmann.house.gov/news/documentsingle.aspx?DocumentID=226594, accessed July 22, 2012; election results from *Statistical Abstract of the United States 2012*, table 410.

2. Lee Fang, "Exclusive: Polluter Billionaire David Koch Says Tea Party 'Rank and File are Just Normal People Like Us,' " http://thinkprogress.org/politics/2011/01/06/137586/koch-teaparty-us/, accessed July 26, 2012.

3. H.J. Res. 1, S.J. Res. 23; see also H.J. Res. 2, H.J. Res. 4, H.J. Res. 5, H.J. Res. 10, H.J. Res. 11, H.J. Res. 14, H.J. Res. 18, H.J. Res. 41, H.J. Res. 87, H.J. Res. 89, and S.J. Res. 24. For an overview of proposals and arguments, see House of Representatives Committee on the Judiciary, 2011, *Balanced Budget Constitutional Amendment*, Report 112–117.

4. H.J. Res. 16, H.J. Res. 50.

5. They include H.R. 25, H.R. 86, H.R. 99, H.R. 123, H.R.185, H.R. 206, H.R. 462, and H.R. 696.

6. Alfred G. Cuzán, 2011, "A Post-Mortem on 'Will Republicans Retake the House in 2010?' " *PS: Political Science and Politics* 44(1): 639-41; Williamson and Skocpol, *Tea Party*, 169; Geoffrey Kabaservice, 2012, *Rule and Ruin: The Downfall of Moderation and the Destruction of the Republican Party, from Eisenhower to the Tea Party* (Oxford, UK, and New York: Oxford University Press, 2012): 4. For quantitative data on the unprecedented conservatism of the

Notes 263

House in 2011, see Thomas E. Mann and Norman J. Ornstein, *It's Even Worse than It Looks* (New York: Basic Books, 2012), 51–8.

7. Skocpol and Williamson, *Tea Party*, 171–2; Mann and Ornstein, *It's Even Worse*, 58–80.
8. This general characterization of late-twentieth-century social movements as being concerned with the defense of consumer lifestyles comes from the tradition of "new social movements" research, though different scholars associated with this tradition would dissent from one or another aspect of this general picture; see, e.g., Alberto Melucci, "The New Social Movements: A Theoretical Approach," *Social Science Information* 19, no. 1 (1980): 199-226; Claus Offe, "New Social Movements: Challenging the Boundaries of Institutional Politics," *Social Research* 52 (1985): 817-68; Hank Johnston, Enrique Laraña, and Joseph R. Gusfield, "Identities, Grievances, and New Social Movements," in *New Social Movements: From Ideology to Identity*, eds. Enrique Laraña, Hank Johnston, and Joseph R. Gusfield (Philadelphia: Temple University Press, 1994), 5-35; Hanspeter Kriesi, Ruud Koopmans, Jan Willem Duyvendak, and Marco G. Giugni, *New Social Movements in Western Europe: A Comparative Analysis* (Minneapolis: University of Minnesota Press, 1995): xviii–xxii.
9. See, e.g., David S. Meyer and Sidney Tarrow, "A Movement Society: Contentious Politics for a New Century," in *The Social Movement Society: Contentious Politics for a New Century*, eds. David S. Meyer and Sidney Tarrow (Oxford, UK: Rowman and Littlefield, 1998), 1-28; McAdam, Sampson, Weffer, and MacIndoe, "There Will Be Fighting in the Streets."
10. No one has directly applied new social movement theories or the social movement society hypothesis to the tax protest movement of the twenty-first century, but many scholars have made arguments about contemporary tax protesters that have some affinities with these perspectives. Zernike, *Boiling Mad*, 50–8, has traced the Tea Party to the middle-class backlash movements of the 1970s. Stuart Wright, *Patriots, Politics, and the Oklahoma City Bombing* (New York: Cambridge University Press, 2011), 54–68, has argued that far-right tax protesters of the late twentieth century had their historical roots in a reaction to the Civil Rights movement of the 1960s; and Lo, *Small Property*, has explained the property tax revolt of the 1970s as a kind of collective consumerism. Such accounts overstate the degree to which the causes of recent tax protest movements must be sought in distinctively late-twentieth-century conditions.
11. This narrative, as ch. 1 showed, has been repeated in very similar form by generations of activists. See, e.g., Arnold, *Desire to Own*, 14; Chodorov, *Income Tax*, ch. 5; Charlton, "Tragic Year," 10; Uhler, *Setting Limits*, 26; Arnn and Norquist, "New Approaches to Tax Reform."
12. The best-known rich people's movements of twentieth-century Europe are the French *Mouvement Poujade* and the Danish *Fremskridtsbevægelse*, both of which quickly abandoned protest demonstrations to found new political party organizations; see Martin, *Permanent Tax Revolt*, ch. 7.
13. This general perspective on the structural opportunities for protest created by the American constitutional order is indebted to Herbert Kitschelt, "Political Opportunity Structures and Political Protest: Anti-Nuclear Movements in Four Democracies," *British Journal of Political Science* 16, no. 1 (1986): 57-85; Kriesi, Koopmans, Duyvendak and Giugni, *New Social Movements in Western Europe; and David S. Meyer, The Politics of Protest: Social Movements in America* (New York: Oxford University Press, 2007).
14. Daniel Alden Reed, "Some Matters of Policy to be Settled Prior to Planning Tax Revision," n.d. [1944?], Cornell University, DAR, Box 1, Folder: 1944 Ways and Means.
15. U.S. Senate Committee on the Judiciary, *Hearing*, April 27, 1954, 50.
16. Amenta, Halfmann, and Young, "Strategies and Contexts"; Amenta, Dunleavy, and Bernstein, "Stolen Thunder?"; Amenta, *When Movements Matter*.

INDEX